PAT CHAPMAN'S

TAJ

P9-DBP-599

GOOD CURRY RESTAURANT GUIDE

Contents

ABOUT THE AUTHOR

Pat Chapman was born in London's *'blitz'*, with a addiction to curry, inherited from his family's six generation connection with India. Already well used to his Gran's curries, he visited his first curry house, Shafi's, Gerrard Street, at the age of six, at a time when there were only three such establishments in London, and six in the whole of the UK. Visits became a regular treat, and confirmed in Pat a passion and a curiosity in the food of India. He was already a curryholic! Following education at Bedales and Cambridge, he did a short stint in the RAF, flying fast jets, then spent several years in industry.

He founded the now world- renowned **Curry Club** in 1982, as the means to share information about recipes, restaurants and all things to do with spicy food. Soon a national network of curry restaurant reporters was established, whose voluntary contributions, led to the publication of the first edition of this highly successful **Good Curry Restaurant Guide Guide** in 1984, and its prestigious awards to restaurants.

Assisted by his wife, Dominique, Pat frequently demonstrates

at major food shows , and appears on TV and radio, and they regularly stage cookery courses and events. His pioneering **'Gourmet Tours to India'** are now well established holidays for afficionados. With sales approaching one million books, Pat is best known as a writer of easy-to-follow recipes, in a succession of popular curry titles, published by Piatkus, Sainsbury's and the BBC.

SOME OF PAT CHAPMAN'S BEST SELLERS

The Curry Club Indian Restaurant Cookbook
Hints, tips and 150 recipes. All your restaurant favourites.

The Curry Club Favourite Restaurant Curries
150 top curry restaurants give their favourite curry recipes.

The Curry Club Balti Curry Cookbook
All Balti's secrets revealed in this best selling 100 recipe book.

The Curry Club 100 Favourite Tandoori Recipes
Everything you need to know, including Tikka Masala curries.

The Curry Club Indian Vegetarian Cookbook
150 vegetarian recipes, all authentic to the Curry Lands.

Curry Club 250 Favourite Curries and Accompaniments
The big book, with a mix of authentic and restaurant recipes.

The Curry Club 250 Hot and Spicy Dishes
Wonderful curries, plus many recipes from around the world.

NAMASTE

FULLY LICENSED AND AIR-CONDITIONED

INDIAN RESTAURANT

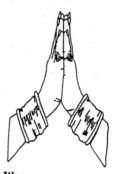

WINNER OF MANY AWARDS
INCLUDING:
THE GOOD CURRY RESTAURANT GUIDE
BEST INDIAN CHEF IN BRITAIN AWARD

COMPREHENSIVE MENU
WITH MANY OLD FAVOURITES, AUTHENTIC INDIAN SPECIALITIES
AND OUR MENU OF THE WEEK CHANGED EVERY MONDAY

SOME SPECIALITY DISHES:
SMOKED SPICED WILD BOAR - CURRIED VEAL STUFFED PANCAKES
STUFFED BABY AUBERGINE - CURRIED FISH COOKED IN YOGHURT
TURKEY TIKKA IN GREEN HERBS - GOAN KING PRAWNS
DUCK CHILLI FRY

Monday to Friday 12pm to 3pm & 6pm to 11pm
Saturday 7pm to 10pm
Sunday & Bank Holidays Closed

30 Alie Street
London E1

0171 488 9242 and 0171 702 1504

Fax: 0171 488 9339

Advertisements

Advertisements appear in this guide only by invitation of the editor, after the restaurants have been selected to appear in it. The inclusion of an advertisement does not therefore either buy entry to this guide, nor does it guarantee an uncritical entry. The advertisers are, to the best of our knowledge, reputable, and their establishments, services or products of good quality. Revenue earned from advertising enables the guide to be priced as low as possible, thus benefiting the buyers of the guide.

Accuracy

The contents of this Guide are as up to date and accurate as possible, but we cannot be held responsible for changes regarding quality, price, menu details, decor, ownership, health offences, or even closure, since our report details were processed.

Connections

The publisher of this guide and the proprietors of The Curry Club wish to make it quite clear that they have absolutely no financial or ownership connections with any of the restaurants mentioned in this guide.

False Representation

Restaurant reports are welcomed from members of The Curry Club and others. We do not pay for reports - they are sent in spontaneously and voluntarily. Our own research and restaurant testing is normally done anonymously, the bill is paid and often no disclosure is made as to our presence. On some occasions, we accept invitations to visit restaurants as 'guests of the house'. We point out, that in no circumstances do we tout for free hospitality, and anyone doing so in the name of The Curry Club is an imposter. We have heard of cases where people claiming to be members of The Curry Club, or GCRG inspectors, request payment and/or free meals in return for entry into this Guide. In such a case, we earnestly advise restaurants to threaten to call the police, for this is attempting to obtain goods and services by false pretences. We would also like to be informed of the names and addresses of such fraudsters. We will not hesitate to take against such people acting illicitly or illegally in the name of The Curry Club or The Good Curry Guide.

Typeset by DBAC in Patatino

Printed and bound by
Lookers Printers,
24 Factory Road, Upton Industrial Estate,
Upton, Poole, Dorset. BH15 5SL   01202 624466

First published in 1995 by Pat Chapman.   01428 658327

Distributed in the UK by Judy Piatkus (publishers) Limited.
5, Windmill Street, London. W1P 1HS .   0170 631 0710

ISBN 0-7499-1407-6

> "Booking a wedding package with Madhu's Brilliant not only relieves you of the tensions but also saves you a lot of time, and money."

The emphasis here is on 'total' - the whole function that pertains to catering services. At Madhu's we pride ourselves in being able to answer most of your needs for food, drinks, decor, venue, entertainment and all the little details at reasonable cost. Doing it yourself can be horrendous chore and expensive. We provide all the services and products to a standard you will be proud of, and that your guests will be impressed by. Whether you are inviting a few hundred guests or even more, utilising our customised package deals save you a lot of hassle and money. Up until a few years ago, there were a few or no professional caterers able to do this. As a complete wedding caterer, Madhu's Brilliant have a solid reputation for quality and good value earned over three generations.

Madhu's brilliant

BRILLIANT PACKAGING...AND MUCH CHEAPER THAN DOING IT YOURSELF

You come in for a preliminary discussion and we take all the problems out of your hands.
- *Cutlery, crockery, linen, glassware, bar staff and decorations, to your specifications.*
- *At the venue we move in and provide the decor, trimmings that will make your wedding truly memorable.*
- *Each menu will be customised to your needs.*
- *Our kitchen, service and bar staff* have a vast experience of Indian Cuisine and are fully briefed so that each one knows enough about the day's menu to handle any questions.
- *We make sure all lighting is at their most enhancing. Dimming or spotlighting at the appropriate moment.*
- *All our food is cooked from fresh, with the majority of dishes cooked on-site.*

TELEPHONE SANJAY OR SANJEEV ANAND FOR INFORMATION ON BRILLIANT PACKAGING WITH THE HOTELS LISTED BELOW. TO BOOK AN INFORMAL MEETING SIMPLY PICK UP THE PHONE AND CALL MADHU'S BRILLIANT ON 081 574 1897 Fax: 081 813 8639 Mobile: 0831 255 155, 39 South Road, Southall, Middlesex UB1 1SW.

We have the capacity, the ambience and facilities to match your needs and these o

Heathrow Park Hotel   The Langham Hilton   The Excelsior Hotel

Madhus Karahi stand makes serving food easier, saves space, keeps food hot and guests can serve themselves easily with what they want, when they want.

...e hotels we have the distinction of tie-ups with.

The Royal Lancaster

The Edwardian International

The Park Lane Hotel

TAJ GOOD CURRY RESTAURANT GUIDE

ASSISTANT EDITOR : DOMINIQUE CHAPMAN
PROOF READER : DAVID MACKENZIE

RESEARCHERS : Karan Bilimoria, Ravi Menezes, Ajay Patel, Arjun Reddy, Iqbal Wahhab.

This guide is possible thanks to the many Curry Club members, and others, who have sent in reports on restaurants. Especial thanks to the following regular, prolific and reliable reporters (apologies for any ommissions, and for the tiny print, necessitated by space considerations!)

A: Martin Abbott, Gloucs; Ray Adams, Kimberley; Colin Adam, Kilwinning; Tony and Lesley Allen, Rugby; Paul Allen, Chatham; MF Alsan, Rugby; G Amos, Wirral; Capt R Ancliffe, BFPO 12; Lisa Appadurai, Benfleet; Robin Arnott, Stafford; Berry Ashworth, Compton Bassett; Allan Ashworth, York; Mrs M Asher, Woodford Green; Darius Astell, Southampton; Dave Ashton, Warrington; JO Ashton, Elland; Michelle Aspinal, Chester; Rachael Atkinson, SW16; Simon Atkinson, N5; Y Atkinson, IOM; Arman Aziz, N4.

B: John Baker, Loughton; Kim Baker, Hatfield; Keith Bardwell, Hertford; Derek Barnett, Colchester; Trevor Barnard, Gravesend; Christopher Barnes, Ashton; Derek Barnett, Colchester; Joanne Bastock, Saltash; Mr and Mrs ML Banks, Enfield; Mike Bates, Radcliffe; Tony Barrel, Hounslow; Ian Barlex, Ilford; Shirley Bayley, Worthing; Joyce Bearpark, Murcia Spain; P Bell, Carlisle; Ian Berry, Goole; John Bentley, Northampton; Ron Bergin, Gerrards Cross; DJ Betts, Bexhill; Brian and Anne Biffin, Fleet; Iain Boyd, Wealdstone; David Bolton, Lichfield; F Boyd, Stranraer; Robert Box, Knottingley; Sean Boxall, Andover; A Boughton, SE27; Sean Boxall, Andover; BH Birch, Hyde; Dave Bridge, Wallasey; John and Susan Brockington, Sutton Coldfield; Alan Boxall, Burwash; Steve Brown, Twickenham; David Brown, Leeds; DA Bryan, York; RC Bryant, Witney; Mark Brown, Scunthorpe; Steve Broadfoot, Anfield; Robert Bruce, Thornaby; Amanda Bramwell, Sheffield; Heather Buchanan, Inverness; Dr TM Buckenham, SW11; LG Burgess, Berkhamsted; A Burton, Weston-super-Mare.

C: Stan Calland, Kingsley; Hugh Callaway, Cleethorpes; Mrs E Campbell, Harrogate; Alex Campbell, Hartley Wintney; Duncan Cameron, Fordoun; Frank Cameron, Dundee; HS Cameron, Wirral; Josephine Capps, Romford; L Carroll, Huddersfield; Peter Cash, Lpl; Paul Chapman, Leighton Buzzard; TM Chandler, Farnborough; Desmond Carr, N8; J Carr, Birkenhead; Madeline Castro, Bury St Edmunds; Hilary Chapchal, Fetcham; Paul Chester, Cuffley; DL Carter, Huntingdon; Mrs M Carter, Colchester; Rajender Chatwal, Bicester; Sqn Ldr PF Christopher, Ferndown; Mrs BM Clifton Timms, Chorley; Billy Collins, Wirral; Peter Clyne, SW11; VA Coak, Penzance; Rhys Compton, Cheltenham; Kim Cooper, Basildon; Dr JC Coppola, Woodstock; Will Coppola, Oxford; Neil Cook, Royston; Mrs J Collins, Portsmouth; A Conroy, Durham; Nigel Cornwell, Orpington; DW Cope, Whitchurch; Roderick Cromar, Buckie; Yasmin Cross, Huddersfield; Robert Crossley, Huddersfield; R Cuthbertson, Southampton; Alexis Ciuszcak, Capistrano Beach, CA; Frank and Elizabeth Crozier, Redruth; Major & Mrs FJB Crosse, Salisbury.

D: Martin Daubney, Hitchin; P Dalton, Wirral; Mr & Mrs PE Dannat, Eastleigh; Jan Daniel, Felpham; Gary Davey, W4; S Daglish, Scarborough; Alasdair Davidson, Heswall; Colin Davis, Tatsfield; Adrian Davies, NW3; Paul Davies, Chiddingfold; Gwyn Davies, Wirral; Mrs G Davies-Goff, Marlow; Peter Deane, Bath; Mrs JC Davies, Leeds; David Dee, Ruislip; Ian Dawson, Mirfield; Elizabeth Defty, Co Durham; R Dent, Bishop Auckland; Les Denton, Barnsley; Richard Develyn, St Leonards; Nigel Peville, Uttoxeter; Richard Diamond, Romsey; RC Dilnot, Broadstairs; S Dolden, Rochester; Keith Dorey, Barnet; James Dobson, Burscough; R Dolley, W11; Anna Driscoll, Cape Province; Sarah Dowsett, Swindon; Diane Duame, Wicklow; Eric Duhig, Hornchurch; Sheila Dunbar, Pinner; James Duncan, West Kilbride; Robin Durant, Brighton.

E: A Edden-Jones, Bristol; CM Eeley, Witney; Bruce Edwards, Norwich; Dave Edwards, Rugeley; Rod Eglin, Whitehaven; Mrs G Elston, Woodley; Anthony Emmerton, Chorley; Mark Evans, Caersws;

F: Gary Fairbrother, Crosby; Hazel Fairley, Guildford; Denis Feeney, Glasgow; Kevin Fenner, Rothley; Stephen Field, Norton; Theresa Frey, Fareham; Duncan Finley, Glasgow; Mrs M Fisher, Woodford Green; Bernard Fison, Holmrook; John Fitzgerald, Great Missenden; Dr Cornel Fleming, N6; KD Flint, Kempsey; Merly Flashman, TN12; Fiona Floyd, Truro; Stephen & Elizabeth Foden, Lynton; Gareth Foley, Porthcawl; Linda Foye, Barry; Chris Fogarty, Enfield; Chris Frid, North Shields; Rosemary Fowler, Midhurst; Steve Frost, Kingston.

G: MJ Gainsford, Burbage; Mrs FE Gaunt, Stonehouse; Brian George, Wolverton; G Gibb, SE21; Robert Giddings, Poole; Andrew Gillies, Edinburgh; Ms D Glass, Liverpool; J Goleczka, Berkeley; AV Glanville, Windsor; Kathryn Grass, Wigan; Rachel Greaves, Tavistock; Bryn Gooding, Corfu; A Glenford, Lincoln; Alan Gray, Erskine; A Greaves, Chesterfield; Dr G Gordon, Kidlington; Nick Goddard, Stevenage; Andrew Godfrey, Seer Green; Bill Gosland, Camberley; David Gramagan, Formby; DC Grant, Enfield; Ian Gosden, Woking; Denise Gregory, Nottinghamshire; DR Gray, SW11; Jonathan Green, Cathays, Michael Green, Leicester; Nigel Green, Orpington; Richard Green, Gerrards Cross; Andrew Grendale, Ingatestone; Sheila Green, Barrow; A Gregor, Boston; Frank Gregori, NW10; M Griffiths, Northampton; Dave Froves, Walsall; Louis Gunn, Chelmsford.

H: Karen Haley, Telford; John Hall, Cullercoats; Andrew Halling, Leigh; Stephen Hames, Bewdley; Tina Hammond, Ipswich; Geoff & Janet Hampshire-Thomas, Kirkland; N Hancock, Derby; Dorothy Hankin, Fordingbridge; Sharon Hanson, Derby; Glynn Harby, Knaresborough; Martyn Harding, Powys; Roger Hargreaves, Stoke; David Harrison, Dursley; Patrick Harrison, Cambridge; J Harman, Brentwood; Paul Harris, BFPO; David Harvey, SE24; John K Hattam, York; John Haynes, Saffron Walden; DI Hazelgrove, West Byfleet; M Hearle, Tunbridge Wells; Kevin Hearn, Newcastle; Terry Herbat, Barnsley; Andy Hemingway, Leeds; George Herridge, W9; J & J Hetherington, Preston; Victoria Heywood, Burton; Roger Hickman, N1; Pat & Paul Hickson, Chorley; Mrs B Higgs, Cotty; Janet Higgins, Blackburn; Mrs S Higgins, Blackburn; Janet Higgins, Blackburn; Alec Hill, Wigan; Daniel Hodson, Abingdon; SC Hodgon; P Hogkinson, Sheffield; Peter Hoes, Bingley; P Howard, Hornchurch; Duncan Holloway, Windsor; Linda Horan, Wirral; Jerry Horwood, Guildford; Bruce Hoverd, Tongham; Mrs J Howarth, Oldham; Kathy Howe, Carlisle; Jan Hudson, Hemel Hempstead; Tom Hudson, Jarrow; Chris Hughes, Wraysbury; SP Hulley, Reddish; Roger Hunt, Sidmouth; Vince Hunt, Manchester; Sheila Hunter, Dundee, Penny Hunter, Brighton; Mrs V Hyland, Manchester.

I: DM Ibbotson, Sheffield; Nick & Mandy Idle, Ossett; Ken Ingram, Leeds; G Innocent, Dawlish; Mrs G Irving, Redditch; Robert Izzo, Horsham.

J: Dr AG James, Wigan; O Jarrett, Norwich; Sally Jeffries, Heathfield; L Jiggins, Dagenham; Paul Jolliffe, Clyst Hydon; G John, Wirral; Maxine & Andrew Johnson, Leiden; Peter Johnson, Droitwich; CML Jones, St Albans; RW Jones, N9; Shirley Jones, SE13; Gareth Jones, Tonypandy; Kate Jones, Leiden; Esther Juby, Norwich.

K: Chris Keardey, Southampton; Anthony Kearns, Stafford; David Kerray, Akrotiri; JS Kettle, Banbury; John Kettle, Dover; Stephen Kiely, N16; David King, Biggleswade; Alyson Kingham,

TAJ GOOD CURRY RESTAURANT GUIDE

Oldham; Peter Kitney, Banbury; J & P Klusiatis, Reading.

L: Martin Lally, Chester; Alan Lathan, Chorley; Jonathan Lazenby, Littlehampton; DH Lee, Waltham Abbey; Jackie Leek, Dartford; Margaret Ann Lewis, Ashford; R Lewis, Rayleigh; David Lloyd, Oswestry; J Longman, Bodmin; Michael Lloyd Jones, Cardiff; John Loosemore, Orpington; Eleanor & Owen Lock, Geneva; DA Lord, Hove; Julia & Philip Lovell, Brighton; AP Lowe, Tolworth; Mrs H Lundy, Wallasey; Graeme Lutman, Herts.

Mac/Mc: David Mackenzie, Twick'm; David Mackay, Twick'm; Deb McCarthy, E6; Patrick McCloy, N8; David McCulloch, NW11; Michael McDonald, Ellesmere Port; David McDowell, Telford; B McKeown, Liverpool; Ian McLean, Brighton; Alan & Jean McLucas, Solihull; Alan McWilliam, Inverurie.

M: Richard Manley, Wirral; E Mansfield, Camberley; Derek Martin, Marlow; DJ Mason, Cleveland; Geraldine Marson, Winsford; E Mansfield, Camberley; Cherry Manners, Hatfield; Gillian May, Bromley; Chris Mabey, Swindon; PR Martin, Southend; DH Marston, Southport; John Maundrell, Tunbridge Wells; LJ Mason, Leeds; Sue & Alf Melor, Hanworth; Simon Meaton, Andover; John Medd, Nottingham; Tim Mee, Harrow; Nigel Meredith, Huddersfield; H Middleton, Coventry; Catherine Millar, BFPO; DR Millichap, Horsham; PJL Mighell, Canterbury; Mr & Mrs P Mills, Mold; Jonathon Mitchell, Alton; Al Mitchell, Belfast; AJ Millington, Woodford; F Moan, Cuddington; Jon Molyneaux, Peterborough; Mrs SE Monk, Gisburn; AV Moody, Portsmouth; DM Moreland, Willington; S Morgan, Feltham; Peter Morwood, Wicklow; Caroline Moss, Solihull; A Moss, Colchester; Mrs L Muirhead, Glasgow; Andy Munro, Birmingham; Joan Munro, Leyburn; RG Murray, Carlisle; Annette Murray, Thornton Cleveleys.

N: Simon Nash, SW11; Mrs PG Naylor, Salisbury; Jeff Neal, Bolton; A Nelson-Smith, Swansea; Liam Nevens, Stockton, Rebecca Newman; Hayey, Clive Newton, Northwich; P & D Nixon, Baildon; Mrs DA Nowakowa, Tiverton; Robert Nugent, SE31; Jody Lynn Nye, Illinois.

O: AM O'Brien, Worthing; Eamon O'Brien, Holland; Pauline O'Brien, London; Elise O'Donnell, Wolverhampton; DC O'Donnell, Wetherby; Mary O'Hanlon, Helensburgh; David O'Regan, Leeds; Jan Ostron, Felpham; Judith Owen, SW6; William & Sue Oxley, Southampton.

P: Trevor Pack, Rushden; RH Paczec, Newcastle; Graham Paine, Coventry; Keith Paine, Tilbury; GJ Palmer, Gainsborough; Angela Parkinson, Clitheroe; Bill Parkes-Davies, Tunbridge Wells; M Parsons, Fareham; Roy Parsons, Richmond; Mrs PA Pearson, Bristol; Mrs G Pedlow, Hitchin; J Penn, Southampton; AJW Perry, Bristol; MJ Perry, E17; Ian Pettigrew, Edinburgh; Christopher Phelps, Gloucester; Diane Phillips, Hyde; Colin Phipps, Scarborough; Sara Pickering, Northolt; Jack Pievsky, Pinner; Susan Platt, Bury; K Pool, Leyland; SR Poole, Runcorn; Steve Porter, Walsall; Alison Preuss, Glencarse; Tim Preston, Barrow; Dr John Priestman, Huddersfield; Jeff Price, Bristol. D Pulsford, Marford; Janet Purchon, Bradford; Steve Puttock, Chatham.

Q: Sheila Quince, E11

R: Diane Radigan, Welling; Clive Ramsey, Edinburgh; RC Raynham, Chelmsford; KJ Rayment, Hertford; Debbie Reddy, W12; CR Read, Epsom; Steven Redknap, Ashford; I Reid, Fife; Lorraine Reid, Edinburgh; Duncan Renn, Dursley; Sean Richards, Dover; Derek Richards, Bewdley; Simon Richardson, Gainsborough; Mathew Riley, SE3; Peter Roberts, Shipston; Margaret Roberts, Rubery; Lindsay Roberts, Lancaster; Stewart & Anne Robertson, Leamington; J & P Rockney, Leicester; KG Rodwell, Harston; John Roscoe, Stalybridge; Brian Roston, Pontefract; Steve Rowland, Matlock; John Rose, Hull; WJ Rowe, DC Ruggins, Chalfont; JA Rumble, Rochford; Mrs EM Ruck, Darlington; Paul Rushton, Nottingham; Bob Rutter, Blackpool; N Ryer, Mansfield; EJ Ryan, Effingham.

S: Pauline Sapsford, Milton Keynes; MR Sargeant, Cornwall; Mark Sarjant, Guildford; GM Saville, Egremont; Mike Scotlock, Rayleigh; Mike Scott, Holmer Green; MJ Scott, SE26; Nicky & Don Scowen, Romford; Tim Sebensfield, Beeston; M Seefeld, W5; Patrick Sellar, Maidstone; Philip Senior, Liverpool; N Sennett, Hull; Mrs DA Seymour, Burnham-on-Sea; Richard Shackleton, Wakefield; Brian Shallon, Camberley; Jeane Sharp, St Albans; Michelle Shaw, Ilford; Deborah Shent, Nottingham; Barrie Shepherd, Bishopstone; Ewan Sim, Leeds; Jennifer Singh, Enfield; Jeff Slater, E6; Else & Harald Smaage, Sauvegny; Hazel Smith, Llandrinio; Gillian Smith, St Andrews; Nora Smith, Cardiff; David Smith, Norwich; Jim Smith, Cork; RB Smith, BFPO; EK Smith, Edinburgh; Denis Smith, Swindon; LP & A Smith, Gibraltar; Colin Snowball, Storrington; Tim Softly, Leigh; Peter Soloman, Middlesbrough; M Somerton- Rayner, Cranwell; M Southwell, Haddenham; Gill Sparks, Halifax; Andrew Speller, Harlow; Andy Spiers, Brighton; R Spiers, Wolverhampton; Chris Spinks, Ilford; John Spinks, Hainault; GD Spencer, Stonehaven; Martin Spooner, Wallsend; Mrs WL Stanley-Smith, Belper; John Starley, Birdingbury; Nigel Steel, Carlisle; Avril Steele, Crossgar; John Stent, Liss; Ian Stewart, Potters Bar; Mrs MB Such FD Sunderland, Plympton; Frank Sweeney, Middlesbrough; Gary Swain, Coventry; Carolyn Swain, Leeds; DL Swann, Parbold; Gill & Graham Swift, Beeston; MS Sykes, Dorrington.

T: Steve Tandy, Cleveleys; Bernard Tarpey, Failsworth; Colin Taylor, Preston; Philip & Vivien Taylor, Cromer; CB Taylor, Wolverhampton; Ken Taylor, Sevenoaks; Roger Taylor, Hamela; Len Teff, Whaddon; DL Thomas, Peterborough; Paul Thomson, Salford; Bill Thomson, Ramsgate; Alan Thompson, Clwyd; Richard Thompson, Rainham; J Thorne, South Benfleet; Mrs H Timblade, Beverley; Bernard Train, Barton; Dr JG Tucker, SW17; Don Turnball, Geneva; Mrs SM Turner, Stroud; R Twiddy, Boston; S Twiggs, Lower Kingswood; Jeremey Twomey, Leamington; John Tyler, Romford;

V: David Valentine, Forfar; Alan & Lesley Vaughan, Paington; Mrs B Venton, Chipstead; Sarah Vokes, Dorking.

W: Phil Wain, Merseyside; R Waldron, Oxon; Alison Walker, Droitwich; Andrew Walker, Aklington; John Walker, Chorley; Dr JB Walker, Burnham; Dr PAW Walker, Wirral; William Wallace, West Kilbride; Alison Walton, North Shields; Pamela Ward, Birmingham; RG Watt, Bromyard; Andy Webb, Aberdeen; Peter Webb, West Byfleet; TG Webb, Peterborough; Nick Webley, Llandeilo; Dave Webster, Gateshead; Andrew Wegg, SW16; John Wellings, Edinburgh; Dave Weldon, Hale; Michael Welch, Reading; J Weld, Eastleigh; LSD West, Torquay; Joyce Westrip, Perth, Australia; Sarah Wheatley, Leavesden; George Whilton, Huddersfield; Andy Whitehead, Swindon; Mr & Mrs DW Whitehouse, Redditch; George Whitton, Huddersfield; Peter Wickendon, East Tilbury; Jennette Wickes, Fleet; PM Wilce, Abingdon; Ted Williams, Norwich; Babs Williams, Bristol; Mark Williams, Bromley; P Williams, St Austell; David Williamson, NW3; BP Willoughby, Devizes; Geoffrey Wilkinson, Orpington; Bob & Eve Wilson, NW2; Dr Michael Wilson, Crewe; Major Mike Wilson, BFPO 140; Mrs AC Withrington, Hindhead; W Wood, Hornsea; Georgina Wright, Nottingham; John Woolsgrove, Enfield; Geof Worthington, Handforth; Clive Wright, Halesowen; Lynn Wright, Newark; Mrs C Wright, Glasgow; D Wright, Rotherham.

Y: Stephen Yarrow, NW11; Rev Can David Yerburgh, Stroud; Andy Young, Penrith; Carl Young, Nottingham; Mrs B Young, Basildon; Mrs E Young, Ilmington.

Introduction

The Good Curry Restaurant Guide (GCRG) is now in its eleventh year (and fourth edition). Its raison d'être is to single out the better restaurants and takeaways. With 8,000 to choose from, the task gets harder than ever (there were 7,000 last Guide and 4,000 the Guide before that). So, regrettably 7,000 do not make it into this Guide. Almost certainly some of them should have done. How come they are omitted?

We rely on a number of sources of information, but by far the most important is the genuine voluntary reports sent in by many people (see pages 8 and 11). We receive over 4,000 reports a year. One report may deal with just one restaurant. Some reporters only write to us once. Another report may contain information on dozens of restaurants. Other reporters write repeatedly. In addition we ask you to list the names of your favourite restaurants, rather than write a full report.

Since our last guide we have therefore received information on thousands of curry restaurants. Such is life, of course, that we do not receive reports on every single establishment. So, yes, it is possible that we've omitted a really good one - and it's bound to be your favourite! So tell us please, we'll know for next time. Equally, though we do our best to filter out 'good' reports on bad restaurants (particularly those written by their hopeful owners). And yes, even after fourteen years in the editor's chair, it is possible that we've been conned and a bad one has slipped into the Guide. Let us know about that too please. No doubt, we'll continue to get irate letters from people, who won't have bothered to read this explanation, telling us that, 'because this or that restaurant was awful when they visited, it casts doubt on the credibility of the entire Guide.' Of course, standards and ownership do change not infrequently in the restaurant business. Equally, staff move around, for numerous reasons. But not one restaurant gets into this Guide unless we have at least one recent good report on it, preferably several.

To get into our TOP 100, the restaurant must have had many recent good reports from different people. I explained this to one Wiltshire restaurant. A few days later and for weeks afterwards the mail delivered a glowing report about this very restaurant, each in totally different handwriting. In normal circumstances such a volume of good reports would have catapulted the restaurant near to top of our TOP 100. The only problem was that every report was a copy, more or less word for word of the first. Did this ernest restaurateur get all his clients to write in? Even the envelopes were similar! As a regular guide entrant, he got in again, but not as a TOP 100.

On another occasion we got nine reports on a Cheshire curry house, including one from a Mr Moan, all in different hands, but written on the same date! As it happens this restaurant had already been selected to enter the elite TOP 100.

Before we even start to select who gets into the Guide we send every one of the 8,000 restaurants a simple questionnaire, mainly to verify our facts, also to remind them we are there. After fourteen years, of bona-fide operations, you would imagine that curry house owners, would clamour to be in it. And indeed some do. More than one restaurant has made veiled hints as to the benefits which would be made available to the editors, if that restaurant was declared the UK's Number One. To those restaurateurs who believe that they can buy this accolade, or even entry into this Guide, we politely request that they save their energy. Should the editor/proprietor accede to such bribes, it would be the end of the credibility of this publication. Our fund raising activities are through booksales, aided by sponsorship and advertisements (see page 5) not through bribes. But not all restaurants are that eager. Some are down-right suspicious of us. And of course, we do get imitators. The current scam is the bogus certificate syndrome. We know of fourteen different operators of such schemes. They approach all restaurants (regardless of quality) with the lure of a 'prestigious' certificate. Every restaurateur wants accolades, and many say 'yes'. They receive their certificate, but along with it, they get an invoice ranging between £100 and £600 for the privilege. The remarkable fact is that so many, otherwise hardened restaurateurs actually are gullible enough to cough up. We have heard of more than one, who pay well over £1,000 per annum for such services. Sadly, apart from the certificate, nothing else whatever is supplied.

However, with so many pretenders vying for a limited pot of gold, it is, perhaps not surprising that some restaurateurs are suspicious of everything. But we are amazed when restaurateurs, on receipt of our questionnaire, phone up and aggressively tell us they want nothing at all to do with our publication. Mohammed of Dundee's Gullistan did so, to advise that in seventeen years of operating he had never heard of The Curry Club, The Good Curry Restaurant Guide or WH Smiths! Neither had the owner of Scunthorpe's Raj heard of us. He said, 'in any case we are in The Good Food Guide.' Neither The Raj nor Scunthorpe appear in recent editions! The Taj Mahal Stockton-on-Tees claimed to have paid Curry Club 'inspectors' to ensure they got into this Guide. If we had inspectors, which we do not, we certainly would not permit them to levy a charge (see page 5). To ensure that the message is understood, we have never paid for diners' reports, nor indeed have we ever received any on this restaurant, which automatically precludes its entry into the Guide.

Perhaps certificates do impress the locals, but readers of this Guide could help the situation by encouraging their favourite local restaurant to avoid paying for certificates, and to support the bona-fide non-charging restaurant guides, by communicating with them. We feel that the production of this Guide should be helpful not only to readers and potential customers, it should also be of use to the restaurants themselves. They have a right to be proud of their entry into this Guide. It is, after all, prestigious to a restaurant to be singled out with a one in seven accolade of excellence from the dining public. All restaurants nominated in this guide will be awarded a free certificate and a window sticker to display if they wish to. The elite will be recognised by special wards.

A good number of our 1,000 have elected to join in our discount scheme, whereby they will give a discount of their choice to Curry Club members in return for a voucher. See page 288 for details.

Finally, I hope this Guide will amuse and entertain you, as well as inform you and guide you to a good curry somewhere in the 1,000 best curry houses across the length and breadth of Great Britain and beyond.

I hope reading its contents will make your mouth water as much as it did mine when I wrote it. I trust that it will take you places that you may otherwise have not tried, where you will enjoy the cuisine of the sub-continent of India at the highest standards.

If this Guide achieves that, it will have done its job.

Bon apetit, and here's to good curries.

Pat Chapman   Founder The Curry Club

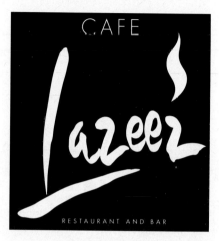

Wine With Curry

Wine journalist and consultant, David Wolfe explodes the myth that fine red wine is spoiled by spicy food.

In Britain today curry and tandoories are often accompanied by lager, but what really goes best with Indian food? Diluted spirits are not everyone's taste nor are fruit drinks. Soured milk drinks such as lhassi are good early in the meal, but too rich for continued drinking. Water is boring, and reacts with some spices to give a metallic twang at the back of the throat. Nor is copious water with rice a good idea. Beer tastes better, but large volumes can be bloating; and for my palate, beer however good, lacks the depth of flavour to match Indian spices - although it cleans the palate effectively.

So for me, and many others, wine is ideal - providing it has masses of flavour. A delicate Muscadet or Beaujolais is delicious; even sweeter wines like German Riesling can be refreshing at the right time and place. But wine, even white wine, is not a thirst-quencher. On the contrary, its high alcohol content makes it dehydrating.

Since white wines generally have less flavour, it must be red to stand up to the spices and herbs. Most wine books say fine wine is spoiled by chillies. But in my own experience, this is not so. The wine and spices do not argue face to face, but slide past each other. As the wine flavour momentarily takes over the palate 'forgets' the chillies; then the chillies return and the wine is forgotten. More likely to spoil the taste of wine is an excess of sweet mango chutney!

For understandable reasons, few Indian restaurant wine lists are outstanding. Here I suggest no individual wines, only types. First house red. Many wines so described have little appeal. Thin, watery bottles become worse with curry; but full flavour, dark wine may go well even if it is rough and coarse.

Some finer reds are also too light. Fine Burgundy is very delicate, but Beaujolais, while light, usually has enough flavour. Better still are powerful Côtes du Rhône wines, and curiously, the clarets of Bordeaux. This is strange, because it is a truism that claret goes best with delicate meat. In choosing remember that basic, cheap claret may be light, and too young. In 1995 the youngest likely to be good is 1992, but 1990 should be even better. Look particularly for the Bordeaux districts of Bourg, Blaye and Saint Emilion; Pauillac and lesser Médocs such as Moulis or Listrac can be excellent too.

And seek out wines of the claret family from other areas. 'Varietals' from Bordeaux grapes, Cabernet Sauvignon and/or Merlot come from southern France, Spain, Italy, Eastern Europe and the New World. Australia is good value, and California is becoming more reasonable. The Rhône grape, Syrah or Shiraz, also makes popular and powerful Australian reds. Rich oaky flavoured Rioja is splendid with curry, but young 'sin crianza' wines (without ageing), good in themselves, may be but too light.

While white wines are lighter flavoured than reds, some do go well with food. White Burgundy, from the Chardonnay grape, has rich fruit and the same grape makes big flavoury wines everywhere. Australian Chardonnays with their rainbow of tropical fruit flavours are often outstanding even if prices are now rising.

If German wine is too sweet, try Alsace, where wines are named for their grapes. Rieslings are drier than German equivalents, Pinot gris is more tasty than Pinot blanc, and the richest is Gewurztraminer. This is often recommended with Indian food, seemingly because 'Gewurz' in the grape's name means 'spicy'. But its spiciness is nearer that of tropical fruit than real spice flavours, and for me its fruitness can clash with the food. White wines, too earthy on their own, or with delicate food, can match rich creamy curries. Look to southern France, Spain, Italy (especially Sicily and Sardinia), even Greece and eastern Europe for these.

Finally, please ignore my advice if you have found by experience that you disagree. But try some of these suggestions if you have not already done so.

Lager With Curry

Iqbal Wahhab speculates that Indian restaurants, having changed the way this country eats, will now change its drinking habits.

That the lads in the provincial high street still use a curry as blotting paper after swilling gallons of beer is, sadly, an image which still persists. But it is less common than it has been in the past. This deplorable British tradition is being eroded. One of the reasons for the turnabout is that customers have found they can enjoy a far better drink in the restaurant than in the pub.

A pint of fizzy, guaranteed-to-get-you-bloated European lager, was the only answer in the past to the question of what to drink with Indian food. The view still persists, even amongst some discerning diners and wine critics. But over the past few years, as restaurants have developed their culinary skills, they have also seen the need to present an authentic and genuine experience to their visitors.

So does the typical dining table in India have pints of gassy, insipid lager floating around? Certainly not! What you will see is genuine Indian beer, and it is increasingly available in Britain. But isn't beer just beer where ever it comes from? Not when it is specifically designed to accompany spiced food.

Cobra Indian Lager, which accounts for over 90% of all Indian beer imported to the UK, is the best example. It has all the qualities one requires in a drink in to accompany curry that are lacking in European brews. The first thing you notice about Cobra is how smooth it is. The beer is brewed by the high-tec Mysore Breweries Limited in Bangalore using an extended double-filtered brewing procedure. Because Cobra is brewed for only export out of India, they use the best malt, maize, yeast, hops and rice. The brewmaster at MBL, Dr S .Cariapa, got his PhD in Czechoslovakia and worked with European breweries before returing to India. So he brings the best brewing technologies to Cobra. The prime importance of this smoothness is that it makes the beer easily drinkable, and irresistable because of its creamy, distinctive taste.

Cobra has a premium 5% alcohol strength and comes in 330ml bottles, though many restaurants serve it in the traditional Indian double- sized 650ml (1.2pints) bottle.There is also a Cobra Silver Label with a lighter, refreshing 4.4% alcohol strength available.

Some restaurants report remarkable Cobra drinking stories. At Khan's in London W2, for example, a group of 12 French businessmen went through 48 large bottles in one lunchtime, and at The Bombay Brasserie, a table of seven went through 30 of them at one sitting! The good thing about the large bottles is that, like wine, it encourages the sharing concept which has already been established with the food

But be warned! When you visit an Indian restaurant, don't just ask for an Indian beer - there are some around with Indian sounding names which are actually brewed in England!

Insist on the best... insist on Cobra!

Iqbal Wahhab , a former journalist with the Independent, as head of a succesful PR company, specialising in restaurants of all types and related products and services, is now the country's foremost practitioner of PR to Indian restaurants.

ROWLEY VILLAGE TANDOORI

**10 Portway Road, (off Throne Road), Rowley
Regis, Warley, Sandwell, West Midlands.
B65 9DB
Telephone: 0121 561 4463**

...Award Winning Restaurant : Fully Licensed...

**OPEN: 7 days a week (except Christmas Day)
HOURS: Sun-Thurs: 5pm-Midnight
Fri-Sat: 5pm-1am**

*Indian cuisine is a combination of subtle tastes.
Fragrant and exotic spices from India are delicately
blended to create the dishes we present to you.*

*Our dishes are of Northern Indian and Bangladeshi
origin and are prepared in our Restaurant exactly as in
our homes.*

*Each dish will have its own distinctive flavour and
aroma which cannot come from any curry powder but
only from spices and herbs specially prepared by
ourselves.*

"Why settle for a taste of India, when The Taj Group can give you the whole banquet?"

Travelling India with us could make you a broader person. Because once you taste the true flavours of this mystical land, you discover that the food of India is sustenance for both body and soul. Every mouthful blends the splendours of the past with a vision for the future in an unforgettable magical reality.

So come with us on a culinary journey through India, from palace to plate, from temple to tea party, and from one extraordinary sensation to another. Only the exquisite restaurants and the immaculately trained chefs of the Taj Group of Hotels can be trusted to take the flavours, the spirit, the magic, the pageantry, the rituals, and the riches of India and blend them subtly and seductively, into a feast for all the senses.

The notion is not entirely original. Travellers have been dining like Kings in this ancient land long before the term *haute cuisine* was coined. But there has never been a better way, or a better time, to savour the pleasures of this earthly paradise than at a table with the Taj. Will you, indeed, want to leave your table to see the splendid stone maidens of Khajuraho, the busy boats bobbing on the mighty Ganges, or that tear-stained, pearl-crowned mighty monument to love, the Taj Mahal? We will not blame you if you can't.

Besides, it is our proud belief that our restaurants vie for your attention with the many spendours of India. Not only are the world's finest and freshest foods used in the creation of each dish, so, too, are the long-lost arts of patience, craftsmanship, and detail. From the fine filigree icing on your French pastry to the way in which flavors are woven like bright silks through your rogan josh (lamb curry), Taj cuisine is an everpresent echo of the artistic and architectural grandeur that surrounds your every step in India.

From a delicate custard apple ice-cream to a perfect Bloody Mary; from a tropical pasta to European sacher torte; from an exquisite vegetarian thali to a magnificent array of barbecued shellfish; our restaurants like India herself, are home to all the arts.

In your own world, you live in the here and now, but in India, we live in eternity. There has been plenty of time to perfect the gentle art of spicing, making the drip by drip decoction of coffee in South India; the catching of fresh seafood, the making of a perfect cup to tea, and the creation of ethereal sweetmeats in Calcutta.

So that instead of bargaining over the brilliant brocades of Rajasthan, the land of Kings, you may relax over a gin and tonic at the Polo Bar at the Rambagh Palace at Jaipur and still aquaint yourself with the fine arts of India.

In Varanasi, you can explore the world's most ancient city and its sacred river one day, and the city's most famous of slow cooked potatoes with over a dozen spices at the Hotel Taj Ganges the next.

As always, it is the colours of India that you will treasure most. The turquoise and vermilion of freshly caught fish at Kerala, the brilliant jewel like cerise and lemon of tropical fruit at Madras. And while nothing is quite as ethereal as a burnt orange sunset over the still waters of Lake Pichola, Upaidur, the colour is caught and held by every dish of delicate Kashmiri saffron tinted rice at the famous Lake Palace.

Colour is everywhere, more vivid than the brilliant piles of spices at the markets and robes of the devout. You will be equally entranced by the faded salmon colours, that tint the whole city of Jaipur, or the Indian ocean crab baked to perfection at the Beach Cafe of The Taj Holiday Village in Goa.

At bustling Bombay, you can tear yourself away from the majesty of the Gateway of India to admire the artistry and grandeur of our famous Indian banquet table at the Taj Mahal Intercontinental, or to feast on the sizzling splendors of the Chinese province of Szechwan without having to pass through the Gateway once again.

Agra means both the romance and majesty of the Taj Mahal, and the candlelight gleaming in a glass of Indian bubbly at your table for two at the Taj View Hotel. Beautiful, tropical Goa gives you brilliant sea views of freshly netted lobsters the size of your arm at the Fort Aguada Beach Resort.

At Paradise Island at the Taj West End, Bangalore, savour a Thai prawn curry over a beautiful pond.

And who could forget the sparkling treasure trove that is Kathmandu, as you sample the authentic flavours of Nepalese cooking at the Taj Hotel De L'Annapurna, or the spicy serendipity that is Sri Lanka at the Taj Sumandra Hotel.

From the rich Moghlai lamb dishes and tantalising tandoori of the north to the sensational seafood, chilli and coconut of the south, we invite you to join us on a gastronomic adventure, and to discover the real jewels in our crown.

We will certainly feed you like royalty if you like. But we would prefer to feed you like a God.

THE TAJ GROUP *of* HOTELS

65 chefs. 12 different Indian

(But, if you insist, we can still make

The past 90 years have seen Indian cuisine at the Taj grow int

a minor industry. From the staple curry-rice served in 1903 t

twelve different Indian cuisines conjured up in our restaurants

we like to think we've done our bit to show the world that India

food goes a little beyond curry-rice. Although if that's what yo

want you'll still get it. At any of the country's finest India

restaurants listed below. Restaurants, though widely diverger

in cuisine, remain solidly similar in name : Taj.

Speciality Indian restaurants at the Taj are : *Handi* (North India

cuisines. 1000 recipes.

you a mean curry-rice.)

Cuisine), Taj Palace Inter.Continental, New Delhi. *Haveli* (North Indian & North-West Frontier Cuisine), The Taj Mahal Hotel, New Delhi. *Tanjore* (North and South Indian Cuisine), The Taj Mahal Hotel, Bombay. *Sonargaon* (Bengali and Lucknowi Cuisine), Taj Bengal, Calcutta. *Raintree* (Chettinad Cuisine of South India), Connemara Hotel, Madras. *Dakhni* (Food from the Deccan and Andhra Pradesh), The Gateway Hotel on Banjara Hill, Hyderabad. *Karavalli* (Coastal Mangalorean, Karwari, Goan and Keralite Cuisine), The Gateway Hotel, Bangalore.

THE TAJ GROUP *of* HOTELS

Market Trends

The bad news is that curry restaurant closures have been continuing apace. It is hard to keep up with closures. Unlike openings, there is no press release to accompany this sad event. It makes it really hard to maintain our records, of course, and we hope that no restaurant in this guide has closed in the period between us receiving its details and entering it into the Guide. We rely very heavily on our reporters to tell us about closures. The good news is that, despite closures, the total number of UK curry houses has grown from 7,000 to 8,000 in the three and a half years since we last published.

Who could have predicated the rise of Balti in the last two years? It has become the buzz word to many, but not to all. Certain food reporters (outside Birmingham) seem to have taken an aversion to it. Madhur Jaffrey declined all knowledge of it in BBC Good Food. 'It doesn't exist in Indian,' she said. As an Indian living in New York, Ms Jaffrey is entitled to her view that every British curry house is an abomination, but it is an opinion not shared by the restaurateurs nor their customers. Balti does exist (albiet in Pakistan - ask Mark Tulley!) And it is thriving in the West Midlands. As to everywhere else, it is true that there is a strong element of 'me-too' going on with restaurants everywhere trying to emulate the Birmingham experience. Some succeed whilst others do not. Given time they may all succeed. Even if there is a little hype involved, it is no worse than that which elevated Pizza into prominence on the British street scene a few years ago. And if it succeeds in getting more Brits converted to curry then so much the better.

Talking of converts, it's now official. Curry is addictive. Says Sydney University's Dr John Preston: 'One taste of Korma leads to a Vindaloo.' And to prove it, he spent three years and thousands of dollars at a succession of Australian curry houses! It's something we curryholics know already, but do we know why? UCLA's Dr Paul Bosland does. He says: 'It's the release of endorphins - the body's pain killers - which give you a feel-good factor when you take chilli. So you take more chilli because it feels so pleasurable. '

British Telecom has done it again, last time it was London, whose codes changed. This time it's every number in the book. R e s - taurant name changes continue to keep us baffled. It is endless and we hope our records are accurate. Whether it is just change for change sake, or whether it is to avoid creditors we cannot say. We can understand Bromley's Carioca becoming the Zanzibar, 'we were fed up with being take for a Karaoke bar.' But why should Llangefni's Gandhi become the Moonlight, or Whitstable's Rajpoot become Whitstable Tandoori, whilst Kent Tandoori becomes the Badsha (Tenterden) equally Enfield's Raj Tandoori, the Aroti. Perhaps our favourite name change is Kokis to Thamoulinee, now in the ownership of Mrs Jasmine Hyacinth.

The recession has hit hard at trade, with some desperate restaurateurs resorting to slashing prices. In some cases it worked, but it's always a dangerous policy if it is uncontrolled, as was graphically demonstrated in Bristol. There it became a price war between certain rival restaurants, so much so that some of them wiped themselves out.

A much more positive attempt to improve trade has been the introduction of home-delivery. Such a service has been part of American culture for ever, it seems. Eventually the pond was crossed, first by pizza deliveries (them again) and now by curry houses. It is a sign of the times

CURRY CLUB

**QUALITY PRODUCTS
BEST SELLING BOOKS**

INDIAN RESTAURANT COOKBOOK
Pat Chapman

250 Favourite CURRIES & ACCOMPANIMENTS
PAT CHAPMAN

BALTI Curry Cookbook
The exciting new curry technique
PAT CHAPMAN

THE CURRY CLUB
HASLEMERE
GU27 1EP

that we prefer the luxury of an on-the-doorstep-service to the tedious wait at the takeaway. We don't even mind paying for it. It's all a question of giving the people what they want.

Congratulations to two outstanding Bangladeshi restaurateurs: Wali Uddin JP (Verandah restaurant - Edinburgh) has recently been appointed Bangladeshi High Commissioner to Scotland and he has been awarded the MBE, by the Queen. Enam Ali, (Epsom's Le Raj) for pioneering the *Dine Bangladeshi* campaign,thus making the British aware of Bangladesh through our curries. Since seven-eighths of our Indian restaurants are not Indian but Bangladeshi, the campaign is appropriate. Let us anticipate some authentic Bangladeshi special dishes emerging nationwide. On a lighter note, we must not omit one of England's latest Lords. Mohammed Abdul Latif, to the Sylhetti manor born, owner of Newcastle's Rupali, is now the honourable Lord of Harpole, near Ipswich. He bought the title. Maybe he'll buy a curry house there too and call it Lord's?

Curry Statistics

Since 1991, the number of UK curry restaurants has grown by 1,000 to 8,000 (an increase of 12 1/2%). Overall, business at the Indian restaurant now accounts for 6% of the entire UK restaurant/takeaway trade, placing it 7th after fish and chips, the pub, the steakhouse, Chinese, hamburgers and Italian. Where it leads all the others is in its astonishing revenue growth of 27% in just one year (93/94). This figure needs is a closer look: Curiously, it is not eating at the restaurant which has increased. Infact it declined by 3% in the year 1993/4. It is eating restaurant curry off the premises which has shown spectular growth during this period. Takeaway accounts for 49% of curry house trade (22% growth). But the most interesting growth is in home deliveries. It has burgeoned by 87% (93/94) to account for 14% of all curry sales.

Between 1991 to 1994 there has been a 26% increase in curry eating. It is estimated that over 2 1/2 million diners visit the Indian restaurant each week. With an average bill of between £12-£15 the total spend is between £1 1/2 to £2 billion. That the curry habit is gained at an early age is shown by the age groups of regulars using the curry house: 23% are between 16 and 24, and 37% are between 25 and 34, whilst 16% are 45-64 and only 2% are over 65. 92% of curry house users prefer evenings. (Saturday night accounts for 25% of all trade, Friday 18%, Thursday 12%). Sunday lunch only accounts for 2%.Indeed all curry house lunch trade amounts only to 9%.

Demographically,18% of A's and B's eat curry at home ,26% of C1's and 26% of C2's do so , while D's and E's eat 29%. As to willingness to try curry amongst the decreasing amount of adults who have not experienced it (yes there are still several millions still awaiting conversion) where as it was 37% in 1992 it is now 42% in 1994. There is a similar growth in ready meals (23% to 27%) and curry recipes (25% to 28%).

The curry scene at the supermarket has seen a 90% growth since 1991. With ingredients and ready meal sales at £400 million a year, it is ahead of the nearest ethnic (Chinese) by a wide margin. Approaching 3 million households cook curry once a week or more. What they cook ranges from microwaving a frozen or chilled ready curry, to cooking a fully fledged curry from a recipe book.£20 million is spent on papadams alone.

Favourite curried ingredient is chicken, which has climbed to 60% (from 52.5%) at the expense of vegetarian dishes which are now at 10%, and meat which is at 20%. Fish and prawn remain at 10%. Chicken Tikka Masala remains the number one dish (15%) with chicken Korma next (7%) and Tikka / Tandoori at 6%.

Main sources: Taylor Nelson and Curry Club User Survey

The Cuisine of the sub-continent

Afghan

Afghanistan's location had always held the strategic key to India until this century, for it was through the solitary mountain passes that the invaders came and possessed India for as early as 3000 BC. Located between Iran (formerly Persia) and Pakistan (formerly NW India) it brought the cuisine of the Middle East to India - and that of India to the Middle east. Kebabs and Birianis, and skewered spiced lamb over charcoal. The only Afghan restaurant in the UK is London's Caravan Serai, W1. ee page 100.

Bangladeshi / Bengali

Most of the standard curry houses in the UK are owned by Bangladeshis and nearly all of those serve standard formula curries, ranging from mild to very hot. Bangladesh, formerly East Pakistan, is located at the mouth of the river Ganges. Before Partition the area either side of the Ganges was Bengal. Today Bengal is the Indian state which shares its border with Bangladesh. In terms of food, Bangladesh is Moslem, so pork is forbidden. The area enjoys prolific fresh and sea-water fish - pomfret, hilsa and ayre, and enormous tiger prawns , and it specialises in vegetable dishes such as Niramish. Until recently, true Bangladeshi / Bengali cuisine was nigh on impossible to find in the UK. With the *Dine ~Bangladeshi* campaign gaining ground, we can expect to find more and more of our Bangladeshi restaurants serving the delights of their own country.

Bombay

Bhel Puri is Bombay's favourite kiosk food. And it has found its way to the UK in the form of Bhel Puri Houses in Drummond Street, Westbourne Grove, Southall, Wembley and other places around London. It is served cold and is delicious. See the entry on page 60 for the Diwana Bhel Puri House, the UK's pioneer of it, for a description

Burmese

Burma, now renamed Myanmar, shares its boundaries with Bangladesh, India, China, Laos and Thailand. Its food is a combination of these styles. Rice is the staple and noodles are popular too. Curries are very hot and there are no religious objections to eating pork or beef or other meats. Duck and seafood are commonly used. The only Burmese restaurant in the UK is the Maymo in London SE 24, see entry.

Goan

Goa is on the West coast of India, about 400 miles south of Bombay. It was established in 1492, by the Portuguese who occupied it until 1962. It is now a state of India where Christianity prevails and there are no objections to eating pork or beef. The food of Goa is unique. Their most famous dish is Vindaloo - but it is not the dish from the standard curry house - it is traditionally pork marinated in spicy Vinegar (the longer the better) then simmered in a chilli hot red curry gravy. Goa also has delicious seafood and fish dishes. There is only one Goan restaurant in the UK, in Putney, SW14, though Goan dishes do appear at the better Indian restaurants.

Gujarati

Gujarat is a sea-board state, north of Bombay. Its population is largely vegetarian. Specialities include much use of yoghurt and gramflour in curries, rissoles and snacks. Gujarati restaurants are prevalent in Wembley, Middlesex, and they pop up elsewhere.

Moghul

The curry from the standard curry house is based on rich creamy dishes developed by the Moghul emperors. No one on earth was richer than the Moghuls, and it was during their time, four centuries ago that Indian food was perfected. Authentically, this style of food should be subtly spiced. It can be found in an increasing number of 'haute cuisine' restaurants around the country.

Nawabi

The Nawabs were the rich royals of the Lucknow area of India, who lived over two centuries ago. Like the Moghuls before them, they perfected a style of cooking which was spicy and fragrant. Called Dum or Dum Puk, it involves cooking the curry or Biriani in a round pot, whose lid is sealed into place with a ring of chapatti dough. The resulting dish is opened in front of the diners releasing all those captured fragrances. This style may be just about to hit the better UK curry restaurant scene.

Nepalese

Nepal, located to the North of India, in the Himalayas, is famous for Sherpas and Gurkhas. The Nepalese enjoy curry and rice, of course, their own specialities are, perhaps less well known. Momos, for example, are dumplings with a mince curry filling. Aloo Achar are potatoes in pickle sauce. There is an increasing, though still small, number of restaurants with Nepalese specials on the menu, particularly in west London.

Pakistani

Pakistan was, until independence in 1947, the north western group of Indian states. Located between Afghanistan and India it contains the famous Khyber Pass. The people are pre-dominantly meat eaters, favouring lamb and chicken (being Moslem, they avoid pork). Charcoal cooking is the norm, and this area is the original home of the tandoor. Breads such as Chupatti, Nan and Paratha are the staple. Balti cooking originated in the northern most part of Pakistan, and found its way to Birmingham centuries later. In general Pakistani food is robustly spiced and savoury. The area called the Punjab was split by the formation of Pakistan, and it is the Punjabi tastes that formed the basis of the British curry house menu. See entry for the Punjab restaurant, WC2. Bradford, Glasgow and Southall have sizeable Pakistani populations.

Persian

It is quite common to see Persian dishes listed on the standard curry house menu. Dishes such as Biriani and Pullao did indeed originate in Persia (now called Iran). Bombay's Parsees came from there, and originated dishes of their own such as Dhansak and Patia. True Persian food is hard to find in the UK, although it is to be found at the Old Delhi, W1.

South Indian

Much of India's population is vegetarian, and the southern part of India is almost exclusively so. Until recently the extraordinary range of vegetarian specialities were virtually unknown in the UK. The introduction of more and more restaurants offering South India fare coincides with the increasing awareness of vegetarianism. Specialities include many types of vegetable curry including Avial with exotic vegetables in a yoghurt base, and Sambar, a lentil- base curry. Other delights include huge thin crisp rice-flour pancakes called Dosas, with a curry filling (masala) and Idlis - steamed rice or lentil- flour dumplings. Restaurants serving this type of food are springing up all around the UK.

Sri Lankan

Sri Lanka is the small pearl-shaped island, formerly Ceylon, at the southern tip of India. Its cuisine is distinctive and generally chilli hot. They eat similar fare to that of South India ie: vegetarian dishes, but they also enjoy meat, squid, chicken and duck. Their curries are very pungent.

THE VEERASWAMY

London's Oldest Indian Restaurant
Established 1927

Truly Authentic Indian Cuisine

AA Rosettes Awards for Good Food 1995

Open: Monday to Saturday
Sunday Closed
12 noon to 2.30pm and 6pm to 11.30pm

Daily Buffet Lunch Available

99-101, Regent Street,
(entrance from Swallow Street)
London. W1

Tel: 0171 734 1401
Fax: 0171 439 8434

THE WORLD'S FAVOURITE BASMATI

Tilda
R·I·C·E

Our Top 100 Restaurants

Which are the country's TOP 100 curry restaurants? We maintain a register of those establishments about which we receive numbers of consistently good reports over the years. There is change from last time, of course, as you would expect after 3 1/2 years. About 20% have been replaced, of which half is due to closures, but the other half due simply to a decline in performance. Of the 'new' entrants (indicated *) who have replaced them, most are long established and have been brought to our attention by reporters. So if there are yet others we have missed, please report to us. For a restaurant to remain in our TOP 100 list we also need your views. Those restaurants highlighted in bold type, are winners of SPECIAL AWARDS.

London	E1	Lahore Kebab House
		Namaste (Best Chef Award)
	N1	Sonargaon
	NW1	Diwana Bhel Poori
		*Great Nepalese
		*Tandoori Nights
		Viceroy of India
	NW5	Bengal Lancer
	SE23	*Babur Brasserie
		Dewaniam
	SE26	**Jehangir (Best Sri Lankan)**
	SW1	Saloos
	SW3	Tandoori of Chelsea
	SW6	*Blue Elephant (Best Decor Award)
	SW7	**Bombay Brasserie (Best Indian)**
	SW10	**Chutney Mary (Culinary Excellence)**
	SW13	*Haweli (Best Chain)
	SW14	Taste of India
	SW17	Sree Krishna
	W1	Anwars
		*Caravan Serai
		*Gaylord, Albermarle Street
		Gaylord, Mortimer Street
		Gopals
		Mandeer
		Ragam
		*Tamarind (Most Promising Newcomer)
		The Veeraswamy
	W2	Bombay Palace
		Diwana Bhel Poori
		Khan's
		*Old Delhi
	W5	Monty's
	W6	**Tandoori Nights (Best Bangladeshi)**
	W8	Malabar
	WC2	*Tandoori Nights
		India Club (Special Award)
		*Punjab
Avon	Bristol	Rajdoot
Berks	Reading	**Bina (Best in the West)**
Bucks	Milton Keynes	**Jaipur (Best in Central England)**
Cheshire	Ellesmere Port	*Agra Fort
Devon	Plymouth	*Kurbani
Essex	Ilford	Jalalabad

(Continued overleaf)

Our Top 100 Restaurants
(Continued)

Hampshire	Liss	*Madhuban
	Portsmouth	Palash
	Southampton	Kutis
Hertfordshire	Abbots Langley	*Viceroy of India
	Cockfosters	*Tandoori Nights
	Royston	British Raj
Kent	Bromley	**Tamasha (Best Menu Award)**
	Chislehurst	*Bengal Lancer
	Folkestone	India
	Orpington	Bombay Braserie
Lancashire	Adlington	Sharju
Leicestershire	Leicester	Curry Fever
		*Friends
Lincolnshire	Boston	Star of India
G. Manchester	Manchester	Ashoka
		Rajdoot
	Ramsbottom	*Moghul Dynasty
Middlesex	Southall	Brilliant
		Madhus Brilliant (Special Award)
		Omi's
		Sagoo and Thakar
	Wembley	Chetna's Bhel Puri
		*Curry Craze
Northumberland	Corbridge	**The Valley (Best in the North)**
Nottinghamshire	Nottingham	Saagar
Oxfordshire	Oxford	*Aziz
		Polash
Staffordshire	Lichfield	Eastern Eye
	Stoke On Trent	*Al Sheikh's
Suffolk	Woodbridge	Royal Bengal
Surrey	Epsom	*Le Raj
Tyne & Wear	Newcastle	Rupali
		Sachins
		Vujon
Warwickshire	Leamington	Ashoka
West Midlands	Birmingham	Days of the Raj
		Maharaja
		Rajdoot
		Royal Naim (Best Balti House)
	Coventry	William IV Pub
	Warley	*Rowley Village
N.Yorkshire	Skipton	Aagrah
W.Yorkshire	Bradford	* Nawaab
	Huddersfield	* Nawaab
	Leeds	Aagrah
		* Darbar
		Hansa's
	Pudsey	Aagrah
	Skipton	Aagrah
Ireland	Dublin	**Rajdoot (Best in Ireland)**
Scotland, Fife	St. Andrews	**New Balaka (Best in Scotland)**
Lothian	Edinburgh	Lancer's
		Verandah
Strathclyde	Glasgow	Balbir's
Wales, Clwyd	Deeside	* **Bengal Dynasty (Best in Wales)**
Gwynedd	Llandudno	* **Bengal Dynasty (Best in Wales)**

A LOVE REQUITED

As the world's most acclaimed Indian restaurant, you probably won't be surprised to hear that we simply adore fine Indian food.

We love the fact that India's finest chefs display their remarkable talents at our restaurant, The Bombay Brasserie.

We are mad about it!

Of the many thousands of guests who return week after week, month after month and year after year, we can't spend enough time in the company of those who share our devotion – a sentiment we know to be undeniably reciprocal.

And even though we regularly welcome the famous, you can be sure that the care and attention we give is without favour.

If you need convincing, ask anyone who has spent some time in our company.

Better still, experience The Bombay Brasserie for yourself. We'd love to see you.

Buffet lunch every day, £14.95. Dinner, average price £30.

**Courtfield Road,
London. SW7.**

**Opposite Gloucester Road Tube.
NCP and cab rank adjacent.**

Reservations: 0171 370 4040 or 0171 373 0971

The A to Z of the Curry Menu

To the first-timer, the Indian restaurant menu is a long and complex document. This glossary sets out to explain many of the standard dishes and items which you will encounter at many a curry house. Spellings of vowel sounds will vary vastly from restaurant to restaurant, reflecting the many languages and dialects of the sub-continent. (See *Masala, Moglai* and *Rhogan Josh Gosht* for some examples.) Our spelling here is as near as possible to the standard accepted way of spelling, when translating phonetically from 'Delhi Hindi' to 'Queen's English'.

A

AAM or AM
Mango

AFGHANI CURRY
Nuts and fruit added for the standard curry house interpretation

ALOO
Potato

B

BALTI
Balti dishes are to be found mainly in the West Midlands, though they are spreading all over the UK. Originally from north Pakistan, the food was spicy and aromatic, not hot, and it was slowly cooked over charcoal in two handled iron pots, called Baltis. These same pots are called Karahi everywhere else.

BENGAL (CHICKEN)
A chicken curry with potato cubes and halves of tomato.

BHAJEE
Dryish mild vegetable curry.

BHAJIA or BHAJI
Deep-fried fritter - usually onion.

BHEL PURI
See Bombay food, page 30.

BHOONA or BHUNA
Cooking process (frying) to produce a dry, usually mild curry.

BINDI
A pulpy vegetable also known as Okra or Ladies Fingers.

BIRIANI
Traditionally rice baked with meat or vegetable filling, enhanced with saffron, served with edible silver foil. The restaurant interpretation is a fried rice artificially coloured, with filling added (see PULLAO).

BOMBAY DUCK
A smallish fish native to the Bombay docks, known locally as Bommaloe Macchi. This was too hard for the British to pronounce so it became Bombay Duck. It is dried and appears on the table as a crispy deep-fried starter or accompaniment to a curry.

BOMBAY MIX
Squiggly dry savoury nibbles, to keep you going at the bar.

BOMBAY POTATO
A popular invention of the curry house. Potatoes in curry and tomato sauce.

BOTI KEBAB
Marinated cubes of lamb cooked in a Tandoor oven.

BARFI
Indian fudge-like sweet made from reduced condensed milk, in various flavours.

BRINJAL
Aubergine, also called Baigan.

C

CEYLON CURRY
At the curry house, these are usually cooked with coconut, lemon and chilli.

CHAT or CHAAT
Literally meaning snack.

CHANA
Chick peas (a large lentil). Can be curried or fried.

CHILLI
The hottest of peppers. If your dish is not hot enough ask for chilli pepper (or cayenne) or pickle.

CHAPATTI
The spelling can vary. A dry 6 inch disc of unleavened bread. Should be served hot.

CHUTNEY
The common ones are onion chutney, mango chutney and tandoori chutney. There are dozens of others which rarely appear on the standard menu. (see SAMBALS).

CURRY
The only word in this glossary to have no direct translation into any of the sub-continent's fifteen or so languages. The word was coined by the British in India centuries ago. Possible contenders for the origin of the word are: Karahi or Karai (Hindi) - wok-like frying pan used all over India to prepare masala (spice mixtures), Karhi or Khadi - a soup-like dish made with spices, chick pea flour dumplings and buttermilk; or Kari - a spicy Tamil sauce; Turkuri - a seasoned sauce or stew, or Kari Phulia - Neem leaves, small leaves, a bit like bay leaves used for flavouring.

D
DAHI
Yoghurt. Used as a chutney, and in the cooking of some curries.

DAL OR DHAL
Lentils. There are over sixty types of lentil in the sub-continent. The common restaurant types are massor (red which cooks yellow), moong, chana and urid.

DHANSAK
Traditional Parsee meat dish cooked in a purée of lentils, aubergine, tomato, and spinach. Restaurants use dal and methi, and sometimes chilli and pineapple.

DO PIAZA
Traditional meat dish. Do means two, piaza means onions. Onions appear twice in the cooking first fried and second batch raw. The onions give it a sweetish taste.

DOSA
South Indian pancake made from rice and lentil-flour. Usually served with a filling.

DUM
Cooked by steaming, eg: Aloo Dum, steamed potatoes. See Nawabi, page 32.

F
FOOGATH
Lightly cooked vegetable dish.

G
GHEE
Clarified butter or margarine used in high quality north Indian cooking.

GOBI
Cauliflower.

GOSHT
Lamb or mutton.

GULAB JAMAN
An Indian dessert. Balls of flour and milk-powder, deep fried to golden and served in light syrup. Cake-like texture.

GURDA
Kidney. Gurda Kebab is marinated kidney, skewered and cooked in the tandoor.

H
HALVA
Sweets made from syrup and vegetable or fruit. Served cold in small squares. Is translucent and comes in bright colours depending on subject used. Orange - carrot; green - pistachio; red - mango, etc. Has texture thicker than Turkish Delight. Sometimes garnished with edible silver leaf.

HASINA KEBAB
Pieces of chicken breast, lamb or beef marinated in spices then skewered and barbecued with onions, capsicum and tomato. Turkish in origin.

I
IDLI
Rice and lentil-flour cake served with a light curry sauce. South Indian in origin.

IMLI
Tamarind. A very sour date-like fruit used as a chutney and in cooking.

J
JALEBI
An Indian dessert. Flour, milk-powder and yoghurt batter, squeezed through a

narrow funnel into a deep-fry to produce golden curly crisp rings. Served in syrup.

JAL FREZI
Sautéed or stir-fried meat or chicken dish, often with lightly cooked onion, garlic, ginger, green pepper and chilli.

JEERA
Cummin seed or powder, hence JEERA CHICKEN, etc

K
KARAHI
A cooking dish. Some restaurants cook in small karahis and serve them straight to the table with the food sizzling inside. (see also CURRY and BALTI).

KASHMIR CHICKEN
Whole chicken stuffed with minced meat.

KASHMIR CURRY
Often, in the restaurant, a sweetish curry using lychees or similar.

KEBAB
Skewered food cooked over charcoal. A process over 4,000 years old which probably originated in the Middle East. It was imported to India by the Moslems centuries ago. (see BOTI, HASINA, NARGIS, SHAMI, SHEEK KEBAB)

KEEMA
Minced meat curry.

KHURZI
Lamb or chicken, whole with spicy stuffings.

KOFTA
Minced meat or vegetable balls in batter, deep fried and then cooked in a curry sauce.

KORMA
To most restaurants this just means a mild curry. It probably derived from the Persian KORESH, a mild stew. The Moghuls made it very rich, using cream, yoghurt and nuts , fragranced with saffron and aromatic spices.

KULCHA
Small leavened bread.

KULFI
Indian ice cream. Traditionally it comes in vanilla, pistachio or mango flavours.

L
LASSI
A refreshing drink from yoghurt and crushed ice. The savoury version is lassi namkeen and the sweet version is lassi meethi.

M
MACCI or MACHLI
Fish. Today fresh exotic fish from India and Bangladesh are readily available fresh.

MADRAS
You will not find a traditional recipe for a Madras curry. It does not exist. But the people of the south eat hot curries. Some original chef must ingeniously have christened his hot curry 'Madras' and the name stuck.

MAKHANI
A traditional dish. Tandoori chicken is cooked in butter ghee and tomato sauce.

MALAI
Cream.

MALAYA
The curries of Malaya are traditionally cooked with plenty of coconut, chilli and ginger. In the Indian restaurant, however, they are usually mild and contain pineapple, and other fruit.

MASALA
A mixture of spices which are cooked with a particular dish. It can be spelt a remarkable number of ways - Massala, Massalla, Musala, Mosola, Masalam etc.

MATTAR
Green peas.

METHI
Fenugreek. Savoury spice. The leaves, fresh or dried, are used in Punjabi dishes.

MOGLAI
Cooking in the style of the Moghul Emperors, whose chefs took Indian cookery to the heights of gourmet cuisine centuries ago. Few restaurateurs who offer Moglai dishes come anywhere near this excellence. True Moghali dishes are expensive and time consuming to prepare authentically. Can also be variously spelt Muglai, Mhogulai, Moghlai etc.

MULLIGATAWNY
A Tamil sauce (MOLEGOO pepper, TUNNY water) well known as a British soup.

MURGH
Chicken.

MURGH MASALA or MURGH MASSALAM
Whole chicken, marinated in yoghurt and spices for hours then stuffed and roasted.

N
NAAN or NAN
Leavened bread baked in the tandoor. It is tear-drop shaped and about 8 to 10 inches long. It must be served fresh and hot. Huge naans (Karak) are offered at Balti houses.

NAAN KEEMA
Naan bread stuffed with a thin layer of minced spiced kebab meat.

NAAN PESHWARI
Naan bread stuffed with almonds and/or cashew and/or raisins.

NARGIS KEBAB
Indian scotch egg - spiced minced meat around a hard-boiled egg.

NENTARA
See Rezala.

P
PAAN
Betel leaf folded around a stuffing - lime paste or various seeds (SUPARI) and eaten after a meal. The leaf is bitter, but the seeds alone are often offered after the meal.

PAKORA
To all intents and purposes, the same and the BHAJIA.

PANEER
Cheese made from bottled milk which can be fried and curried (Mattar Paneer).

POPADOM or PAPAD
Thin lentil- flour wafers. When cooked (deep fried or baked) they expand to about 8 inches. They must be crackling crisp and warm when served. If not, send them back to the kitchen and deduct points from that restaurant. They come either plain or spiced with lentils, pepper, garlic or chilli. There are many ways to spell popadom.

PASANDA
Meat, usually lamb, thinly beaten and cooked in a creamy curry gravy.

PATIA
Restaurant curry with thick dark red sweet and sour sauce. Based on a Parsee dish.

PHAL
The hottest curry invented by the restaurateurs, also known as Bangalore Phal.

PICKLE
Pungent, hot pickled vegetables essential to an Indian meal. The most common are lime, mango , brinjal and chilli.

PRAWN BUTTERFLY
Usually a large king prawn - marinated in spices and fried in batter.

PRAWN PURI
Prawns in a hot sauce served on a puri bread. Though sometimes described as Prawn Purée it is not a purée.

PULLAO
Rice and meat or vegetables cooked together in a pan until tender. In many restaurants the ingredients are mixed after cooking to save time. (see BIRIANI).

PULLAO RICE
The restaurant name for rice fried with aromatic spices, and coloured yellow.

PURI
A deep fried unleavened bread about 4 inches diameter, it puffs up when cooked and should be served at once.

Q
QUAS CHAWAL or KESAR CHAVAL
Rice fried in ghee flavoured and coloured with saffron.

R
RAITA
A cooling chutney of yoghurt and vegetable. eg: cucumber, to accompany the meal.

RASGULLA
Walnut-sized balls of semolina and cream-cheese cooked in syrup (literally meaning

INDIAhh!

<u>All this</u>
<u>and curry too.</u>
<u>Aahh…heaven.</u>

For details of all holidays in India, send for
a free colour brochure. To: The Government
of India Tourist Office, 7 Cork Street,
London W1X 2LN. Tel: 071-437 3677/8.
Fax: 071-494 1048.

- - - - - - - - - - - -

Name_____

Address_____

_____

_____

TAJ GOOD CURRY RESTAURANT GUIDE

juicy balls). They are white or pale gold in colour and served cold or warm.

RASHMI KEBAB
Kebab minced meat inside an omelette net.

RASMALAI
Rasgullas cooked in cream. Served cold. Very rich, very sweet.

REZALA
Lamb cooked in yoghurt, subtly spiced with herbs, chillies, tomatoes and ginger.

RHOGAN JOSH GOSHT
Literally meaning lamb in red gravy. Traditionally in Kashmir, lamb is marinated in yoghurt, then cooked with ghee and aromatic spices. It should be creamy but not hot. The curry house version omits the marinade and uses tomato and red pepper to create a red appearance. There are many ways of spelling it, Rogon, Roghan, Rugon, Rugin, Rowgan, Ragan etc. Just, Joosh, Jash etc, Goosht, Goose, Gost etc.

ROTI
Flat bread of any type.

S
SABZI
Vegetable.

SAG or SAAG
Spinach.

SAMBALS
A Malayan term describing the side dishes accompanying a meal. Sometimes referred to on the Indian menu.

SAMBAR
A hot and spicy, runny south Indian vegetable curry made largely from lentils.

SAMOSA
Celebrated triangular deep fried meat or vegetable patties, good as starters or snacks.

SHAMI KEBAB
Minced meat round rissoles.

SHASHLIK
Cubes of skewered lamb.

SHEEK KEBAB or SEEKH
Spiced minced meat, skewered and grilled.

T
TANDOORI
A style of charcoal cooking originated in north west India (what is now Pakistan and the Punjab). The meat is marinated in a reddened yoghurt sauce, then skewered and placed in a tandoor (clay oven). Originally it was confined to chicken and lamb (see BOTI KEBAB and TIKKA) and naan bread. It now applies to lobster, prawn etc.

TARKA DAL.
A tasty, spicy lentil dish, the Tarka being a crispy fried garnish.

TAVA
A heavy steel rimless frying pan.

THALI or TALI
A set of serving bowls (Tapelis) on a tray (Thali) used by diners in India.

TIKKA
Literally, a small piece. eg: Chicken Tikka, is a Tandoori-cooked piece of chicken.

TINDALOO see VINDALOO.

U
URID
A type of lentil, its husk is black and it comes whole, split or polished. Available as a dhal dish in some restaurants.

V
VINDALOO
A fiery hot dish from Goa. Traditionally it was pork marinated in vinegar with potato (ALOO). In the restaurant scene it now comes to mean just a very hot dish. Also sometimes called BINDALOO or TINDALOO (even hotter).

Y
YAKNI
Mutton.

Z
ZEERA
(or JEERA). Cummin . Zeera Gosht is lamb cooked with cummin.

What We Need To Know

We need to know everything there is to know about all curry restaurants in the UK. And there is no one better able to tell us than those who use them. We do not mind how many times we receive a report about a particular place, so please don't feel inhibited or that someone else would be better qualified. They aren't. Your opinion is every bit as important as the next persons.

Ideally we'd like a report from you everytime you dine-out – even on a humble takeaway. We realise this is hard work so we don't mind if your report is very short, and you are welcome to send in more than one report on the same place telling of different occasions. You can even use the back of an envelope or a postcard, or we can supply you with special forms if you write in (with an S.A.E. please).

If you can get hold of a menu (they usually have takeaway menus to give away) or visiting cards, they are useful to us too, as are newspaper cuttings, good and bad and advertisements.

So, please send anything along with your report. Most reports received will appear, in abbreviated form in the Curry Magazine (the Curry Club members' quarterly publication). They are also used towards the next edition of this guide.

We do not pay for reports but our ever increasing corps of regular correspondents receive the occasional perk for us. Why not join them? Please send us your report after your next restaurant curry.

Thank you

Pat Chapman
Founder The Curry Club

County Index

ENGLAND

GREATER LONDON

Greater London, established in 1965, absorbed Middlesex and parts of Essex, Herts, Kent and Surrey. For GL towns / boroughs in these affected areas please see the relevant county (see index on page 49).For the purpose of this guide we define London by its well known 1870's, post codes. We run alphabetically as follows: E, EC, N, NW, SE, SW, W and WC.

LONDON E

E1 - BRICK LANE

This area was once predominantly Jewish, containing tailors and cab drivers and salt-of-the-earth street markets. More recently it has become home to the country's largest Bangladeshi community. All around the area you will find small, very cheap curry restaurants and cafes. The most prolific street is the long and narrow Brick Lane, running between Shoreditch and Aldgate East tube stations. It has become a centre for cheap and cheerful curry cafés, snack bars and restaurants run by the thriving community. (To emphasise its roots you'll also find an all night fresh-baked bagel shop where cab drivers queue for sustenance). As for curry, most of the establishments are unlicensed and are fairly spartan and you can bring your own. The number of curry houses has grown from nineteen in 1986 to twenty four in 1994, reflecting exactly the growth of curry houses nationally. Here we single out seven on Brick Lane.

BENGAL CUISINE   **CC DISCOUNT**
12, Brick Lane. E1.   **0171 377 8405**
Well established in Brick Lane terms (1980) operating all day between noon and midnight. Good prices enhanced by that fact they will give a discount to Curry Club members at their quieter times, see page 288.

BHEL POORI BRASSERIE
63a, Brick Lane. E1.   **0171 377 6412**
Unusual for Brick Lane in that it serves Bhel Poori (see glossary) and South Indian dishes. Indeed it is all vegetarian. JT says, 'The decor was extremely eye catching with black chairs complementing the pink table-cloths and neatly laid out tables. The main course 'Chef's Thali', was the choice for three out of four in our party, which was exceedingly good value. Eight small pots of carefully prepared vegetable curries and side

IF YOU WOULD LIKE TO JOIN OUR DISCOUNT SCHEME SEE PAGE 288

dishes surrounded a larger central dish of Pullao Rice. Although the Bhel Poori restaurant is not licensed, customers are welcome to BYO from the off licence opposite. A welcom addition to Brick Lane.'

CLIFTON TANDOORI
126, Brick Lane. E1.   **0171 377 9402**
The Clifton remains an institution and unlike its Brick Lane counterparts it thrives on its touristic reputation. Some would say it exploits it. We have reports of prices considered to be high for the area. JS felt it was, 'Cashing in. At 90p for mango chutney and ditto for mixed pickle plus service charge.' Others adore the place. MR tells us, 'The nubile wall paintings are still there and the staff friendly and helpful.' And JW loved the Brains Masala and Squid and the main course which she says, 'Could not be faulted. We were delighted.'

NAZRUL
128, Brick Lane. E1.   **0171 247 2505**
'Portions are not enormous but still we left feeling full though not bloated. It offers a café style service and decor rather than a restaurant. Always appears to be busy - particularly popular with students.' AS.

SONAR GAON
161Brick Lane. E1.   **0171 729 7835**
'The food is first class. It does not swim with fat and everything is beautifully cooked. Best Nan I have ever tasted. Dal Tarka superb.' JBO.

SHAMPAN
79, Brick Lane. E1.   **0171 375 0475**
This is rather more your typical Bangladeshi run High Street curry house than typical Brick Lane. It is licensed and 'up-market' with all the curry favourites supplemented such specials with Betki, Rup, Arr and Rhui (Bengali fish) and the unique Shatkora Gosht /Murgh, meat or chicken given a sour flavour with with this lemon-like Sylheti citrus fruit.

SWEET AND SPICY
40, Brick Lane. E1.   **0171 247 1081**
'I regularly visit this wonderful eatery on my jaunts down to East London. A canteen style service, grab a tray and fill up from the dishes of the day plus a whole host of snacks. A compact eating area, with jugs of water kept constantly filled. Excellent value, sometimes high on chilli but a place I would always recommend.' BG.

ELSEWHERE IN E1
HALAL
2, St Mark Street. E1.   **0171 481 1700**
'The Halal which claims to be East London's oldest and has other branches nearby - 88, Aldgate High Street for example. I have visited on numerous occasions over the last seven years, during which time it has come very slowly 'upmarket'. The place is usually crammed between 12 noon and 2pm (especially Fridays). The menu is ample but not extensive and they provide set regular daily specials - good value. The Halal is worth a visit if you want a good value, no nonsense meal without any trimmings.' NG.

LAHORE KEBAB HOUSE   **TOP 100**
2, Umberton Road. E1.   **0171 481 9737**
Other branch, 248, Kingsbury Road, Kingsbury. NW9. Strings of reports all concur that the Lahore Kebab House remains in the TOP 100 category. Here is RMMA's report which is typical of them all. This is a place that has a deservedly high reputation among those who work 'in the city'. It has extremely basic furnishings - truck stop café style formica and vinyl

downstairs and equally basic wood upstairs. The menu is similarly basic - chicken tikka, meat tikka, chicken korai, meat korai, usual vegetables - sag aloo, vegetable curry, lentils. However, don't be fooled by this into giving it the go-by - the food is excellent, the chicken tangy with lemon grass, the meat also delicious. You get rotis automatically and a salad plate to pick at while your waiting for food - which is not long at all. Prices are pretty good too, especially when you consider that it does actually lie within the City and tends to be frequented by men in suits. Portions size good to extra- good and we were hungry. Definitely worth a visit.' Even the super-critical Dr CF rates it highly! Though not so its branch in NW9 (see entry).

NAMASTE   TOP CHEF AWARD   TOP 100 - CC DISCOUNT
30, Alie Street. E1.   **0171 488 9242**

It's really great to be first to bring to the public notice a really great establishment. We did this in our last guide for the Namaste. In fact, I can reveal now that we wrote the accolade before its chef had even started working arrived in England. And we gave Chef Cyrus our, 'UK Top Chef Award' too. Of course I'd known Chef Cyrus for many years and witnessed his outstanding cooking in the Taj Hotels Fort Aguada complex in Goa. Now the Namaste secret is out, and Chef Cyrus is virtually smothered with food guide awards. Indeed, he is now not just chef, he is owner, with his wife Parveen.And I've given him our TOP CHEF AWARD for the second time running.

The restaurant seats seventy-two with an additional eight outside, weather permitting. Being located in the City, it does a really busy lunch trade on Mondays to Fridays, the service of which is supervised by Parveen, herself a Taj trained caterer. Evenings are busy too, although Saturdays are often quieter and on Sunday they close completely. The reason for the restaurant's popularity is not the location (it isn't glamour-ous) it is quite simply the food. Chef Cyrus remains head and shoulders over all the others, the number one curry chef in the UK. He is a Parsee trained in classical Indian cooking. He has worked all over India, and in particular in Goa. Above all, he is a remarkable innovator. He seems able to take any ingredient and turn it into something magical - the hallmark of the great chef, of course. His a-la-carte menu simply bristles with originality. True, the unadventurous can pick Onion Bhajia, Samosa and Shami Kebab for starters and follow with Pullao Rice, Naan bread and Chicken Tikka Masala and a superb meal you'd have too (although unlike everywhere else in Britain these items are now well down on the Namaste popularity list). And that's because there are so many other items on the menu competing for your choice. For example, your eye would be caught by some truly extraordinary items. Starters like Chilli Cheese Garlic Toast for example or Shinanio Balchao - mussels in a Goan sauce, or Tangri Piri Piri - Tandooried chicken drumsticks - delicious, of course and completely devoid of red food colouring.

For main course you could try Kerla Nandu - crab curry or Galhina Xacutti - Goan chicken curry, or Parsee Lamb Liver and Kidney Curry. And that's just a few of the wonders on offer! But there's more:

A Chef's Speciality menu is changed every week. And it is here that Cyrus' flair and originality bursts out. For example, how about for starters: Tandoori Pineapple - cubes of fresh pineapple marinated and cooked in the tandoor way or Madras Blazers - hot pancakes stuffed with diced curried veal, Chole Paó - the Indian version of baked beans on toast - only here it's spicy chickpeas in a hot bread roll. And then most remarkable of all perhaps: Tandoori Beef or Pork Sausages, of which Cyrus says, 'interesting but delicious'. And yes they are ordinary British sausages marinated and cooked, Tandoor method.

Main courses now top of the Namaste popularity list include curries made from vension, goose, sweetbreads, grouse and pheasant as well as the more conventional ingredients: chicken, duck, lamb and beef dishes, but all cooked to unusual authentic Indian recipes. One of the most popular ingredients is Wensleydale Wild Boar - in such guises as Jungli Maas Dhuanaar - where a haunch is marinated in a masala smoked over whole spices eg: cinnamon, cardamom, cloves etc, then slowly oven roasted before being sliced and served with shredded mango pickle (home made, of course). Wild boar also features in a pickle and says Cyrus, 'It's so popular, there's never any to take home.'There's a home delivery service available.Having found a reliable supplier, he even promises to be able to supply the, till now, elusive oyster dish mentioned in our last guide. Rawa Kalwa - oysters marinated in Goan Piri Piri masala - dipped in dry semolina and crisply flash fried, served with a hot garlic dip.!

This is Indian cuisine extraordinaire. Our advice is that you forgo your regular standard favourite and try everything for yourself. This restaurant gives discounts to Curry Club members, see page 288 and page 4. Watch for a change of address during the lifetime of this guide, and a possible restaurant name change, but follow Cyrus wherever he goes.

RAJ TANDOORI
129, Leman Street. E1.   **0171 702 1168**
'The Raj is a small restaurant and typical of many such places around the Aldgate area, supplying basic good value food without the frills. The menu is standard without being boring. The decor is standard 'red flock' (hooray! keep it! - Ed) and the comfort level is perfectly adequate, as is the service - never had cause to complain. I have used the Raj many times as it is across the road from my office and prices reasonable.' NG.

E4 - HIGHAMS PARK
PURBANI
34, The Avenue, Highams Park. E4.   **0181 531 8804**
'I don't visit this very often but I am never disappointed. They have catered well for me when we have ordered special meals for large groups. It continues to be of good quality' BG.

E6 - EAST HAM
EASTERN EYE   **CC DISCOUNT**
269, High Street, East Ham. E6.   **0181 470 8078**
DMcC visits here, 'Many times,' and she never has, 'Any complaints.' Mabud Mussain, who also owns the Himalaya, 178, The Grove, Stratford. E15, offers discounts to Curry Club members, see page 288.

YAAL
404, Barking Road, East Ham. E6.   **0181 471 6744**
Here's something different for East London. The Yaal serves Sri Lankan and South Indian dishes, worth a try. For those who must 'play safe' there is a big range of 'standard' curries.

E10 - LEYTON
RAJ BRASSERIE   **CC DISCOUNT**
322, Lea Bridge Road, Leyton. E10.   **0181 539 8504**
Owned by Messrs Miah (manager) Musabbir and Haque (chef), the Raj has a full complement of favourite Tandoori and curry dishes with comprehensive vegetarian section. Will give discounts to Curry Club members, see page 288.

TO FIND OUT HOW TO JOIN OUR DISCOUNT
SCHEME SEE PAGE 288

TANDOORIAN RECIPES   CC DISCOUNT
434, High Road, Leyton. E10.   **0181 556 2475**
Iqbal Hussain's quaintly named 'Tandoorian Recipes' has a large and
comprehensive menu with some nice specials (Butter Chicken gets the
thumbs up from AR). Also has vegetarian section, and Balti comes to E10
with some thirty dishes. This restaurant will give discounts to Curry
Club members, see page 288.

E11 - LEYTONSTONE
VICEROY OF INDIA
High Road, Leytonstone. E11.   **0181 989 6158**
'The food here is excellent. The actual curry comes sizzling on a plate, not
in a dish and therefore portions are gi-normous. The Sag Creme is divine
- very rich but gorgeous - and all chicken is white meat. The Chicken
Dhansak is also very highly recommended. Booking advisable' MS.

E14
RAJ BOY   CC DISCOUNT
564, Commercial Road. E14.   **0171 791 3535**
Opened last year (1994) and gaining a good reputation locally with
standard curry cuisine done well by owner manager Abdul Kalam. This
restaurant will give discounts to Curry Club members, see page 288.

E17
GANDHI TANDOORI
267, Hoe Street, Walthamstow. E17.   **0181 505 3212**
It's MJP's, 'Firm favourite. The restaurant has recently introduced Balti
food. Our meal was excellent. Pleasant decor, friendly service which can
be slow at times even when the restaurant is quiet.'

E18
ROSE OF INDIA   CC DISCOUNT
65-67, High Road, South Woodford. E18. **0181 989 8862**
The Rose has been operating for 17 years now under Messrs Miah and
Hoque. It offers a good range of favourite tandooris and curries. This
restaurant will give discounts to Curry Club members, see page 288.

LONDON - EC

EC1
RAVI SHANKAR
442, St John Street, Clerkenwell. EC1. **0171 833 5849**
The only London EC restaurant to get into this guide. Others fell by the
way with a plethora of poor reports. We'd like more reports on EC
please. However, we're pleased to keep Ravi Shankar in. It delighted
Mrs DRC with its South Indian vegetarian menu which, 'Appeals to me
so choosing is always agonising. We ended up with a Vegetarian Thali
and a starter of yoghurt, spices and what appeared to be small pieces of
idli, which was delicious, spicy, sweet and sour all at once. Our Paper
Dosa, with usual relishes was absolutely marvellous and served very
eye-catchingly, vertically, curved around the back of the stainless steel
platter with the relishes in front, rather than the more usual roll laid on
the plate. I don't know how they got it to stand upright.' DRC.

LONDON - N

N1

ANGEL CURRY CENTRE
5, Chapel Market, Islington. N1.   **0171 837 5727**

'Menu as one would expect. I've been many times and the quality of food is excellent. Chicken Dhansak (my favourite) particularly good. Portions reasonable and service always courteous. Excellent value.' RStH.

EVA 11
41 Newington Green Road, N1.   **0171 704 2279**

The second of three Eva's (number one is in Drummond Street, NW1 and Eva 111 is in Hackney Road E2. The owners are hoping for a nationwide chain. Good reports so far, but we'd like to hear more.

INDIAN VEG BHEL POORI HOUSE   CC DISCOUNT
92/93, Chapel Market, Angel. N1.   **0171 837 4607**

Nurus Safa's, 'Eat as much as you like', fixed price buffet lunch - £3.25 and dinner £3.50 remains outstanding value for money. NS says, 'Seven of us took advantage of the lunchtime buffet (and most of us went back for seconds!). A nice range of flavours nothing too oily. Couscous instead of (as well as!) rice made a nice change. Service OK, restaurant clean and well frequented. Lhassi was lovely!'. Discount for Curry Club members at their quieter times, see page 288.

MILAN INDIAN PURE VEGETARIAN   CC DISCOUNT
52, Caledonian Road, Kings Cross. N1.   **0171 278 3812**

Mr and Mrs Verma (manager and chef respectively) own this good value vegetarian eatery which is open on weekdays from noon to 10pm (Saturday 12 noon to 2pm and 6pm till 10pm, Sunday closed). They will give a discount to Curry Club members at the 'Eat as much as you like', buffet, see page 288.

RAJMONI INDIAN CUISINE   CC DISCOUNT
279, Upper Street, Islington. N1.   **0171 354 3821**

We welcome Kalam and Jamal's Rajmoni to the Guide. It's a standard curry house which has been operating far more than five years and has attracted a strong local following. They will give Curry Club members a discount, see page 288 and have branches at Ampthill, Beds (Rajgate) and SW6 (Villa, Bombay).

SONARGAON   TOP 100 - CC DISCOUNT
46, Upper Street, Islington. N1.   **0171 226 6499**

'On a training course in Islington a few of my colleagues from Manchester, knowing I am a curry addict, asked if I knew any good curry restaurants in the area. I opened my Good Curry Guide and to my great delight found that the Sonargaon was just around the corner from the training course. Off we went and had what proved to be one of the best meals any of us had ever had. The Manchester lads know their curries as they are regular visitors to the Rusholme area and to a man they declared that the Sonargaon was well worth its TOP 100 rating. We were met at the door by an extremely friendly waiter who invited us in. Service and atmosphere were good, and we enjoyed a variety of excellent dishes. The Pall Masala turned out to be hot enough for me and the taste was out of this world. One of my colleagues had Chicken Jalfrezi and voted it one of the best ever. The Chicken Tikka starter also received wide acclaim while the Nan bread, although not particularly large, was the tastiest I've had. The Lamb Roghan Josh, Chicken Tikka Masala and the Prawn Puri starters were all well appointed. It is rare to go to a restaurant with such a large group and find that to a man everyone reckoned it to be one of the best ever.' BG. And we are pleased to keep the Sonargaon in our TOP 100. Will offer a discount to Curry Club members, see page 288.

N3 - FINCHLEY
KARAHI HUT
164, Ballards Lane, Finchley Central. N3.   0181 346 5947
Delicious food and many tempting offers as well.

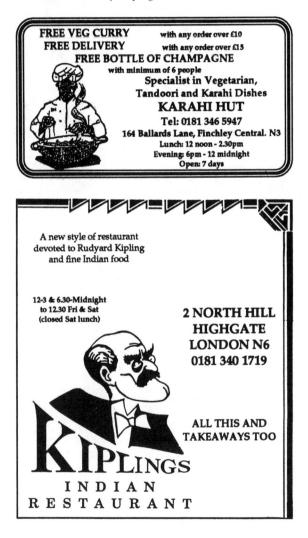

RANI
3, Long Lane, Finchley. N3.   **0181 349 2636**
Jyoti Pattni's vegetarian menu, with its specials (cooked by his wife and
his mother) makes this restaurant different. 'Home made chutneys are
excellent as are the breads. Portions are fairly modest but made with high
quality produce and spices. Staff is friendly and helpful. Most enjoyable
vegetarian meal.' MF.

N4
SUNDERBAN   **CC DISCOUNT**
50, Blackstock Road. N4.   **0171 359 9243**
'This is a basic, standard - but clean curry house. Decor - flock. Service
is very good if you mention Curry Club. We have been here on numerous
occasion the food is always excellent.' AS. Will offer a discount to Curry
Club members at their quieter times, see page 288.

N6
KIPLINGS   **CC DISCOUNT**
2, North Hill, Highgate. N6.   **0181 340 1719**
This fairly new venture (1993) is from the Stanley Krett stable (see Bengal
Lancer, NW5). It has quickly established itself a good reputation with
everything, 'As it should be.' JE. Curry Club members will get a discount
at their quieter times, see page 288.

N8 - HORNSEY
ALALIAH   **CC DISCOUNT**
163, Priory Road, Hornsey. N8.   **0181 348 4756**
The Jalaliah has been in business for 20 years under Moen Uddin's
ownership. The menu follows the curry formula so you can expect to find
all your favourites here. It remains, 'Inexpensive and very good.' Curry
Club members will get a discount at their quieter times, see page 288.

JASHAN   **CC DISCOUNT**
19a, Turnpike Lane. N8.   **0181 340 9880**
The change of ownership here had already been detected by certain of
our scribes. CF wondered if it means a change of chefs from the previous
Indian brigade, after reporting on several very satisfactory visits followed by one, where he was with a large group of fellow doctors, many
themselves Indian, who were served below par food. However, AS tells
of, 'Generous portions with really fresh tasting Murgh Chaat followed by
Mild Creamy curries and wonderful side dishes.' GG considers it, 'The
best he's been in.' and others sing equal prasies. It is evenings only and
closed Sundays. We'd certainly like your views. The current owner RD
Khagram also has an involvement in the Tandoori Nights, WC1 and
NW1. Will give a discount to Curry Club members, see page 288.

MEGHNA   **CC DISCOUNT**
55, Topsfield Parade, Tottenham Lane, Crouch End. N8. 0181 348 3493
The Megna's wedge shape lends itself to a spacious typical Indian-arch
type of decor. Its menu in the hands of chef Moynul Haque, is comprehensive and has a full complement of standard items plus specials
Lemon Chana Chicken is the unsual favourite of FS. The all day Sunday
help-yourself-to-as-much-as-you-like-buffet is favourite of several other
reporters. Owner Omar Khan will offer a discount to Curry Club
members, see page 288. Branch: Palace Tandoori, 42, Craven Park Road,
Harlesden. NW10.

TO FIND OUT HOW TO JOIN OUR DISCOUNT SCHEME
SEE PAGE 288

N11
NEW ARJUN
35-37, Friern Barnet Road. N11.   **0181 368 1504**
The restaurant is welcomed back to the Guide as the New Arjun, although it has had the New bit for some time and the Arjun itself has been around since 1978. Its supporters enjoy the comprehensive tandoori and curry items under the safe hands of chef Miah.

N12 - NORTH FINCHLEY
CURRY ROYAL   CC DISCOUNT
932-934, High Road, North Finchley. N12.   **0181 445 1650**
Mr Abdul Choudhury's Curry Royal opened as early as 1970 and it has always attracted favourable reports. One regular likes the Garlic Chicken and another asks whether Chicken or Meat Kushboo is unique to this restaurant. It is flavoured with herbs and fresh corinal (sic) which we believe is indeed unique. Abdul will give a discount to Curry Club members, see page 288.

FINCHLEY PAN CENTRE
15, Woodhouse Road, North Finchley. N12.   **0181 446 5497**
A tiny Indian snack bar frequented by Indians and is open daily noon to 10pm (Friday 3.30pm to 10pm and closed on Tuesdays). Kebabs, samosas, veg rissoles etc very inexpensive and with friendly service.

N13 - PALMERS GREEN
DIPALI
Aldermans Hill, Palmers Green. N13.   **0181 886 2221**
A regular entrant in the guide of which Mr and Mrs MLB say 'The food is beautifully cooked using fresh spices and the finest ingredients. The portions are generous and the dishes imaginatively created. The decor is very pleasant and the management and staff are very professional and friendly. The Prawn Dansak and the Chicken Jal Ferezi (sic) are our favourites with Chana Masala and the Sag Aloo, but really we have enjoyed everything we have tried on their menu.' MLB.

N14 - SOUTHGATE
ROMNA GATE TANDOORI
14, The Broadway, Southgate. N14.   **0181 882 6700**
Everyone remarks on the decor. 'Impressive,' 'Outstanding.' The room is made spectacular and intimate by the skillful use of elegant coloured glass, mini waterfalls and wrought iron work. The little service bell on each table is a good idea. 'The glass screens each side of the table cut out cigarette smoke from other diners.' DCG. We do hear about it getting very busy particularly at peak times, which is always taxing for the best run restaurants, and occasionally leads to a less than perfect occasion. However, reporters are more than happy with all aspects of the Romna.

N15
GUPTA BHEL PURI   CC DISCOUNT
460, West Green Road. N15.   **0181 881 8031**
If you enjoy Bhel Puri (see glossary) Gupta's is for you. It's a vegetarian establishment but the food is inexpensive satisfying and very more-ish. It's open daily from 11am to 11pm. A discount will be given to Curry Club members, see page 288 for details.

TO FIND OUT HOW TO JOIN OUR DISCOUNT SCHEME
SEE PAGE 288

N16 - STOKE NEWINGTON

RASA
55, Church Street, Stoke Newington. N16.　　　　0171 249 0344

'Owned by Das, who was formerly the manager at Spices, on the same street. Specialises in Southern Indian Vegetarian cooking. Decor is very relaxing, with about fifteen tables. On my one visit so far, I had Thayir Vadal as a starter. This is fried urid bean doughnut marinated in freshly spiced yoghurt. For my main course I had Moru Kachiathu, a Travancore speciality of yoghurt curry prepared with green banana and sweet mangoes, served luke warm (as it should be, apparently) on Lemon Rice. Both dishes were new to me and were delicious!' DS.

LANCERS　　　　　　　　　　　　　　　　CC DISCOUNT
18, Church Street, Stoke Newington. N16.　　　　0171 254 4429

A standard curry house which has been operating since 1989 and now has a regular following. We hear of a menu full of old favourites with a good vegetable selection as well. Owner Sunawar Ali offers a discount to Curry Club members at his quieter times, see page 288.

SPICE OF ASIA　　　　　　　　　　　　　CC DISCOUNT
56, Stoke Newington. N16.　　　　　　　　　0171 923 4285

Another Stoke Newington standard curry house with a formula menu consisting of many a tandoori and curry favourite. Mr Chowdhury the owner has recently introduced Balti to his menu (as well as to the restaurant's name). The first in the area. He also offers a discount to Curry Club members at his quieter times, see page 288.

N19

RAJ VOGUE　　　　　　　　　　　　　　　CC DISCOUNT
34, Highgate Hill. N19.　　　　　　　　　0171 272 9091

Abed Choudhury is still there with his manager Abdur Rahman and chef Suruk Miah, and yes Ken Livingstone (who's he?) and Spurs football stars(and who are they?) are also still there, we're told. The food is still good too and GG confirms it is, 'Excellent including the Kebab Platter.' Curry Club members will be given a discount at their quieter times, see page 288.

RAJ OF INDIA
10, Station Road, Winchmore Hill. N21.　　　　0181 360 9543

JS advises us not to be, 'Fooled by the tatty exterior of this restaurant. Inside is a traditional (red flock wallpaper), largish - 20 tables, Indian eatery. The food wheeled in on a wooden trolley is superbly cooked and nicely presented. There is nothing lavish or exotic about the food or surroundings but don't let that detract from a very pleasant meal. The dishes are not very spicy so if you like the food hot you can go for the Vindaloo without ordering a gallon of water. The waiters were helpful and pleasant and did not mind waiting at least 10 minutes while we pondered and asked their advice.' JS.

The editor of this Guide welcomes your views on the restaurants and take-aways we list in its pages, and on any you visit anywhere. Please send your reports to : The Editor, P.O. Box 7, Haslemere, Surrey, GU27 1EP. Please enclose an addressed envelope if you want a reply.

LONDON - NW

NW1 - DRUMMOND STREET

I often get asked where the best restaurants are. It's one reason for producing this Guide. As far as London is concerned, Drummond Street is one area which I recommend. Just behind Euston Station, it is easy to get to. It is short and will not win any awards for beauty. It lacks the ethnic glamour of Southall and Wembley ,or the intensity of purpose of Brick Lane, but it is a small concentrated sector of extremely good Indian food. There are greengrocers and delis supplying Indian ingredients, and a dozen or so takeaways and restaurants. Here in alphabetical order is our Drummond Street selection:

AMBALA SWEET CENTRE
112, Drummond Street. NW1.   **0171 387 3521**
10am to 11pm. The Ambala started trading in 1965. It specialises in savoury snacks (Pakoras and Samosa etc), Indian sweets (Halva, Jalebi, Gulab Jamun, Barfi etc) and a few curries. All are to take out only. Established initially for the Asian trade it now has branches in Birmingham, Bradford, Luton, Leicester, Derby, Slough, Tooting, Wembley, Leyton, East Ham, Southall, Finchley, Glasgow and Manchester. Drummond Street is the flagship. All branches serve identical items at identical prices. The quality is first class and the prices are always reasonable. Be prepared to queue.

CHUTNEYS
134 Drummond Street, Euston. NW1.   **0171 388 0604**
One of three Drummond Street restaurants in the same ownership (see also Haandi and Ravi Shankar). They are all licensed and this one serves vegetarian only food.

DIWANA BHEL POORI   **TOP 100**
121,Drummond Street, Euston. NW1.   **0171 380 0730**
Midday to 11pm. It pioneered Bombay pavement kiosk snack food in the UK and is now much copied. Bhel Puri is a tantalising cold mixture of crispy, chewy textures, sweet, hot and sour tastes. Crunchy savoury squiggly biscuits share the bowl with diced potato, puffed rice (mamra) and fresh coriander (dhania). Lace it together with yoghurt, tamarind (imli) sauce, chilli sauce and coriander chutney and you have it. You might continue your meal with a dosa pancake filled with sambar curry boosted with fresh coconut and mustard seed chutney. It's all vegetarian and it's all fabulous and it's all authentic. Try the Diwana's legendary Kulfi. A recent expansion now provides more seats upstairs but despite the re-dec Diwana retains its title as the best of its type. It is functional, café-style, unlicensed, open all day and above all, it's still very cheap. 'I recommend the 'Paper Dosa' for its spectacular appearance. The highlight of our meal was the 'Falooda' - an Indian 'knickerbocker glory' - probably the best in London. You wouldn't want to linger too long over your meal at Diwana - the seats are uncomfortable wooden benches - however the quality of the food outweighs the numbness in your backside!' DB. Despite the extra room you should still expect a queue (especially at peak hours). Probably the best value in London... and don't forget to 'bring-your-own! (no corkage charge). It remains high in our Top 100.

HAANDI
161, Drumond Street, Euston. NW1.   **0171 383 4557**
In decor terms it's the smartest of the Chutneys, Haandi, Ravi Shankar trilogy. It has all the South India favourites but this is the only one of the three to offer meat dishes. 'Upon ordering the waiter asked if we would like a complimentary glass of white wine or onion bhajia starter. A further special offer was a 50% off the total bill.' JT.

GUPTA CONFECTIONERS
100, Drummond Street. NW1.   **0171 380 1590**
Overshadowed, undoubtedly, by the Ambala up the road, Gupta is none-the-less a very good snack and sweet take-away. Vegetable only Samosas and Pakoras, plus a delightful Pea Kebab are inexpensive and freshly cooked in the kitchens behind. Their sweets achieve a lightness of touch and seem to avoid the taste of tinned evaporated milk, which sometimes spoils those made by others. There is another Gupta branch at Watford Way, Hendon.

RAAVI KEBAB
125, Drummond Street, Euston. NW1.   **0171 388 1780**
Open 1230 to 11pm, it's very much a meat place as its name suggests. 'Had three roti which were freshly made, very good and moist. Main course was Haleem, which was described as a very special dish from the sub-continent cooked with meat, wheat, lentils and spices - very nice and spicy. The rest of the menu wasn't extensive with five grills, four specials, four meat, three curry, four vegetable dishes. Worth a visit and seemed to be patronised by local Asians.' GH.

RAVI SHANKAR
133, Drummond Street. NW1.   **0171 388 6458**
Open all day (midday to 11pm) and the least pretentious of the Chutneys, Haandi group (and the first), it is slightly (but only just) more upmarket. Otherwise similar in most respects to the Diwana (see above) which it followed into Drummond Street. It is licenced but prices are still very reasonable and it is usually busy. Recommended are the two thali set dishes - the Mysore and the Shankar, and the Shrikhan dessert. Branch in EC1.

ELSEWHERE IN NW1

GREAT NEPALESE   **TOP 100 - CC DISCOUNT**
48, Eversholt Street, Euston. NW1.   **0171 388 6737**
A regular entrant to the guide and justly so. It is one of London's few Nepalese restaurants (see page 32) but unlike many of these, the Great actually has a Nepalese chef (Masuk) and owner (Manandhar) and more particularly it has a decent number of Nepalese specialities on the menu. Masco Bara (black lentil pancakes) Mamocha (steam cooked meat pastries) and Kalezo Ra Chyow (chicken liver) are three such starters. Main courses include Dumba (mutton), Pork Bhutwa, and Hach Ko (duck) curries. There is also a range of eleven Nepalese vegetable dishes. Couple those to 16 'standard' curry house vegetable dishes and the vegetarian will be spoilt for choice. In addition the 'Great' does all the standard curries and Tandoories, from Phal, 'very very hot,' to Shali Korma, 'very very mild.' For consistency, reliability and for a range of choice plus quality that is way above average, we are pleased to promote the 'Great' into our TOP 100.

TO FIND OUT ABOUT HOW YOU CAN JOIN THE CURRY CLUB MEMBERS' DISCOUNT SCHEME, PLEASE TURN TO PAGE 288.

NW1
MUMTAZ
4 Park Road, NW1.   **0171 706 2855**
'"Very" is perhaps the keyword to describe Mumtaz. The restaurant is very smart, very clean - the food was very excellent and very expensive. I think its worth the extra cost. Chicken Tikka Masalla was very!' DW.

TANDOORI NIGHTS   TOP 100 - CC DISCOUNT
108, Parkway, Regents Park. NW1.   **0171 482 1902**
'Referring to the Guide I came upon this small air-conditioned restaurant. It was around 7pm and I was starving. Started with excellent Shami Kebab and salad and a glass of Indian lager. After a decent interval, arrived a delectable Lamb Pasanda and Pillau Rice with the usual Chutney and Popadoms. Staff polite if a little distant. Finished with a Mango Kulfi and coffee. The prices not all that expensive.' AE-J. Branches: Tandoori Night Cockfosters, Herts and Covent Garden, WC2 (see entries)All three jointlyointly in our TOP 100. See page 39.

VICEROY OF INDIA   TOP 100 - CC DISCOUNT
3-5, Glentworth Street. NW1.   **0171 486 3515**
The Viceroy's period of uneven-ness seems, thankfully to be over. Following the change of ownership (now by the Gaylord, Albemarle Street group) and judging by the increasing amount of positive praise from our correspondents, it is undoubtedly London's most elegant curry establishment. It is large (150 seats) yet has a feeling of spaciousness. Once you have found it (off Marylebone Road, the exterior, with its marble facing and copper Hindi dome is very inviting. Inside the marble theme continues with pillar facings, steps and counter tops, skilful use is made of natural brick walls and York floor-tiles, Indian wood carvings, paintings and artifacts. Round and square tables, some in bays, are crisply adorned and plants are dotted around to provide relief. One main feature is the tandoori kitchen which is on view behind glass. We point out that this is an Indian operation (rather than Bangladeshi) and the kitchens, under Chef K Ram, turn out what at first may appear to be a small choice in the menu, just five starters, eight Tandoori items and an equally careful selection of main course dishes breads and rices with nary a Phal, Vindaloo, Madras, Dhansak or Tikka Masala in sight. Spicing is gentle and subtle but is geared up on request. Our advise is to request it, or you may find tastes too subtle. The Viceroy has long been one of the regular haunts of London's well-heeled Indian diplomatic and commercial community. Prices are above average, as you'd expect, but this is eased with a discount for Curry Club members, contact the manager Mr PK Dey and see page 288. Deservedly high in our TOP 100.

NW2
SHAMA   CC DISCOUNT
66, Cricklewood Broadway. NW2.   **0181 450 9052**
The Shama is one of those places which local communities thrive on. It's small (50 seats) and comfortable, but not plush. Owned by Messrs Rawat (manager) and Ahmed (chef) the food is competent and inexpensive. Two more advantages you can BYO (bring your own drink) and Curry Club members will be offered a discount, see page 288.

NW3
BELSIZE TANDOORI   CC DISCOUNT
58, Belsize Lane. NW3.   **0171 794 8643**
You'll find all your favourites at M Rasheed's Belsize Tandoori plus one or two unusuals. We hear tell of meat curry with bamboo shoot and Bengal Beef Musalla (sic) for example.

CURRY MANJILL
34, England's Lane, Hampstead. NW3.   **0171 722 4053**
A typical curry house with a typical menu boosted by some nice specials. Pomphret Mosalla (sic) and Koliza Bhuna (chicken liver in a creamy sauce). There are some Balti dishes here too.

CURRY PARADISE
49, South End, Green End. NW3.   **0171 794 6314**
'Served us well for over ten years. Unfortunately, recent indoor redecoration has lessened seating power, increasing likelihood of sitting next to smokers. A pity. Otherwise, superb Phals - fire-eaters' dream! An excellent and extremely reliable curry house, reasonably priced.' DMcC.

FLEET TANDOORI   CC DISCOUNT
104,Fleet Road, Hampstead. NW3.   **0171 485 6402**
'A good restaurant for those seeking a dependable, quiet and inexpensive meal. The Sunday Buffet is a must for those who wish an alternative to meat and two veg. An additional attraction is the 'Special' on the menu - Pomfret Fish, which comes either tandoori or for those with a rich palate, bathed in a curry sauce flavoured with a multitude of spices. They offer a 10% discount to Curry Club members at any time!' AD.

NW4
PRINCE OF CEYLON
39, Watford Way. NW4.   **0181 202 5967**
There are precious few Sri Lankan restaurants in London and, whilst the Prince has a pretty much standard menu with Tandooris and Curries, it also has a number of Sri Lankan specials such as Lumpri (chicken, meat and egg) Hoppers (pancakes) and Ambul Thial (spicy fish dish). The Ceylon Squid curry is unusual too. Most people like a change (so our reports say) but find the Prince's, 'Service prompt and pleasant. The waiters found it hard to explain the dishes so we ended up with huge quantities which we were unable to finish as we were too full. We pronounced ourselves well satisfied with the quality of the meals.' GGP.

NW5
BENGAL LANCER   TOP 100 - CC DISCOUNT
253, Kentish Town Road. NW5.   **0171 485 6688**
Stanley Krett and Akram Ali's brain child brasserie, now ten years on, pioneered a wave of Raj 'reminiscence' theme restaurants. The Lancer soldiers on, attracting good reports a-plenty. 'This is a restaurant whose standard has remained consistently high. Always a pleasure to visit. The service is efficient, but not obtrusive and the quality of food very high, thus guaranteeing that we will be visiting again shortly.' DM. 'A monthly outing of the Jubilee Line Extension Project curry clan. Good food presented with some style even when faced with nine very hungry people. Service good, portions reasonable. Highlights from the menu included Potato Chat and Jeera Chicken. The Peshwari and Keema Naan were also extremely good.' PC. 'A genuine classy restaurants with an excellent menu range. Liver Hazra, liver cooked and tossed in spices, rich and almost a meal in itself. Unusual, good and great taste. Tiger Wings are chicken drumsticks tandoori style. Service first class, attentive and despite a packed peak time Saturday night they kept checking up to see if we required anything else. Food up among the best for quality, portions more than adequate and at value for money prices. Deserves its rating in the TOP 100.' AS. Some criticism though about the service charge, the £1 cover charge and 'lighting too intense for an intimate dinner.' DW. It has a branch (Kiplings, N6). It remains in our TOP 100. The discount for Curry Club members will go some way to offset these minor criticisms, see page 288. See advertisement, overleaf.

The Bengal Lancer

INDIAN BRASSERIE

253 Kentish Town Road
London NW5
Telephone: 0171 485 6688

Serving nouvelle Indian cuisine

12-3 & 6.30-Midnight to 12.30 Fri & Sat closed Sat lunch

INDIAN LANCER
        CC DISCOUNT
56, Chetwynd Road. NW5.
        0171 482 2803
A small newish (1989) restaurant which under the ownership of MY Hashmi, has become a very popular local curry house.

SHAHANA TANDOORI
        CC DISCOUNT
343, Kentish Town Road, Kentish Town. NW5.
    0171 485 5566
Owner ME Muslim is on hand in this popular local curry house. It too is relatively new (1988) and is offering a discount to Curry Club members, see page 288.

NW6
GEETA SOUTH INDIAN
57, Willesden Lane. NW6.
        0171 624 1713
It's vegetarian food at which Geeta excell, Dosas, Idlis, Upamas Karela (bitter gourds) drumsticks (long pithy marrow which you suck to extract the tender flesh), Rasams, Sambars and more. It's all fine stuff served in less than glamourous surroundings to a thoroughly devoted following. Actually they do have meat and tandoori items on their menu and a drinks licence - and all at reasonable prices. Even the 10% service charge doesn't dent them.

SURYA
        CC DISCOUNT
59-61, Fortune Green Road, West Hampstead. NW6.
    0171 435 7486
This tiny thirty four seat restaurant really packs 'em in. Run by the husband and wife Tiwari team, he front of house - she the chef, there's no room to move, almost literally - it's always full. The dish of the day (it changes daily) excites several of our regulars at this vegetarian licensed restaurant. We have heard well of Gujarati dishes such as Patra and

Kaddu Kari (see page 32) and inexpensive prices. It opens 6pm to 10.30 daily and for Sunday lunch. They have a branch - Shree Ganesha, 4, The Promenade, Edwarebury Lane, Edgware, Middx.

VIJAY
49, Willesden Lane, NW6.   **0171 328 1087**
Vijay heads up towards its 30th year it boasts a loyal following of regulars who know they'll get, 'Very nice tasty food.' B & WW. Reasonable prices. Like Geeta's it pioneered South Indian Vegetarian food in London.

NW7
DAYS OF THE RAJ   CC DISCOUNT
123, The Broadway, Mill Hill. NW7.   **0181 906 3363**
The Days' extensive menu appears to be formula stuff from Kurma (sic) to Phal etc, available in the form of chicken, lamb, beef, prawn, king prawn and vegetables. But a closer look provides a number of 'unique' dishes. What are Noorane, Sherajee, Kushboo, Dilkush and Bakhara curries for example? Each available in the six above forms (the menu explains their attributes), they are clearly house inventions. As is Days of the Raj, gently cooked with pineapple, lychees and sultanas in a thick creamy sauce sprinkled with nuts. It sounds like a fruit salad but is, we're assured, 'Really quite delicious, the chicken quite succulent, and mild enough for my boss who is a curry novice.' GC. Owner Khalam Matin and his chef S Miah are to be applauded. A little experimentation with new ingredients could take this restaurant to higher planes. Maybe this is just the place to offer some real Bangladeshi dishes. Meanwhile, it is more than a 'safe-bet' curry house. It is very smart indeed and is a place to go for an enjoyable meal out. The give a Curry Club members' discount at their quieter times, see page 288.

BRENT TANDOORI   CC DISCOUNT
24, High Road, Willesden Green. NW0.   **0181 459 0649**
This takeaway only is reported as being clean, generous, prompt and efficient. The food is evidently well liked and the prices reasonable. Owner Monojir Alo welcomes Curry Club members to whom he will give a discount at his quieter times, see page 288.

NW10
ANNE MARIE AT
THE TASTE OF THE TAJ   CC DISCOUNT
4, Norbreck Parade, off Hanger Lane, Ealing. NW10.   **0181 991 5366**
I got rapped on the knuckles by Anne Marie herself a couple of guides back for failing to state that her previous restaurant was in Ealing Common. I merely said Ealing. I thought, being born and bred in Ealing and having lived there a number of decades, that I know Ealing well. Now I'm risking it all again. For Anne Marie's own venture, which has been going since 1989 isn't in Ealing... it's in NW10 (but it used to be W5). So, please don't sue me Anne Marie, because the North Circular Gyratory keeps getting rebuilt and postcodes keep shifting. In fact, by agreement, we have placed her ad and map in the W5 section, on page 95. She says herself it's, 'Essential to phone and ask for directions because the front access is now closed.' But find it you should, and avail yourself of a personalised service and advice that some of Anne Marie's regulars have known and delighted in for 25 years. First timers will discover (if they listen to her) that it's the memsahib's personal touches that make this very ordinary looking menu into a welcoming taste experience. Chef Nazrul converts it all into stimulating cuisine. We hear of a. 'Fabulous fresh Chicken Dapeaza (sic) floating in fresh glistening onions.' CR and 'A rather unexpected delicacy of touch in the courgette Bhaji.' RG. Anne Marie will give a discount to Curry Club members, see page 288 and 93.

KADIRI KITCHEN   **CC DISCOUNT**
26, High Road, Willesden. NW10.   **0181 451 5525**
It's a small place (thirty-six seats) which has been around for a long time
(since 1974). Sayed Kadiri's 150 item menu surely has something for
everyone, 'Including Fish Curries (Wednesdays only) and a great selection of Paneer dishes, eg: Paneer Chilli Masala.' GB. Mr Kadiri will give
a discount to Curry Club members, see page 288.

SABRAS
263, High Road, Willesden Green. NW10.   **0181 459 0340**
Here's hoping Mr and Mrs Desai survive their current financial problems. - The Ed.

NW11
GURKHA BRASSERIE   **CC DISCOUNT**
756, Finchley Road. NW11.   **0181 458 6163**
One of the best places to go for Nepalese food. Owner/Chef Hari KC is
often on hand to explain what's what amongst the Gurkha's Nepalese
specials. The regular curries are, 'Pretty darned good too.' SW. Will give
a discount to Curry Club members, see page 288. Branch: Gurkha
Brasserie, W1.

LONDON - SE

SE1

BENGAL CLIPPER
11-12, Cardamom Building,
Shad Thames, Butlers Wharf. SE1.   **0171 357 9001**

A new restaurant (1994) sited amidst trendy Terence Conran restaurants opposite St Katherine's docks. Money has been lavished on decor to produce a room with clean lines and pleasing appearance. A grand piano indicates that there is live entertainment. The menu looks promising. The results are less rewarding. The site is not Thamesside with a view, like the Conran restaurants - it's a block back and has no 'view'. The piano playing is so loud for the adjacent tables as to be annoying. The food doesn't quite live up to its promise. It lacks zest, with every dish having a same-taste-syndrome, born of a rather spiritless communal hot-pot sauce. It was early days when we visited. In fact we were invited to opening night - but after dozens of well-heeled guests had arrived the 'event' was cancelled leaving perplexed and vexed people on the door step. It was rather like the Marie Celeste: everything was ready to go, except there was a full crew but no food, no drink and no convincing explanation on offer. Our return trip left much to be desired. Gauche waiters spilt drinks, and delivered wrong dishes without joy to our table. Items were missed. We thought long and hard about whether or not to omit this restaurant from the Guide but decided to include it in the sincere hope that things improve, following such an enormous investment. We welcome reports.

CASTLE TANDOORI
200-201, Elephant and Castle Shopping Centre. SE1.   **0171 703 9130**

Mr Uddin's Castle is a spirited place and a regular entrant in our Guide. Open noon to 1am daily (extended to 2.30am on Fridays and Saturdays) we know of no longer hours in London. So, if you're an insomniac curryholic or just a late night reveller note this place well. The menu is pretty much formula (135 items) but includes duck, lamb chops and trout in various curry guises. Reports tell of the value for money.

SE3 - BLACKHEATH

TILDA
120, Lee Road, Blackheath. SE3.   **0181 244 4848**

NC tells us that things here are, 'Good and very good in a pleasant, smallish restaurant offering value for money.'

SE5 - CAMBERWELL

CAMBERWELL TANDOORI   **CC DISCOUNT**
22, Church Street, Camberwell. SE5.   **0171 252 4800**

Our regular correspondents continue to vote for the Camberwell. They tell of some unusual items, eg: Kebab-E-Coxbazza (sic) a fish dish from that region of Bangladesh (Cox's Bazaar!). Equally liked is their Murug-E-Makoney (sic) a type of Chicken Tandoori Masala. We noted one Balti dish (presumably) on the menu... Balthee (sic) chicken! Chef Juned and owner manager Sam Huda give a discount to Curry Club members, see page 288.

NOGAR   **CC DISCOUNT**
59, Denmark Hill. SE5.   **0171 252 4846**
Until recently (93) this was the Akash. Now, as the Nogar, it is owned and managed by K Hussain, with A Islam as chef. 'We liked the idea of Chicken Flaming (whole breast mediumly (sic) cooked.. sizzling with a flame of Sambuca. And we liked it when it came.' BK. We liked the move towards Bengal fish specials (there are four), we also note a Balti dish here. A discount is offered to Curry Club members, see page 288.

SE9 - ELTHAM

JIBON SATHI   **CC DISCOUNT**
52, High Street, Eltham. SE9.   **0181 265 0406**
Evenings only at this curry house (6 to 11.30pm). It opened in 1979 under owner manager AB Choudhury and changed name from the Luna fairly recently. The food remains excellent, we hear the service experienced and competent. Will offer a discount to Curry Club members, see page 288.

MAHATMA TANDOORI   **CC DISCOUNT**
156, Bexley Road, Avery Hill, Eltham. SE9. **0181 859 7954**
The Mahatma has a chatty menu which explains fully many of chef Miah's formula curries. A good all rounder where you should not be disappointed. They offer a discount to Curry Club members, see page 288.

WELL HALL TANDOORI   **CC DISCOUNT**
373, Well Hall Road. SE9.   **0181 856 2334**
A competent curry house owned and managed by Tuahid (front) and Abdul (chef) Ali and Muhan Miah. They offer a discount to Curry Club members, see page 288. See page 66.

SE10

TASTE OF INDIA
57, Greenwich Church Street, SE10.   **0171 858 2668**
Standard curries from a formula menu. Reports welcomed.

SE13

BABU SAHEEB
406-408, Lewisham High Street, SE13.   **0181 244 2112**
A smart place and quite large too with bar, 100 seats and a further 100 seater party room. 'An extensive menu, which particularly appeals to me because of the vegetarian option for almost every dish. I have been going to this restaurant for the last five years and every dish I have tried has been delicious. The service is always excellent ans the atmosphere relaxing. All my friends whom I have taken to Babu Saheeb have enjoyed their meals and many have returned, and I therefore feel it deserves a mention in your book.' BR.

BENGAL BRASSERIE   **CC DISCOUNT**
79, Springbank Road, Hither Green. SE13. **0181 244 2442**
'A nice little menu,' is how CT describes it, containing a few originals. Awshi Lamb contains lamb chop and red pumpkin. The spinach in Lobster Saghee makes this, 'A fine dish.' ES. And others enjoy the Sea Thali with its emphasis on seafood. They do a range of Pizza too with curry toppings - 'Great for that quick home-delivered snack.' AH. Owned by Syed and managed by Jahed Ahmed. They offer a discount to Curry Club members, see page 288.

CHANDPUR   **CC DISCOUNT**
134, Lee High Road, Lewisham. SE13.   **0181 473 8222**
The extremely popular Spice of Life has moved along Lee High Road to
reopen as the equally popular, Chandpur. Owned by Harris Miah, with
the cooking by Jilad, we hear that, 'It still serves superb food, excellent
value, friendly, jolly service and a real treat. Now larger with very smart
decor but they still took the trouble to telephone and let us know that
Tandoori fish was on the menu.' GM. The party atmosphere remains and
they give discounts to Curry Club members, see page 288.

DIL RAJ
33, Staplehurst Road, Hither Green. SE13.   **0181 297 8989**
Well recommended takeaway only, hours 4.30pm to 11.30pm. Formula
curries, with one or two Nepalese items at fair enough prices.

SE19

GOLDEN CURRY CENTRE   **CC DISCOUNT**
86, Anerley Road. SE19.   **0181 788 9997**
Another takeaway only, with lunch time and evening hours (to midnight). Owned by M Ali (front) and Johur Ali chef they give a discount
to Curry Club members, see page 288.

PASSAGE TO INDIA
232,Gipsy Road. SE19.   **0181 670 7602**
'I have been eating here for eight or nine years. It is still excellent. I ate
there last week and had a wonderful meal.' GG.

SE22 - EAST DULWICH

MIRASH
94, Grove Vale, East Dulwich. SE22.   **0181 693 1640**
'A crisp and smart interior,' says VG . Formula curries include all the
favourites. Value for money Sunday set lunch.

SURMA
42, Lordship Lane, East Dulwich. SE22.   **0181 693 1779**
One of the older (1976) curry houses in the area. No suprises. A
competent place. Branch: Joy Bangla Curry House, 39, Denmark Hill.
SE5.

SE23 - FOREST HILL

BABUR BRASSERIE   **TOP 100 - CC DISCOUNT**
119, Brockley Rise, Forest Hill. SE23.   **0181 291 2400**
You're struck straight away by its striking and really attractive white
Muglai - arched frontage, each arch enhanced by hanging baskets and
floor tubs. The white decor continues inside, offset by air force blue chair
upholstery. Dining is intimate in a screened area or in the conservatory.
The menu is a careful compilation of well known favourites with an
above average selection of unusuals. Aloo Choff is a mashed potato and
vegetable rissole rolled in chopped cashew and fried, for a starter. The
delicious and unusual Patra (see glossary) is also superb as a starter.
Main courses include the gorgeous traditional Parsee dish, Sali Jardaloo.
Here lamb is slowly cooked with savoury spices enhanced with the sweet
and sour tastes dried apricots (jardaloo) and honey. The dish is garnished with straw potatoes (sali). Poodina Gosht included mint in the
cooking. Vegetable are well represented with Dum Tori (courgettes and
amchur - sour mango powder) and Kadoo Masala (red pumpkin). All
owner chef Enam Rahman's cooking is bright and fresh. Front of House
is equally bright and fresh under the careful supervision of owner

manager Emdad Rahman. Watch out for their regular cuisine festivals and special offers. It is plentiful attention to details (such as the gold-credit-card-style visiting cards) good food, service and ambiance which has gained this restaurant promotion into our TOP 100. They offer a discount to Curry Club member, see page 288.

DEWANIAM   **TOP 100**
133-5, Stanstead Road, Forest Hill. SE23.   **0181 291 1218**
We are sickened to hear of the arson attack which gutted this restaurant. The Babur (see above) also suffered an arson attempt. Luckily damage was minimal there. So the Dewanian has been closed for months (at the time of writing) but will hopefully be opened by the time you read this. We await the results with excitement, but as owners Rashid Ali and Fozlu Miah (chef) promise the menu and atmosphere will be the same but the decor will be new and, 'very, very good.' It's the menu which we have been extolling for years. And where this guide goes others follow. So the Dewaniam is now no stranger to accolade. Sometimes this can rock the boat and a much vaunted establishment can become complacent. Not so the Dewaniam. All our reports glow with contentment. We repeat what we've said in our previous guide: we know of no other Indian restaurant which has such a wide choice of ingredients permanently on its menu. You can, of course, have a thoroughly good meal choosing old standard favourites (chicken lamb, prawn etc). But there are some truly outstanding alternative choices. Game is represented by pheasant, quail, duck, hare and venision. Don't panic about Heron Tikka, however - it's not that elusive, well-loved river bird - it's 'marinated deer meat barbecued in the tandoor.' (The Hindi/Urdu word for venison is Heeran!). Lamb brain is unusual and worth a try. Chef Fozlu is an innovator. His skilful use of alcohol matches anything you'd find in the French repertoire. Mugli Batak, for example, is duck cooked with mince, egg, cream, green herbs and red wine. But it's not just red wine which appears in a number of dishes - white wine enhances the Tandoori Trout marinade - brandy is used as a flambée (for tandoori pheasant or quail) and Tia Maria as a marinade in chicken Indropuri. There's one Bangladeshi fish dish Fish Masallah (sic), and a no compromise vegetable dish (Sabzi Satrang - okra, bitter gourd, sour tinda and aubergine). I'd like to see the Dewaniam add more really authenic Bangladeshi dishes, (without of course removing any of their exisiting dishes). Despite its enforced shut down, I am retaining this restaurant high in our TOP 100.

MAYMYO
127, Dulwich Road. SE24.   **0171 326 4789**
We are delighted that Gerald Andrews is back with a new restaurant. It's the country's only Burmese restaurant. Don't go for the decor, but do go for the food. Burmese food is the link between Indian and Thai. Our advice is that you ask the staff to recommend choices if it's new to you.

SE25 - SOUTH NORWOOD
JOMUNA BRASSERIE   **CC DISCOUNT**
165, Portland Road, South Norwood. SE25.   **0181 654 9385**
A medium sized (forty-four seats) standard curry house with all the good old favourites, plus some Balti dishes. Owner E Ali offers a discount to Curry Club members, see page 288.

MANTANAH THAI CUISINE
2, Orton BLgs, Portland Road, South Norwood. SE25.   0181 771 1148
Well regarded in the area is this Thai restaurant. 'You can binge yourself silly on chilli.' RD. Yes, we hear that some of the dishes are hot - as they should be, of course. Good green or red curries and much more, (123 items on the menu in fact).

SE26 - SYDENHAM

JEHANGIR   **TOP 100**
67, Sydenham Road, Sydenham. SE26.   **0181 244 4244**

The room is gorgeously decorated with vaulted archways, marble floors, hand painted ceiling, complete with huge colonial fan, mahogany carvers and Wedgwood crockery. The menu is astonishing. It runs to 10 pages and contains a massive 143 numbered items. It is a combination of Indian (North and South) and Sri Lankan, with a touch of the Maldive Islands thrown in. Everything is exceptionally well described. There are twenty three starters. Hot Tempered Prawns are indeed hot and the Gothamba Roti a thin bread, is indeed silky. There are eight types of Dosai (urid and rice flour pancakes), idlis and three hoppers. Main courses include thirteen chicken, twelve lamb and ten seafood dishes, many of which use imported Sri Lankan fish. Breads, rice and biriyanis (sic) are followed by one of the most remarkable vegetarian selections we've seen. Over twenty-three dishes. Nice touches here include perfumed face towels and chocolate mints. They are extremely good with customer care. On the special occasions - cards, flowers, cake or champagne is given by the management. Reports received since we last told all this, are generally in agreement with our description. 'Everything you say about this is correct. It is superb and I have used this restaurant about five or six times since discovering it in August 1992.' GG. MJS disagrees with both our guide and the Sri Lankan Embassy's recommendations. His report was so awful that I can't repeat it (except that he considered it made our guide 'suspect'. We wonder if he was at the same restaurant). RP enjoyed the Sunday Lunch Buffet but was cross that the £8.00 it cost was enhanced by an, 'Unadvertised and ever unpopular 12.5% service charge.' GCM enjoyed it too but was disappointed, 'Not to be greeted by the ladies in saris.' Have they gone for good now? No they haven't! Mrs Kughan, wife of the owner is the chef and there is at least one waitress in a sari serving drinks. We're happy to keep the Jehangir in its TOP 100 slot.

LONDON - SW

SW1
KUNDAN
3, Horseferry Road. SW1.   **0171 834 3434**
There are 117 seats at the Kundan (and 200 or so at the House of Lords and
632 at the Commons). And like as not you'll spot many a political 'name'
in there all enjoying right-wing-raitas with Commons seeds and red
Vindaloos or Matar Peers perhaps. Our Honourable and Right Honourable members enjoy curry so much, they've even formed a branch of The
Curry Club at their House, and are frequently seen practising at the
Kundan. Owner Nayab Abbasi enjoys all this, of course, and given half
a chance he'll explain to you about the loud bell that rings here from time
to time. Standard food not cheap but such delights wouldn't be and it is
Westminster!

SALOOS   **TOP 100**
62/64, Kinnerton Street, Knightsbridge. SW1.   **0171 235 4444**
I get more reports about Saloos from my Indian friends, than about any
other restaurant. Curious really. Because I do mean Indian. And Saloos
is very much Pakistani, owned by M Salahuddin (who wrote me a kind
letter inviting me to lunch in April 1992, which I never fulfilled, then
threatened to sue me, on another matter, in July 1992. Never mind - such
is the price of fame. The matter was dropped). But despite such activity
and maybe because of its idiosyncrasies, of which more below, I continue
to admire and promote Saloos in our Guide, as I have for twelve years.
As I say it is immensely popular with London's well educated wealthy
Indians, who ignore politics when it comes to good food. And in their
opinion there is precious little good Indian, let alone good Pakistani food
in Britain. On the evening of our visit, we found the first-floor restaurant
nearly full, its clientele composed of the afore mentioned Indians, plus
some Arabs and whites. 'Drinks orders for gin and tonic (£5.50 each)
were taken promptly and delivered by a very nervous young man. The
wine (Mouton Cadet £18.50) was opened with no grace and if there had
been any sediment at the bottom of the bottle it was now distributed
equally among the liquid. The glasses weren't even as nice as the ones
you can collect with ESSO vouchers. The restaurant atmosphere wasn't
the usual one of diners chatting and eating, clinking of glasses. It
reminded me of breakfast time in a large hotel: eating with not much
talking.' DD. Despite the large, genial head-waiter's habit of telling us
what we were about to order (Chicken Shashliks were doing a roaring
trade it seemed) we were finally allowed to choose for ourselves. Seated
near the back stairs - the route to the kitchen - provided us with a fair
measure of cabaret. The ordering system is to throw a copy of the chit
down the stairs with a screech. It is collected by an unseen minion and
later is transferred into food, carried aloft up the stairs by a seen minion,
complete with long white marigold gloves, who silently waits until the
head waiter takes these offerings from him. Time after time he appeared
with a two foot long Chicken Shashlik skewer in each hand. These were
ceremoniously carried aloft by the Maitre'D who proudly delivered
them to the appropriate table. Watching these proceedings as well as us,
was a well dressed gentleman who spent his time preparing bills, raising
his eyes to the heavens and from time to time muttering in our direction.
I took him to be Mr Salauddin himself. And what about the food? Meat
predominates. Lamb and chicken is Halal, of course, and being the major
part of Pakistani repertoire, it is the same at Saloos. Vegetarians be

warned! There is a comprehensive Tandoori section providing succulent natural coloured divinely flavoured offerings. Our lamb chop (£9.90) and Shami Kebab (£10.50) were both lean and melt in the mouth. The Chicken Shashlik looked equally good. From the select range of main courses we chose the hard-to-find (but acquired taste) Hyderabadi dish - Haleem (£10.50) - pounded meat cooked with wheat, supplied complete with a DIY spice kit of chillies, ginger, garam masala and onion tarka, which you add yourself. It was, however, rather undefined in flavour. The Chicken Jalfrezi (£10.50) was the weak link, with too much ginger and rather stringy overcooked chicken The Pullao Rice (£3.95) was superb and definitive. Aloo Paratha (£3.90) was fantastic. It is essential to book. The elegant Farizeh Salahuddin (daughter of the house - she can be heard out of hours on the answer machine) handles bookings with considerable aplomb. Our bill for two with an aperitif, wine, starter, main course and coffee came to £100, including cover charge of £1.50 and 15% service charge, which makes it probably the most expensive Pakistani, Indian or Bangladeshi restaurant in the UK. The place is an institution and is worth at least one visit. Open: Monday to Saturday 12 noon to 2.30pm and 7pm till 11.45pm. Remains in our TOP 100.

WOODLANDS
37, Panton Street. SW1.   **0171 930 8200**
'Made very welcome. I particularly like Southern Indian food so I am delighted Woodlands is back to its original form. We were very happy with all the dishes we had, well spiced and presented. Also glad to have a choice of Indian desserts. Good value.' HC.

SW2

BHANGRA BEAT
17-21, Sternhold Avenue, Streatham. SW2.   **0181 678 0965**
Sam Khan's Romford branch has been such a sizzling success (see entry in Essex) that he has repeated the formula in Streatham. See also page 41.

LANCER OF BENGAL   **CC DISCOUNT**
220, Brixton Hill, Brixton. SW2.   **0181 674 4736**
It's a small place (40 seats) but it serves the formula curry (preceded by an 'exotic' cocktail). Home delivery also available. Akal Ali's restaurant gives discounts to Curry Club members, see page 288.

SW3

PLANET POPPADOM
366, King's Road, Chelsea. SW3.   **0171 370 3377**
Cashing in, perhaps, on the razzmatazz surrounding the Planet Hollywood concept, Mohammed Yusuf's Planet Poppadom opened shortly afterwards, without the super stars and the hype of the former. I suppose its name was bound to be applied by someone and it does have some alliterative charm. It's a smallish place and has been starkly decorated in black, white and chrome, with a bar and an on-view open cooking section on one side. Aromas and funky music fill the air. Pictures of the Planets adorn the walls to remind you of the theme. Billed as Chelsea's first Balti Brasserie and Bar, it has a range of some 20 Baltis on offer, although those we were offered on opening day were indistinguishable in flavour from formula curries. Tandoori, Onion Bhaiji, Vegetable Samosas and Biriani plus sundries complete the menu. Planet is undoubtedly designed for, and already popular with the Chelsea 'set'. But we'd like to see rather more confidence in the spice department. Open noon to midnight, Thursday to Sunday (4pm to midnight Monday to Wednesday).

TANDOORI OF CHELSEA   **TOP 100**
153, Fulham Road, Chelsea. SW3.   **0171 589 7617**

This elegant basement restaurant quietly goes about its business without fanfare or hype. It is, and always has been, since it opened in the sixties, a leader in style, from its carefully selected small number of dishes, to its decor and wine list. It is, of course, the Indian (see page 30) owned by A Rajan, whose quote in our last guide amused many and is worth repeating (excuse the pun). 'Good wine does go with well cooked Indian food. It is not overpowered by subtle spicing,' he says. 'That is why we have Chateau Latour on the menu.' Asked if one should drink lager with his food he exploded, 'Certainly not, spice and gas don't mix!' 'An indisputably smart place where dressing up is part of the fun.' Says EB. The food is indeed subtly spiced, but the chefs will step up both spice levels and chilli heat if requested. Here is what one of our ace reporters (Mrs DRC) says. 'I've walked by this restaurant dozens of times and always admired the Indian dressed doorman and imagined the basement restaurant would be attractive. This week found ourselves driving right by at the right time, wanting a quick meal and there was a parking space right outside, so took the opportunity to find out what the interior is like. Yes, it is very attractive, elegant Indian style, and we were made very welcome in the totally empty restaurant. Other diners soon arrived but it was never more than half full, which seemed a shame for such a good restaurant. The food was superb, menu fairly limited, much less for a vegetarian than is usual in Indian restaurants. Every dish we had was marvellous, service was good, prices fair for the quality and area. We were very impressed.' The restaurant remains firmly in our TOP 100.

SHAHEEN OF KNIGHTSBRIDGE   **CC DISCOUNT**
225, Brompton Road. SW3.   **0171 581 5329**

Formula curries right there on Brompton Road, not a chupatti throw from Harrods. Good Bangladeshi stuff from Chef Mustafa Kamal, with one or two 'unusuals.' The Maahn Dal is a Gujarati special with black lentils, ginger, tomato and chillies, and Mango Lassi is a favourite with some. It's a small place (40 seats) and prone to tourists. Owner AK Trehan will give a discount to Curry Club members, see page 288.

SW4 - CLAPHAM

MAHARANI
117, High Street, Clapham. SW4.   **0171 622 2530**

Clapham's first curry house, opened long before the place became trendy. It has kept up with the trends though, and serves highly competent formula curries, indeed owner SU Khan was one of the pioneers of the formula. The Sunday lunch buffet is the new 'institution' there. 'Quite a lot of different dishes available for the Sunday Buffet. I enjoyed it at the time but afterwards on reflection, the food was a bit bland.' RP. (It's a common problem with buffets - they are cooked to a large scale and cannot be the same as individually cooked dishes - Ed).

SW5

NIZAM
152, Old Brompton Road, South Kensington. SW5.

CC DISCOUNT
0171 373 0024

It is Miss Sumaira Lateef-Mian managerial warmth and efficiency and M Jabbar's good cooking coupled with a bamboo and plant 'outdoor' light-and-airy decor which makes the Nizam 'a favourite place to go.' MM. The Sunday 12 noon to 5.30pm (£7.95) Eat all you can is popular - as is the a la carte choice. Curry Club members will get a discount, see page 288.

STAR OF INDIA
154, Old Brompton Road, South Kensington. SW5.　　0171 373 2901

Every one talks about the decor - the murals, the stars, the lighting, the flora and the prices. 'Such luxury doesn't come cheap,' said owner Reza Mohammed and as the place is always full to bursting (booking essential) he's reaping the benefits, we presume. And we applaud such theatre. Dining out is supposed to be fun and escapist. Says Mrs MF, 'Very expensive, however seeing that the place was packed on a Friday night. Food good, portions very small. The starters - Samosas, Onion Bhajis and Chicken Chaat were just put on the plate with no garnish at all. The main courses were good though a plain meat dish alone was £7.50. £1 cover charge per person.' None-the-less, a place for all curryholics to visit.

SW6

BLUE ELEPHANT　　WINNER OF SPECIAL AWARD　　TOP 100
4-6, Fulham Broadway, Fulham. SW6.　　0171 385 6595

Talking of escapism (see Star of India entry) the Blue Elephant has to win the top decor award. The frontage is fairly nondescript with its blue neon competing with that of the pub next door. Go inside you get a warm welcome from the hosts and hostesses in national costume. There's a bar and a cloakroom. Nothing out of the ordinary here. It is when you proceed into the restaurant that you realise this is no ordinary place. Ahead of you is the jungle: literally hundreds of strategically placed plants. Bamboo on the walls and ceiling, and pagodas transport you at once from Fulham to Phuket. And just when you think you've seen it all, you realise there's more. The restaurant goes on and on. Small bridges traverse ponds inhabited by golden carp and lillies. Waterfalls tinkle gently down. The perfumes from exotic flowers fill the air. Little Thai houses surround the walls, and different dining areas have different characteristics. Some are secluded, some communal. Yet despite being gigantic (it has a massive 250 covers) one is simply not aware of its size and it somehow manages to retain a feeling of intimacy, and the blue elephant motif appears again and again - in the carpets, in the tablecloths, on the crockery and the display cabinet amongst items for sale and on the menu.

What of the menu? Well, there are two actually (three, if you count the wine list). One is the main menu, the other is the Vegetarian menu. The main menu contains seventeen starters, five soups and thirty four meat, chicken, duck and seafood dishes. Chilli heat is indicated with elephant symbols (three for hottest) on the menu, and there are a number of Thai curry dishes. For those who like to try a wide range of dishes the Banquet for £25 (without soup) £28 (with) provides a massive selection of dishes although you need a large party to take advantage of this. Smaller groups, even singles, can sample a selection of starters and main course dishes by ordering 'Pearls' and 'Royal Platter'. The Blue Elephant flies in fresh produce every week. Ingredients such as lemon grass, aubergine, green pepper, chillies, holy basil and banana leaves (they make disposable doilies from them), orchids and galangale combine to produce those memorable Thai fragrances. And flying in their own ensures a freshness unmatched in rival Thai restaurants. Portions are more than ample. Service is gracious, smiling and accurate. Don't forget to book - it is always full. Parking is nigh on impossible so go by taxi. (it's opposite the tube - but if you can't afford a taxi you might as well forget the Blue Elephant). It's a top price restaurant, (for Indo-Thai that is, but still much less than Roux / Little / Hilton type places). Expect to pay between £30 to £50 per head depending on how lavish your extras are, and that may not include the 15% service charge and £1.50 cover charge. The food at the Blue Elephant is spot on. The place has become an institution. For two or three hours you can escape from the world in here. It is fun and it is theatre. What more can one ask? High in our TOP 100.

MAMTA
692, Fulham Road. SW6.   **0171 736 5914**
A rarity in the area - a Gujarati vegetarian (licensed) establishment. Fans, ask the waiters to 'spice it up' or else it can be a mite bland. Reports please.

NAYAB
309, New Kings Road. SW6.   **CC DISCOUNT**
                                        0171 731 6993
Owner Praveen Rai is quite a wag. He'll regale you with many a tale about his travels and his ability. 'There isn't a chef in India (or indeed in Britain) whose particular talents are safe from Parveen's scrutiny.' he tells us. His really quite up-market menu is full of, 'some dishes you won't recognise and some that you will.' Masha - onion skins filled with spiced cabbage, celery and black-eyed beans, Baked Squid, Lasooni Lamb Rara (sharp and hot) and Meat Dhaba Wala Lamb cooked in bone marrow stock and mince (ask Rai to tell you about this) are some of the former. A substantial quota of vegetable dishes is also on offer. Woe betide you if you order a Phal. Mr Rai's menu tells us it comes from the Hindi phrase 'Bhund Phar' meaning 'bottom-ripping.' Manager Ms N Kapre (Naz) handles all Rai's exuberence with grace and efficiency making the Nayab a popular place. Open 6.30 to midnight it gives a discount to Curry Club members, see page 288.

TIFFIN
541a, Kings Road, Chelsea. SW6.   **0171 610 6117**
Formerly the Kabana, the recently opened Tiffin is billed as the world's first 'Indian tapas Bar and Brasserie'. It is designed to appeal to the Chelsea set. To tiff, it seems, means to sip. And there is a satisfying list of soft drinks including several lassis and Nimboo Pani - fresh lime and soda - try it with salt! and alcoholic beverages amongst which are Indian beer and champagne. Tiffin's menu has a careful selection of snacks (tiffins) from the tandoor as well as old favourites such as samosas. Chholey Garam is unusual - it is a Punjabi hawkers dish with chickpeas in a spicy sauce served piping hot on a dried leaf plate. The a la carte selection of main courses is small but has 'something for everyone'.

SW7 - KENSINGTON
BALTI'S
The London Esthetique, 41, Queen's Gate Terrace. SW7. 0171 581 3019
Just what an esthetique is, you'll have to ask when you visit. The mystery is no less incongruous when you find Baltis (not known for their oppulence) served in the most upmarket setting - a beautiful room (don't miss the plaster work on the ceiling) in the former MI5 building, now a women only health spa. Not expensive, especially as it is BYO. Evenings only. Closed Sunday. Reports please.

BOMBAY BRASSERIE   BEST INDIAN RESTAURANT
Courtfield Close, Courtfield Road, Kensington. SW7.   **0171 370 4040**
Known affectionately by its fans as the BB, and stepping into its thirteenth year, with more confidence than ever (yes it all began in 1982 - doesn't time fly!). The Taj Group's marketing director Camelia Panjabi,

whose brainchild the BB, was explains that she wanted to get away from standard Punbaji food served then in nearly all Indian restaurants, both in the UK, and in India. 'I wanted to launch regional Indian cuisine in England - homestyle Bombay dishes such as Patrani Macchi, fish with green chutney, baked in a banana leaf, and streetside food - Sev Batata Puri for starters, and regional main course dishes, such as Jardaloo Sali Boti and garnished with potato straws)'CP. These and many other similar authentic dishes have remained on the menu all these years and are always in demand. It is the regional specialities which you should go for when you visit. Of course the BB does some well known Punjabi dishes too. Tikka, Kebabs and Tandoori come luscious and succulent and devoid of artificial food colouring. Familiar main courses include Rogan Josh, Chicken Tikka Makhani and Biriani. There are plenty of vegetarian choices and several set meal Thalis. If the BB went through a down patch a few years ago, it certanly is on top form now. We've had so many good reports on the BB over the last three years. Here are extracts from a few: 'A little piece of upper class India right in the heart of London, that's how I would describe THE BOMBAY BRASSERIE in a few words. My grandfather's job as a chef took him all over India, and I would often hear him tell of the Tiffin rooms. The Bombay Brasserie is exactly how I imagined them, the atmosphere, the decor, the staff, everything. I proceeded to the lunch buffet table and helped myself to a little of everything, which I placed on an outstandingly large dinner plate, (none of your tea plates here) and sat down to an exceptional lunch. The only fault, if any, was that the waiter forgot to inform me that a Nan would also be provided with the meal, and consequently I'd almost finished my meal when it arrived.Still not to worry, it just meant that I would have to get seconds to eat with it. Then I sampled some of their delicious fruit salad. After which I simply sat back and soaked up some of that magic atmosphere, which I doubt if any one could re-create just anywhere. I think that the building has got to be just right, which incidentally you would not detect from the outside of the building, with its high ornate ceilings and ceiling fans and huge Indian paintings etc. I thoroughly enjoyed myself at this restaurant and would recommend it to anyone.' MB. 'Well, what can I tell you about the interior of this wondeful restaurant? It must be like stepping back in time to when the British occupied India. Everyone in my party was extremely impressed, and put instantly at their ease. It is a little difficult to say exactly what we all ate that night but nobody had any complaints. The service was excellent and the quality of food, and its presentation was first class. One of the party had the lobster (to make sure he spent ALL the £25.00 min charge!) and thoroughly enjoyed it.' MD. 'I have never been disappointed here. You do have to pay for the quality here, but for a special occasion it is worth it.' NS. 'A fabulous buffet lunch. Special offer for £5! Can you imagine that? Of course, it's not normal curry house fare and would normally set you back a good £25.00..... and even then it is great value for money. Everything is so elegant and unhurried, almost like the upper classes at play from years gone by. The food is brilliant. Even at full price it is an experience that you have to try once.' JL.

The difference between authentic regional Indian cooking and curry house offerings has in the past caused some criticism. But we have received almost none recently. NDM gives a fair assessment of this view. 'Wonderful decor and ambience. Slight initial disappointment at the food, tempered by the realisation that this was probably owing to the fact that I am unused to the 'genuine article'. Overall: a good, if somewhat expensive experience.' NDM. General Manager Adi Modi tells me that he is currently having to turn up to 80 people away every day. So booking is essential. If you prefer the conservatory ask for it when booking. To lessen disappointment, plans are afoot to add another 80 seats. The Bombay Brasserie, despite being a large machine, operates very smoothly with a very experienced team. It has the benefit of an even bigger operation and team in the form of its owners the Taj Hotel Group.

Despite the arrival of a good many new contenders on the Indian restaurant scene, none has quite managed to topple the BB from its position of excellence. And despite a close run from our last guide's over all winner, The Bombay Brasserie is at the top of our TOP 100.

CAFE LAZEEZ
23-29, Old Brompton Road, Kensington. SW7. **0171 581 9993**
Opened in 1992, since the last guide was published, to a blaze of publicity, which hailed the Lazeez (meaning 'delicate and aromatic, pleasing to the senses, delicious to taste) as a new type of Indian restaurant. In fact it is in two parts - an upstairs restaurant with illuminated tented ceiling, and the much starker downstairs café. The latter has a short but adequate menu whilst upstairs has a much longer menu. Consultant chef Ms Sabiha Kasim sister of owner Zahid Kasim has attempted to bring home Indo-Pak cooking to Brompton Road. The menu offers many favourite dishes, plus some 'evolved' originals (such as Officer's Chops - marinated in soya and honey), with a promise of fresh raw ingredients cooked to order. Comments received indicate a generally satisfied clientele, and it is indisputably popular with tourists and the local Chelsea set, although we have found in our visits a patchy quality to both food and service. Still, a place worth visiting which we're hopeful will improve with experience. Reports welcomed. See page 16.

DELHI BRASSERIE
CC DISCOUNT
134, Cromwell Road, South Kensington. SW7. **0171 370 7617**
Opened in 1986 and now well established and popular this 60 seater is unusual for the area in that is open all day, from noon to 11.30pm. Chef Ram Singh's food is 'particularly tasty.'GH. Owner Mr A Jabber and manager K Choudhury gives a discount to Curry Club members, see page 288.

KHAN'S
3, Harrington Road, South Kensington. SW7. **0171 584 4114**
'Decor very attractive, Indian in a modern way. We were made very welcome, and all the food was above average and prices very reasonable for central London.' DRC.

KWALITY
CC DISCOUNT
38, Thurloe Place. SW7. **0171 589 3663**
Sultan Khan's Kwality has been in operation since 1984. 'In appearance, very old fashioned, typical flock wallpaper, standard Indian restaurant china, but we were pleasantly surprised. We were made very welcome and the service from start to finish was efficient, professional and very friendly. All the food, by chef Gafur, was above average. Gulab Jamun, fine. Good to see it on the menu, one of my grumbles is the shortage of Indian sweets in Indian restaurant, a selection of International style ice creams is a lazy way out.' DRC. The restaurant give a discount to Curry Club members, see page 288.

MOTI MAHAL
3, Glendower Place, South Kensington. SW7. **0171 584 8428**
An old hand, established in 1956, and it knows its business, serving according to DRC, 'food ranging from very good to excellent.'

SW8
BIRAJ
CC DISCOUNT
266, Wandsworth Road. SW8. **0171 622 0455**
Formerly the Wandsworth Tandoori now the Biraj, it is open 6pm to midnight evenings only - closed Tuesday. This reflects the fact that it is family (Choudhury) run, and we hear of fresh home-style cooking. Gives discount to Curry Club members, see page 288.

QUEEN'S STAR   CC DISCOUNT
39, Queen's Town Road. SW8.   0171 622 7228
Established in 1980 and recently refurbished. Mr M Tafader's restaurant
has a comprehensive menu selection including Baltis. The restaurant
give a discount to Curry Club members, see page 288.

SW9

OLD CALCUTTA   CC DISCOUNT
64a, Brixton Road, Oval. SW9.   0171 582 1415
Owned and managed by Mrs Syeda Rafia Khatun, this restaurant is good
value (try the cheap set meals) and enterprising (ask to see the publicity
about Bishop Tutu amongst others). The wide ranging menu serves Balti
amongst many favourites. The restaurant will give a 10% discount to
Curry Club members on takeaways. See page 288.

The Old Calcutta Tandoori

THE FAMOUS INDIAN RESTAURANT

Open Daily. Noon to 2.30pm 6pm to Midnight. All Day Sunday Buffet.
Booking is Advisable. All Parties Catered for. Fully Licensed.

0171 582 1415

64a BRIXTON ROAD, OVAL,
LONDON SW9 6BP

10% DISCOUNT ON TAKEAWAY   FREE HOME DELIVERY
ON COLLECTION ONLY   (3 MILES - £15 MIN)

SONARGAON   CC DISCOUNT
260, Brixton Road, Brixton. SW9.   0171 274 5422
Named after one of Bangladesh's ancient cities, the Sonargaon is in the
same ownership (Karim, Khan and Islam) as the erstwhile Maharani
SW4 and NW! and Taste of India, 334, Kennington Road, SE11. Such a
pedigree ensures good quality. The restaurant gives a discount to Curry
Club members, see page 288.

SW10 - CHELSEA

CHUTNEY MARY   SPECIAL AWARD WINNER   TOP 100
535, Kings Road, Chelsea. SW10.   0171 351 3113
Looking back over the three years that have passed since this publication
made Chutney Mary number one, I notice that three parallel things
occurred in 1992. Firstly, the restaurant got busy, full in fact, almost all
the time. Secondly, the service, though sincere, was frequently inefficient
forgetful or downright stupid. One reporter (JL) raved about the place
on his first visit, but was told when he subsequently wanted to book his
group of twelve that they, 'wouldn't take a group of more than 10 on
Friday or Saturday.' As a consequence, continues JL, 'I don't suppose I
shall go again if I'm only welcome when it suits them.' JL asks what I feel
about this. I have to say that I totally agree with him. DBAC can see it
from the other side. Large parties can and do get very noisy and selfish.
They can ruin the atmosphere in the restaurant for the rest of the diners,
just because they are large and therefore will be paying a large bill they
think they're entitled to behave badly. So, DBAC does not 'totally agree'
with JL or PC. Other reports from that period tell of various lapses in
service. MB was much harsher. 'My love affair with Chutney Mary

ended when I found lager cost £5 a pint, and though some of the food was excellent I found other dishes too bland. (The lamb Cutless and the Akurie - scrambled egg). Other reporters had various minor niggles, and it is the price both a restaurant and a restaurant reviewer have to pay when you make a restaurant Number One. People's expectations are that much higher - disappointments that much greater. And it is fair enough. As the reviewer I passed the comments on to the restaurant, and the management, to be fair to them, acted, (People like JL, for example, were contacted and amends were made). But their most important action was to replace all the waiting staff. The team is now headed by Joe Mirrelson (ex Dorchester) and the remainder of the team is Indian, and very highly trained. Since this change, two or more years ago, I get no more complaints about service, and the place is still full to bursting. So what about the food? The menu is a brief document. Nothing on it resembles a standard 'curry house' of course, but I believe most diners are aware of that. Chutney Mary still alludes to being the first 'Anglo-Indian' restaurant - indeed I believe it remains the only such establishment. And true there are still one or two Anglo-Indian dishes which my late grandmother may or may not have been familiar with in her days in the Raj. But 'Anglo-Indian' it is not. Chef Hardev Singh Bhatty, and his brigade of five chefs are very much Indian, and so is their food. I am often asked what Chutney Mary means by 'Anglo-Indian' and I really am not sure I can explain satisfactorily. I see Chutney Mary as an Indian restaurant - ie: it serves Indian food. But it does not serve standard 'Indian restaurant food.' Says AJM, 'The food was good and extremely well presented, it was difficult to compare the restaurant / food to the normal local 'curry house' because it would be like comparing good pub food to the Ritz. Both are excellent in their own right. The prices are far more expensive than you normally pay but you get what you pay for!'
Chutney Mary's strength comes from the personal attention lavished on its food by the person whose concept it was, Namita Panjabi. As a director of cuisine, she is frequently to be seen checking out the chefs and dining at the restaurant. The resulting food is as close to Indian home cooking as you could get in any restaurant. See page 9. We are pleased to give Chutney Mary our SPECIAL AWARD for culinary excellence.

SW11 - BATTERSEA

BATTERSEA TANDOORI
515, Park Road, Battersea. SW11.　　　　　**0171 585 0487**
'Fairly standard menu but the food is well cooked and always arrives at the table hot. Quantities are very generous and prices reasonable.' DRG.

BATTERSEA VILLAGE RICKSHAW
27-29, High Street, Battersea. SW11.　　　　　**0171 924 2450**
'We were made welcome and service was efficient and professional. Standard menu with fair prices. Very light and crispy Onion Bhaji. Absolutely wonderful Chicken Makhani. Had to try the Kadu - pumpkin - very good. One of the best Mutter Panir, very creamy and rich, superb. Chef very heavy handed with the lurid red colouring.' DC.

PANAHAR
184, Lavender Hill. SW11.　　　　　**0171 228 8947**
'Quiet service, good menu range, very comfortable and attractive environment.' PC.

BALTI HOUSE
76, Northcote Road. SW11.　　　　　**0171 924 2347**
Free bottle of wine with every takeaway over £15.00. What a great deal, go and take them up on their offer! Reports please.

◆ Chef Manzoor Ahmed ◆

FINALIST
of the
INDIAN CHEF OF THE YEAR
invites you to sample his
WORLD FAMOUS CUISINE
at the

TABAQ

47 Balham Hill, London. SW12 9DR
Tel: 0181 673 7820/673 2701

SW12 - BALHAM

TABAQ
47, Balham Hill, Baltham. SW12.   **0181 673 7820**
Owned by M & M Ahmed, one is front of house manager and the other head chef in the kitchen, but which one is which? 'Too expensive. Food was mediocre with fancy and complex names being attached to standard dishes.' Dr TMB. Seats fifty diners, so booking at the weekend is necessary. Hours: 6pm till midnight.

SW13 - BARNES

HAWELI   **TOP 100 - CC DISCOUNT**
7, White Hart Lane, Barnes. SW13.   **0181 876 4441**
Owned by Manju Chowdhury who is also head chef. One of an extensive chain of upmarket curry houses. Pat has been a consultant chef, cooking with Manju in the kitchens of this very branch. They worked out a new and exciting menu (ever heard of a Red Korma!!) and added Balti to the range of dishes available. So, with such expert advice how could we not give this restaurant a TOP 100 award? Haweli (meaning Palace) gets very busy at the weekends so booking is advisable. Manager, Basu Patel will give a discount to Curry Club members, see page 288. Hours: 12.30pm to 3pm and 6pm till 11.30pm. See page 15.

TANDOORI GRILL   **CC DISCOUNT**
188, Castelnau, Barnes. SW13.   **0181 748 1515**
Hours: 12 noon to 2.30pm and 6pm to midnight. Branches: Sopna, 175, High Street, Hampton Hill, Middx. Bilas, 4, Broad Street, Teddington, Middx. Gives a discount to Curry Club members, see page 288.

SW14

TASTE OF THE RAJ   **TOP 100**
130, Upper Richmond Road West. SW14   **0181 876 8326**
A modern upmarket curry house, well above average, run by the articulate Shawkat Ahmed (call me Chris). 'The food came in delicious waves and the time went by easily.' PC. Remains in our TOP 100.

SW15 - PUTNEY

BANGLADESH CURRY MAHAL   **CC DISCOUNT**
29, Upper Richmond Road, Putney.SW15   **0181 789 9763**
Bangladesh appears in the title of this restaurant, but what about the food, does Bangladehi food appear on the menu.? Reports please. Proprietor, M Nurul Islam will give a discount to Curry Club members, see page 288. Hours: 12 noon to 3pm and 6pm till midnight. Branch: Putney Tandoori, 137, Lower Richmond Road, Putney.

GANGES
205, Lower Richmond Road, Putney.SW15

CC DISCOUNT
0181 789 0357

A small and cosy restaurant seating thirty-four diners. Menu contains all your usual favourites such as Jalfrezi, Pasanda and Madras. Korahi (sic) dishes are also there. Owner and manager, Mr B Ahmed will give a discount to Curry Club members, see page 288. Hours: 12 noon to 2.30pm and 6pm till midnight. Home delivery service available.

MA GOA
299, Upper Richmond Road, Putney. SW15.

0181 780 1767

'Good friendly staff. Bhajee Pala Feast(for vegetarians), good, so was the Beach Barbecue (grilled chops, wings, steaks, liver and kidneys). Fish Caldin and the Goan Machiwalla (fish c urry) were bland. Galinna Kodi (chicken curry) and the Goan Batata (potatoes) were reasonable. All were loud in praise of the Sada Pullao. Overall we like it, but thought it wasn't proper Goan. However, recommended with the advice "be more Goan".' Dr CF. Home delivery service available.

PUTNEY TANDOORI
137, Lower Richmond Road, Putney.SW15

0181 788 4891

Proprietor, Mr Ahmed runs a very good restaurant serving competent curries to a famous local clientele. Hours: 12 noon to 2.30pm and 6pm till midnight.

SW16

ANARKALI BALTI HOUSE
229, Streatham High Road. SW16.

CC DISCOUNT
0181 769 3012

'It had been some time since we had been to the Anarkali and a take-away menu popped through the door was enough to prompt us to order a delivery. The food standard was high and very tasty. Balti is on the menu.' SN & RA. Proprietor, Mr M Miah will give a discount to Curry Club members, see page 288. Hours: Monday to Saturday 12 noon to 2pm and 5.30pm till midnight. Sunday 12 noon till 3pm and 7pm till midnight.

MEMORIES OF INDIA
109, Mitcham Lane. SW16.

0181 677 8756

A small and pleasant restaurant seating a cosy thirty-six diners, booking is necessary at the weekends. Hours: 12 noon to 2.30pm and 5.30pm till 11.30pm. Branch: Rajdoot, Ontario, Canada.

SHAHEE BHEL POORI VEGAN
145, London Road. Norbury. SW16.

CC DISCOUNT
0181 679 6275

One of a few Indian restaurants to offer vegan food. Manager, SA Rahim will give a discount to Curry Club members, see page 288. Hours: 12 noon to 2.30pm and 6pm till 11pm.

SPICE COTTAGE
78, Streatham High Road, Streatham. SW16.

CC DISCOUNT
0181 677 1719

Seating is divided on two floors. Manager, Praful Shah will give a discount to Curry Club members, see page 288. Hours: evenings only, Monday to Saturday 6pm till midnight, Sunday 5pm till 11pm.

SW17 - TOOTING

JAFFNA HOUSE
90, High Street, Tooting Broadway. SW17.

0181 672 7786

Sri Lankan dishes and South Indian too. Unlicensed, very cheap, good food served noon to 11.30pm.

KOLAM   CC DISCOUNT
58-60, Upper Tooting Road, Tooting. SW17.   0181 767 2514
South Indian delights are listed on the menu. Tamarind Rice sounds good. Tuesday to Sunday 12 noon to 2.30pm and 6pm till 11pm. Manager, S Rajakumar will give a discount to Curry Club members, see page 288. Hours: Friday and Saturday till midnight.

PEACOCK TANDOORI   CC DISCOUNT
242, Upper Tooting Road, Tooting. SW17.   0181 672 8770
Established in 1988 and has built up a local local crowd who can rely on the Peacock for a good curry. Proprietor, Yogi Anand, will give a discount to Curry Club members, see page 288. Hours: 12 noon to 3pm and 6pm till midnight.

SREE KRISHNA   TOP 100
192-194, Tooting High Street, Tooting. SW17.   0181 672 4250
A South Indian restaurant, menu contains all the usual curries but it specialises in food from Kerala. 'It has lost a little something though the food remains good, it is also quite cheap.' GG. Hours: 12 noon to 3pm and 6pm till 11pm. Branch: Ragam, 57, Cleveland Street, London. W1. Remains in our TOP 100.

SW18 - EARLSFIELD
NAZMIN   CC DISCOUNT
398, Garratt Lane, Earlsfield. SW18.   0181 946 2219
A standard curry house serving all your favourite standard curry house food at reasonable prices. Manager, A Rashid will give a discount to Curry Club members, see page 288. Home delivery service available. Hours: 12 noon to 2.30pm and 6pm till midnight.

SW19 - WIMBLEDON
NIRVANA   CC DISCOUNT
277, Wimbledon Park Road. SW19.   0181 780 2406
Proprietor, MA Mannan will give a discount to Curry Club members, see page 288. 10.20am to 3pm and 6pm till midnight.

SW20
INDIAN GOSSIP
20, Leopold Road, Wimbledon. SW20.   0181 946 0586
'Aiming at upmarket type clientele - open airy restaurant in pastel blue. Dhansak very rich and spicy.' SN.

NAZ   CC DISCOUNT
554, Kingston Road, Raynes Park. SW20.   0181 542 1608
All your regular curries at this establishment. Set meals look good value for money. Will give a discount to Curry Club members, see page 288. Home delivery service available. Evenings only: 6pm till midnight.

LONDON - W

W1

ANWARS
64, Grafton Way. W1.

TOP 100
0171 387 6664

A cafe, open from 10am to 10pm, owned by Pakistani Punjabis, whose gutsy, spicy food is redolent of Southall. Make your choice from the serving counter, from the dishes of the day, then carry your tray to a formica table and enjoy it. It's not licensed, BYO accepted. It has good local Asian patronage. 'Good, cheap and unpretentious. Friendly helpful hosts. The place for a London fix.' GH.Remains in our TOP 100.

CARAVAN SERAI
50 Paddington Street, W1.

TOP 100
0171 935 1208

The UK's only Afghan restaurant. A very nice touch is free hot Pakoras with chutney, given at the beginning, while you examine the menu. Try the Logery - leg of lamb, flavoured with spices and saffron, or the Sekonia (skewered lamb, cooked in the tandoor).Ashaks are pastries, filled with a spicy leek and mince filling, with yoghurt. Kohi is roast lamb, spiced with Char Masala and blackcurrant. End with Carrot Kulfi or Coconut Halva. The service is exemplary, as is the presentation. The food is superb, although portions are on the small size. In our TOP 100.

GAYLORD
16, Albemarle Street. W1.

TOP 100 - CC DISCOUNT
0171 629 9802

Both Gaylords (see next entry) emphasise that they no longer have a connection. This one was opened in 1973 and is owned by H Hariela and and managed b y VK Bammi. The cooking by S Mal is refined and very Indian . The breads are, 'the lightest, brightest ever.' DR. Some unusual Kashmiri specialities such as Goshtaba and Rista both Koftas and both, 'delicious.' KC. Worldwide branches . See page 288.In our TOP 100.

GAYLORD
79-81, Mortimer Street. W1.

TOP 100 - CC DISCOUNT
0171 580 3615

The Mortimer Street Gaylord's opening in 1966 heralded the pioneering of Indian 'haute-cuisine' in the UK.A smart location and expensive decor had not figured in curry reataurants 30 years ago.. It claims to be the first restaurant to have used a Tandoori oven in Britain. 'The decor is very attractive, the welcome and service friendly, the food very good. The spicing was better than any restaurant we know, the only criticism was that the flavours of vegetable dishes were too similar. We were im-pressed and loved the bustly atmosphere. As well asAsian diners, there were singles too, all made welcome and happy with the restaurant. Owner Mangat R Lama . See pages 288 and 86 . In our TOP 100.

GOPALS
12, Bateman Street. W1.

TOP 100
0171 434 1621

Chef NT Pittal's golden touch brought first the Lal Qila then the Red Fort to currinary prominence. Such were his talents that it was not surprising that he went solo in Soho, using his nick-name, Gopal to christen his venture. That was five years ago. It was a justifiable success, and has not ceased to attract satisfied reports. 'Lovely fresh flavours.' DM. 'Aloo Gobi and Mushroom Bhaji good and the Peshwari Nan the second best in the world.' PD. 'Murgh Goa very tasty.' JW. 'Dishes outstanding. As good as any restaurant I've been to.' JL. Gopal's remains high in our Top 100. In 1994, Gopal opened a branch in E1 (see entry) and he recently engaged the celebrated wine expert, David Wolfe to create a new wine list. It's a refreshing document, which should open the eyes (and hopefully the mouths) of many a wine snob (see page 17 and overleaf).

GURKHA BRASSERIE   CC DISCOUNT
23, Warren Street. W1.   0171 383 4985

'Genuine Nepalese restaurant . Superb decor with Gurkha photos on the walls (including owner Hari KC's father with the Queen at a regimental do). The thatched hut decor transports your straight to Nepal, as does the food. Nepalese food is very different and must be sampled. Momos (spicy dumplings) are highly recommended as arer all the dishes.' GH. Try the Choala cold lamb with garlic... hmmm!' DL. Branch at 756, Finchley Road, NW11. Discounts for Curry Club members, see page 288.

HARE KRISHNA
Hanway Street. W1.   0171 636 5262

Vegetarian South Indian food available from 12 noon to 12 midnight, and licensed. 'All acceptable average and absolutely fantastic value for money.' DRC. We do hear of slow service, so you may have to be a little patient for your bargain.

INDIAN YMCA CANTEEN
41 Fitzroy Square, W1.   0171 387 0411

This is one of my favourite eating holes, decidedly unlicensed. It's the downstairs canteen for the YMCA residents, many of whom are Asian students. Apart from continental breakfast, the food is just basic unsophisticated curry, school- dinner style. I've been using it for years. Outsiders are welcome. Take a plastic tray, join the always busy queue. Point to your choice of curry which is unceremoniously dolloped onto your plate. Top up with chapatties, tea or coffee and pay at the till. It's absurdly cheap... it's hard to exceed £4. Then jostle for space at a formica table. The food may not be brilliant, but the company can be, when you share your table with talkative friendly students. Highly recommended. Strict hours: lunch 12.30 to 1.30. Dinner 7 to 8 pm. No bookings.

KANISHKA   CC DISCOUNT
161, Whitfield Street. W1.   0171 388 0860

Owner Jagdish Vitish's is very smart and very Indian, with goodies from all over the country. On two floors, ground and basement, it is as busy at lunch as dinner, so booking is essential. AS found helpful staff and loved the food but, 'for the price the portions were not large enough.' RA felt the tables were too close together, and she too finds it expensive... 'but considering the ingredients used and the quality of the dishes, we felt the price was reasonable. I ordered the turnip dish as a dare, and it was outstanding... easily the best dish on the table.'

MAHARANI
77, Berwick Street, W1   0171 437 8568

A very reliable curry house with reasonable prices for Soho.

MANDEER   TOP 100 - CC DISCOUNT
21, Hanway Place. W1.   0171 323 0660

There are two parts to Mr and Mrs Ramesh Patel's vegetarian Mandeer - the no frills canteen, packed with lunchtime office workers (no booking, long queues but worth it for value and quality) and the Ravi Shankar, the smart place alongside where you go to linger over Chef Daudbhai's food. 'From the moment the papadams arrived, we knew we were in for a veritable sensation of a meal. We were not disappointed. It was fantastic.' AS. We do hear of some over lingering ie long waits and erratic service, but we are happy to keep the Mandeer in our Top 100. See page 288.

NEEL AKASH
2, Hanway Street. W1.   0171 580 9767

'Despite its rather drab setting, we went in and had a truly outstanding lunch. Portion size was just right too. We left feeling completely satisfied but not over-full, which is a rare experience for any restaurant.' RA.

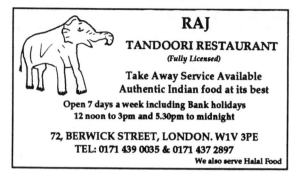
NEW DIWAN I AM
60-62, Blandford Street. W1.   0171 935 39

Long standing curry house serving competent food to a loyal following.

RAGAM SOUTH INDIAN   TOP 100
57, Cleveland Street. W1.   0171 636 9098

Popular and small (booking addvisable) with 36 upstairs, 20 downstairs.It does serve a range of standard curries and good though they are, our advice is to ignore them and concentrate only on the South Indian specialities. DB adores the Rasam and the Dosas. JL adores the Kaalam (orange coloured mango yoghurt and the 'very hot' Uthappam. It remains safely in our Top 100. Branch at Sree Krishna Tooting, SW17.

RAJ TANDOORI   CC DISCOUNT
72, Berwick Street. W1.   0171 439 0035

I used to work at Oxford Circus and came here four times a week, when it was the Islamabad. The Methi Gosht was nice and bitter, Bhajees crisp and the Phal, hot! All ample portions and excellent value. I moved jobs and did not visit for four years, but when I did recently, I was recognised as soon as I walked in, and was given a welcoming free pint, plus a brandy at the end.' GC. Discounts for Curry Club members, see page 288.

RED FORT
77, Dean Street, Soho. W1.   0171 437 2525

Amin Ali, once the doyen of the media, has made a brave effort to revive the fortunes of his Red Fort since his unfortunate insolvency some three years ago. Not only is there new decor, much needed after a decade of heavy use, there are new ideas flowing, of which the regular food festivals are the best. The results have been, at times, rewarding. Not withstanding, we have some disatisfaction about service, and the editors themselves recently used the venue to entertain a prestige group, and found a lack of zest in the food, the staff and Mr Ali himself.

TAMARIND (MOST PROMISING NEWCOMER AWARD) TOP 100
20, Queen Street, Mayfair, W1   0171 629 3561

Tamarind opened in late 94, to a blaze of publicity, yet to be matched in daily paying attendances. As with any new venture, it has yet to settle down. But one has to note a degree of timidity in many areas. Its entrance, for example, is uninviting to the point of invisibility. Its front door, though doubtless costing a fortune, at night resembles a sheet of blockboard. When you have decided it is the door, and you enter, the welcome is good, and the staircase down to the action is no obstacle.

The dining room is spacious, and the 80 seats do not feel cramped. The decor, in tones of blonde, gold, copper, brass and pine, is Mayfair, not Madras, subdued, not sub-continent. The main feature is two long glass wall panels, displaying some rather plain, palid pink sari silk. But why not some exquisitely embroidered Kanchi Puram silks? . I was smitten by the specially commissioned wrought-iron chairs until editor DBAC

---

warned that their rough edges could easily snag nylons, skirts and saris.

Chef Atul Kochar is young and Oberoi trained. His food is of the highest standard, and over three visits, improving as he settles in. His spicing is light and delicate, and some of his work innovative. Chicken Liver Masala is a spicy melt-in-the-mouth appetiser, though the Aloo Chaat Anarkali was devoid of taste. Bhuna Ghost and Hari Machli fish were both truly Indian in their delicacy. Bharwan Aloo, potato stuffed with nuts raisins and spices was masterly. Raj Soor heads the service with a huge team of attractive, smiling young men and women. Their keenness to please sometimes results in collisions, crashing of trays and glasses, and other gauche mishaps, born of inexperience. And times will get more testing as attendances grow from tiny acorns to full houses.Given confident backing , sufficient time, and a new front door, and providing it nurtures its personnel, especially, Chef Kochar, Tamarind will be as delightful a restaurant as its name. To help it on its way we are placing it our Top 100 and giving it our most promising newcomer award.

THE VEERASWAMY   TOP100 - CC DISCOUNT
99-101, Regent Street. W1.   **0171 734 1401**

London's oldest Indian restaurant, dating from 1927, became a London institution. A few years ago it slithered into a decline, matching that of the British Empire, a part of which it so admirably represented. Sarova Hotels of Kenya came to the rescue in 1986. Under the sprightly management of Paul Baretto, The Veeraswamy has regained much of its old glory. It is as much the haunt of American and Japanese tourists as of British afficionados, though these days rather less of 'old hands', home from their life of luxury in the Raj. The menu is modern Indian, with a selection of dishes from all over the country. Chef Sona Bedi is capable, and all aspects of the restaurant are smooth and experienced. It remains safely in our Top 100. It is inevitably not cheap, but Curry Club members can avail themselves of their discount , see page 288. See also page 33.

W2

BOMBAY PALACE   TOP 100
50, Connaught Street, Hyde Park Square. W2.   **0171 723 8855**

Starters include Alu Papri, thin potato crisps with yoghurt, tamarind and curry. Chooza Pakoras, spicy chicken fritters. Shammi Kebabs, succulent and superb. Main courses include the Bombay Palace's unique Murgh Keema Masala, minced chicken breast, lightly sautéed in ginger, garlic, onion, tomato, green peas, yoghurt and spices. 'Everyone in my group of nine were very pleased to be introduced to the Palace although many thought it expensive. I found that sometimes, less than best cuts of meat had been used, and they sent vegetable dishes down automatically. This had to be stopped because, although they weren't ordered they would be charged for. I don't like the Rice and Naan order to be done automatically either, but the waiter insisted on bringing, 'a selection,' for the table. One the whole, the food is very good, but service pushey. (They serve Cobra Lager).' MD. Others are more laudatory in their reports, indeed it is several reviewers' favourite Indian restaurant. We are happy to retain the Bombay Palace in our TOP 100. See page 90.

GANGES
101, Praed Street, Paddington. W2.   **0171 723 4096**

Thirty years on and still going strong. 'A small restaurant seating thirty, an inexpensive pleasant meal in pleasant surroundings and good friendly service.' BP-D.

GOLDEN SHALIMAR   CC DISCOUNT
6, Spring Street,. W2.   **0171 262 3763**

Well established standard curry house. Owner chef, Gulab Ambia and manager Gulab Mohammed gives a discount to Curry Club members, see page 288.

GATEWAY TO SUPERB INDIAN CUISINE

Bombay Palace ®

India's Culinary Ambassador
Established 1979

THE LARGEST AND PERHAPS FINEST
INTERNATIONAL CHAIN OF

INDIAN RESTAURANTS

IN THE WORLD

**KNOWN FOR AUTHENTIC NORTH INDIAN COOKING,
SERVICE AND AMBIENCE**

Bombay Palace

50, Connaught Street,
London. W2.
0171 723 8855
0171 258 3507

NEAREST UNDERGROUND - MARBLE ARCH

**DAILY BUFFET LUNCH, AIR CONDITIONED
'PALACE SUITE' FOR PRIVATE PARTIES
EASY PARKING AVAILABLE**

BRANCHES
* NEW YORK * WASHINGTON DC * BEVERLEY HILLS *
HOUSTON * ATLANTA * TORONTO * MISSISSAUGA *
MEXICO CITY * MONTREAL * KUALA LUMPUR *
BUDAPEST

INDIAN CONNOISSEURS
8, Norfolk Place. W2.

CC DISCOUNT
0171 402 3299

Opened since our last guide. A smart frontage reveals a bright and airy small (forty seats) interior, so booking advisable, with a 'big' menu. Yes, it has all your favourites, but it's not often you are offered Bangladeshi fish (Ayre and parrot fish) or Venison Bhoona. The even more adventurous could plump for Khashi Gazar (goat with carrot), Tandoori Pheasaeant (sic) or grouse. Adventurous stuff from chef Kabir Miah. Discounts for Curry Club members, see page 288. Branch: Golden Orient, E11.

OLD DELHI
48, Kendal Street. W2.

TOP 100
0171 724 9580

You'll often find so called 'Persian' dishes on the standard curry house menu. There is a centuries-long link between Persia (now Iran) and Indian. Biriani, Patia, Pullao, Patia, Dhansak, and more, all had their origins in Persia. But to most curry houses, these dishes are merely a modification to formula curries. Not so at the Old Delhi, whose owner manager is Iranian. You can certainly get superbly cooked curries in its superb setting, but venture further, and try at least some of the rather less spicy but authentically cooked Iranian specials. Faisenjan (chicken marinated, then cooked in a purée of pomegranate, spices and nuts) goes divinely with Saffron Rice and Doog (minty lhassi). A must for serious spicy food afficionados. Awarded our TOP 100 cachet.

WESTBOURNE GROVE - W2
This street is home to many curry houses. Three are worthy of mention:

DIWANA BHEL POORI HOUSE
50, Westbourne Grove. W2.

TOP 100
0171 221 0721

An equally succesful branch of the Drummond Street, NW1, flag ship serving crispy delicious cold Bombay Kiosk food. See entry NW1 for menu details. Inexpensive, very busy and in our TOP 100.

KHAN'S
13-15, Westbourne Grove. W2.

TOP 100
0171 727 5420

Khan's is the most difficult restaurant to review. I'll explain: It's a love it or hate it place - there's no inbetween. You'll probably love the decor. It's a fairy land room whose high, cloud-painted ceiling is supported by a forrest of gilt palm trees. There is a huge Hindi-arched mahogany bar and countless tables with pink cloths and black bentwood chairs. It is huge (over 300 seats on two floors) and it as full at lunch time as dinner. Apparently it is not unusual for them to do 1000 covers a day. And there in lies the problem. This sheer volume results in an American-style 'have-a-nice-day / take-it-or-leave-it', attitude. Even Americans are shocked and my files continue to bulge with complaints mostly about the inaccurately delivered orders and missing items, but occasionally about undesirable cabarets such as brawling customers with the waiters joining in. As first impressions count, we would not recommend it for a curry first timer nor to demure foreign tourist groups. But for seasoned curryholics, it is an institution and decidedly not to be missed. Indeed, Khan's has built up a very large customer base of regulars who frequently come from far and wide. This recent report from Colchester's DB is typical: 'Another enjoyable visit to Khan's - a huge busy restaurant with bags of atmosphere. Chilli Chicken Masala - excellent spicy taste, also the Lamb Bhuna Ghost. Reasonably friendly service this time which wore off when the place got busier - we had to ask five times for our pudding! Overall Khan's represents excellent value, and is highly recommended.' And from PD, 'I'm a regular here and if they don't make a mistake on my order and blame me for it, I'd think I was somewhere else!' Despite all this we'll go along with the majority and retain Khan's in our TOP 100. But maybe owner, Salman Khan, usually on hand, should consider implementing operational improvements. Tell him yourself. He's articulate and funny.

Khan's

**13-15, Westbourne Grove.
London. W2
0171 727 5420**

7 Days A Week -
12pm to 3pm & 6pm to Midnight

SULTAN TANDOORI BUFFET
57, Westbourne Grove. W2.

**CC DISCOUNT
0171 792 2565**

The 150 seat Sultan opened in 1993, under Messrs Khan and Majid, with a successful eat-all-you-can £6.99 - 20 dish (menu changed weekly) self-serve buffet. Included in the price are table served Popadoms and starters. The bonhomie from all this tummy-bursting good value, spreads to the waiters, who are 'always pleasant.' ED. Talking of the tummy, as if all this isn't enough, on Tuesdays there's an added attraction - Cathy the International Belly Dancer. And as if it isn't cheap enough already, the owners promise Curry Club members a discount, see page 288. Branches: Kebabish, Wembley, E7 and Manor Park.

W3 - ACTON
ACTON TANDOORI
138, Churchfield Road, Acton. W3.　　　　　　　　**0181 992 4583**
'Good Nepalese food. Corn Bhajee and Jeera Chicken huge and delicious.' MD. 'Simply outstanding.' SA.

W5 - EALING
CLAY OVEN
13, The Mall, Ealing. W5.

**CC DISCOUNT
0181 840 0313**

Still one of Ealing's favourites. Go for Bhadur Chelleri's cooking and owner Vinod Khanna's discount .See page 288. Branch: Ealing Cottage, 76, Uxbridge Road, W13.

MONTY'S
1, The Mall, The Broadway, Ealing. W5.

**TOP 100
0181 567 8122**

Still ahead on points as Ealing's most popular with a full range of standard curries plus some Nepalese specials.Remains in our TOP 100.

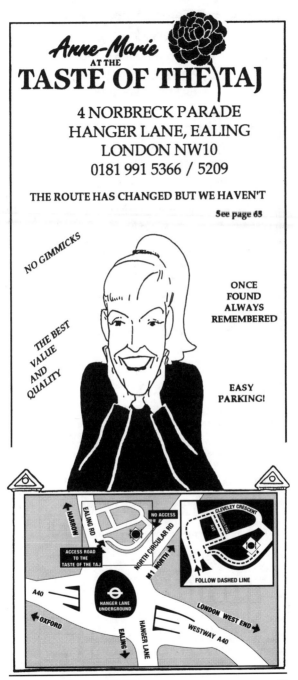

SAMRAT
52, Pitshanger Lane, Ealing. W5.

CC DISCOUNT
0181 997 8923

A welcome curry-hole in the Pitshanger area, and serving the full range of curry favourites. Owner manager, Horuf Miah. See page 288.

YAK AND YETI
185, South Ealing Road, Ealing. W5.

CC DISCOUNT
0181 568 1952

Another good Nepalese in the area. Chef Rajesh Maharajar's specials are the thing to choose for something different. No Yak or Yeti on the menu but lamb or chicken Bhutawa or Swadilo and Momo (dumplings with tomato pickle) make a nice change. Manager, MB Thapa gives discounts to Curry Club members. See page 288.

ZAYKA INDIAN CUISINE
8, South Ealing Road, Ealing. W5.

CC DISCOUNT
0181 566 5662

'Rafiq Karim (proprietor) and staff could not have been nicer. Their service was superb and so was their food.' MS. Fresh Carrot Chutney with the Popadoms, tasty starters (Gurda Masala - kidney) and 'great Chicken Ginger!' Gives a discount to Curry Club members, see page 288.

W6 - HAMMERSMITH

ANARKALI
303, 305, King Street, Hammersmith. W6.

0181 748 1760

'Good honest food and nothing too startling.' DL. Branch: Rajdoot, W6, 291, King Street, W6 gts same comments from DL.

AZIZ
116, King Street, Hammersmith. W6.

CC DISCOUNT
0181 748 1826

Enjoyed by many as one of Hammersmith's safest bets for good formula curries. Owner Daya Patel will give discounts to Curry Club members. See -page 288. Branch: Askew Tandoori, 129, Askew Road, W12. See entry.

TANDOORI NIGHTS   SPECIAL AWARD - TOP 100
319, King Street, Hammersmith. W6.   **0181 741 4328**
Mr Modi Udin's Tandoori Nights still gets the best in the area vote from
our reporters. One local couple goes on a King Street curry crawl, lucky
them, from time to time - a kind of bindi-bender, I suppose, taking in
them all, but they always find the Tandoori Nights their favourite. 'The
bright white fascade is as inviting as the manager and his staff. The pink
decor is relaxing, and the food is curry house at its best.' IW. The editors
agree, having visited here for the first and second birthday parties of Mr
Modi Udin's twins. Remains in our TOP 100. With the 'Dine Bangladeshi' movement gaining ground, we are delighted to give it SPECIAL
AWARD as a prime example of a well crafted Bangladeshi curry house.

W8

MALABAR   **TOP 100**
27, Uxbridge Street. W8.   **0171 727 8800**
The menu hasn't changed at the Malabar since it opened in 1984. After
all, why change a good thing? It's short yet wide ranging: from Philouries
(batter fried prawns) and Hiran (venison) starters to Long Chicken
(medium hot with cloves and ginger) One of our more discerning well
travelled frequent reporters says, 'This is a real find thanks to your guide.
After so many recent formula curries, it's a treat to see different offerings
on the menu and all superbly cooked. The Murgh Makhani and Keema
Nan are among the best I have tasted, and the 'menu for two' delivers a
substantial and economical feast.' JPL. Jo Chalmers has now been joined,
front of house by her daughter Sophie and we get constant praise for their
customer care. Remains very high in our TOP 100. See page 96.

W9

RAJ BRASSEREI   **CC DISCOUNT**
536, Harrow Road. W9.   **0181 960 4978**
'Thoroughly decent curry house in all respects.' DR. Manager A
Khalique gives a discount to Curry Club members, see page 288.

W12

ASKEW TANDOORI
129, Askew Road. W12.   **0181 749 3379**
In the same ownership as W6 Aziz (see entry) and just as chapatti chuck
away, the Askew is equally popular. We hear that the Bangalore Phal is
indeed, 'extra very hot' (sic). Owner, Daya Patel. See page 288.

W13

LAGUNA   **CC DISCOUNT**
127-129, Uxbridge Road, West Ealing. W13.   **0181 567 6211**
SK Lamba's Laguna continues to please West Ealing. Its 140 seats are
often all taken which says it all. See page 288.

SIGIRI
161, Northfield Avenue, Northfields. W13.   0181 579 8000
It's a pleasure to tell that the Sigiri is, according to reports, thriving. It's
Sri Lankan, and there are precious few in the whole UK. Attractive
enough decor and sensible serving create a good atmosphere. The food's
good too, with squid or pork (devilled they say, but if you like it hot and
spicy, tell'em - the devil is quite a mild chappie at the Sigiri). Hoppers,
(Apa), Dosa and Uppaamas - and don't forget the Coconut Chutney. All
good Sri Lankan stuff and all at good prices.

W14

KHAN SAHI BALTI HOUSE   **CC DISCOUNT**
142, West Cromwell Road, West Kensington. W14.   0171 371 2077
N Rafiq and K Sheikh were quick off the mark to offer Balti to West
Kensington. As in Brum, you can get Balti anything but at rather higher
prices (it is Kensington after all and it is smart). 'All eight of us enjoyed
the Baltis and Nan Breads, though service was slow.' MD. The ownwer
give a discount to Curry Club members, see page 288.

LONDON - WC

WC1 - HOLBORN
GANPATH
372, Grays Inn Road. WC1.   0171 278 1938
Ignore the meat / chicken north Indian food and order the South Indian
vegetarian dishes for good inexpensive meal.

RED PEPPER   **CC DISCOUNT**
65, Red Lion Street. WC1.   **0171 405 8072**
Cute name and good pedigree (Chutney's, Ravi Shankar and Handi in
same ownership). Some good unusual dishes on offer: Pattice (spicy
potato rissoles) and Shakoothi (sic) Goan chicken, with plenty of red
chilli pepper, are but two. ManagerMujeeb Sayeed offers a discount to
Curry Club members, see page 288.

WC2

ALDWYCH TANDOORI   **CC DISCOUNT**
149, The Strand. WC2.   **0171 836 3730**
Syed Khan's restaurant continues to be a 'safe-bet' formula curry house.
'All food above average, except our Onion Bhajia, which was a bit
stodgy,but everything else was spicy and particularly good.' DRC. Mr
Khan gives a discount for Curry Club members, see page 288.

THE INDIA CLUB   **SPECIAL AWARD**   **TOP 100**
143, The Strand. WC2.   **0171 836 0650**
For the serious curryholic, this place simply cannot be bettered. In the
three years since the last guide was published, we literally have received
more reports on the Indian Club than on any other restaurant. One
reporter (JL) uses it for his, 'alternative Christmas lunch.' DRC 'never
misses the opportunity to eat here. MG finds it, 'economical, reliable and
unchanging.' DB, a frequent user, found 'the Chilli Bhajias blew his socks
off, but will return.' PD thinks it, 'excellently tacky.' JL: 'the food is
straight-forward and excellent.' We editors think nothing of doing the
100 mile round trip simply to eat at the Indian Club. It's cheap and café
style, with laid back, friendly waiters. It's unlicensed so you can BYO.
There is some nonsense about joining their club (cost £1.10) to enable you
to buy Cobra Lager at the so called hotel residents' bar. We duly paid up,
to the unquenchable amusement of the elderly bar waitress, who,
inbetween cackles, advised me that the waiters 'know nothing'. It's all
part of the charm. The India Club has been there since 1950. Find the
door-width entrance, (there's a new sign, gold on black, saying 'India
Restaurant and Hotel', otherwise nothing has changed since it opened,
including, I do believe, the bar maid! - and I've been going here for 35
years). Climb the narrow stairs.(In typical Indian style, the owners do
not see the need to redecorate - it's clean enough though). The first floor
is hotel reception (singles £29, doubles £39). Old hands stock up with
Cobra here, then proceed up another floor to the L-shaped restaurant.
Flaking paster, no table-cloths, flies a-buzzing, bare charms, pictures
askew. 'Someone has been round straightening the pictures, including
Ghandi's! Let up hope that this is just a prank not official policy.' LO1.
And shortly after: 'Ghandi is askew again - thank heavens!' LO1. We
greatly prefer the South Indian Rasam (served in a tea cup with saucer -
hot as hell), Sambar, Masala Dosa and Coconut Chutney. Don't over
order: the portions are generous. I could go on and on writing. There
isn't enough space. Suffice to say in fourteen years I've never received
a poor report on the food. A unique achievement. Despite its quirks,
(which gives it a, 'charm of its own.' CD), it decidedly remains right up
there at the very top of the TOP 100 tree.Indeed, I'm tempted to make the
country's Number One. Instead I am giving it a SPECIAL AWARD for
its ability to have survived unchanged, yet so excellent, for so long. The
last words go to PD: 'Long may the Club remain open.'

MAHARAJA OF INDIA   **CC DISCOUNT**
19a, Charing Cross Road. WC2.   **0171 930 8364**
Open noon to midnight (useful to know). Bazlur Rashid (Salim) has a
small tightly run chain of good quality Bangladeshi restaurant. (also
Piccadilly Tandoor and Maharaja Tandoori both Denman Street, W1,
Iman Brasserie, Rupert Street and Strand Tandoori, Bedford Street, WC2.
Above average dishes. Discounts for Curry Club members,see page 288.

PUNJAB
80-92, Neal Street, Covent Garden. WC2.

TOP 100 - CC DISCOUNT
0171 240 9979

In the same ownership (the Maan family) since it opened in 1947 in , Aldgate. It moved to its present site in 1951, and is the oldest Punjabi restaurant in the UK. Sadly, its founder Gurbocham Maan died recently, having reached his century. Now in his son's capable hands, the Punjab was one of the original pioneers of the curry formula. Only here it is done as it has always been done, and as it should be. It is spicy, savoury and very tasty. One of its former regulars used it twice a day, five days a week, for forty years, before retiring (GL). This astounding claim (can anyone better it? - let me know) got Geoff onto a BBC-TV Noel Edmonds programme with Pat Such is their loyalty to the place that they have their own club, the Punjabbers'. Should have always been in our TOP 100. Mr Maan gives discounts to Curry Club members. See page 288.

ROYAL BOMBAY CHEF
6-8, May's Court, St Martins Lane. WC2.

CC DISCOUNT
0171 240 6263

Owner chef Kuldeep Makni's claim to fame is that he was indeed a royal chef - not in Bombay though - to the King of Nepal.. His menu si fascinating to read and better still to taste. How about Bakre-de-Tang - sliced lamb marinated in rum, cognac and red wine and spices, served with a hot sauce. It sounds like a cocktail but we're assured is a Punbaj speciality. It is just one of many exciting choices. 'The food is excellent.' DRC. Discount for Curry Club members. See page 288.

ROYALS
7-8, Bow Street, Covent Garden. WC2.

0171 379 1099

Sited next to the Royal Opera House keeps it busy with pre-theatre dinners (3 course for under £10) and served swiftly and deftly.

SHAN
200, Shaftesbury Avenue. WC2.

0171 240 3348

'Tiny Gujerati café which looked more like a kiosk. When I visited, the proprietor's wife was helping her two daughters to practise reading English - I showed them the Guide and they read that instead! Tasty food an excellent value.' GH. Hours: 12 noon to 9.30pm. Closed Sundays.

STRAND TANDOORI
45, Bedford Street. WC2.

CC DISCOUNT
0171 240 1333

Competent food. Manager, S Rashid gives CC discounts. See page 288.

TANDOORI NIGHTS
35, Great Queen Street, Covent Garden. WC2.

TOP 100 - CC DISCOUNT
0171 831 2558

Owner Mrs Yasmeen Rashid opened her first Tandoori Nights in Cockfosters, Herts (see entry) in 1988, and her second in NW1,months later. In 1993 she opened this branch, with Mr Hilary Fernandes from Goa as manager, and chef Ram Chandra. The food is 'all very good, the prices reasonable. We were more than pleased.' DRC. In addition to his authentic Indian food, Chef cooks a distinctive Indo-Chinese range of dishes, which are now on the menu, and worth trying for a different experience. We are happy to place Mrs Rashid's three Tandoori Nights into our TOP 100. Discount for Curry Club members. See page 288.

TASTE OF INDIA
25, Catherine Street, Covent Garden. WC2.

CC DISCOUNT
0171 836 2538

'Obviously catering for the theatre set, it gets busy pretty early. The food is of a high standard. Very attentive service, although this mainly revolved around the supply of drinks.'JL. 'Smart waiters and reasonable prices. Some unusual items - like barbequed trout and quail, but it was a shame that the spicing and flavours were cautios and catering for visitors.' DRC. They will 'spice it up if you ask, though. Owner, Mahtab Chowdhury gives a discount to Curry Club members. See page 288.

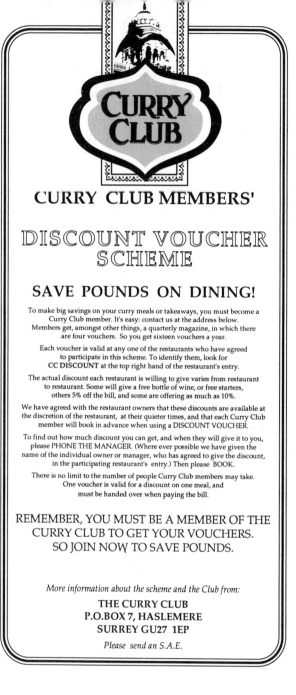

CURRY CLUB MEMBERS'

DISCOUNT VOUCHER SCHEME

SAVE POUNDS ON DINING!

To make big savings on your curry meals or takeaways, you must become a
Curry Club member. It's easy: contact us at the address below.
Members get, amongst other things, a quarterly magazine, in which there
are four vouchers. So you get sixteen vouchers a year.

Each voucher is valid at any one of the restaurants who have agreed
to participate in this scheme. To identify them, look for
CC DISCOUNT at the top right hand of the restaurant's entry.

The actual discount each restaurant is willing to give varies from restaurant
to restaurant. Some will give a free bottle of wine, or free starters,
others 5% off the bill, and some are offering as much as 10%.

We have agreed with the restaurant owners that these discounts are available at
the discretion of the restaurant, at their quieter times, and that each Curry Club
member will book in advance when using a DISCOUNT VOUCHER.

To find out how much discount you can get, and when they will give it to you,
please PHONE THE MANAGER. (Where ever possible we have given the
name of the individual owner or manager, who has agreed to give the discount,
in the participating restaurant's entry.) Then please BOOK.

There is no limit to the number of people Curry Club members may take.
One voucher is valid for a discount on one meal, and
must be handed over when paying the bill.

REMEMBER, YOU MUST BE A MEMBER OF THE
CURRY CLUB TO GET YOUR VOUCHERS.
SO JOIN NOW TO SAVE POUNDS.

More information about the scheme and the Club from:

**THE CURRY CLUB
P.O.BOX 7, HASLEMERE
SURREY GU27 1EP**

Please send an S.A.E.

ENGLAND

AVON

BATH

THE BENGAL BRASSERIE
32, Milson Street, Bath.

CC DISCOUNT
01225 447906

'It just shows the wide difference between individuals' taste buds. My wife thought that the food here was better than the Rajpoot, Argyle Street. She still talks lovingly about the Chicken Bhoona. I did not like this food. I thought my Dhansak had no flavour and the sauce was over thick. The portions were large and the service good.' EM. 'One plate specials good value.' PD. This restaurant gives discounts, see page 288.

THE EASTERN EYE
11, Argyle Street, Bath.

01225 622323

Mr & Mrs NDT visiting from Holland said, 'Brilliant, excellent, delicious. We ordered starters, main course (Lamb Pasanda) and a brilliant Mataar Paneer, made with spinach which was really good. The manager is from Bengal and talked to me very enthusiastically and even gave me some tips (dry your paneer, as soon as you have made it so as to preserve it). Well, sorry to ramble on, I cannot recommend this restaurant too highly for a really innovative menu.' Others, slightly less enthusiastic, have complained about good food but expensive tiny portions, 'The Pullao Rice was so small I had to order a second at £1.80'. DY.

JAMUNA
9-10, High Street, Bath.

CC DISCOUNT
01225 464631

'Beautiful upstairs views over orange grove and Bath Abbey. Decorated in soft pinks. Small table for 2 people. Plastic trailing ivy could soon look dusty and greasy. Starter - Chicken Tikka, portions small, Bhuna Chicken, standard lamb curry, vegetable Bhajia and plain boiled rice. Mild. Reasonable. Average curry house taste. Sweets extra. eg: Bombay Kulfi, Pistachio with bed of almond ice cream. Good size, gorgeous, my wife said. Gulab Jamun OK. Will return. Good and friendly service.' PD. This restaurant gives discounts for Curry Club members, see page 288.

RAJPOOT
4, Argyle Street, Bath.

CC DISCOUNT
01225 668833

'Very smart restaurant. I liked the doorman dressed in Indian costume. Food was superb. I had a Chicken Dhansak which was quite wonderful. My wife had a Bhoona which had flavours not experienced before. Only slight reservation was that the portions were not over generous, but the taste more than made up for that. An excellent restaurant and one that I will certainly visit again.' EM. If all the reports we received were like this we would have retained Rajdoot's TOP 100 status. Unfortunately reliable reporters such as DL, DRC, DY and TB talk of long waits, cold food, overbooking, busy staff (one reporter talks of 'mission impossible', it was so busy). These are the problems of success. Chef Zeraguai's food is still up to scratch, but proprietor Ahmed Chowdhury, who also has a stake in the Bengal Brasserie and The Jamuna, whilst certainly trying to satisfy everyone, should take note of these rumblings, and sort out the problem. PD says, 'The Rajpoot seems to be my yardstick. I've never had such delicious tasty food. Very friendly staff and owner. Always very mild, but will cook to individual tastes and strengths with a little persuasion.' Discounts for Curry Club members, see page 288.

BRISTOL

LAL JOMI PAVILLION
Coldharbour Lane, Redland.

CC DISCOUNT
0117 924 4648

'Excellent food, excellent service, though occasionally a little slow when pushed. We've never had a poor meal off their extensive menu. Try the Jalfrezi, Chicken Tikka Biriani or Makhani. I've been here many times, comfortable, usual decor but nice booths to hide in. Book at weekends.' AW.

THE NEW TAJ TANDOORI
404, Gloucester Road, Horfield.

0117 942 1992

Takeaway only, evenings only. Says AJWP. 'I have been eating Indian food for 35 years and in the last 10 years or so, I thought my palate had become jaded since all the normal Indian restaurant food tended to taste the same and was indifferent in flavour, not like it used to be in the 50s and 60s. However, the New Taj has restored my faith. It is first class.' Owned and run by Parvin Rayman, a Bangladeshi Moslem woman described by all our reporters as helpful and friendly. Her takeaway is spotless, decorated with flowers and serving fresh tasty food.

PUSHPANJLI
217a, Gloucester Road, Bristol.

01117 924 0493

'A wonderfully informal yet smart Gujarati vegetarian restaurant fitted with formica tables and plastic chairs, with all food displayed under a glass counter. All food is home cooked, a huge variety of starters, Dhal Bhajia, Samosa, Kachori, Bateta Wada, Mogo Chips, all superb. Large assorted pickle tray offering wide choice and lovely Papads. Masala Dhosas enormous helping with Sambar and coconut chutney. Many lovely vegetable curries, rice and breads. I visit this restaurant several times a month and it is truly brilliant in all aspects listed above.' DR. 'My number 1 restaurant, great vegetarian food which I cannot fault. Bhel Puri great, portions good, sweets are very indulgent. They hold buffet evenings where you help yourself for £10-12 ish, eat until you drop. A quality restaurant.' JM.

RAJDOOT
83, Park Street, Bristol.

TOP 100 - CC DISCOUNT
0117 926 8033

Now in its 25th year Rajdoot continues to reign supreme. The owner Mr Des Sarda is Indian. As most restaurants are Bangladeshi run, Rajdoot's food may come as a surprise to some. It is much truer to the authentic food you'll find in homes in Northern India. It is this very fact which leads to the disappointment which is expressed to us by a small percentage of Rajdoot's diners who simply do not find the food to their expectations. The complaints, and I stress again that they are few, but they are persistent, are that the food is bland. It's the same at all four Rajdoot branches (see Birmingham, West Midlands, Manchester and Dublin). Your editor has personally dined in all four on several occasions and I have to say that I find it excellent on all counts. But the 'disappointed' reporters must be addressed. Typical is one from JW. Writing on A3 note paper (that's large!) as if to ensure I'd read it, he tells of his 50th birthday treat with a friend. He felt that the portions were too small and the Naans were soggy and half the size of any elsewhere. 'We ordered three more (at £1.95 each) to make up.' He also would prefer that the waiter leaves the rice dish on the table rather than takes it away with rice still on it. Of course the prices are higher than average - it is easy to spend £25 to £30 a head. However, there are Chef's Recommendations - set meals from £13.50 per person, including a vegetarian platter. On the plus side we have had numerous reports praising Rajdoot's. This is part of one which is typical for a Bristol resident: 'Have paid this restaurant several visits and keep going back for more! The cooking is good, the meals nicely spiced if a little mild for my taste. They do, however, serve delicious Indian sweets. I particularly enjoy the Gulab Jamun. We had an excellent meal washed down with 2 bottles of house red wine. Polite service, good food, atmosphere and the smell of incense are what makes it for me!! No wonder it's in the top 100 restaurants in the roundup. Go for it.' AEJ. We confirm this enthusiastic view and recommend that you ask for the food to be spicy, if that's your bag. Mr Sarda will give a discount to Curry Club members, at his quieter times, see page 288.

SHEESH MAHAL   **CC DISCOUNT**
13a, Gloucester Road, Bishopston.   **0117 942 2942**
A typical curry house which has been in the same ownership since 1979 and with sufficient 'satisfied' reports to ensure its entry to the guide. This restaurant will give discounts for Curry Club members, see page 288.

SITAR
61, High Street, Westbury-on-Trym.   **0117 950 7771**
'Still providing good quality food with a very good value takeaway discount.' GC

TANDOORI NIGHT
86, Broad Street, Staple Hill.   **0117 970 1353**
'This is where I proposed to my now fiancée!! After all that was over, we settled down to order a meal that included melt in the mouth Chicken Tikka starter and Shami Kebabs. This preceded her usual Chicken Tikka Massalla and my Lamb Vindaloo. Both main meals were beautifully cooked as were the accompanying rices. First time I'd tried Banana Naan, now I can't get enough. Well priced, good portions and friendly staff. Almost wholeheartedly recommended.' A E-J.

CLEVEDON
MOGHULS TANDOORI
33 Old Church Road, Clevedon.   **01275 873695**
Continues to provide good, competent standard menu curries. Gives 10% discount on takeaways. Recommended as safe bet by several correspondents including PJ who 'adores the Pakistani Basmatic' rice (for asthmatics perhaps?) and is amused by 'Samusas.'

MIDSOMER NORTON
SHAPLA INDIAN TAKEAWAY
42, High Street, Midsomer Norton.   **01761 411887**
A takeaway only in an attractive stone-faced building. LT liked especially their Dandag (sic) and had not previously heard of their chicken lamb or prawn Dim (sic) '(cooked with egg in a sauce)'. Neither have we.

SITAL
112, High Street, Midsomer Norton.   **01761 411375**
Along the street from the Shapla is another takeaway only - the Sital. Open 5pm to 11.30pm Wednesdays to Mondays and 'very good especially their Prawn Dansak - lentil soft, but not a mushy mess.' says PD. It has the usual tandoori/tikka/curry menu but, unusually for the area, it does 40 Balti dishes, the owners, it seems, having come Birmingham.

PORTISHEAD
SPICY AROMA TANDOORI   **CC DISCOUNT**
Clarence House, High Street, Portishead.   **01275 845413**
The former Bay of Bengal restaurant has adopted this catchy and appropriate name, unique (at the moment at any rate) among curry houses. Their not over-long menu includes a number of unusual specialities such as Cobra Salon (chicken, lamb, egg, tomatoes and mushroom) and X'cutti (pronounced dja-cewt-ee) from Goa. This restaurant will give discounts for Curry Club members, see page 288. See advertisement, overleaf.

Spicy Aroma

TANDOORI RESTAURANT

Purveyors of Genuine Taste

Clarence House, High Street,
Portishead, Bristol BS20 9YP

TELEPHONE 01275 845413

THORNBURY

MOGHULS BRASSERIE
High Street, Thornbury, Bristol.   01454 416187

A E-J tells us he was Moghul's first customer a few years back when it opened. He has told us in a number of reports how much he likes it.

MUMTAZ INDIAN   CC DISCOUNT
7, St Mary's Centre, Thornbury, Bristol.   01454 411764

Evenings only. The Mumtaz is on two levels. The downstairs seating area and small bar are for takeaway customers and perusal of the menu. The restaurant is situated upstairs. 'Menu not too extensive, but food extremely good and large portions. Clean European style decor and music! Very helpful staff and friendly. Would go back.' WW. KB was less enthusiastic about the decor and other reports talk of standard curries of generous proportions. A E-J found the Phal too hot on one occasion and too mild on another although his fiancée 'loves the Kormas'. This restaurant gives discounts for Curry Club members, see page 288.

WESTON-SUPER-MARE

AVON TANDOORI   CC DISCOUNT
16, Waterloo Street, Weston-super-Mare.   01934 622622

Formerly the highly-rated Anarkali, this became the Avon Tandoori in 1988 when it changed hands to Shahim Miah. The restaurant's menu contains all the old favourites plus a few surprises including Tandoori Trout Masala and a sprinkling of Balti dishes. This restaurant will give discounts for Curry Club members, see page 288.

CURRY GARDEN   CC DISCOUNT
69 Orchard Street, Weston-super-Mare   01934 624660

We said of this restaurant in our previous guide that it is a standard archetypal curry house. The menu contains all you would expect to find. We're pleased to say they've now added a few Balti dishes, but not so pleased to find that they refused a CC member (GC) his discount, despite agreeing to it in the last guide. Anyway they've agreed to do it again - so here's hoping!! See page 288.

VICEROY
57, Whitecross Road, Weston-super-Mare.   01934 628235

Weston's relative newcomer (1989) is also a newcomer to the Guide, and there because of a number of glowing reports about excellence of food, service, decor etc. It is AB's favourite restaurant. He says, 'They make every effort to ensure satisfaction, and as regular customers a personal touch is always given, remembering names, favourite drinks etc. Always willing to provide dishes not on the menu.' He would perhaps prefer larger portions and GC was shocked to find Kingfisher lager at £3 a pint but he does enjoy the food and the pond in the restaurant, which houses a collection of Coi Carp and a working fountain. This restaurant was visited by Anthony Hopkins of Silence of the Lambs fame recently. (Brings a whole new meaning to Chef Special - Ed).

BEDFORDSHIRE

BEDFORD

ALAMIN
CC DISCOUNT
51-51a, Tavistock Street, Bedford. **01234 327142**
Previously in the guide as the Sonali, the present ownership under
Gulzar Miah commenced in 1992, and from the reports we've received
the restaurant is maintaining the good food service standards. This
restaurant will give discounts for Curry Club members, see page 288.

AMRAN TANDOORI
CC DISCOUNT
53b, Harpur Street, Bedford. **01234 352359**
We welcome Shabbir Raja's Amran back to the guide, and we presume
and rather hope that he has not removed the red flock wall paper and Taj
Mahal pictures which adorn the walls. Precious few Indian restaurants
now have that once celebrated trade-mark and it would be a pity if the
Amran changed its erstwhile ways. Established in 1958, the Amran has
consistently served competent and good curries. See page 288.

CHOUDHURY TANDOORI
32, The Broadway, Bedford. **01234 356162**
Its menu encompasses everything you'd expect to find at a standard
curry house plus a bit more... Tandoori Trout, Balti dishes and Badshahi
Mosala are some. Says JO, 'We had a takeaway from here while visiting
friends in Bedford. Quality on the whole very good, quantities rather
variable, ranging from meagre to generous. Service was efficient and
friendly. Comfort and decor looked OK - wouldn't mind eating in.

THE GRAND
39, Tavistock Street, Bedford. **01234 359566**
The Grand continues on its reliable and competent way satisfying a
number of our regular reporters.

MAGNA TANDOORI
50, Tavistock Street, Bedford. **01234 356960**
Messrs Chowdhury and Mohammed's Magna continues to serve consistently good curries, at fair prices, so it is a favourite haunt of several of
our correspondents.

MAGNA TANDOORI NO: 3
199, Bedford Road, Kempston, Bedford. **01234 840416**
Sister to the Magna (see previous entry) this restaurant is a bit out of
Bedford centre (about 2 1/2 miles south west). The owners, menu and
therefore the comments are as above. One diner, JLG talks of good Meat
Dhansak, and Bombay Potato but found the Meat Vindaloo bland.

SPICES OF BENGAL
84, Tavistock Street, Bedford. **01234 356220**
The owner, Fakhrul Islam, is the chef at this takeaway only establishment
which usually means good quality food. This was the first time we've
heard of Labu (chicken, meat or prawn cooked with a spicy sauce in lime
pickle). Free delivery in 7 miles radius. 10% discount if you collect.

TO FIND OUT ABOUT HOW YOU CAN JOIN THE CURRY CLUB MEMBERS' DISCOUNT SCHEME, PLEASE TURN TO PAGE 288.

TANDOORI NIGHTS
84, High Street, Clapham, Bedford.   **01234 211452**
Clapham is a large village 3 miles north of Bedford. Tandoori Nights is a relatively new (1992) takeaway evenings only operation with a useful free home delivery service. You get a 10% discount if you collect it yourself. Ms DG likes the on-view kitchen and enjoyed her Vindaloo. She also enjoyed her discount and the free popadom she got whilst waiting. She says, 'My dad had the Chicken Curry and Onion Bhajiee which he pronounced excellent. My Gran, was is 82, and wary of more 'exotic' foods, was given a meat curry (it was beef) and loved it. I shall visit it whenever I'm in that area.'

DUNSTABLE

TASTE OF INDIA   **CC DISCOUNT**
135, High Street South, Dunstable.   **01582 602697**
We know there are plenty of curry restaurants in Dunstable. Unfortunately we seem to get precious little reporting on them - so please get cracking in this area. Meanwhile, it's the Taste of India which has picked up the vote this time. The food is in the hands of Shomshor Ali who after more than 25 years at it, knows exactly how to please the curry palate. Owned by Montaz Ali. Gives discounts to Curry Club, see page 288.

LEIGHTON BUZZARD

AKASH TANDOORI
60, North Street, Leighton Buzzard.   **01525 372316**
Two PC's (not the editor) applaud the Akash, one tells us, the mango chutney is the best he's tasted. And the other says, 'The Akash has been our local for the past 5 years and is generally on the good side of average. Decor is good and the restaurant is air-conditioned. Service is always good, hot crisp popadoms and chutneys appear almost instantly. The menu is limited but the Lamb Pasanda and the Methi Chicken are perennial favourites, accompanied by Niramish or the Buttery Keema Naan which have become something of a speciality.'

LUTON

ALANKAR   **CC DISCOUNT**
276, Dunstable Road, Luton.   **01582 410374**
The Alankar is in a beamed mock-Tudor house, complete with tower (don't expect Hampton Court though - it's strictly thirties). Inside, our reporters tell us, you'll find a menu with all the favourites. Owned by Dilip Odera they will give discounts to Curry Club members, see p288.

MEAH TANDOORI   **CC DISCOUNT**
102, Park Street, Luton.   **01582 454504**
Named after the owner, Moklish Meah, who also own Biggleswade's Biggles Tandoori, this is a standard curry house with a typical menu offering all the curry favourites competently. It also offers discounts for Curry Club members, see page 288.

SHALIMAR CURRY HOUSE
129, Dunstable Road, Luton.   **01582 29753**
Says BG, 'After a hard evening's work in Luton (this must really be the town that God forgot!) we end up at the Shalimar. It is like a transport café, formica top tables, plastic seats, glass fronted bar. The proprietor, Mr Khan, was very pleasant. Kebabs good and well spiced - a hot mint chutney. Chicken Curry with quite a lot of tomato but not so much chicken - meat curry was better. Naan breads were very good. Not licensed.' Maybe God forgot about Luton, but where else can you get a curry takeaway at 4am, 7 days a week?

BERKSHIRE

BRACKNELL

PASSAGE TO INDIA
3, Market Place, Bracknell.   **01344 485499**
More reports are requested from this area. The few we have speak well of the Passage. PJ thinks it is 'good', (praise indeed from this much travelled curryholic!). It has a wide-ranging menu and home delivery.

READING

BINA   BEST IN THE WEST AWARD & TOP 100 - CC DISCOUNT
21, Prospect Street, Caversham, Reading.   **01734 462116**
We've all seen the claim by many a curry house that here is the 'finest Indian cuisine in your area'. Usually it's far from the truth - but not at the Bina. Since it opened (just too late for inclusion in our last edition) we've heard nothing but praise for the place. This is largely due to the energetic management from its young Bangladeshi proprietor, Abdul Miah, helped by a strong family connection with the UK curry trade. Here in a few extracts is what our reporters think. 'The outside is appealing and the inside continues the theme. It is clean and smart, but very comfortable. The waiters were welcoming and efficient. Suprisingly, the manager apologised for the service being slow. We didn't notice. We arrived early on Bank Holiday Monday. By 8 o'clock the restaurant was filling up. The menu offered a wide selection of starters, main courses, sundries and vegetables. The prices were a little higher than average, but the food was well worth it... fresh, tasty and well presented. The quantities were good. The food was served in small korais and so the meal was piping hot. The Chicken Pakoras were particularly impressive and contained large pieces of chicken and were very crispy. The Nan Breads were excellent, especially the Peshwari which was full of lovely sultanas. Overall the standard of the rest of the meal was consistently good.' SR. 'The surroundings are very pleasant and the staff welcoming and friendly. During my last visit, I had an interesting and most enjoyable chat with the Bangladeshi owner, Abdul Miah. The service is just about right - not too rushed, yet not too slow. Most importantly, of course, the food is quite exquisite and a little hotter than the average. I would certainly recommend the 'Puri Path' as a starter. This is the chef's own recipe of liver cooked with spices, served on a fried Indian bread. Quite delicious and worth visiting the Bina to sample this dish alone. Although the Bina is perhaps a little more expensive than other curry restaurants in the area, it is more than worth the extra. Ladies will also appreciate the rose presented to them upon leaving.' MW. 'Both the Butter Murg and Murg Shashlick are excellent and Keema Pilau a must. Good quantities - we normally end up leaving some. We each received a Christmas card with a offer for a free bottle of wine in January or February. When redeemed we received a very acceptable bottle of Piat d'Or. Our group of diners varies from 3 to 6 people. We found the Bina by chance when we were looking for somewhere to eat one Sunday. Now it's any excuse to go there for a meal.' SM. Not only does it deserve TOP 100 rating, the Bina gives discounts for Curry Club members, see page 288, and page 39. We are also giving the Bina our BEST IN THE WEST (of England) AWARD.

EVEREST TANDOORI
9, Meadway Prect, Honey End Ln, Tilehurst, Reading. 01734 583429
Says MW, 'Although the decor and service are nothing special, the cuisine is extremely good. The portions are enormous and you need to be careful not to over-order. Probably not a place for eating on your own - you need a few friends to help you.' And SP says, 'Promoted as a

Nepalese restaurant, it has plenty of seating and is quite busy on midweek visits. I had popadoms for starter with pickles. Main course Chicken Tikka Massala, really good, full rich flavour right through the meat. Vegetable curry also very good. Rice aromatic and fluffy.'

GARDEN OF GULAB
130-134, Wokingham Road, Reading.   01734 667979
'The food is excellent and I particularly like the Lamb Korai. For those who like it hot, the Vindaloo certainly leaves the taste buds tingling. What makes this restaurant a particularly enjoyable place to visit, however, is the friendliness of the staff with nothing being too much trouble. Indeed, I remember one occasion when I and a few friends had enjoyed our evening so much, that we had missed the last bus home. Upon asking if we could ring for a taxi, the owner said that there was no need as he would arrange for someone to take us home. A nice gesture .MW.

SUNARGAON TANDOORI   CC DISCOUNT
Unit 3, Underwood Road, Calcot, Reading.   01734 571184
Rahim Ullah's Sunargaon has been trading since 1986. It is a small restaurant (38 seats) operating evenings only and offering all your favourite curries at reasonable prices, made even better with discounts for Curry Club members, see page 288.

SLOUGH
ANAM TANDOORI AND BALTI HOUSE   CC DISCOUNT
1a, Baylis Parade, Oatland Drive, Slough.   01753 572967
A typical competent curry house owned by Javeed Ali and open evenings only. 'Baltis are a speciality here and very tasty too.' RE. Will give discounts to Curry Club members, see page 288.

TWYFORD

GAYLORD CC DISCOUNT
26, London Road, Twyford. 01734 345511

Says AVG, 'The service is friendly and good humoured. . My companion chose Moglay Chicken, absolutely superb. A waiter even came over to ask her if the chicken was too strong - I think he meant tough - but it was perfect. M Ullah also owns the Maharajah in Yateley and Lightwater's Raj Rani. His Gaylord gives discounts to CC members, see page 288.

WOKINGHAM

ROYAL INDIAN TANDOORI CC DISCOUNT
72, Peach Street, Wokingham. 01734 780129

Our reporters tell us of a thoroughly competent restaurant serving standard curry house food. Last time we reported that prices were high (Wokingham is the UK's wealthiest town!), but three years on the Royal's prices are as good as any other restaurant out of London town. Owner A Khalique will give discounts to Curry Club members, see page 288.

BUCKINGHAMSHIRE

BEACONSFIELD

BUCKS TANDOORI
7, The Broadway, Penn Road, Beaconsfield.   **01494 674580**
Says MS, 'I am a regular and I mean most Friday nights. The food here
is Nepalese style and is freshly prepared, so do not expect to get in and
out in record time. The service is comfortably good with friendly and
polite waiters, the decor is good, and they can accommodate about 80
hungry people. Every Sunday there is a buffet - eat as much as you can
for £7.50 per person without drinks, superb value for money. Hot towels
and 'after-curry mints' round off a very good and enjoyable meal.
Everything that has been tried is excellent, and well worth a visit. Special
events take place throughout the year. Bucks Tandoori has kept a
consistently good standard of food for a number of years - so much so that
you will want to tell your friends.' MS. See previous page.

MOGHAL TANDOORI   **CC DISCOUNT**
8, Warwick Road, Beaconsfield.   **01494 674280**
'Refurbished since its entry in our previous guide to a very high degree
of comfort. Menu is extensive and contains some unusual dishes.
Dalbura (starter) was described by the waiter as 'chicken burger', not far
from the truth. But very nicely spiced, very filling! I had not come across
Kabuli Kofta Bahar either, this also was very nice. All the food was very
tasty, generous portions and piping hot. Will return.' DM. Dabir
Ahmed's restaurant gives discounts to CC members, see page 288.

BUCKINGHAM

DIPALEE   **CC DISCOUNT**
18, Castle Street, Buckingham.   **01280 813925**
A regular entrant into our guide because it is a well established (1980)
curry house under the watchful ownership of Salique Ahmed. We still
hear about people enjoying the special Khurzi Chicken or Lamb (48
hours notice required). We also hear about other tasty dishes. 'I had
Methi Chicken in a very tasty sauce.' JG. 'The food is always good,
portions large.' M and AJ. This restaurant will give discounts to Curry
Club members, see page 288.

BURNHAM

AKASH TANDOORI   **CC DISCOUNT**
21, High Street, Burnham.   **01628 603507**
Foysol Ahmed's Akash is a regular entrant in these pages. Indeed our
regular correspondent of many years who wishes to remain anonymous
now claims to have eaten his way round the menu over 10 times - every
dish at least once. The menu contains all the old favourite dishes and we
continue to get 'safe bet' reports. This restaurant will give discounts to
Curry Club members, see page 288.

CHESHAM

DELHI DURBAR
131, Broad Street, Chesham.   **01494 783121**
SJW has, 'visited this restaurant on many occasions. Brilliant food, good
selection. Huge portions small restaurant. Very friendly staff. Decor a
bit dark and tacky, typical prices. Mushroom Rice £1.80, Chicken Madras
£3.50, Samosas £1.50. Staff get to know their regulars and go out of their
way to chat, joke and be extremely pleasant.'

FLACKWELL HEATH
EMPIRE OF INDIA
CC DISCOUNT
3a, Straight Bit, Flackwell Heath.
01628 530304
A pleasant smallish (42 seats) curry house, open evenings only, and serving all the standard curries and tandooris competently, according to our reporters, with generous portions. Owned by Fokruz Zanel. This restaurant will give discounts to Curry Club members, see page 288.

GREAT MISSENDEN
TANDOORI NITE
CC DISCOUNT
56, High Street, Great Missenden.
01494 866953
Moti-or Rahman's Tandoori Nite has been operating since 1986 and has built up a regular trade of satisfied customers, some of whom tell us they don't need to go anywhere else for their favourite curries. This restaurant will give discounts to Curry Club members, see page 288.

HIGH WYCOMBE
CURRY CENTRE
CC DISCOUNT
83, Easton Street, High Wycombe.
01494 535529
A long standing restaurant (1970) which since 1980 has been owned by A Musowir (manager) and MA Mali (chef). Whenever the owners are personally looking after front of house and kitchen respectively, you can be sure of getting of their best (or at least you know who to tell if not). They also own the Indian Delight Takeaway at 189, Farnham Road, Slough. Curry Centre will give discounts to CC members, see page 288.

ELACHI
188, Cressex Road, High Wycombe.
01494 510810
Elachi, as all good cooks know, means cardamom. Under the same ownership as The Bina in Reading, see separate entry. It opened February 1995. An extremely pretty restaurant with hand painted figures on the walls reminiscent of Michael Angelo. The menu is equally interesting with quite a number of new dishes. We wish Adbul great success with his new venture. Reports are welcomed.

MILTON KEYNES
Britain's most developed new city has its fair share of curry houses including an exceptional one (the Jaipur). Many offer a home delivery service. Indian traveller and curry expert Brian George wonders whether MK has become 'a city of bed-ridden curry addicts'. Here are the pick of the city's curry houses as rated by a good number of our contributors.

AKBER TANDOORI
CC DISCOUNT
10/12, Wolverton Road, Stony Stratford.
01908 562487
Well established (1983) owned and managed by Messrs A & M Nasir Uddin (who also own the Agrabad, 67, West Street, Boston, Lincs). No surprises here and no bad shocks either. It's a competent curry house enjoyed greatly by some, and it will give discounts to Curry Club members, see page 288.

THE CASA DE GOA
3, Stratford Road, Wolverton.
01908 227097
Says BG, 'A new restaurant. I must give this a mention even though I fear it may not last long. The proprietor, Mr Fernandes, is from Goa. The food, too, is Goan and is quite wonderful... a very small menu includes Salmon Curry, Beef Assad, Pork Fry and a Goan Prawn Curry. Vegetarian dishes are also excellent, notably spinach, bhindi and an excellent dal. No breads served here, only pulao Rice, which is the best I have ever had at a restaurant in the UK. Expect to pay around £10 to £12 per person without drinks. Quite different from the usual Indian restaurant.'

GOLDEN CURRY

TANDOORI INDIAN RESTAURANT

Fully Licensed

LUNCH 12pm to 1.30pm
DINNER 5.30pm to 11.30pm
Thur to Sat 5.30pm to Midnight

THURSDAY NIGHT
BANQUET
FIVE COURSES FOR £8.50

4, DUNCOMBE STREET,
BLETCHLEY, MILTON KEYNES. MK2 2LY
01908 377857

GOLDEN CURRY
4, Duncombe Street, Bletchley.

CC DISCOUNT
01908 377857

MK's oldest established curry house (1971) has been under Kalamdar Ali's ownership since 1982 with Iskander as head chef. They've been dispensing competent curries for years there to the contentment of a good number of regulars, one of whom delights in their Porota (sic) and Papa Dam (sic). They do a free home delivery service and will give discounts to Curry Club members, see page 288.

JAIPUR   AWARD WINNER AND TOP 100 - CC DISCOUNT
502, Elder Gate, Central Milton Keynes.

01908 669796

Mr A Ahad's Jaipur restaurant in the centre of MK has set a very high standard since it opened in 1987. We awarded it a TOP 100 cachet in the last edition. Since then we have received a veritable bombardment of good reports, and not one of them was bad. 'Outstanding! Everything from the decor to presentation was first class. The 'loos' were so clean you could have eaten your meal there.' says BG. We're not quite going that far but we agree they are immaculate. So too is the decor. It's very plush in shades of pink, reflecting its namesake city - Jaipur - in Rajasthan a city where all the buildings are pink-coloured made from the local sandstone. Walls, chairs, tablecloths, ceiling (the centrepiece of which is a gorgeous chandelier) are a gorgeous pink, a colour which we know appeals to one of our most prolific restaurant reporters (JL). SC from Sussex, who is not a Jaipur regular was slightly less enamoured about the decor, 'On my way from Newcastle to Hemel Hempstead I was thinking of somewhere to stop for the night. I chose MK to visit this restaurant. It was a good choice. The restaurant mirrored the town - squeaky clean and a little lacking in atmosphere.' But he goes on, 'The central fountain was a nice touch. I tried the Chicken Jaipur and very nice it was too with a rich sauce that didn't overpower everything. I also tried Cobra lager for the first time. A most enjoyable meal.' BG, one of our staunchest reporters (he's a teacher who regularly does school exchanges with India so knows a great deal about the real thing) reckons the Jaipur to be right at the pinnacle of excellence. He says, 'First, the food is excellent. The menu is not as extensive as the standard High Street restaurant and everything is cooked exquisitely. The proprietor, Mr Ahad, is consistently looking for improvement and has visited India and Bangladesh to enlist the services of new chefs. New dishes are always being added to the menu and the quality just keeps on rising. It has a proven reputation over time. The waiter service is efficient and attentive but is now overpowering. Supari and sweets are served at the end of the meal and hot towels to freshen up. The Jaipur is innovative. A low-calorie menu is available for weight watchers. There are regular 'special events' menus to celebrate festivals and anniversaries. Musicians and dancers have graced these evenings. Recently the Jaipur catered for an Intercity express from Euston to Wolverhampton, a wonderful improvement on British Rail sandwiches! All round, the Jaipur is an outstanding restaurant.' BG. We certainly agree. Furthermore it gives discounts to Curry Club members, see page 288.See advertisement inside front cover. We are pleased to give the Jaipur our BEST IN CENTRAL ENGLAND AWARD.

LALBAGH TANDOORI   CC DISCOUNT
47, Aylesbury Street, Fenny Stratford, Bletchley.   01908 271494
A comfortable sized restaurant (forty) which has been trading since 1988 as a safe bet competent curry house. This restaurant will give discounts to Curry Club members, see page 288.

MOGHUL PALACE
7, St Paul's Court, High Street, Stony Stratford.   01908 566577
'Owners have migrated from Birmingham and have introduced the first Balti selection to the area, albeit in what may be a more sophisticated form than seen in Birmingham. The location is an old Monastery school where monks once beat knowledge into the sons of local gentry. A monkish Order of Sybarites could feel at ease here now. Despite being a fairly new venture, they already seem to have a numerous and regular clientele. Personally, I think they well merit inclusion in your Guide.' LT. About the setting, BG from Camberley tell us, 'It is unusual and very pleasant, retaining the features of the monastery wood panelling, stonework etc. There is a spacious reception area with armchairs and comfortable sofas where you wait to be seated. The restaurant itself is fairly large and was very busy when we visited. Service and food quality were both excellent although portions were on the small side. I had my usual favourite, Chicken Jalfrezi. It was very tasty as were the Chicken Madras, Thali Special and Chicken Biryiani. The Thali was delicious.'

THE NIGHT OF INDIA   CC DISCOUNT
38, The Square, Wolverton.   01908 222228
BG says, 'My local town, I have to include this. Cheaper than most local restaurants and very long opening hours, into the early hours of the morning, so ideal for that late supper or early breakfast. It is good and always worth a visit.' And as others agree with you Brian, we're delighted to see the Night of India stay in the Guide to please the MK night owls (it stays open until 2am!) Not surprisingly perhaps it doesn't do a lunch trade. K Kapoor, the owner is frequently present and will give discounts to Curry Club members, see page 288.

MYSORE
101, High Street, Newport Pagnell.   01908 216426
'Now does free home delivery in a seven mile radius. Minimum order £9.95, free bottle of wine on home delivery order over £17.95. 10% discount on takeaway prices if you collect! Says BG, 'I had vegetable Thali £7.95, interestingly different from the usual selection - Sabji Jalfrezi, Baigan Bartha, Aloo Gobi, Bindi Bhajee, Dall Tarka, mixed Raita, Naan and Rice. It was very good - I particularly liked the Dall, but their Dall and Chapatti have always been among my favourite Indian food.' BG. See advertisement, next page.

ROSE OF INDIA   CC DISCOUNT
6, Duncombe Street, Bletchley.   01908 641115
Owned by three Mr Alis, one of whom is chef and related to the Golden Curry (see earlier) on the same street. Just 30 seats here and similar contented reports received. This restaurant will give discounts to Curry Club members, see page 288.

WENDOVER
THE PRINCE OF INDIA   CC DISCOUNT
10-12, Aylesbury Road, Wendover.   01296 622761
We've actually received no reports on the Prince since our last edition, but because it has been in our guide since edition one (1984) we see no reason to take it out now. Owned by Rafiqual Haque. This restaurant will give discounts to Curry Club members, see page 288.

CAMBRIDGESHIRE

CAMBRIDGE
GOLDEN CURRY
106, Mill Road, Cambridge.   **01223 351027**
'Unobtrusive street-side appearance should not put off. Greeting friendly, even on a busy Saturday night. Chicken Dansak was rich and hot, and the Chicken Shashlik had a wonderful taste. Very pleasant surroundings - divided into booths. Everything piping hot - including the plate.' JB.

KOHINOOR   CC DISCOUNT
74, Mill Road, Cambridge.   **01223 323639**
'You'd think Mill Road was Cambridge Curry Alley,' says one reporter, 'with good restaurants up and down it.' The Kohinoor is a regular GCRG entrant. It gets the thumbs up from MB. 'Yes, the peacock tapestries would seem to have disappeared, since the last guide. I was shown to my table by a very polite and attentive waiter. Lamb Rogan Gosht, very tasty, Pilau rice excellent ' PH thinks it is, 'outstanding, beautifully presented and every dish flavoursome.' JB was less flattering finding lunchtime service, 'poor with bored waiters but most delicious Chicken Tikka.' Will give discounts to Curry Club members, see page 288.

TAJ TANDOORI   CC DISCOUNT
64, Cherry Hinton Road, Cambridge.   **01223 248063**
A relative newcomer (1992), SA Haque's Taj Tandoori has a standard heat-graded menu with all your curry favourites, plus one which caught AB's, eye, Tandoori Chum Chum. (No, we don't know what it is either). This restaurant will give discounts to Curry Club members, see page 288.

ELY
SURMA TANDOORI   CC DISCOUNT
78, Broad Street, Ely.   **01353 662281**
An old friend on these pages, having been in every edition of this Guide since we started in 1984. This is what you say about it. 'You will find the Surma on the main road out of this delightful historic city. I ordered Shami Kebab, which really was more like a Rashmi as it comes complete with an omelette on top of it - which was very tasty and juicy. The Chicken Madras was absolutely full of flavour.' MB. And forteacher BG, 'My annual visit to the Surma - a fieldwork trip with hundreds of vibrant students!! While they munch their sandwiches in the cathedral car park, a colleague and I enjoy a takeaway as we supervise. A very acceptable lunch. I like the layout of the restaurant too, plenty of nooks and corners.' This restaurant will give discounts to Curry Club members, see page 288.

PETERBOROUGH

BOMBAY BRASSERIE   **CC DISCOUNT**
52, Broadway, Peterborough.   **01733 65606**
We welcome this restaurant to the Guide for this first time. Owned in
1988 by Rony Choudhury and Mahbub Khan (front manager and chef
respectively), we hear of a very attractive red-brick interior with a brass-
work bar as a feature. RG finds, 'the food quality very good, quantities
generous, service excellent, in a comfortable restaurant with an easy
atmosphere.' Others talk of the good quality Sunday lunch buffet. This
restaurant will give discounts to Curry Club members, see page 288.

INDIA GATE   **CC DISCOUNT**
9, Fitzwilliam Street, Peterborough.   **01733 346485**
Remains in the guide by popular request. Shah Nanaz's Indian Gate
appeals, it seems, to a solid core of regulars, some of whom talk of the
'elegant decor full of Eastern trinkets and atmosphere.' The menu
consists of a full house of curry favourites, competently cooked and
served. Will give discounts to Curry Club members, see page 288.

SHAH JEHAN
18, Park Road, Peterborough.   **01733 348941**
New to the guide because of reports like this. 'My wife and I visit the
place whenever we can. The decor, staff, service and food are fantastic.
We cannot fault the place.' DLC. And, 'The Tandoori was juicy and crisp,
the Dhansak just the right spicy hot. The Bhaji was a little small but we
were very hungry. You get first class service. ' DLT

TAJ MAHAL   **CC DISCOUNT**
37-39, Lincoln Road, Peterborough.   **01733 348840**
'Mohammed Shabeer is owner and manager and Gulfraz Khan head
chef. Between them since 1983 they have built up a good solid regular
trade producing competent curries. This restaurant will give discounts
to Curry Club members, see page 288.

ST IVES

KUSHIARA
21, Bridge Street, St Ives.   **01480 465737**
'Although we live approximately 15 miles away from St Ives, whenever
we are celebrating a special occasion (such as my birthday this time), we
always return to this restaurant. The manager, Ali, always remembers
our names and where we live. The tablecloths are so white you can see
your reflection in them and the service is excellent. Value for money is
good. I will continue to visit it time and time again.'NC.

It is the purpose of this Guide to report trends, to note
the bad things, and praise the good. Entry into any
guide, big or small, famous or little known, can affect
a restaurant, sometimes adversely. But a guide c an do
no more than report facts. Clients ultimately are the
lifeblood of a restaurant. And clients should make their
views known - praise and complaints alike - to the
restaurant, there and then, not next day. They should
also inform us of their views.

CHESHIRE

Please Note:
We have adhered strictly to the official county of Cheshire here. Please look also at the entries for Greater Manchester and Merseyside (see index page 49) for other restaurants within the former Cheshire boundary.

CHESTER
THE ASIA   **CC DISCOUNT**
104, Foregate Street, Chester.   **01244 322595**
MB would like the owners to 'smarten the place up'. He goes on, 'At first sight one could be forgiven for thinking that this restaurant was probably not worth the effort. The decor is a little on the drab and tired side, but the Shammi Kebabs were a delight, Chicken Madras one of the tastiest I've ever tasted. My colleagues sampled Chicken Tikka Masala, wonderful!!! Naan Bread first class. Pilau Rice comes with the meal and was excellent. Parking a bit of a problem.' SRP says, 'The menu at first was a bit of a let-down as I am a vegetarian. My first impression was that people such as myself were not well catered for. The only vegetable dish listed was Vegetable Biriani. When I ordered, I found they were prepared to have a go at anything I asked for. I found the service to be quick and pleasant as I was very soon shown to my table where the starter was already waiting. I enjoyed my evening at The Asia and would recommend it to anyone looking for good food at a fair price in a pleasant environment.' This restaurant will give discounts to Curry Club members, see page 288.

CHESTER TANDOORI
39-41, Brook Street, Chester.   **01244 347410**
Everyone has their local favourite and this one is no exception. MA and ML say: 'Their Chicken Jalfrezi is superb - masses of tender, marinated meat in a spicy sauce with onions, peppers and fresh chillies, and always huge portions. Naan Bread is fresh and fluffy and Pullao Rice perfect. After the meal you are given fresh orange wedges and chocolate mints plus a flower for ladies. The decor is simple and understated, and the service very friendly and discreet. Also to be recommended at this restaurant are their Chicken Korai and Chicken Madras.'

STEP IN INDIA   **CC DISCOUNT**
130, Foregate Street, Chester.   **01244 346431**
Evenings only but open late (1am Sundays, 2am weekdays, 2.30am Fridays and Saturdays), which could be useful for night owls and insomniacs. It will give discounts to Curry Club members, see page 288.

CREWE
THE BOMBAY
31, High Street, Crewe.   **01270 214861**
The Bombay retains its place in the guide because we hear, 'The service is friendly and helpful, and the larger portions and better quality merit the slightly higher price one pays.' MW.

SURMA
36, Nantwich Road, Crewe.   **01270 214878**
We hear of 'good meals at reasonable prices,' IG ,and that they now serve Balti dishes. Reports welcomed.

ELLESMERE PORT
THE AGRA FORT   **TOP 100**
1-7, Cambridge Road, Ellesmere Port.   **0151 355 1516**
New to the guide, the Agra Fort has attracted a large number of good reports (including a batch of nine, each sent in separately, from nine different people all on the same date!). We don't think this is the owner and his relatives - but they all speak of excellence. Despite the fact that one of these is from an F Moan we don't think it's a hoax. In fact, we've had many other reports. 'It's not a normal restaurant. The owner is a complete enthusiast.' DL. 'I spent the New Year with my side of the family at Ellesmere Port. Always when I am home on leave, our first evening was spent at an Indian restaurant, on this occasion the Agra Fort at Ellesmere Port. We were all very favourably impressed. The service was friendly and efficient, the servings generous, and the food amongst the best I have ever tasted in an Indian restaurant. We ordered dishes ranging from a Vindaloo for myself, a Madras for my mother and Balti dishes for the remainder of our family. Everyone of us thoroughly enjoyed the meal and thought very good value for money - so much so that we returned shortly after and were not disappointed. My thanks to the manager, whose relaxed and humourous 'patter' helped set the scene, and his staff for two most pleasant evenings. I look forward to the next occasion.' MW. Because of all the 'superlative' reports we have received with (unusually) no moans (excuse the pun) we have placed this restaurant into our TOP 100 category. 'Business lunch, Onion Bhajia and Chicken Madras with boiled rice, wheeled to my table and the sauce was reheated on a burner, result was piping hot. Well presented and superb value.' DB. 'Pleasant reception area, courteous staff escorted us to a nicely laid out and clean table. A good evening out, good value for money, recommended.' HSC.

NORTHWICH
CASTLE HILL TANDOORI
18-25, Chester Road, Northwich.   **01606 783824**
'It is well appointed with traditional Sylhelti Art adorning the walls. Above average formula curries from very helpful friendly staff.' SC. MJG is a regular there. He says, 'It was very impressive again, with quick cheerful service. My 18 month old grand-daughter was made welcome and a fuss of by the waiters. Large quantities, well presented food.'

SANDBACH
TAKDIR
11, High Street, Sandbach.   **01270 763823**
This was the Sapna in our last guide, but continues with its new name to serve competent curries. 'The restaurant is opposite a very old cobbled square which contains the Sandbach Cross. I had Chicken Dansak which was quite good. My wife had a Dupiaza, which she described as excellent.' TM. 'Had a good meal here. They do one Balti special dish here - it's tasty but not like you get in Birmingham.' GM.

WINSFORD
KESAAN
23-24, Queens Parade, Winsford.   **01606 862940**
PO'B says she, 'Cannot fault it in any way, whatever we have. Food first class with ample portions. Staff are excellent, very friendly and service is A1. We have used this restaurant for at least 5 years and never had cause for complaint.' Dr MW says, 'The place is spacious, light and airy and has the unusual feature of a central elevated enclosed table within the dining area. We especially enjoyed the selection of both non-vegetarian and vegetarian dishes served on a thali. Highly recommended'

CLEVELAND

HARTLEPOOL

THE DILSHAD
49a, Church Street, Hartlepool.   **01429 272727**
The Dilshad gets good reports usually, but then it will get a poor one
(from the same reporters too). So, we conclude that it is generally good.
'Onion Bhajia fresh and tasty, Sri Lankan Chicken hot indeed, very hot.'
GKP. 'Chicken Tikka Masala lush, Vegetable Pillau very good.' ED.
More comments welcomed.

STOCKTON-ON-TEES
THE ROYAL BENGAL   **CC DISCOUNT**
Prince Regent Street, Stockton-on-Tees.   **01642 674331**
Again few reports to hand about the Royal Bengal but those received
seem happy with it. It has been going since 1977, a sufficient age to give
it maturity and sensible management from M Faruque and Chef partner
Abdus Subhan Khan.Discounts to Curry Club members, see page 288.

TAJ MAHAL   **CC DISCOUNT**
90-92, Yarm Lane, Stockton-on-Tees.   **01642 615923**
Another evenings-only establishment (daily 6pm to 1am) about which
one reviewer raves about his takeaways. DM, 'tried the Balti but found
the service rather fussy.' Owned by Moti Khan, managed by Heera
Hussain, cooking by Sma Chandi. Discounts to Curry Club, see page 288.

CORNWALL

FALMOUTH
HANNAN TANDOORI
47, Arwenack Street, Falmouth.   **01326 317391**
It takes its name from its owner, Rabbani Choudhury Hannan, we're
told. It retains its colourful decor and attractive image and we have
received several good reports about it since our last guide. But Curry
Club members will have to ask Mr Hannan or his manager Ruhel Ahmed
why he has ceased to give discounts to Curry Club members.

HELSTON
THE TAJ
The Old Cinema, Wendron Street, Helston.   **01326 562752**
We've received just one report on this place from DW of Rotherham who
says, 'Excellent food, friendly service, the Chicken Phal is quite possibly
the hottest in the West! Worth a round trip of 550 miles!!' Is he right?

LAUNCESTON
LAUNCESTON TANDOORI
4, Western Road, Launceston.   **01566 774842**
A comprehensive menu with everything the curryholic needs at reasonable prices, all of which pleases PJ.

LOOE

THE MOONLIGHT
Fore Street, East Looe.   **01503 265372**
Reasonable prices and food ranging from 'a bit mild' to 'excellent'. Says
CY, 'The thing that stands out most though was the service. Quick, polite
and friendly. How about this... The waiter came to replace my cutlery
after I had eaten my Nargish Kebab. I was extremely surprised to see that
he had obviously noticed that I am left handed. Without any comment
he set my new cutlery out for a left handed diner. A small thing perhaps
but I've never come across it before even at top restaurants.'

NEWQUAY

THE NEW MAHARAJAH
39, Cliff Road, Newquay.   **01637 877377**
Vasant Maru's restaurant has the unusual distinction of having Indian
(rather than Bangladeshi) chefs. One is from South India, the other
Nepal. The restaurant has, 'fresh and tasty food with unusual items such
as Patra (rolled leaves in batter).' Mr Maru must have heeded our advice
in the last guide because according to MRS. 'The portions are now fine.
I was certainly satisfied, with my large appetite!'.

PENZANCE

TAJ MAHAL
63, Daniel Place, Penzance.   **01736 66630**
Tastefully decorated in an 'olde' bow-fronted building, by Messrs Hannan
and Amir. Say A and VL, 'Recently we visited Penzance and had a very
pleasant meal in the Taj Mahal. The food was very good. Do not agree
with your reporter who says the place is cramped.' More reports
welcomed.

ST AUSTELL

THE TAJ MAHAL
57, Victoria Road, Mount Charles, St Austell.   **01726 73716**
'There are so few Indian restaurants in Cornwall,' says CL, 'that we travel
a 26 miles round trip to go to the Taj and it's worth it for friendliness, good
food and comfort. They do need to learn to make decent coffee though!'
Regulars comment on generally good food though can be 'variable on
flavour'. PW. SP can't fault it on a one-off visit.

SALTASH

SALTASH INDIAN
23-25, Lower Fore Street, Saltash.   **01752 848194**
We deliberated about whether to take this one out of the guide or leave
it in. Reason: we get reports from regulars who find the service slow and
unsmiling. 'Despite the fortune we've spent going 2-3 times a week over
three years they still don't know our names. We now only use the
takeaway service.' JB. However, JB, PJ and others tell of superb food.

TRURO

TAJ MAHAL
19, Old Bridge Street, Truro.   **01872 41330**
Evidently according to local reportage, the new ownership is shaking off
the Taj's previous reputation. 'One of our party had never eaten Indian
before but was 'converted' via her Chicken Passanda, .' FF. Our well-
travelled scribe JL says, 'The meal was typical of what I call an 'every
town should have one' restaurant. It was a reasonable standard at
reasonable prices. There was nothing very outstanding, but equally
nothing was below average. The sort of place you're glad to go into.

CUMBRIA

BARROW-IN-FURNESS

MONIHAR   **CC DISCOUNT**
252-254, Dalton Road, Barrow- in-Furness.   **01229 431947**
In our previous guide as the Taj Mahal, it is now (since 1992) Masud
Ahmed's Monihar. TP says, 'At last a decent curry house in Barrow.' SG
visits, 'fairly often,' She is, 'impressed by the food and hospitable staff.'
They now offer Balti. Gives discounts to CC members, see page 288.

SUNARGON   **CC DISCOUNT**
36, Dalton Road, Barrow-in-Furness.   **01229 430061**
Situated on a corner site is Barrow's other curry house, which has been
in business since late 1991 under AF Choudhury. Regulars speak well of
it and it will give discounts to Curry Club members, see page 288.

CARLISLE

ASHUKA
23, West Tower Street, Carlisle.   **01228 593763**
'They do a special Balti night the first Monday in each month which is
excellent value for money. Portions very generous.' NS.

DHAKA TANDOORI   **CC DISCOUNT**
London Road, Carleton, Carlisle.   **01228 23855**
Says local man NS. 'This restaurant is my favourite in the city. The food
is always of a very high quality and the servings are generous. The staff
are always very polite and friendly. Their Lamb Pasanda is the best I
have ever tasted and their Pulau Rice is very fragrant.' Others agree 'Still
the best food in the City. Lamb Pasanda is simply the best. High prices
but the food is exceptionally good.' NS. Fazrul Karim's Dhaka will give
discounts for Curry Club members, see page 288.

THE VICEROY
Rigg Street, Shaddongate, Carlisle.   **01228 590909**
Several correspondents believe this to have taken, 'pole position in the
Carlisle curry house grand-prix.' AY. 'It's near the castle just out of the
city centre and not easy to find. The outside resembles a garage
workshop,' continues AY, 'but there is a transformation when you step
inside. You start in a conservatory, where you can browsw over a drink,
Bombay mix, and the huge menu. There you'll find most Indian
favourites, plus Balti, Thalis, and Jalfrezi.' RGM says it all adds up to,
'Carlisle's most popular Indian with an excellent selection of vegetarian
meals.' 'Very popular because of its consistent high standards even
when they run off their feet. Quality meals with a very friendly staff and
manager.' NS.

COCKERMOUTH

KNIGHTS OF INDIA
7, Old Kings Arms Lane, Main Street, Cockermouth.   **01900 827419**
A full curryhouse menu with a good selection of house specials makes
this a favourite of local reporter RE, who says, 'This one is first class. It's
a good curry restaurant - my friends agree with me. The Chicken Tikka
with garlic is superb.'

PENRITH
CAGNEYS TANDOORI
17, King Street, Penrith. **01768 67721**
Standard curry menu with 'quality spot on,' says RE who goes on to say
that, 'it was well worth the 70 mile round trip to try Cagneys.' AY found
that takeaways got priority which caused his table order a long wait, but
still thinks it's the only decent Indian restaurant around for miles.

WHITEHAVEN
ALI TAJ
34, Tangier Street, Whitehaven. **01946 693085**
We asked for reports on this restaurant and we got them. Plenty of them.
Most were from locals who all agree that it is a good quality restaurant,.
GMS felt there was, 'plenty of choice' though RE would like, 'a few more
house specialities.' It is however still his favourite, 'improving with age.'
We think the menu is quite comprehensive containing all the curry and
tandoori favourites but with Sri Lankan and Balti specials. One Lon-
doner (DC) was not only impressed with the food but with the waiters
'who,' he says, 'are walking football encyclopedias.'

WINDERMERE
EAST BENGAL
Royal Hotel, Queen's Square, Bowness-on-Windermere.
015394 47709
A relatively new venture this. MB says of it, 'The restaurant to the Royal
Hotel situated next door. Decor is sparse and shoestring budget type.
The food was not the best in the world, but then again I suppose not the
worst either. Still, it satisfied a craving for a while. Service was fair,
parking a real headache.' JW was more impressed, 'The portions were
generous, the food very tasty.' Although somewhat untried yet, we've
included this restaurant in the guide because of the paucity of curry
restaurants in the area. We welcome reports.

It is the purpose of this Guide to report trends, to note
the bad things, and praise the good. Entry into any
guide, big or small, famous or little known, can affect
a restaurant, sometimes adversely. But a guide c an do
no more than report facts. Clients ultimately are the
lifeblood of a restaurant. And clients should make their
views known - praise and complaints alike - to the
restaurant, there and then, not next day. They should
also inform us of their views.

DERBYSHIRE

ASHBOURNE

RAJAH
1-5, Digg Street, Ashbourne.   **01335 342537**
Remains a popular restaurant with its locals, according to reports .

CASTLE DONINGTON

TANDOORI NIGHTS
43-45, Borough Street, Castle Donington.   **01332 853383**
It opened in 1991 and has attracted good comments. It is formula curry
with a standard curry menu and free delivery service as well.

BELPER

GANGES BRASSERIE
East Mill, Bridgefoot, Belper.   **01773 826625**
'The setting is beautiful,' says WLS-S, 'as it overlooks a weir' She goes on,
'The food is really nice, fresh and well cooked with fresh vegetables. As
we don't eat meat this is especially important to us and it makes a nice
change. The service is very friendly and helpful.'

CHESTERFIELD

ISMAIL'S EASTERN INN
57, Chatsworth Road, Brampton, Chesterfield.   **01246 558922**
MB says of it, 'Decor is to the very highest standard in soft pinks and reds
and soft piped non-Indian music in the background all go to make a very
relaxed atmosphere indeed.' 'It is a consistently good smart up-market
restaurant. For starters I had Shami Kebab, full of flavour, followed by
Chicken Jalfrezi, again full of flavour, accompanied by Pilau Rice and
Chapatis. All of which is served by very friendly waiters promptly.'

DERBY

ABID TANDOORI
7, Curzon Street, Derby.   **01332 360314**
'This particular evening the food was delicious. It always is, but tonight
the dishes were really on form. The dishes are always very generous and
the service is always quick and the waiters are helpful. The restaurant is
comfortable but by no means up-class, just right.' NH.

ADNAN BALTI AND TANDOORI
196-198, Normanton Road, Derby.   **01332 360314**
One of several curry houses on this road, the Adnan has now added some
20 Balti dishes to its already comprehensive menu.

FULLMOON TANDOORI
278, Normanton Road, Derby.   **01332 298298**
'I visited with a large group of people efficiently handled by the staff.
Very good standard of food. I had the Fullmoon Special Biryani -
delicious and nicely presented.' AT.

TO FIND OUT ABOUT THE CURRY CLUB DIS-
COUNT SCHEME, PLEASE TURN TO PAGE 288

MELBOURNE ARMS AND CUISINE INDIA
92, Ashley Road, Derby.   **01332 864949**

'The restaurant is housed in a listed building so you have the sights and smells of Indian food in an Olde English surrounding. It does evenings only. There were five of us in the group and we all had something different from the extensive menu. We were impressed with the quality of both the food and the service and the cost was very reasonable. It was a very pleasant and novel experience. .' DRC.

SHABAB BALTI HOUSE   **CC DISCOUNT**
11, Curzon Street, Derby.   **01332 341811**

M>Rashid's Shabab still does a full curry house menu, but has now changed its name to include 25 or so Balti dishes. Our reporters welcome these additions. SR calls the place, 'a winner' and JRM thinks it is 'superb' They do a home delivery service and their evening only hours go from 6pm to 2am, Sunday to Tuesday and to a remarkable 3am the rest of the week. Shabab will give discounts to Curry Club members, see page 288.

LANGLEY MILL
MEHRAN
2, Cromford Road, Langley Mill, Nr Heanor.   **01773 531307**

Popular establishment, serving tasty curries with a branch in Mapperley, Nottingham. See entry in that county.

MATLOCK BATH
ABID TANDOORI   **CC DISCOUNT**
129, Dale Road, Matlock Bath.   **01629 57400**

'The Abid Tandoori is situated in the very pleasant spa town of Matlock Bath, nestling on the river Derwent in the Peak District of Derbyshire, with its many pleasant walks and even a cable car to take you to the top of the cliffs , and if all that does not work up an appetite then nothing will. The Abid is quite a pleasant little restaurant with seating for approximately 70 people. It has a comprehensive menu with surprises such as Maranjee Gosht, diced lamb cooked in red wine. I went for Karahi Gosht, chunks of lamb, cooked with fresh garlic, ginger, tomatoes and spices, served in a Karahi, which was excellent.' MB. Others speak of excellence, although regular SDR's most recent report suggest a change of chef, and 'different tastes.' Reports please. Evenings-only Mohammed Bashir's restaurant gives discounts to CC members, see page 288.

MATLOCK BATH BALTI & TANDOORI   **CC DISCOUNT**
256, Dale Road, Matlock Bath.   **01629 55069**

'Until recently this restaurant was known as Shahi Mahal, but has undergone a complete refurb, and has emerged as The Matlock Balti, complete with Kashmiri chef, and very nice it all looks as well, with rich reds against a pure white-walled background. All, from what I sampled at any rate - very tasty, served by very friendly waiters. Well worth a visit.' MB. A view echoed by others. Naveed Khaliq's evenings-only restaurant will give discounts to Curry Club members, see page 288.

RIPLEY
SHEEZAN TANDOORI   **CC DISCOUNT**
11, Church Street, Ripley.   **01773 747472**

All your usual curry and tandoori favourites are here at Mohammed Sharif's Sheezan. So is Mr Sharif who is both a partner and the manager. He also gives discounts to Curry Club members, see page 288.

TO FIND OUT HOW TO JOIN OUR DISCOUNT
SCHEME SEE PAGE 288

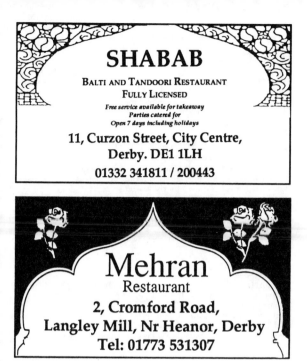

DEVON

AXMINSTER
SITARA   CC DISCOUNT
2, West Street, Western Parade, Axminster.   **01297 32256**
Luthfur Rahman is both owner and chef. His Sitara opened in 1993 (it
was formerly the Empress of India) and will give discounts to Curry Club
members, see page 288.

BARNSTAPLE
GANGES IX
The Old Railway Station, The Strand, Barnstaple.   **01271 23372**
The setting is quaint and noted by our correspondents, who find the food
OK (PJ).

DAWLISH
DAWLISH TANDOORI
12, Brunswick Place, Dawlish.   **01626 863144**
One local regular has put in an impassioned plea for the excellence of this
restaurant. So for Mr GI, here it is. Others agree?

EXETER
GANGES
156, Fore Street, Exeter.   **01392 72630**
It is a place to get a formula curry, but not, we're told, part of the Ganges
restaurant chain.

ILFRACOMBE

RAJAH   **CC DISCOUNT**
5, Portland Street, Ilfracombe.   **01271 863499**
Ralph Wild is the owner chef here assisted by his son James. It has been going since 1986, operates evenings only and will give discounts to Curry Club members, see page 288.

PAIGNTON

GANGES
Hyde Road, Paignton.   **01803 551007**
Neither is this one part of the Ganges chain. Obviously the name Ganges is big in the West Country. PJ finds it, 'brilliant', others say that its quality and crowding suffer during tourist season.

THARIK'S   **CC DISCOUNT**
379a/b, Torquay Road, Preston, Paignton. **01803 664116**
Some of our reporters have brought A Hoque's Thariks to our attention. We'd like to hear more. This restaurant will give discounts to Curry Club members, see page 288.

PLYMOUTH

KURBANI   **TOP 100 - CC DISCOUNT**
1, Tavistock Place, Sherwell Arcade, Plymouth.   **01752 266778**
Owner Mr AM Tarafder and his energetic son, coming from a long tradition of curry restaurateuring have, in their decade of trading, established themselves as a restaurant which is different from the run of the mill curry house. Even the chef is a Tarafder, so it is truly a family business. And in many respects it attempts to achieve a 'home-cooking' style to a restaurant discipline. Since the sad demise of the Khyber, also run by a Tarafder, many regulars have switched their allegiance to the Kurbani and we now receive more reports on this restaurant than any other for miles around. As we said last time, it is elegantly decorated in beige, buff brown and magnolia. Stained-glass peacocks and picture mirrors depict Indian village life and that of the Moghul courts. The walls are painted in magnolia, the tables have a darker shade of magnolia slips on white tablecloths. Gold-coloured spoon-backed mahogany chairs make the setting very attractive. The many special dishes, some unusual ones, include Goshtaba - a Kashmiri meat-ball dish, Kuta Gosht, spicy pounded steaks, Aam Gosht, beef curried with mango and Machli Ka Salan, salmon cutlets in tandoori sauce, to mention a few. Lovers of safe bets will find a range of familiar curries and there is a wide choice of set four-course diners. But our advice is to be adventurous and try a special or three. You'll enjoy, we hope, the freshness of the herbs and spices and lightness of touch from Mr Tarafder. Don't forget to request the home-made pickles. If you've left enough room for desserts, you may wish to venture into their home-made world of the Zelapi (Indian crispy pancake), Gulabzam (sic) (milk sponge in syrup) and Bhadam Khir (a kind of almond rice pudding). We believe in full marks for trying and a genuine and successful attempt to break from 'formula curry', and so we award this restaurant our TOP 100 status. This restaurant promises discounts for Curry Club members, see page 288.

RAJ INDIAN   **CC DISCOUNT**
101, Mayflower Street, Plymouth.   **01752 660628**
and
TAJ INDIAN   **CC DISCOUNT**
49, Mayflower Street, Plymouth.   **01752 669485**
We put these two together. Not only are they on the same street, they are both owned by Syed Lutfus Rahma. GMO tells of, 'a lovely meal with really helpful waiters.' Both restaurants give discounts. See page 288.

TAVISTOCK

GANGES VI
9, West Street, Tavistock.   **01822 616731**
The Roman numerals tell us that this is part of the Ganges chain. RG loves their Peshwari Naans and finds everything to her liking.

TIVERTON

GATE OF INDIA
52/54, Fore Street, Tiverton.   **01884 252380**
Competent restaurant even if JL finds the Taj Mahal arches 'hideous' (I wonder how you'd find the real thing then John!). He did find the breads, Korma and Kashmiri Gosht 'excellent'. Mr Ali Chand, the owner chef will give discounts to Curry Club members, see page 288.

TORQUAY

BELGRAVE TANDOORI   CC DISCOUNT
57, Belgrave Road, Torquay.   **01803 292301**
It's an evenings only, takeaway only place but if long distance truck driver PJ gives it the thumbs up, and he does, then so do we. And it will give discounts to Curry Club members, see page 288.

PEARL OF INDIA   CC DISCOUNT
Scarborough Road, Torquay.   **01803 201220**
It must be the largest curry house in the West (of England) with 200 seats. It is a sister to Paignton's Thariks (see earlier) in the same ownership (Mr A Hoque) and the Pearl restaurant will give discounts to Curry Club members, see page 288.

SYLHET
63, Market Street, Torquay.   **01803 298095**
Another evenings only, takeaways only establishment with free home deliveries, and has been visited by PJ (thumbs up again!). JG, 'enjoyed it all,' and LSDW points out that they have a 'superb' selection of Balti

TAJ MAHAL   CC DISCOUNT
47, Abbey Road, Torquay.   **01803 295163**
Torquay's oldest Indian restaurant (1964) has been in MA Choudhury's hands all this time. Now celebrating its 30th year it is a safe-bet competent curry house. LSDW finds the rice portions 'a bit small' otherwise most things are OK. This restaurant will give discounts to Curry Club members, see page 288.

DORSET

BOURNEMOUTH

THE EYE OF THE TIGER
207, Old Christchurch Road, Bournemouth.   **01202 780900**
Formerly a Momtaz branch. We hear of good quality food and service here.(PJ). See their advertisement, bottom of prev ious page.

LALBAGII   CC DISCOUNT
188, Charminster Road, Bournemouth.   **01202 536742**
It's a popular place locally, serving competent curries. Owned by SS Aktar, it is managed by Roni Miah. This restaurant will give discounts to Curry Club members, see page 288.

MOGHUL DYNASTY
865, Christchurch Road, Boscombe, Bournemouth.   **01202 422634**
'The distinguishing feature of this restaurant is that you can have Lobster anything! Our meal was tasty and competently spiced. Well worth the journey out of town.' LO1. 'The best in Bournemouth.' DN.

SHAH JAHAN   CC DISCOUNT
728, Christchurch Road, Boscombe, Bournemouth.   **01202 399355**
Formerly the Momtaz. 'The speed of the service was notable considering there were so many of us. The standard of the meal was certainly more than competent and well presented.' MS. This restaurant seats fifty four and manager Mahidur Rahman would be very pleased to see you every day between 12 noon to 2.30pm and 6pm to 2.30am. This restaurant will give discounts to Curry Club members, see page 288.

TAJ MAHAL   CC DISCOUNT
42, Poole Road, Westbourne, Bournemouth.   **01202 761108**
Korai and Pilaw Rice dishes are this restaurant's specialities. It is a large restaurant seating ninety-five. 'We use this restaurant for takeaways. The food smelt delicious. The car was checked for rogue air fresheners and windows securely closed. The interior fan was switched to 'heat feet', with brown bags placed on the stained rubber mat in the warm passenger footwell for maximum nasal enjoyment. The meals tasted as good as they smelt, and we reluctantly left the cleaned foil containers to perfume the nearby skips.' LO1. 'This was probably the first Indian restaurant I ever visited back in the 1960's. It's changed surprisingly little since then.' JL. This restaurant will give discounts to Curry Club members, see page 288.

WESTBOURNE TANDOORI   CC DISCOUNT
42, Seamoor Road, Westbourne, Bournemouth.   **01202 767142**
Owned by AA Chowdhury and seats fifty-two. Managed by Anwar and open between 12 noon and 2.30pm, and 6pm till midnight. This restaurant will give discounts to Curry Club members, see page 288.

CHRISTCHURCH

STARLIGHT INDIAN CUISINE   CC DISCOUNT
54, Bargates, Christchurch.   **01202 484111**
Seats forty-two and open from 12 noon to 2.30pm and 6pm to midnight, seven days a week. Specials include, Starlight Delight, dishes cooked with liqueur, cream and herbs. Korai dishes also feature on the menu. This restaurant will give discounts to Curry Club members, see page 288.

GILLINGHAM
GILLINGHAM TANDOORI
The Square, Gillingham.

01747 822579

Opening Hours: 12 noon to 2.30pm and 6pm to 11.30pm. This restaurant will give discounts to Curry Club members, see page 288.

POOLE
IMRAN TANDOORI TAKEAWAY
409as, Ashley Road, Parkstone, Poole.

01202 716560

Takeaway only. Evenings only. Same ownership as the Rajpoot, 69, High Street, Poole. Opening Hours: 5.30pm to midnight, Monday to Thursday, Friday and Saturday they stay open till 12.30am. This restaurant will give discounts to Curry Club members, see page 288.

GANDHI
359, Ashley Road, Parkstone, Poole.

01202 722813

Free home delivery service. 10% discount for customers collecting their own takeaways. Open 7 days a week 12 noon to 2.30pm and 6pm to 11.30pm, Friday and Saturday nights open till midnight.

RAJPOOT
69, High Street, Poole.

01202 682152

Same ownership as Rajpoot, 409a, Ashley Road, Parkstone, Poole. Seats eight-five. Open from 12 noon to 2.30pm and 6pm to 11.30pm, Friday and Saturdays till midnight. 'This place hangs all its many certificates in the reception area and is clearly proud of its status. Jam packed to the point they were even having difficulty seating guests in their reception area! Seating is divided, rather like railway compartments, and between each 'carriage' they have etched glass. The meal was fantastic. Chicken Ceylon was exactly the right blend between sharpness and flavour.' JL. This restaurant will give discounts to Curry Club members, see page288

DURHAM

CROOK

INDIAN COTTAGE TAKEAWAY
18, Church Street, Crook.   **01388 768066**
Opening hours: 5.30pm to midnight, seven days a week. 'Good' PJ

DARLINGTON

GARDEN OF INDIA
43, Bondgate, Darlington.   **01325 467975**
'Restaurant is smart and considerably extended in 1994. Service good
and friendly. Tarana dishes cooked in red or white wine, flambéed with
a liqueur of your choice, served with rice or nan. Chicken Tikka Korahi
brought on sizzler. Ladies receive a carnation before they leave.' ED.

JEWEL OF ASIA   **CC DISCOUNT**
Imperial Centre, Grange Road, Darlington.   **01325 483998**
A jewel of a menu according to PJ who is a regular there when in the area.
Managing owner, P Singh gives a discount to Curry Club embers at his
quieter times, see page 288. Opening hours: Monday to Saturday 12 noon
to 2.30pm and 6pm to midnight and Sunday 6pm to midnight.

PRINCE OF INDIA
204, Bondgate, Darlington.   **01325 468920**
'Chose the restaurant's special starters, too much to eat before the main
meal. Large portions, Jalfrezi brought on sizzler, well presented. ED.

SEEMA EXPRESS   **01325 482100**
No published address because it's a delivery service only. Evenings
5.30pm to 12.30am daily (1am Friday and Saturday). For those who like
to know DMc tells us it's in the kitchen of the Garden of India (sic).

SHAPLA
192, Northgate, Darlington.   **01325 468920**
'Brilliant.' PJ.

SITAR   **CC DISCOUNT**
204, Northgate, Darlington.   **01325 360287**
Sister restaurant, Garden of India, Bondgate, Darlington. 'Decor is
tastefully exotic and luxurious, the service splendid and when it comes
to the food, the menu covers a wide range of regional dishes, including
some old favourites but especially many intriguing newcomers. Fresh
Fish of the Day, marinated and pan-fried in butter.' EMR. 'Food of a very
high standard. Nan breads exceptional.' ED. Ashok Bhagat, owner, will
give a discount to Curry Club members at his quieter times, see page 288.

SPICE ISLAND
90, Surtees Street, Darlington.   **01325 365575**
'Portions are expensive but large. North Indian style food rather than
Bangladeshi.' DM.c Takeaway only. Opening hours: evenings only 5pm
till midnight, till 12.30am on Friday and Saturday.

DURHAM

MOZ'S
30, Front Street, Framwellgate Moor.   **0191 384 3672**
'Ample portions, Brinjal and Sag Bhaji side dishes, both excellent. King
Prawn Dhansak, the best I've had for ages. The owner, Moz, is very nice
too.' ED. 'Mr Moz's takeaways have become a Sunday evening institution. Service is friendly, ask for chicken breast. Recommended D,Mc.

SHAHEEN'S
The Old Post Office, 48, North Bailey.   **0191 386 0960**
Formerly Bebes. 'Consistently been my favourite Indian that I have ever
been to. Caters for all the usual tastes, Rogan Josh, Bhuna, Madras etc.
A small and very personable restaurant.' AF.

SHILDON
RAJAH   CC DISCOUNT
00, Main Street, Shildon.   **01388 772451**
'Situated on the first floor over a fish bar. Gives the feeling of an old
Indian officers mess, with panelled walls ,old wood- framed pictures,
and the occasional pair of cross swords protecting a coat of arms. Menu
fairly extensive and prices reasonable. I toyed with ordering a Vindaloo,
but ordered a Chicken Madras, which was at least the strength of a
Vindaloo, thank God I didn't order one. Really very tasty and nothing
left. Service first class, food on the whole wonderful.'MB. Sister: Sabu's,
199, Newgate Street, Bishop Auckland, Co Durham. Takeaway open in
1977 by Abdul Subhan. Seats fifty people. Opening hours: 12 to 2.30pm
6pm to 12 midnight. Menu contains all the regular favourites . 10%
discount for takeaway . Mr Subhan gives discount , see page 288.

STANLEY
MONJU TANDOORI   CC DISCOUNT
33, Park Road, South Moor, Stanley.   **01207 283259**
Sister restaurants: Golden Gate, 11, South Burns, Chester-le-Street, Co
Durham and Birtley Tandoori, 7, Arndale House, Durham Road, Birtley,
Tyne and Wear. Monju Tandoori has a delivery service. Mrs Miah,
owner, took over Monju in 1991. She runs a small restaurant seating
thirty diners. Her chef, Mr Uddin, serves all the regular favourites, and
she gives a discount to Curry Club members , see page 288.

ESSEX

*Part of Essex was absorbed by Greater London in 1965. We note affected
boroughs with the letters GL.*

BARKING GL
CURRY CENTRE   CC DISCOUNT
6, North Street, Barking.   **0181 591 2809**
This a relatively small Indian restaurant, seating forty diners. This
restaurant will give discounts to Curry Club members, see page 288.
Opening hours: 12 noon to 2.30pm and 5.30pm to midnight. Afruz Miah
gives a discount to Curry Club members, see page 288.

BENFLEET
AKASH
219, High Road, Benfleet.   **01268 566238**
'A small and welcoming restaurant. Service is friendly and prompt,
waiters keep a discreet distance while you are eating. I have a restrictive
diet and need my curries to be as oil free as possible, the chef is very
happy to do this for me.' LA.

MUMTAZ

Quality Tandoori Cuisine

MUMTAZ MAHAL
10 ESSEX WAY
BENFLEET
ESSEX

TEL: 01268 751707

MUMTAZ MAHAL   CC DISCOUNT
10, Essex Way, Benfleet.   01268 751707
A cosy place with ninety seats, split upstairs and down. Standard menu
but very competently cooked. Owner, Abdur Rashid will give a discount
to Curry Club members, see page 288.

STAR OF INDIA   CC DISCOUNT
14, Benfleet Road, Hadleigh, Benfleet.   01702 559450
Well established popular restaurant serving all the favourites. Manager,
Mr Rahman, will give a discount to Curry Club members, see page 288.

TANDOORI PARLOUR
63, Hart Road, Thundersley, Benfleet.   01268 793786
'Good, larger than average Shami Kebab. Loads of onions with Sheek
Kebab. Nan had the most garlic I have seen or tasted in a bread. Portions
were if anything too large. We left feeling bloated.' PH. 'Can seat 200,
live piano music with a special set menu. Dinner dance at the weekend.
Magician entertains at our table.' RL.

TASTE OF INDIA   CC DISCOUNT
261, High Road, Benfleet.   01268 758327
Seats 42. Manager, Abdul Gofur will give a discount to Curry Club
members, see page 288. Hours: 12 to 2.30pm and 5.30pm till midnight.

BILLERICAY
RAGLA   CC DISCOUNT
6, High Street, Billericay.   01277 624996
Formerly the Polash. Seats 80, a large restaurant. This restaurant will
give discounts to Curry Club members, see page 288. : 12 to 2.30pm and
6pm to 11.30. Branch: Codsall Tandoori, The Square, Codsall, Staffs.
Owner, L Uddin, gives a discount to Curry Club members, see page 288.

BRAINTREE

BRAINTREE CURRY PALACE
28, Fairfield Road, Braintree.

CC DISCOUNT
01376 320083

Well established restaurant seating forty diners. Owner, MA Noor will give discounts to Curry Club members, see page 288. Opening hours: 12 noon to 2 o'clock and 6 o'clock till 11 o'clock.

BRENTWOOD

VICEROY
110, High Street, Brentwood. 01277 212830

'A little more expensive than other restaurants. Excellent Chicken Tikka with a superb sauce. Vegetable, rice and breads were all of a good standard.' ED. 'Very attractive Tudor building, matched by excellent food. Chicken Jalfrezi was delicious.' DO'R. We have, however, had a few poor reports as regard to the service and friendliness of the staff.

BURNHAM-ON-CROUCH

POLASH
169, Station Road, Burnham.

CC DISCOUNT
01621 782233

Seats sixty-eight diners. Under same ownership since 1984. This restaurant will give discounts to Curry Club members, see page 288. Opening hours: 12 noon to 2.30pm and 6pm to 11.30pm. Sister restaurant, Polash, 84-86, West Road, Shoeburyness, Essex. Manager, Mr SA Motin will give a discount to Curry Club members, see page 288.

CHADWELL HEATH GL

BHANGRA BEAT BALTI
108, High Road, Chadwell Heath.

CC DISCOUNT
0181 590 2503

Formerly the Tandoori Cottage. Now very popular in its new trendy ownership, complete with Baltis. This restaurant will give discounts to Curry Club members, see page 288. Opening hours: 12 noon to 2.30pm and 6pm to midnight. Sister restaurant: Bhangra Beat, 17-21, Sternhold Avenue, Streatham, London. SW2. See ad on page 41. Owner, Shamin Khan will give a discount to Curry Club members, see page 288.

CURRY KING
212, High Road, Chadwell Heath. 0181 597 4374

'Home delivery service available. They have a good clear voice on the phone, delivery takes about 20 minutes and the food is very good in quality. Onion Bhajee are huge. Free bottle of Coke and free popadoms with our order. The same size meal in any local restaurant would be double the price.' DS.

MALONCHO
27, Station Road, Chadwell Heath. 0181 590 6837

'We were not disappointed. Service attentive even with a brisk takeaway service. Prices reasonable. Opening hours: Monday to Thursday 12 noon to 2.30pm and 6pm to midnight. Friday and Saturday 12 to 2.30pm and 6pm to 12.30pm and Sunday 1pm to 2.30pm and 6pm till midnight.' JT.

RANI BAUGH
1039, High Road, Chadwell Heath. 0181 590 5342

'Another very good local of mine. Portions and service very good. Recommend the Biriani and Chicken Madras, and breads.' IB. 'Piping hot Chicken Tikka and Prawn Puri. Creamy Korma, but Dhansak heat can vary. Portions are always generous.' DS. Opening hours: Monday to Sunday 12 noon to 2.30pm and 6pm to midnight. Friday and Saturday they stay open till 12.30pm.

COLCHESTER

CURRY INDIA
119-121, Crouch Street, Colchester.   01206 762747
'Every aspect of this restaurant and staff is impeccable. Menu is both
extensive and reasonable in price. Superbly prepared and served food.'
AM. Owner, Mr Khan, will give a discount to CC members, see page 288.

INDUS MAHAL BALTI HOUSE   **CC DISCOUNT**
59, East Street, Colchester.   01206 860156
Well established and popular curry house, serving competent curries.
This restaurant will give discounts to Curry Club members, see page 288.
Hours: 12 noon to 2.30pm and 6pm to 12 midnight.

DAGENHAM GL

CURRY MAHAL
27, Gorsebrook Road, Dagenham.   0181 592 6277
'Special Chicken Curry was medium strength, with onions, capsicum,
egg and tomatoes, highly flavoured without being too hot. Worthy of its
place in the guide.' JT.

INDIA PASSAGE
612, Longbridge Road, Dagenham.   0181 597 8331
'Is a really very good standard type of restaurant. It is near to where my
in-laws live, so we pop in quite regularly. Chicken Ceylon is lovely, as
is the Chicken Vindaloo and they do a wonderful Onion Raitha at 95p.'

SHAJHAN TAKEAWAY   **CC DISCOUNT**
670, Rainham Road South, Dagenham.   0181 592 0502
Owner/chef Abdul Jobbar gives a discount to Curry Club members, see
page 288. An evenings only establishment, serving competent curries for
takeaway. Hours: 5.30pm till 11pm.

HALSTEAD
HALSTEAD TANDOORI
73, Head Street, Halstead   01787 476271
Opened in 1977 and still in the same ownership. All the favourites served
completely in this 34 seater. Hours: 12 noon to 2pm and 6pm till 11pm.

HARLOW
RAJ LODGE   CC DISCOUNT
38, High Street, Old Harlow.   01279 626119
Opened in 1987. Seats eight diners between two rooms, upstairs is
available for large parties. This restaurant will give discounts to Curry
Club members, see page 288. Opening hours: 12 noon to 2.30pm and
6.30pm till 11pm. Tables are almost on top of each other. Good news,
a new menu. Chicken Achari - a revelation, overflowing with flavour it
really lived up to its reputation.' AS. Manager Faruque Harun gives a
discount to Curry Club members at his quieter times, see page 288.

HORNCHURCH GL
PASSAGE TO INDIA   CC DISCOUNT
99, Upminster Road, Hornchurch.   01708 437533
'Food excellent and service prompt and efficient. Lamb Tikka Balti
superb, presented in the traditional wok with an abundance of sauce.' JT.
'Considering how busy they were, the meal was served quickly, with
such speed that it took us a minute to sort out what we had. Meal itself
was very good, but not in the exceptional category it was on our last visit.'
PH. A problem that a lot of restaurants suffer from, when they are just
too full to serve customers properly. Opening hours: 12 noon to 2.30pm
and 6 till midnight. See ad on page 46. Mr Uddin will give a discount to
Curry Club members, see page 288.

TASTE OF BENGAL   CC DISCOUNT
194, High Street, Hornchurch.   01708 477850
'Decor very swish and food surpassed expectations, Best starter, King
Prawn Butterfly. The staff were really helpful and didn't mind us taking
nearly three hours over our meal on a busy evening.' PW. This report is
typical of all received, see ad on page 46. Owner, Jamal Uddin will give
a discount to Curry Club members, see page 288.

ILFORD GL
JALALABAD   TOP 100
247, Ilford Lane, Ilford.   0181 478 1285
'Have yet to find anywhere remotely up to the Jalalabad's standard.
Chicken Tikka remains unique in its quality, the vegetables crisp and
fresh and an excellent Jalfrezi has been introduced. The portions are still
enormous.' IB. 'Methi Gosht outstanding. Aubergine and Bhindi of the
highest quality. Nans and Puris light and puffy - gorgeous.' MF.

KURRY POT   CC DISCOUNT
237, Cranbrook Road, Ilford.   0181 518 2131
Malay. Formerly the Penang. A tiny exclusive restaurant seating twenty
six diners. Owners, MS Manku and Chef Mrs Manku will give discounts
to Curry Club members, see page 288. Hours: 11.30 am till 11.30pm.

LEIGH-ON-SEA
SHIMA   CC DISCOUNT
56, The Broadway, Leigh-on-Sea.   01702 76411
A good and reliable standard curry house. Manager Badrul Uddin will
give discounts to Curry Club members, see page 288. Opening hours: 12
noon to 2.30pm and 6pm till midnight.

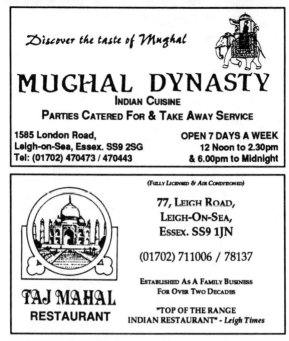
MUGHAL DYNASTY   CC DISCOUNT
1585, London Road, Leigh-on-Sea.   01702 470373
An upmarket pretty restaurant in shades of green. Large chandeliers
hang from the ceiling. Seats fifty-six diners. Hours: 12 to 2.30pm and
6pm till midnight. Owner/ Nazam Uddin gives discounts to Curry Club
members at his quieter times. See page 288.

RAJAH TANDOORI   CC DISCOUNT
25, Broadway West, Leigh-on-Sea.   01702 714281
Formerly Samrat. This restaurant will give discounts to Curry Club
members, see page 288. Opening hours: 12 noon to 3pm and 6pm till
midnight. Seats sixty diners. Sister branch: Samrat 309, Mitcham Road,
Tooting, London. SW17. Tel: 0181 672 6560. Manager Raj will give a
discount to Curry Club members, see page 288.

TAJ MAHAL
77, Leigh Road, Leigh-on-Sea.   01702 711006
A well established curry house (1973) owned by Nazam Uddin. Decor
Medieval Indian. 'Good atmosphere, good food and good service.' JT.

MALDON
THE RAJ
24, Mill Road, Maldon.   01621 852564
Formerly Tandoori Garden of Maldon. 'Crisp Popadoms and flavourfull
Chicken Tikka Masala and Chicken Special.' AS. 'A pleasant low key
local restaurant with prices to match, but above average cooking.' JW.

MANNINGTREE
INDIA VILLAGE   CC DISCOUNT
3-5, South Street, Manningtree.   01206 394102
Popular local curry house, serving all the old favourites. Manager MM
Ali will give discounts to Curry Club members, see page 288.

ROCHFORD

ROCHFORD TANDOORI **CC DISCOUNT**
45, North Street, Rochford. **01702 543273**
'Quite a lot of original dishes and very pleasant staff.' JR. Seats 50 covers.
Opening hours: 12 noon to 2pm and 6pm till midnight. Owner, Azir
Uddin will give a discount to Curry Club members ,, see page 288.

ROMFORD GL

INDIA GARDEN **CC DISCOUNT**
62, Victoria Road, Romford. **01708 762623**
Originally opened in 1970 and under the present management since
1975. A medium sized restaurant seating fifty-four diners. Manager,
Yeabor Ali will give discounts to Curry Club members, see page 288.
Opening hours: 12 noon and 6pm till midnight. Sister restaurant: Rupali,
10, Guildway , off Inchbonnie Road, South Woodham Ferrers, Essex.

SAFFRON WALDEN

NEMONTHON
18, George Street, Saffron Walden. **01799 522739**
'Our local producing the excellent standard of food and service' JH.

SHOEBURYNESS

POLASH **CC DISCOUNT**
84-86, West Road, Shoeburyness. **01702 293989**
Proprietor, M Khalique will give discounts to Curry Club members, see
page 288. Opening hours: 12 noon to 2.30pm and 6pm till 11.30pm. Sister
restaurant: Polash, 169, Station Road, Burnham-on-Crouch, Essex.

SOUTHEND-ON-SEA

ANAND
363-365, Victoria Avenue, Southend-on-Sea. **01702 333949**
Formerly the Himalaya Punjab. 'Our favourite Indian, which we have
frequented for the last four years without mishap! Decor is pleasant if
rather functional. Seating is limited so book for weekends.' PM.

PANAHAR **CC DISCOUNT**
295, Victoria Avenue, Southend-on-Sea. **01702 348276**
Seats seventy diners. Owner, Syed Hassan will give discounts to Curry
Club members, see page 288. 12 noon to 3pm and 6pm till midnight.

SOUTH WOODHAM FERRERS

NAWAB **CC DISCOUNT**
1, Chipping Row, Reeves Way, S Woodham Ferrers. **01245 321006**
Formerly Curry Garden. Seats seventy two diners. Opening hours: 12
noon to 2.30pm and 6pm till midnight. 'Chicken Tikka Chilli Masala
with extra chilli, rather good. Service slow.' LG. Managing owner,
Agefor Ullah will give discounts to Curry Club members, see page 288.

WESTCLIFF-ON-SEA

MOTI MAHAL **CC DISCOUNT**
186, Station Road, Westcliff-on-Sea. **01702 332167**
'Gets my money any day. Thanks heavens for the Moti Mahal.' GC. A
smallish restaurant seating thirty two diners. Managing owner, Shahidur
Khan will give discounts to Curry Club members, see page 288. Hours:
12 noon to 2pm and 6pm till midnight.

GLOUCESTERSHIRE

BERKELEY

BERKELEY TANDOORI
17, Canonbury Street, Berkeley.   **01453 511166**
'Absolutely superb.' JG. 12 noon to 2pm and 5pm till 11.30pm.

CHELTENHAM

EVEREST MOGHUL
3, Portland Street, Cheltenham.   **01242 221334**
'A modern and clean restaurant seating 50 diners Home delivery service. Simply delicious Sheek Kebab followed by a first class Lamb Rogan Josh.' MB.

INDIAN BRASSERIE   **CC DISCOUNT**
146, Bath Road, Cheltenham.   **01242 231350**
Formerly the Dilraj. Seats fifty-six diners. A pretty restaurant decorated in pastel shades with cane furniture. Mr A Rakib, the manager will give discounts to Curry Club members, see page 288. Opening hours: 12 noon to 2.30pm and 6pm till 11.30pm. Sister restaurant: Dilraj Tandoori, 37, Long Street, Dursley, Glos, telephone for reservations: 01453 543472

INDUS TANDOORI   **CC DISCOUNT**
266, Bath Road, Cheltenham.   **01242 516676**
RC's opinion,'the best in Cheltenham. Decor is pleasant as is the atmosphere. Very succulent Chicken Tikka served on a crisp bed of lettuce followed by Lamb Vindaloo, exceptionally flavoured.' Owner and manager, Noorl Allam will give a discount to Curry Club members, see page 288. Opening hours: 12 noon to 2pm and 6pm till 11.30pm, Sunday 6pm till 11.30pm.

KASHMIR TANDOORI AND BALTI
1, Albion Street, Cheltenham.   **01242 524288**
'Menu - good selection, many Balti dishes. Very good and tasty food. Free Popadoms and chutney/pickles! Service indifferent.' JG. 'Quality and service good, menu and decor very good, quantities OK.' RHA.

MUNIRA
60, Upper High Street, The Strand, Cheltenham.   **01242 516677**
For comments see Tewkesbury entry. Opening hours: 12 noon to 2.30pm and 6pm till 11.30pm, Friday and Saturday till midnight.

CINDERFORD

AKASH
92, High Street, Cinderford.   **01594 827770**
'A small restaurant seating about forty-two. Decor is to a high standrad and spotlessly clean. Tasty Shami Kebabs if a little small followed by a quite excellent Meat Madras with lashings of fresh coriander.' MB.

TO FIND OUT ABOUT HOW YOU CAN JOIN THE CURRY CLUB MEMBERS' DISCOUNT SCHEME, PLEASE TURN TO PAGE 288.

CIRENCESTER
CASTLE TANDOORI AND BALTI
1, Farrwell Close, Cirencester.   **01285 658987**
'Lamb Madras Balti rather too hot for my liking with plenty of fresh green
chilli apparent. Chicken Tikka Pasanda, delicately spiced and creamy.
Korma, mild and rich creamy texture. Naan freshly cooked and piping
hot. All was served politely, . CP.

CASTLE TANDOORI

1 FARRELL CLOSE
CASTLE STREET
CIRENCESTER
GLOUCESTER
Tel: (01285) 658987

RAJDOOT   **CC DISCOUNT**
35, Castle Street, Cirencester.   **01285 652651**
A pretty green and yellow restaurant seating fifty-two diners and also
doing a home delivery service. Hours: 12 noon to 2.30pm and 6pm till
midnight. Owner and manager Fozlur Rahman will give a discount to
Curry Club members, see page 288. Sister restaurant: Biplob, 12-14,
Wood Street, Old Town, Swindon, Wiltshire.

DURSLEY
DILRAJ
37, Long Street, Dursley.   **01453 543472**
'I visit this restaurant as often as once a week and have never had
anything less than an excellent meal or takeaway. Tandoori Machli
folowed by Chicken Madras or Dhansak with Madras Dal Sambar being
an exciting and different side dish. Rashid and Rakib have fitted in to the
local community, one waiter plays cricket with the local club.' DH. 'Our
favourite restaurant. The food, and we have tried most of the dishes, are
always excellent and well prepared.' FG. Hours: Sunday to Thursday 12
to 2.30pm and 6pm till 11.30, Friday ? Saturday to midnight.

GLOUCESTER
INDIAN DYNASTY
72, Westgate Street, Gloucester.   **01452 385386**
'Menu well presented, clear, helpful and clean. Quantities more than
enough, service 1st class, comfort and decor very good. I cannot speak
highly enough of this restaurant.' NF.

VICEROY INTERNATIONAL
88, Westgate Street, Gloucester.   **01452 310366**
'Meal had been pre-booked in advance, our starters arrived almost
instantaneously. Chicken Tikka succulent and superbly spiced. Methi
Gust delicately spiced, Prawn Bhuna, good sized prawns cooked in a
carefully spiced sauce. Food bright red - the restaurant preference.' CP.

LECHLADE
BRITISH RAJ
Burford Street, Lechlade.   **01367 252952**
Formerly the Gulshan. "Comfortable and intimate atmosphere. Friendly and efficient, no delays but sufficient time given betwen courses.' C & SR. Owners Junab Ali and Abdul Aziz will give a discount to Curry Club members, see page 288. Opening hours: 12 noon to 2.30pm and 6pm till 11.30pm. Sister Restaurant: Castle Tandoori and Balti Restaurant, 1, Farrell Close, Castle Street, Cirencester, Glos.

LYDNEY
MADHUMATI TANDOORI
3, Cavendish Building, Hill Street, Lydney.   **01594 842283**
'This restaurant is smart and clean. Decked out in old cottage style complete with coach lamps on the walls. Chairs are well padded and very comfortable in red velvet. I think the chef got a little carried away with my Madras, it was a real-fork melter. Portions plentiful and Naan fresh and light, Prices a little high.' MB.

MORETON-IN-MARSH
MORETON TANDOORI
High Street, Moreton-in-Marsh.   **01608 650798**
'An excellent meal in pleasant surroundings. Service quick and efficient. Balti Vegetable Bhoona very especially good. Decent sized starters.' JM. Opening hours: 12 noon to 2.30pm and 6pm till 11.30pm.

NAILSWORTH
PASSAGE TO INDIA
Old Market, Nailsworth.   **01452 834063**
'On entering I was met with a wonderful aroma of spices. Lamb Phal and
Pilau Rice well cooked, well balanced but so huge, I couldn't eat it all.'
AEJ. 'A very tastefully decorated restaurant with friendly and courteous
staff. Food is freshly cooked and mouthwatering. I will return.' ST. 'A
bit expensive, but with it, food very good.' PJ. Opening hours: 12 noon
to 2.30pm and 6pm till 11.30pm.

STONEHOUSE
TUDOR TANDOORI KITCHEN
High Street, Stonehouse.   **01453 792022**
'Converted Tudor house, food excellent, good Keema Naan, first class
staff.' PJ. Opening hours: 12 noon to 2pm and 5.30pm till midnight.

STROUD
JEWEL IN THE CROWN   **CC DISCOUNT**
22, Gloucester Street, Stroud.   **01453 765430**
'A small restaurant which consistently gives excellent quality food,
always white juicy breast meat and lovely deep flavours to all dishes.
Service is occasionally slow and disorganised.' JM. Home delivery
service available. Opening hours: 12 to 2.30pm and 6pm till 11.30pm
including bank holidays. Owner Mohammed Yasin will give a discount
to Curry Club members, see page 288. Sister restaurant: Shelan Balti
Palace, 73, Blackwell Street, Kidderminster.

TEWKESBURY
TEWKESBURY TANDOORI
32, Barton Street, Tewkesbury.   **01684 850746**
Home delivery service available. Opening hours: Monday closed,
Tuesday to Thursday 5 o'clock till 11.30pm, Friday and Saturday 5pm till
midnight. Saturday and Sunday lunch 12 noon till 2pm, Sunday 6pm to
11.30pm.

MUNIRA   **CC DISCOUNT**
69, Church Street, Tewkesbury.   **01684 294353**
'Should be in the TOP 100,' (should it? Ed) 'absolutely first class. Gor-
geous food, friendly staff.' PJ. Reports on this and its branch welcomed
Opening hours: 12 noon to 2.30pm and 5.30pm till 11.30pm - Friday and
Saturday till midnight. Sister restaurant: 60, Upper High Street, The
Strand, Cheltenham, Gloucs. Reservations: 01242 516677.

The editor of this Guide welcomes your
views on the restaurants and take-aways
we list in its pages, and on any you visit
anywhere. Please send your reports to :
The Editor, P.O. Box 7, Haslemere, Surrey,
GU27 1EP. Please enclose an addressed
envelope if you want a reply.

H & W

HEREFORDSHIRE AND WORCESTERSHIRE

Please note these counties will become independent again during the lifetime of this Guide.

BEWDLEY
THE RAJAH
8, Load Street, Bewdley.   **01299 400368**
'Food is excellent and the people extremely friendly offering a high standard of customer service.' SH.

BROMYARD
BOMBAY PALACE   **CC DISCOUNT**
22, High Street, Bromyard.   **01885 488668**
Opened in 1992 under the ownership of Mr Sofik Miah. Seats sixty diners. Opening hours: 5.30pm till midnight. 'The friendliest restaurant in town. Food can only be described as first class, a pleasure to look forward to on a night off.' RW. 'Their food and service are excellent.' CT. This restaurant will give discounts to Curry Club members, see page 288.

DROITWICH
MOGHUL   **CC DISCOUNT**
17, St Andrews Street, Droitwich.   **01905 794188**
Home delivery service. Hurray! Opening hours: Sunday to Thursday 5pm to midnight, Friday and Saturday 5pm till 1am. Abdul Matin will give discounts to Curry Club members, see page 288.

EVESHAM
HUSSAIN'S
13, Vine Street, Evesham.   **01386 47227**
'One of the most memorable meals out we've had. Tastefully decorated, creating a nice friendly atmosphere. Food superb, Chicken Tikka tender and moist with lots of salad.' JS. 'Excellent Popadoms with super accompaniments.' RA. Branch in Stratford-on-Avon.

HEREFORD
KAMAL
82, Widemarsh Street, Hereford.   **01432 278005**
Home delivery service available. Opening hours: Sunday to Thursday 12 noon to 2.30pm and 6pm till midnight. Friday and Saturday 12 noon to 2.30pm and 6pm till 1am. 'Needed a fix, Chicken Ceylon excellent.' PJ.

KIDDERMINSTER
NEW SHER E PUNJAB   **CC DISCOUNT**
48, George Street, Kidderminster.   **01562 740061**
Evenings only at Puran Singh's restaurant which has been open a long time (1971). Satisfactory reports generally though one tells of good food but poor service (DR). More reports welcomed. This restaurant will give discounts to Curry Club members, see page 288.

MALVERN

ANUPAN
85, Church Street, Malvern.　　　　　　　　　**01684 573814**
'Friendly efficient service, decor pleasant and comfortable. Chicken Tikka Masala, excellent flavour, not too hot, good sized portion. Chicken Patia, not on menu, was also excellent.' DR.

PERSHORE

SHUNARGA　　　　　　　　　　　　　　　**CC DISCOUNT**
44, High Street, Pershore.　　　　　　　　　**01386 555357**
This restaurant has a cocktail area which seats between ten and fifteen people. The restaurant itself seats fifty-four diners. Opening hours: Sunday to Thursday 12 noon to 2pm and 6pm till midnight, Friday and Saturday 12 noon to 2pm and 5.30pm till 12.30am. Owner, Mosnul Hoque's will give discounts to Curry Club members, see page 288.

REDDITCH

AKASH　　　　　　　　　　　　　　　　**CC DISCOUNT**
31-33, Unicorn Hill, Redditch.　　　　　　　**01527 62301**
Opening hours: Monday to Saturday 12 noon to 2.30pm and 5.50pm till midnight, Sunday 1o'clock till midnight. Akil Choudhury's restaurant will give discounts to Curry Club members, see page 288. Other branches: Balti Raj, 41, Unicorn Hill, Redditch, Worcestershire; Tilla Balti Takeaway, 1242, Evesham Road, Astwood Bank, Redditch, Worcestershire and Taste of India, 1240, Aldridge Road, Great Barr, Birmingham.

AKASH
TANDOORI & BALTI RESTAURANT
BALTI BUFFET NIGHT MONDAY 6.30-10.30
Booking Always Advisable
10% DISCOUNT FOR TAKEAWAY
(Have yours delivered for £1.00)
OPEN 7 DAYS A WEEK MON-THUR 12-2.30pm-5.30pm-Midnight
Fri & Sat 12-2.30pm - 5.30pm-1am Sun 1pm-Midnight
CHILDREN WELCOME
31-33 UNICORN HILL, REDDITCH. TEL: (01527) 62301

DHAKA
19, Beeley Road West, Redditch.　　　　　　**01527 61815**
Takeaway / delivery service only. Evenings only. 'Waiting area for takeaway is warm and comfortable where we can relax and enjoy spicy Bombay Mix whilst watching TV or reading magazines. The staff are very friendly and always helpful. Our tastes vary each week but we particularly like their Tandoori Chicken Masala.' DW.

MAHARAJAH TANDOORI AND BALTI　　　**CC DISCOUNT**
17-21, Unicorn Hill, Redditch.　　　　　　　**01527 64594**
A wide range of Curries and Baltis at Sheikh Elahee's sixty seater restaurant. Sunday to Thursday 6pm to midnight, Friday and Saturday 6pm till 1am. Will give discounts to CC members, see page 288.

ROSS-ON-WYE
OBILASH
19a, Gloucester Road, Ross-on-Wye.   **01989 567860**
A smallish restaurant seating forty. Some unusual dishes on the menu include: Shathkora Curry and Ada Lembu Curry. Opening hours: 12 noon to 2pm and 6pm till midnight.

TENBURY WELLS
SHAMRAJ BALTI HOUSE   **CC DISCOUNT**
28, Cross Street, Tenbury Wells.   **01584 819612**
Seats fifty diners. Opening hours: 12 noon to 2.30pm and 6pm till midnight. Manager, Lokon Miah, will give discounts to Curry Club members, see page 288. Other branches: Shapla Tandoori, 17, Tower Street, Ludlow, Shropshire and Shapla Balti, 58, Broad Street, Ludlow, Shropshire.

ASHLEYS
BALTI RESTAURANT

11, TYTHING,
WORCESTER. WR1 1HD

01905 611747

WORCESTER
ASHLEY'S BALTI HOUSE   **CC DISCOUNT**
11, The Tything, Worcester.   **01905 611747**
Opening hours: 5.30pm to midnight, Friday and Saturday they stay open till 1am. Sunday Buffet lunch available between midday and 5pm. Balti dishes also served. Owner, M Ashfaq, will give discounts to Curry Club members, see page 288.

PASHA INDIAN CUISINE ·   **CC DISCOUNT**
56, St John's, Worcester.   **01905 426327**
'Restaurant has a well lived in look about it, with Laura Ashley wall paper and drapes yet still with a distinctive Indian theme. Food first class. Sheek Kebab, creamy yoghurt sauce on a crisp bed of salad. Lamb Roganjosh (sic) absolutely delicious. Well worth a visit.' MB. Opening hours: 12 noon to 2pm and 5.30pm till midnight. Partner, S Rohman will give discounts to CC members, see page 288.

PURBANI   **CC DISCOUNT**
27, The Tything, Worcester.   **01905 23671**
Established 1979, the Purbani has built up a strong reputation with its regulars. 12 noon to 2pm and 6pm to midnight. Managing partner, Abdul Haie, will give discounts to CC members, see page 288.

TO FIND OUT ABOUT HOW YOU CAN JOIN THE CURRY CLUB MEMBERS' DISCOUNT SCHEME, PLEASE TURN TO PAGE 288.

HAMPSHIRE

ALDERSHOT
ASHRAM
2, Wharf Road, Ash Vale, Aldershot.   **01252 313638**
'Should have been in the last guide - since it is a bhaji-throw away from
Pat Chapman in Haslemere. Depending on when the head chef is
working, the food can range from outstanding to mediocre. Star dishes
are Chicken Shashlick, Prawn Puri, Tandoori & Chicken Tikka Karai.' JH.

JOHNNIE GURKHA'S   **CC DISCOUNT**
186, Victoria Road, Aldershot.   **01252 28773**
'Glad to see the restaurant is still as seedy as ever, although it's not quite
so easy to accept since the prices are now as much as anywhere else. Mint
sauce is excellent. Famous Dil Kusa Nan - an enormous bread topped
with cherries and coconut.' PD. 'Food is very plentiful, beautifully
cooked and spiced and nothing was left!' JW.

ALTON
ALTON TANDOORI
7, Normandy Street, Alton.   **01420 82154**
'Food is very good and in plentiful quantities.' JM. 'My husband ordered
King Prawn Madras but there were no king prawns left so he settled for
Prawn Madras, with plain rice. It was the hottest Madras he had ever
had, verging on Vindaloo. Chicken Bharta was delicious.' JW.

ASHURST
EURO ASIA INDIAN CUISINE   **CC DISCOUNT**
179, Lyndhurst Road, Ashurst.   **01703 292885**
Formerly Red Fort. Managing Partner Azad Miah will give a discount to
Curry Club members at his quieter times, see page 288. Opening hours:
6pm till midnight, seven days a week. Other branches: Prince of Bengal,
42, Pylewell Road, Hythe. Dynasty, 57, Brookley Road, Brockenhurst.
Lal Quilla, 135/136, High Street, Lymington.

BASINGSTOKE
CURRY PARADE   **CC DISCOUNT**
4, Winchester Street, Basingstoke.   **01256 473795**
Originally opened as a restaurant since 1978 and under the present
ownership since 1985. Hours: 12 noon to 2.30pm and 6pm till midnight.
Owner Shelim Ahmed gives a discount to Curry Club , see page 288.

THE SPICE
149a, Pack Lane, Kempshott, Basingstoke.   **01256 56480**
'A small restaurant seating thirty diners. Nicely furnished. Absolutely
delicious Tandoori Chicken Morrissa, very hot, lots of chillies.' JW. 'My
reference restaurant. Excellent quality food and the best Chicken Tikka
Masala. Always a warm welcome.' GC.

EASTLEIGH
GREAT MOGHUL
1, High Street, Eastleigh.   **01703 612018**
'Quantities were generous, service excellent, very comfortable. Always
receive extras, mango chutney, onion salad etc especially with large
orders.' PD. Opening hours: 12 noon to 2.30pm and 6pm till midnight.

FAREHAM
FAREHAM TANDOORI
174a, West Street, Fareham.   **01329 286646**
'Food, presentation and service were all excellent, quantities were perhaps, slightly larger than average.' MP.

FLEET
GULSHAN
264-266, Fleet Road, Fleet.   **01252 615910**
One of JW's favourite local restaurants. 'Madras is hotter than the norm!
Delicious, plentiful, nicely flavoured food, service attentive. Discreet
decor with soft lights.' JW.

GOSPORT
TASTE OF INDIA   **CC DISCOUNT**
5, Bemisters Lane, Gosport.   **01705 601161**
Formerly Dilshad. Owner Abdul Khalique has run this small forty seater
restaurant since 1992 and will give a discount to Curry Club members at
his quieter times, see page 288. 12 noon to 2.30pm and 5pm till midnight

HAMBLE
LAST VICEROY   **CC DISCOUNT**
4-7, High Street, Hamble.   **01703 452285**
'Last year it was gutted. New and clean kitchens, new carpets, new
decorations and now excellent food. Firmly recommended.' BF. Opening times: 12 noon to 2pm and 6pm to midnight. Owner Mrs Begum
Bahar will give a discount to Curry Club members, see page 288.

LISS
MADHUBAN   **EDITORS CHOICE - TOP 100**
94, Station Road, Liss.   **01730 893363**
One of the editor's local haunts. A pretty blue restaurant with glittering
chandeliers and golden fountain. If you order a brandy, they serve it to
you supported by a brass swan with flame. 'A lovely welcoming
restaurant. Decor is light, pleasant and relaxing. Staff are very friendly
and remember your name even after some considerable time between
visits. Food is the best, Jalfrezi is so good I can't bring myself to order
anything else.' JM. 'I was met at the door and welcomed in by the head
waiter and was immediately struck by the decor. Service impeccable and
the food the best.' JS. 'Toilets were actually the best I have ever found,
spotlessly clean.' JO. In our Top 100.

NEW MILTON
BALTI MAHAL
5, Westcroft Parade, Station Road, New Milton.   **01425 628868**
'Plaint tasteful decor. Plentiful, first class food.' DH. Hours: Monday to
Saturday 12 to 2pm & 6pm to 11.30pm, Sunday Buffet 1pm to 9.30pm.

PETERSFIELD
RIVER KWAI THAI
14-18, Dragon Street, Petersfield.   **01730 267077**
Pretty bar upstairs. Waitresses dress in traditional Thai costume. Not a
cheap restaurant. At the time of writing this guide we were having the
house replastered. Richard Bishop, plasterer extraordinaire, who lived
in Petersfield, visited this restaurant and thought it a great place and
recommends it to everyone, 'You'll love it.' So do we. Branch in Southsea.

PORTSMOUTH

GANDHI   **CC DISCOUNT**
139-141, Kingston Road, North End, Portsmouth.   **01705 811966**
A huge restaurant seating 110 diners. Portsmouth Football Club eat at
this establishment on a regular basis. 'Thali excellent value for money.
Free popadoms and chutneys. Lamb Madras very tender, wonderful
flavour.' JC. 'Chicken Dhansak superb, well flavoured with an excellent
Sag Aloo. It was a pity to see the boring dessert menu of ice-creams.' JH.
Owner Mr KA Khan will give a discount to Curry Club members at his
quieter times, see page 288. Hours: 12 to 2.30pm and 6pm till midnight.

GULSHAN   **CC DISCOUNT**
128, London Road, North End, Portsmouth.   **01705 660045**
A long established restaurant, since 1978. seats fifty six diners. Opening
hours: 12 noon to 3pm and 6pm till midnight. Owner Moklisur Rahman
will give a discount to Curry Club members, see page 288.

NEW TAJ MAHAL   **CC DISCOUNT**
54, Kingston Road, Buckland, Portsmouth.   **01705 661021**
A small restaurant seating 40 diners. Owner Moshod Miah, since 1965,
will give a discount to Curry Club members at his quieter times, see page
288. Opening times: 12 to 2.30pm and 6pm till midnight.

PALASH   **TOP 100 - CC DISCOUNT**
124, Kingston Road, North End, Portsmouth.   **01705 664045**
The Palash continues to maintain a position of high regard amongst its
visitors. Partners Mazid, Mukith and Kadir divide the roles of ownership, management and cheffing between them, achieving a formula of
care and quality which has worked well since the restaurant opened in
1981. We hear good reports about all the specials, one writer raving
about the Indian fresh-water fish dishes (CVM). The Palash remains in
our TOP 100. Managing owner Abdul Mukith, since 1981 will give a
discount to Curry Club members at his quieter times, see page 288.
Opening hours: 12 noon to 2pm and 5.30pm and 11.30pm. Other
branches: Palash Takeaway, 65, London Road, Cowplain and Bombay
Express Balti House, 79, Albert Road, Southsea.

STAR OF ASIA   **CC DISCOUNT**
6, Market Way, City Centre, Portsmouth.   **01705 837906**
Hours: 12 to 3pm and 6pm till 1am. A small restaurant seating forty.
Owner Abdul Mothen will give a discount to CC members, see page 288.

RINGWOOD

CURRY GARDEN
10, High Street, Ringwood.   **01425 475075**
'Very good' PJ. Standard curry house, offering a wide range of heat-
graded curries. Hours: 12 noon to 2.30pm and 6pm till 11.30pm.

SOUTHAMPTON

KOHINOOR
2, The Broadway, Portswood, Southampton.   **01703 582770**
Now run by Jehangir Miah, nephew of Kuti Miah and say W and SO, 'We
have known him for some time and the food is as good as Kuti's.' See
below.

KUTI'S BRASSERIE
37-39, Oxford Street, Southampton.   **01703 333473**
'Decor, service and atmosphere exuded quality.' PB. 'Impressed by good
service - fast, efficient, polite. Decor - tasteful and clean. Food excellent,
well cooked and presented.' JG. Owned by Kuti Miah , see next page.

KUTI'S INDIAN CUISINE TOP 100 - CC DISCOUNT
70, London Road, Portswood, Southampton. 01703 221585
'Very impressed by the good service, fast, efficient and polite. Tastefully decorated, a nice clean atmosphere. Food well cooked and presented - excellent.' JG. And so say all of the reports we've received. It's a sixty-six seater with a high standard of decor, with cabin seating, smartly attired waiters ('in Noel Coward jackets' JL). Owned and managed by Kuti Miah, hence its name, it remains deservedly in our TOP 100. Kuti will give a discount to Curry Club members ,see page 288.

SURMA
44, London Road, Southampton. 01703 227492
'Sue said the Onion Bhaji was the best she'd tasted, light and crispy outside and not stodgy inside.' MB.

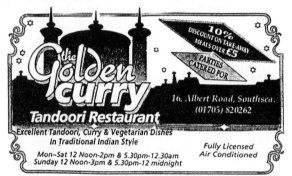

SOUTHSEA

GOLDEN CURRY CC DISCOUNT
16, Albert Road, Southsea. 01705 820262
Following our last guide entry we had an impassioned letter from owner Salim Ullah emphasising that by closing at 12.30am (midnight Sundays) this, 'actively discourages the after pub trade,' and that, 'they succeed in maintaining a quiet pleasant and relaxed family atmosphere.' And we're sure you are right, Mr Ullah. Mr Ullah will give a discount to Curry Club jmembers at his quieter times, see page 288. Hours: Monday to Saturday 12 to 2pm and 5.30pm to 12.30am, Sunday till 3pm & 5.30pm to midnight.

MIDNIGHT TANDOORI CC DISCOUNT
101, Palmerston Road, Southsea. 01705 822567
Seating a massive ninety-two diners, this restaurant opened under the present ownership of Nazrul Islam in 1989, who will give a discount to Curry Club members, see page 288. Hours: Monday to Saturday 12 noon to 2.30pm and 6pm to midnight, Sunday 12 noon to 12 midnight.

PURNIMA CC DISCOUNT
54, Albert Road, Southsea. 01705 826343
A comprehensive range of curries. Seats forty-four diners. Owner Elias Miah will give a discount to Curry Club members, see page 288. Hours: Sunday to Thursday 12 noon to 2.30pm and 6pm to 1 am, Friday 6pm to 2.30am andSaturday 12 noon to 2.30pm and 6pm till 2.30am.

STANDARD CC DISCOUNT
8, Albert Road, Southsea. 01705 811307
Southsea's oldest (1959) and it has remained ever popular with succeeding generations of curry lovers. Stays open very late (until 2.30am) which

pleases the night owls. Owner D Miah gives Curry Club members a discount, see page 288.

RAJDULAL TAKEAWAY CC DISCOUNT
60, Fawcett Road, Southsea. **01705 820862**
An evenings only establishment, 5pm till midnight. Owner, manager and head chef, Mr Choudhury, who opened up his restaurant in 1980, will give a discount to Curry Club members, see page 288.

RIVER KWAI CC DISCOUNT
27A, South Parade, Southsea. **01705 732322**
Sister restaurant to the River Kwai in Petersfield. Seats approximately 100. Opened in 1991. Head chef Aipolij. Hours: Monday to Saturday 12 noon to 2.30pm and 6pm till 11pm. Manageress, Mrs Phillis Griffiths, will give a discount to CC members, see page 288. Branch: Petersfield.

TASTE OF BENGAL CC DISCOUNT
17, Albert Road, Southsea. **01705 827342**
A small forty seater restaurant. Owner Moklis Ali will give a discount to Curry Club members, see page 288. Hours: Sunday to Thursday 12 noon to 2.30pm and 6pm to 12.30am, Friday 6pm to 2am, Saturday 12 noon to 2.30pm and 6pm to 2am

WINCHESTER

GANDHI
163, High Street, Winchester. **01962 863940**
'My local. I think its the best for food and service, even though it's a touch more expensive than the others. I go back again and again, I just can't seem to get enough curry!' PB. 'Superb ambience. Most of the tables (50-60 covers) arranged for four in cabins, which can be partitioned by curtains - very unusual but very nice for a young couple in need of a quick cuddle before a curry! Chicken Phall - the hottest ever! The food in general was excellent more than compensated for confused service. There were no hot towels or mints. My son and his mate were very contented with their meal. In my opinion, when the manager can get his act together on service, the quality and quantity of food is one of the best and deserves an entry in the Guide.' BPD.

SUHELS BALTI HOUSE
8, St Georges Street, Winchester. **01962 862838**
Jalfrezi Balti - Hot!, large Keema Nan. Good meal except for "higgledy-piggledy" service, A bit cramped.' JM.

HERTFORDSHIRE

Part of Hertfordshire was absorbed by Greater London in 1965. We note affected boroughs with the letters GL.

ABBOTS LANGLEY

ABBOTS LANGLEY TANDOORI　　　　　**CC DISCOUNT**
Langley Road, Abbots Langley.　　　　**01923 260402**
A pretty restaurant with hanging plants from the ceiling, colonial fans and large golden chandeliers and fish tank, which makes it a very smart seventy seater indeed. 'Spotlessly clean and inviting. We were shown to a table close to the aquarium which was built in to the adjacent wall. This immediately relaxed us after a somewhat hectic football match. Service was attentive but not pushy and they put themselves out to please and succeeded. Food, beautifully prepared and cooked perfectly. Onion Bhaji was very big. My son's Chicken Tandoori was brought in hot and sizzling and tasted marvellous. Hours: 12 noon to 2.30pm and 6pm till 11pm. Owner, Gulam Ambia will give discounts to Curry Club members, see page 288. Branches: Shefford Tandoori, 8, High Street, Shefford, Bedfordshire.

VICEROY OF INDIA　　　　　**TOP 100 - CC DISCOUNT**
20, High Street, Abbots Langley.　　　　**01923 262163**
Opened in 1989 and we have featured this restaurant in our Club magazine's pages before. Curry Club member, DM from Marlow raves about this place. 'A lovely restaurant, busy but we had prebooked our table. We ate, Onion Bhajees - four tiny, cute little bhajees!. Hash Tikka, yummy; Lamb Bhoona, rich tasty gravy; Mushroom Rice - which wasn't on the menu, but they didn't mind whizzing it up and a garlic nan (I smell now!!) And the all essential mints afterwards, not the After Eights, oh no!! Suchard Twlights!!!' SW. 'On another night we had the most disappointing meal, I think it was an off night.' SW. 'Decor reasonable. Layout and general cleanliness are impeccable. Always fresh carnations on the table. Highly impressed with the food. Popadoms are fresh and served within seconds as are the drinks. Level of service, my only criticism.' NC. Hours: 12 noon to 2.30pm and 6pm till 11pm. Managing partner, Ronney Rahman will give discounts to Curry Club members, see page 288. Awarded a TOP 100 status for DM as much as anyone! See previous page for advertisement.

BARNET GL
SHAPLA TANDOORI　　　　　**CC DISCOUNT**
37, High Street, Barnet.　　　　**0181 449 0046**
A smart restaurant seating fifty diners. A popular local. Hours: 12 noon to 2.30pm and 6pm till 11.30pm. Owner, SI Ahmed will give discounts to Curry Club members, see page 288. Branch: Sonali, Barnet.

BERKHAMSTED
AKASH　　　　　**CC DISCOUNT**
307, High Street, Berkhamsted.　　　　**01442 862287**
'We particularly like the level of personal service - you are greeted at the door, coats taken, napkins placed in your lap, staff are attentive without hovering, they top up your wine glass.' LB. Hours: 12 noon to 2.30pm and 6pm till midnight. Owner, Foysol Ahmed will give discounts to Curry Club members, see page 288.

CURRY GARDEN   CC DISCOUNT
29, High Street, Berkhamsted.   **01442 877867**
'An old converted pub, lovely low beams and cosy booths. We were very impressed with everything, will most definitely be back.' SW. This restaurant will give discounts to Curry Club members, see page 288.

BUSHEY

INDIA GARDEN
88, High Street, Bushey.   **0181 950 2061**
A comprehensive menu including a range of good value Baltis. Live music Thursdays - jazz on Sundays. Hours: 12 noon to 2.30pm and 6pm till midnight.

CHESHUNT

OLD POND TANDOORI   CC DISCOUNT
1, Manor Croft Parade, College Road, Cheshunt.   **01992 620554**
Formerly Taj Tandoori. We hear of good food and value for money at the Old Pond. Hours: 12 noon to 2.30pm and 6pm till 11.30pm. Friday Saturday and Sunday they stay open till midnight. Sunday Buffet - eat as much as you like from 12.30pm to 5.30pm. Children get a discount. Manager, Abdul Malik will give discounts to CC members, see page 288.

COCKFOSTERS GL

TANDOORI NIGHTS   CC DISCOUNT
27, Station Parade, Cockfosters.   **0181 441 2131**
Formerly Saheli Tandoori. A good and reliable restaurant seating sixty diners. Owner, Mrs Yasmeen Rashid first opened this establishment in 1988, she will give discounts to Curry Club members, see page 288. Hours: 12 noon to 2.30pm and 6pm till 11.300m. Sister restaurants: Tandoori Nights, 108, Parkway, London. NW1 and Tandoori Nights, 35, Great Queen Street, Covent Garden. WC2. See entries and ad on page 39.

HARPENDEN

ANARKALI
1a, Harding Parade, Station Road, Harpenden.   **01582 769317**
A small but smart and modern establishment with a large modern frontage which is home to several exotic palm and rubber plants. It seats about forty diners. 'An extensive menu with well over 100 dishes to choose from. Popadoms and chutneys arrive, fresh and prompt. Tandoori starters 1st class. Main courses full of flavour with fresh succulent Nans. Only criticism, the waiters insistence to try and rush through.' MB.

HEMEL HEMPSTEAD

HEMEL TANDOORI   CC DISCOUNT
51-55, Waterhouse Street, Hemel Hempstead.   **01442 242937**
'Splendid menu and one of the few to do duck.' PJ. Hours: 12 noon to 2.30pm and 5.30pm till midnight. Branch: Guru Tandoori, 5, Bridge Street, Hemel Hempstead. Manager, Mr M Rahman will give discounts to Curry Club members, see page 288.

PARADISE TANDOORI   CC DISCOUNT
79-81, Waterhouse Street, Hemel Hempstead.   **01442 243595**
'The Pasanda, cooked with wine was just divine.' MS. A sixty seater restaurant. Hours: 12 noon to 2pm and 5.30pm till midnight. Owner, M Ruez, opened in 1988, will give discounts to Curry Club members, see page 288. Branch: Raja Tandoori, Hemel Hempstead, see below.

RAJA   **CC DISCOUNT**
84, London Road, Apsley, Hemel Hempstead.   **01442 252322**
'They deliver at no extra cost and the service was fast. Food arrived
piping hot within the 30 minutes. Portions were large and very tasty.
Prices average for the area.' JH. 'Surroundings both spacious and
intimate. Portions were generous and waiter brought the food sizzling.'
JP. A discount is available to Curry Club members, see page 288.

HERTFORD
GURU
6, Parliament Square, Hertford.   **01992 551060**
'There is always ample food to eat, always served promptly. The food is
always very good quality and you can ask to inspect the kitchen at any
time.' KR. Hours: 12 noon to 2.45pm and 6pm till midnight, seven days
a week, including bank holidays. There is a free delivery service or if you
can pick up your own takeaway there is a discount of 20%. Every Sunday
is a Buffet served from 12 noon to 6pm.

MOYURI
15, Castle Street, Hertford.   **01992 581069**
'A small restaurant seating thirty diners. Popadoms were served with six
chutneys - three standard and three unusual. Standard menu with some
specialities. Portions enormous, struggled to finish despite not having
starters. Massalla Nan was great.' KB. 'Arrived at 11.15 to find the
waiters attempting to throw out some rather drunk potential customers!
Fortunately you soon learn the trick which is to appear sober when you
enter an Indian restaurant! Service - like lightning. Food - excellent,
quantities and quality well above average.' PC.

HITCHIN
INDIA BRASSERIE   **CC DISCOUNT**
36, Bancroft Road, Hitchin.   **01462 433001**
Reliable food and service at this small restaurant seating thirty-eight
diners. Hours: lunch 12 noon to 2.30pm except Friday, evenings 6pm till
11.30pm, Friday and Saturday open till midnight. Proprietor Chef, MJ
Chowdhury will give discounts to Curry Club members, see page 288.

RANI
80, Hermitage Road, Hitchin.   **01462 450635**
'My husband and I have eaten at the Rani on numerous occasions over
the years and had even more takeaways. Waiters friendly and courteous.
Food portions are ample, served hot with spice and flavour.' GP. Hours:
Sunday to Thursday 12 noon to 2.30pm and 6pm till 11.30pm - Friday and
Saturday 12 noon to 2.30pm and 6pm till midnight.

LETCHWORTH
CURRY GARDEN   **CC DISCOUNT**
71, Station Road, Letchworth.   **01462 682820**
A large restaurant seating seventy-two diners. Formerly the Eurasia, it
now has a 'huge' friendly menu.' MT. Sunday buffet from 12 noon to
5.30pm. Hours: 12 noon to 2.30pm and 6pm till midnight. Head Chef and
owner, Afiz Ullah will give discounts to Curry Club members, see page
288. Branches: Curry Garden, 29, High Street, Berkhamsted, Herts;
Curry Garden, 141, Uxbridge Road, Rickmansworth, Herts; Curry Garden, 69, Katherine Drive, Dunstable, Beds and Curry Garden, 307,
Hornchurch Road, Hornchurch, Essex.

TO FIND OUT HOW TO JOIN OUR DISCOUNT SCHEME SEE PAGE 288

RADLETT
RADLETT INDIA CUISINE
70e, Watling Street, Radlett.   **01923 856300**
'Started with Chicken Chockro Vorty - strips of marinated chicken, grilled, served with salad - exceptional!! Jeera Kata Garlic Chicken - brilliantly tasty, no cloying curry gravies. Nan, chewy and delicious.' CJ.

RICKMANSWORTH
MODHUBON   **CC DISCOUNT**
9, Penn Place, Northway, Rickmansworth.   **01923 711101**
Popular with its local following. A small restaurant seating forty diners. Hours: 12 noon to 2.30pm and 6pm till 11.30pm. Manager and owner Ekbal Hussain will give discounts to Curry Club members, see page 288.

ROYSTON
BRITISH RAJ   **TOP 100 - CC DISCOUNT**
55, High Street, Royston.   **01763 241471**
Last time I confessed that I had not visited the British Raj and I confess I still haven't. However, I still have a soft spot for it and Mr Choudhury's sense of humour. His new menu is still a document for bed time reading

British Raj Restaurant
(Thalia Specialities)

55, High Street,
Royston, Herts.

Established 1976

01763 241471

TAKES THE LID
OFF INDIAN FOOD

12pm to 3pm & 6pm to Midnight
Every day

and it will bring a smile to your lips. "We've had it our business to put more on the menu for the Happy Eater." "Bring the family in and loosen your belt." "Remember curry enhances your appetite while you eat until unknowingly you find yourself overloaded." "The tastefulness is terrific" And is it? Well according to the many good reports received - yes it is. 'An excellent meal and deservedly in the TOP 100. Ate chef's recommendations - a mountain of food. We left feeling bloated - our own fault. Paan Liqueur should be tried - if only for the experience!' AS. The menu contains starters, main meals - 3 pages of them. There are third course - desserts - four courses - finishers (coffee / liqueurs) and the remarkable fifth course, unique to the Raj, a Hukkah (Hubble Bubble) pipe, so you can smoke your way out of the meal. Chef J Ali's specials include some unusuals, and the various Thalia (sic) meals are all well illustrated. We did receive one snorter of a report which took us to task for making it into a TOP 100 establishment. But it was alone among many good reports so I'll stick my neck out again and give the British Raj my editorial idiosyncratic TOP 100 award for the second time around. Children are welcome, "they get small meals." Proprietor, NU Choudhury, knows all too much about marketing and produces a great booklet about his restaurant, featuring the menu, recipes, celebrities, diagrams and maps. Will give a discount to Curry Club members, see page 288.

ST ALBANS

ALBAN TANDOORI
145, Victoria Street, St Albans.   **01727 862111**
A sixty six seater restaurant owned and managed by Mr Choudhury.
Opening hours: 12 noon to 2.30pm and 6pm till midnight. 'Pleasant
decor, comfortable surroundings. Swift and attentive service. Superb
King Prawn with green chillies and ginger.' Capt RA.

MUMTAJ   **CC DISCOUNT**
115, London Road, St Albans.   **01727 858399**
Originally opened as a restaurant way back in 1965. Present owner,
Muklasur Rahman took over in 1983 and has established himself as a
reliable source of Indian cuisine. Seats forty four diners in two rooms
partitioned by an archway. Hours: 12 noon to 2.30pm and 6pm till
11.30pm. Sunday buffet 12 noon to 3pm, children get a discount. This
restaurant will give discounts to Curry Club members, see page 288.

SAWBRIDGEWORTH

STAR OF INDIA
51, London Road, Sawbridgeworth.   **01279 726512**
'Waiters were very friendly, ensuring everything was OK. Onion and
Cauliflower Bhajees were superb. Special Chicken Passanda and Chicken
Madras very good, but Madras could be hotter.' KB. 'My all time
favourite Indian restaurant. Food is average priced but the quantities are
very generous (Onion Bhajias the size of melons).' DW.

STEVENAGE

SHEPHALL TANDOORI TAKEAWAY   **CC DISCOUNT**
20, The Hyde, Stevenage.   **01438 360520**
A wide range of curries are, 'well done here.' PJ. Owned, since 1991 by
N Hussain and A Hoque, the former is front of house, the latter the chef
behind the scenes. They will give discounts to Curry Club members, see
page 288. Branch: Huntingdon Indian Takeaway, 144, High Street,
Huntingdon. Hours: 5pm till midnight, Friday and Saturday till 12.30am.

TRING

JUBRAJ   **CC DISCOUNT**
53a, High Street, Tring.   **01442 825368**
The special dinners for two are talked about at this large restaurant
seating ninety diners, situated adjacent to the town car park. Hours: 12
noon to 2.30pm and 6pm till 11.45pm. Manager, Monnan Miah will give
discounts to Curry Club members, see page 288.

WARE
NEELAKASH
1-3, Amwell End, Ware.   **01920 487038**
'Quantities, quality and service was good. Only one complaint, 'The mango chutney was like treacle!!' PC. 'Brightly decorated, genuine carnations on the tables. The meal, Sunday buffet, was enjoyable.' AS.

WATFORD
ALI BABA TANDOORI
13, King Street, Watford.   **01923 229793**
'Plenty of food with each dish, Vindaloo was excellent, the freshest Nan bread I have ever had.' AM.

BOMBAY TANDOORI   **CC DISCOUNT**
36, Market Street, Watford.   **01923 225768**
Free delivery takeaway service in the Watford area. Hours: seven days a week, 12 noon to 3pm and 6pm till midnight. Manager, 3A Khan, will give discounts to Curry Club members, see page 200.

JAIPUR   **CC DISCOUNT**
37, Market Street, Watford.   **01923 249374**
A large restaurant seating ninety diners under the ownership of Mohammed Abullaes since 1989 and now well established with its loyal regulars. Hours: 12 noon to 2.30pm and 6pm till midnight. Mr Abullaes will give discounts to Curry Club members, see page 288.

WELWYN GARDEN CITY
RAJ OF INDIA
16, Hall Grove, Welwyn Garden City.   **01707 373825**
'Decor is light and airy. The staff are helpful and even smile and joke with you. Generous quantities of food, served promptly. Chicken Balchara including rice was loaded with flavour.' KB. Hours: 12 noon to 2.30pm and 6pm till 11.30pm, until midnight on Friday and Saturday.

HUMBERSIDE

Note: For the purposes of the guide, we combine North and South Humberside.

BARTON-ON-HUMBER
GANDHI TANDOORI
28, High Street, Barton-on-Humber.   **01652 634890**
'Tandoori dishes are excellent, with Chicken Tikka worth singling out. Curries are distinctive and aromatic.' BT.

CLEETHORPES
AGRAH
7-9, Seaview Street, Cleethorpes.   **01472 698669**
A sixty-five seater restaurant, owned by Bashir Miah since 1979. A well established and reliable curry house. Hours: 12 noon to 2.30pm and 6pm till midnight. Branch: Helal Tandoori, Mercer Row, Louth, Lincs and Shaki Mahal Takeaway, 6, Pinfold Lane, Grimsby.See ad. overleaf

TASTE OF PUNJAB
9-11, Market Street, Cleethorpes.　　　　　　　01472 603720
'An easy to read and comprehensive menu, which the owner, Mr Sagoo, is only too happy to help you with. From the initial Popadoms to the final coffee, the quantities are just right.' HC.

GRIMSBY

ABDULS TANDOORI　　　　　　　　　　**CC DISCOUNT**
152, Victoria Street, Grimsby.　　　　　　　01472 356650
'I have been using the place when I'm in town, never had a bad meal, absolutely brilliant.' PJ. Branch: Eastern Delights, 43, Market Place, Cleethorpes. Owner, Abdul Salique will give discounts to Curry Club members, see page 288. Hours: seven days a week, 12 noon to 2.30pm and 6pm till midnight, Friday and Saturday till 12.30am.

HULL

BALAKA　　　　　　　　　　　　　　**CC DISCOUNT**
133, Chanterlands Avenue, Hull.　　　　　　01482 442119
A medium sized restaurant seating fifty-four diners. Balti specials on the menu. Hours: 12 noon to 2pm and 6pm till midnight, till 1am on Friday and Saturday. Managing owner, A Hamid will give discounts to Curry Club members, see page 288.

TANDOORI MAHAL　　　　　　　　　**CC DISCOUNT**
589, Anlaby Road, Hull.　　　　　　　　　01482 505653
A medium sized restaurant seating sixty two diners, serving reliable and competent curries with all the usual accompaniments. Hours: 12 noon to 2pm and 6pm till midnight. Owner, Abu Maksub will give discounts to Curry Club members, see page 288.

POCKLINGTON

TANDOORI MAHAL
Railway Street, Pocklington.　　　　　　　01759 305027
'One of our two favourites. Lamb Passanda is mild but tasty and their Zalfrezi is also worth a special mention.' BT.

SCUNTHORPE

RAHMAN'S TANDOORI
143, Frodingham Road, Scunthorpe.　　　　　01724 841238
'They serve first class food and service.' SR.

KENT

*Parts of Kent were absorbed by Greater London in 1965. We note affected towns/
boroughs with the letters GL.*

ASHFORD

CURRY GARDEN   CC DISCOUNT
31, Bank Street, Ashford.   **01233 620511**
'Service was very efficient and food was of a high quality, portions were
ample.' JSK. Owner, Bajloor Rashid, will give a discount to Curry Club
members, see page 288. Hours: 12 noon to 3pm and 6pm till midnight.
Branch: Shapla, 36, Harbour Street, Whitstable, Kent.

TANDOORI NIGHTS   CC DISCOUNT
9, Torrington Road, Ashford.   **01233 636681**
Partner, Ziaul Ahmed, will give a discount to Curry Club members, see
page 288. Hours: 12 noon to 2pm and 5.30pm till 11.30pm.

BARNEHURST GL

JHAS TANDOORI   CC DISCOUNT
158c, Mayplace Road East, Barnehurst.   **01322 555036**
Opened in 1989 by KS Jhas, an evenings only establishment seating forty-
five to fifty diners. Hours: 6pm till 11.30pm, until midnight on Friday
and Saturday and closed all day Sunday. Mr Jhas has agreed to give a
discount to Curry Club members, see pa ge 288.

BECKENHAM GL

ROSE TANDOORI   CC DISCOUNT
406, Upper Elmers End Rd, Eden Park, Beckenham.   **0181 650 0919**
A small and friendly restaurant seating just thirty-eight diners. Serving
all your old favourite curries and accompaniments. Managing partner,
Keenu Mul Islam, will give a discount to Curry Club members, see page
288. Hours: 12 noon to 2.30pm and 6pm till 11.30pm.

BEXLEY GL

ALBANY   CC DISCOUNT
44, Steynton Avenue, Albany Park, Bexley.   **0181 309 7254**
On Sundays and bankholidays they serve special set lunches and set
dinners. Manager, S Alom, will give a discount to Curry Club members,
see page 288. Branches: Mahatma Tandoori, 156, Bexley Road, SE9.

RUCHI   CC DISCOUNT
58, Steynton Avenue, Albany Park, Bexley.   **0181 300 0200**
The Ruchi opened way back in 1986 and has established itself as a good
reliable and competent restaurant seating fifty-six diners. 'A well organ-
ised restautant with an enormous takeaway trade. Service was friendly.
Breads were the best feature.' JL. Owner, Madan Lal Prashar, will give
a discount to Curry Club members, see page 288. Hours: 12 noon to 2pm
and 6pm till 11pm, until midnight on Friday and Saturday.

BIGGIN HILL GL

RAJ
187, Main Road, Biggin Hill.   **01959 572459**
'Intense and worthy competition from the other local restaurants have
led to a keener pricing policy, larger portions and a distinct lack of
complacency in terms of quality. Albert at this restaurant still produces
the best meals in the area.' LO1. Hours: 12 to 2.30pm ; 6pm to11.30pm.

BROMLEY GL
CHANDNI
123-125, Mason Hill, Bromley.   **0181 290 4447**
'Another excellent meal in convivial surroundings. Their Dhansak is
superb and their Black Lentil Dal is worth trying.' JL. Hours: 12.30pm
to 2.30pm and 6pm till 11pm, Friday and Saturday till 11.30pm and
Sunday closed. Fully air-conditioned. Also at: 174, Pembroke Road,
Ballsbridge, Dublin 4. Eire.

SHANTI   CC DISCOUNT
419, Bromley Road, Downham, Bromley.   **0181 461 4819**
Established in 1989 by Panna Dhar. Opening hours: 12 noon to 2.30pm
and 6pm till midnight. Kurzi Lamb on the menu at 24 hours notice,
priced at a huge £49.95. Manager, Syed Abdul Mannan will give a
discount to Curry Club members, see page 288.

TAMASHA   SPECIAL AWARD   TOP 100
131, Widmore Road, Bromley.   **0181 460 3240**
This is an Indian restaurant and not a Bangladeshi one. Tamasha means,
'something worth seeing', and we agree with MW's comments. 'Needs
to be seen to be believed, it's very impressive. Decor is brilliant. The
tables are well spaced and there isn't a chance of pushing your chair
(which are of quality) back into someone else. Samosas were the largest
I've seen as a starter, served with salad and tamarind sauce. Tikka Masala
- lovely flavour. Manchoori - made with chopped chillies, not too hot,
just about right. Bombay Aloo - huge portion. Overall - exceptional,
large portions that were well presented and full of flavour.   Service
polite, precise and helpful.' M W. A deserving new entrant to our TOP
100. The Tamasha is located, incidentally at a local hotel. A useful tip for
Kent curryholic travellers.We are pleased to give the Tamasha ourBEST
MENU AWARD, in recognition of their very pretty menu.

ZANZIBAR
239, High Street, Bromley.   **0181 460 7130**
Formerly Carioca and has its name change because owner Ken Modi was
fed up with Karaoke requests. The small exterior belies the massive
interior seating 120, which includes a mock Pullman railway carriage.
Baltis are included amongst the curries. Closed on Sunday evening.

CANTERBURY
GANDHI   CC DISCOUNT
36, North Gate, Canterbury.   **01227 765300**
Standard curries here. Owner, Nurul Islam Khan, will give a discount to
Curry Club members, see page 288. Hours: 12 noon to 2.30pm and 6pm
till midnight.

CHISLEHURST GL
BENGAL LANCER   CC DISCOUNT- TOP 100
15, Royal Parade, Chislehurst.   **0181 467 7088**
'Another very competent meal, with my Chicken Tikka Biryani being
excellently spiced. My daughter had a cold and we suggested she try a
Madras, after all, she's fifteen now and really ought to have sampled
some of the spicier meals. They produced an absolutely perfect one for
her and it cleared her cold too. Vegetables were particularly good on this
occasion "done but not done in" as my Gran would say!' JL. Given TOP
100 status on the strength of JL's many accolades. Will give a discount to
Curry Club members, see page 288.

FIND OUT HOW TO JOIN OUR DISCOUNT SCHEME ON PAGE 288

DEAL

BENGAL DINERS
53, The Strand, Walmer, Deal.

CC DISCOUNT
01304 363939

A popular local establishment. Managing partner, Azad Ali will give a discount to Curry Club members at his quieter times, see page 288. Hours: 12 noon to 2pm and 6pm till 11.30pm, daily. Fax for a copy of their menu or book a table on 01304 368888.

DOVER

LIGHT OF INDIA
Burlington House, Town Wall Street, Dover.   **01304 241066**

A pretty and large (100 plus diners) restaurant furnished with blue upholstery and gold curtains and table cloths. 'Menu is pretty standard but the food is of a high quality. Portions are ample. Prawn Puri was full of prawns, excellent value.' JSK. Hours: 12 to 2.30pm and 6pm 11.30pm.

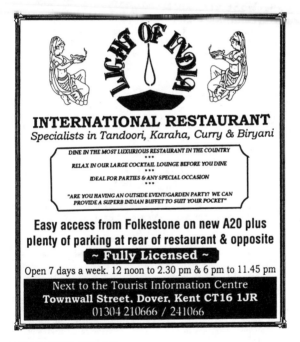

EAST PECKHAM

RED FORT
14, Hale Street, East Peckham.

CC DISCOUNT
01622 872643

'A spacious restaurant in a country setting. Food, all large quantities served on hot plates by uniformed waiters. This is a place to take visitors, very impressive, we think so anyway and we shall return.' NG. A huge restaurant seating ninety-eight diners. Under the present ownership since 1989, so a well established and reliable curry house serving competent curries with all their accompaniments. Managing partner, Mr Mainuzzaman, will give a discount to Curry Club members, see page 288. Hours: 12 noon to 2.30pm and 6pm till 11pm.

FOLKESTONE

INDIA   CC DISCOUNT- TOP 100
1, The Old High Street, Folkestone.   01303 259155
Opened back in 1985 and seats fifty diners. 'Most delicately spiced and
tasty Dhansak curry, I have had in years. Pullao Rice was uncoloured
and garnished with coriander and coconut, Naan bread was hot and
crisp!.' NG. Chef proprietor, A Ashraf, will give a discount to Curry Club
members at his quieter times, see page 288. Hours: 12 noon to 2.30pm and
6pm till 10.30pm, closed on Mondays. Remains in our TOP 100.

PRINCE OF INDIA   CC DISCOUNT
23, Risborough Lane, Cheriton, Folkestone.   01303 276298
A sixty seater establishment, serving reliable curries. Hours: 12 noon to
2.30pm and 6pm till midnight. Owner, Mr Sirajul Islam will give a
discount to Curry Club members, see page 288.

GRAVESEND

MEOPHAM TANDOORI   CC DISCOUNT
2, The Parade, Wrotham Rd Meopham, Gravesend.   01474 812840
Comprehensive menu with all the favourites. Managing owner, (since
1985) Jahir Ali, will give a discount to Curry Club members at his quieter
times, see page 288. Hours: 12 noon to 2.30pm and 5.30pm till 11.30pm.

BLUE ELEPHANT CURRY INN

98 KING STREET
MAIDSTONE, KENT
01622 756094

**NEW NAME . NEW MENU . NEW DECOR . NEW DISHES
FROM YOUR OLD FAVOURITE CURRY HOUSE**

Try Our New Balti Dishes

MAIDSTONE

BLUE ELEPHANT CURRY INN   CC DISCOUNT
98, King Street, Maidstone.   01622 756094
Maidstone's oldest restaurant, opened way back in 1965, and still under
the same ownership. Seats fifty diners. 'Since their refurbishment, the
prices are now reflecting this. Have tried Dhansak, Bhoona, Vindaloo
(Bloody hot) all excellent, full marks, just wish the prices were lower. 40
pence extra for breast chicken only.' NG. Owner, ST Meah will give a
discount to Curry Club members, see page 288. Hours: 12 noon to 2.15pm
and 5.45pm till midnight - Monday to Saturday. All day Sunday Buffet.
Branch: Joshan of Wye, 2-4, High Street, Wye, Ashford.

RUCHITA
73, Tonbridge Road, Maidstone.   01622 674140
'We have had many takeaways (10% discount) , but now they deliver.
Food is always 1st class, large portions.' NG. Hours: 12 noon to 2pm and
5.30pm till midnight.

SHAMRAT BRASSERIE CC DISCOUNT
36, Upper Stone Street, Maidstone. 01622 764961
'Chicken Jalfrezi - extra hot, superbly hot. I rate this one as one of the best
I have visited. It appeals to me as a fire-eater!!' BP-D. 'Always an
excellent welcome from all the staff. Warm on a cold night. Popadoms
and pickles, Dhansak with rice included, Tikka Patia again rice included,
sizzling Tikka, Cauliflower Bhajia and Naan, bottomless coffee, liqueurs,
orange slices, Suchard Mints, hot towels and an excellent house white
wine. How do they do it!' PS. 'The warmth of a real blazing fire and
Bombay Mix helped thaw me out whilst I looked through the menu.
Quality, tasty, large portions of food.' NG. Plentiful accolades for the
Shamrat Brasserie. Discount to Curry Club members, see page 288.

ORPINGTON GL
BOMBAY BRASSERIE TOP 100
76, High Street, Green Street Green, Orpington. 01689 862906
A large restaurant seating ninety diners. Under the ownership of H Miah
and J Ali since 1906. 'Another excellent Chicken Tikka Biryani, accompanied by their superb bread products. My son's Chicken Tikka Masala
was brilliant too.' JL. 'Chicken Tikka Kebabs absolutely mouthwatering.
My daughter dropped her Popadom on the floor and before we'd
realised it a waiter produced a fresh one.' JL. Hours: 12 noon to 3pm and
6pm till midnight. Rated into the TOP 100 at request of JL.

CURRY HOUSE CC DISCOUNT
24, Station Square, Petts Wood, Orpington. 01689 820671
If you go down to Petts Woods today you're sure of ... Some old
favourites including Sik (sic) Kebab and Vinderloo (sic). Opening hours:
12 noon to 3pm and 6pm till midnight. Managing partner, B Wahab,
(since 1970) will give a discount to Curry Club members, see page 288.

RAJ OF INDIA CC DISCOUNT
4, Crescent Way, Orpington. 01689 852170
'As usual a maddening mixture of very good (Chana Panir and Chicken
Tikka) and mediocre (Onion Bhaji). One day they'll get it right on the
same day and then they'll be unbeatable!' JL. 'Smart restaurant. They do
me an ultra hot Phall, which somtimes is too hot to eat in one sitting, so
I have the rest for breakfast!. Aubergine Bhaji is worthy of a mention.'
PW. 'Our kitchen had just been gutted and we couldn't face trying to
cook. Dhansak and lamb Tikka Masala were superb but the meat lacked
quality' JL. Owner manager, Mr Muzibur Rahman, will give a discount
to Curry Club members, see page 288. Hours: 12 noon to 2.30pm and
6pm till midnight. Branches: Raj of India, 23-25, High Street, Swanley,
Kent; Raj of India, 2, Bell Road, Sittingbourne, Kent; Raj Bari, 7, Tubs Hill
Parade, London Road, Sevenoaks, Kent; Maharahaj, 84, High Street,
Bexley, Kent; Raj of India, 9-10, Neptune Terrace, Sheerness, Kent and
Juboraj, 84, Warley Hill, Brentwood, Essex.

RAMSGATE
CURRY PALACE CC DISCOUNT
17, Harbour Street, Ramsgate. 01843 589134
Opened in 1988, by Mr Khan and Mr Rahman. A medium sized, fifty
seater, restaurant serving all your old favourite curries and accompaniments. Mr Rahman will give a discount to Curry Club members, see page
288. Hours: an evenings only establishment - 6pm till midnight.

ROCHESTER

BENGAL BRASSERIE   CC DISCOUNT
356, High Street, Rochester.   **01634 841930**
'Reasonable portions, good flavours. We enjoyed our meal and everything was alright for us!' S & VP. Managing owner, Shahin Ali, has agreed to give a discount to Curry Club members, see page 288. Hours: 12 noon to 2.30pm and 6pm till midnight. Branch: Bexley Tandoori, 77a, High Street, Bexley.

TASTE OF TWO CITIES
106, High Street, Rochester.   **01634 841327**
'This restaurant just gets better and better everytime I visit. ' PA.

SINGAPORA   CC DISCOUNT
51, High Street, Rochester.   **01634 842178**
Opened in 1990 by Dr and Mrs Shome. A huge restaurant seating 150 diners. A good range of Singaporean food including curries. Open daily: 11am till 3pm and 6pm till 11pm. Sunday 11am through to 10.30pm. Branches under the same management: Singapore Garden, 73, Brewer Street, Maidstone and Gordon Hotel, 91, High Street, Rochester. Will give a discount to Curry Club members, see page 288.

SIDCUP GL

BLACKFEN TANDOORI   CC DISCOUNT
33, Wellington Parade, Blackfen Road, Sidcup.   **0181 303 0013**
A pleasant competent curry house. Owned by Muzammil Ali since 1983, who has agreed to give a discount to Curry Club members, see page 288. A friendly restautant seating forty-eight diners. Hours: 12 noon to 2.30pm and 6pm till midnight.

OVAL BRASSERIE   CC DISCOUNT
49, The Oval, Sidcup.   **0181 308 0274**
'Meat Samosas were very small, but tasted lovely.' MW. Manager, Afsar has agreed to give a discount to Curry Club members, see page 288. Open from 12 noon to 2.30pm and 6pm till 11.30pm.

SWANLEY

BENGAL LANCER   CC DISCOUNT
3, Station Road, Swanley.   **01322 662098**
Formerly Lalquila and still a popular curry house. Seats forty eight diners. Owners, Hiron Miah (chef behind the scenes) and Feruz Ali (front of house manager) will give a discount to Curry Club members, see page 288. Open from: 12 noon to 2.30pm and 6pm till midnight.

SHAAN   CC DISCOUNT
9, High Street, Swanley.   **01322 666011**
Formerly the Viceroy. A large restaurant seating seventy-six dinners. We hear of enjoyable meals here. There is also a large hall in the basement of the restaurant which could be hired for private buffet parties. Head waiter, NA Sanjania has agreed to give a discount to Curry Club members, see page 288. Hours: 12 to 2.30pm and 6pm till midnight.

TONBRIDGE

SIMLA CUISINE   CC DISCOUNT
2, Church Road, Paddock Wood, Nr Tonbridge.   **01892 834515**
A smart place, inside and out with a good menu. The set meal appeals to some. Hours: 12 noon to 2.30pm and 6pm till 11pm. Friday and Saturday till 11.30pm. Abdul Miah, managing owner has agreed to give a discount to Curry Club members, see page 288. Branches: La Lipu Cuisine (below). Happy Cuisine, Tonbridge. Hafsa Cuisine, Pembury.

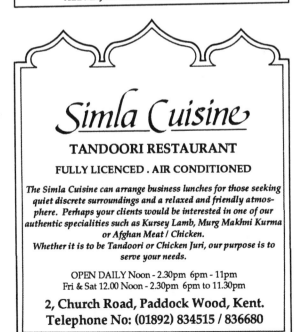

TUNBRIDGE WELLS
LA LIPU CUISINE
CC DISCOUNT
69, London Road, Southborough, Tunbridge Wells. 01892 534182
A sixty-five seater restaurant, with a smoking and no smoking area.
Hours: 12 noon to 2pm and 6pm till 11pm. Owner, Makhan Miah, will
give a discount to Curry Club members, see page 288.

WESTERHAM
SHAPLA
CC DISCOUNT
20, London Road, Westerham. 01959 563397
'A warm welcome from a large staff in smart green striped shirts.
Delighted to see a blackboard with specials. Chicken Nilgiri and Chicken
Bhapali Quite spicy, large helpings, very tasty.' GM. Hours: 12 noon to
2.30pm and 6pm till 11.30pm (weekdays), midnight (weekends). Owned
by Anil Kumar and Shekhor Tarat, who have agreed to give a discount
to Curry Club members, see page 288. Branches: Tamasha, 131, Widmore
Road, Bromley and Shajus, Adlington, Lancashire. See page 173.

WEST WICKHAM GL
OLD CALCUTTA
CC DISCOUNT
54, Croydon Road, Coney Hall, West Wickham. 0181 462 9416
Generally good comments. Partner, Dewan Faizul Islam, has agreed to
give a discount to Curry Club members, see page 288. Hours: 12 noon to
2.30pm and 6pm till 11.30pm, Friday and Saturday till midnight.

WHITSTABLE
SHAPLA
CC DISCOUNT
36, Harbour Street, Whitstable. 01227 262454
'A Saturday night, and very crowded. I expected this after the marvellous meal we had last time. The atmosphere was great, but I think the
chef was struggling.' JL. A forty seater establishment, owned and
managed by Mr S Rahman, has agreed to give a discount to Curry Club
members, see page 288. Hours: 12 noon to 2.30pm and 6pm till 11.30pm.

WYE
JOSHAN OF WYE
2-4, High Street, Wye. 01233 812231
'Quantities of food - while not piled high - are on the generous side average.
A very friendly welcome and service. Value for money is reckoned
outstanding - even more so if you become a member of the tiffin club.'
RCD. One Balti dish on the menu - spelt Bhalti. Infact there are a number
of intriguing dishes on the menu. And for regulars there is their Tiffin
Club. Hours: Monday to Saturday 12 noon to 2.30pm and 6pm till
midnight.

Joshan of Wye
SUPERIOR BENGALI CUISINE

Distinguished for subtlety & delicacy of spicing

Daily Lunch & Dinner with Full Á La Carte Menu
Sunday All Day 'Tiffin' Buffet 'Pick and Choose' from Good Selection of
Tasty Starters and Main Course Dishes

Remember, Joshan means "Celebration"

THE TIFFIN CLUB
2-4, HIGH STREET, WYE, NR ASHFORD.
TELEPHONE (01233) 812231
Please telephone during normal restaurant hours to receive free copy of our menu & Tiffin Club details.

INDIAN · CUISINE

20 LONDON ROAD, WESTERHAM, KENT.
TELEPHONE: WESTERHAM 63397/62163

Indian Take Away

PARTIES CATERED FOR

**178, CHORLEY ROAD, ADLINGTON.
TEL: 01257 474630**

OPENING HOURS:
SUNDAY TO THURSDAY
4PM TO 11.30PM
FRIDAY & SATURDAY
4PM TO 12 MIDNIGHT

**All food prepared in full
view of customers**

EXCLUSIVE RAJ CUISINE

Church Street, Adlington,
Chorley, Lancashire. PR7 4EX
(01257) 481894/482514

Monday - Thursday
12.00 - 2.00pm &
6.00pm - 11.00pm

Friday & Saturday
12.00 - 2.00pm &
5.30pm - 12.00pm

Sunday - All Day
Self Service Buffet
from 12.00 - 4.30pm

LANCASHIRE

We have adhered strictly to the official county of Lancashire here. Please also refer to the entries for Greater Manchester and Merseyside (see index page 49) for other restaurants within the former Lancashire boundary.

ACCRINGTON

SAGAR II
217- 219, Whalley Road, Clayton-le-Moors, Accrington.   **01254**
                                                                   871700
A largish restaurant seating ninety diners. 'Have visited this restaurant many times, both sit in and takeaway and the food is excellent, very fresh and expertly presented, always brought to the table piping hot.' JH. Hours: 12 noon to 2pm and 6pm till 11.30pm. Branches: Sagar I, 61, Church Street, Blackrod, Bolton and Sagar Premier, Clayton Brook Road, Bamber Bridge, Preston.

ADLINGTON

SHARJU   **TOP 100 - CC DISCOUNT**
Church Street, Adlington.   **01257 481894**
A huge restaurant (a converted church) seating 150 diners. 'Huge portions of everything. Decor and surroundings very comfortable and relaxing.' BC-T. 'Chicken Shahee, chicken and minced lamb with tomatoes, onion and peppers - medium hot with Pillau rice and fried onions. There is only one word which covers the experience 'magnificent'.' DB. 'Madras is very hot but with bags of flavour right down to the last grain of excellent Pillau rice, all helped down with a Naan bread of the highest quality.' MB. Partner, P Dhar, will give a discount to Curry Club members, see page 288. Hours: 12 noon to 2pm and 6pm till 11.30pm, Sunday 11pm. Remains in our TOP 100. Branches, Shanti, 466, Bromley Road, Bromley, Kent. See previous page .

SHAPLA TAKEAWAY
178, Chorley Road, Adlington.   **01257 474630**
'I have been addicted to Indian food from an early age and wonderful to have this need satisfied on my doorstep. Quality and freshness are unquestionable.' AL. 'Menu is various and offers a wide range of food, which is excellent.' AH. Hours: Sunday to Thursday 4pm till 11.30pm, Friday and Saturday 4pm till midnight. See previous page.

BLACKBURN

BALTI HOUSE   **CC DISCOUNT**
1-3, High Street, Rishton, Blackburn.   **01254 887386**
A massive establishment seating one hundred and twenty diners and serving Balti everything and anything. 'We were well received in this very good and large restaurant. Kitchens are on view behind large glass windows, clean, full of stainless steel. Food very good indeed, rounded off by a glass of Indian liqueur.' IS. Opened in 1982 by Mr Asab Ali, who has promised to give a discount to Curry Club members, see page 288 for details. Hours: 5pm till midnight.

SHAJAN
Longsight Road, Clayton-le-Dale,Blackburn.   **01254 813640**
'King Prawn Bhaji, Khari Lamb and Pomfret are all my particular favourites. Probably the best Parathas anywhere! - they just melt in the mouth.' PH. Hours: Monday to Thursday 12 noon to 2pm and 5.30pm till 11.30pm, Friday and Saturday till midnight, Sunday 1pm till 11pm.

BLACKPOOL

FAYEZ TANDOORI AND BALTI HOUSE
82, Victoria Road West, Cleveleys, Blackpool.   **01253 853562**
'Food as great as always. Popadoms, warm and crisp and a selection of
pickles. Maharajah Fort Special - superb, huge portion of off-the-bone
Chicken and Lamb Tandoori Masala served with excellent vegetable
Pullao Rice garnished with strips of tomato, cucumber, cress and coconut. The manager resembles a Pakistani George Michael!' BR. Hours: 12
noon to 2.30pm and 6pm till midnight, Friday and Saturday till 1am and
Sunday 12 noon till midnight. There is also a taxi food delivery service.

BURNLEY

AGRA
Horse Hill Farm, Hapton, Nr Burnley.   **01282 770113**
'A most impressive converted barn in the last place you'd expect to find
a restaurant, let alone an Indian. Someone has gone to long lengths to
create a rich and comfortable Indian atmosphere. Food was as good as
the interior. Chicken Tikka and Shammi Kebabs were perfect. Chicken
Tikka Makahan and Royal Bengal Special both excellent mopped up
with a large succulent Nan. Well recommended.' MB.

SHALAMAR   **CC DISCOUNT**
56, Church Street, Burnley.   **01282 34403**
A huge well reported restaurant seating 120 diners. Hours: Monday to
Thursday 5.30pm till 12.30am, Friday and Saturday 5pm till 1am, Sunday
5pm till 12.30am. Owner, A Majeed gives a discount . See page 288.

CARNFORTH

FAR PAVILION
25, Bye Pass Road, Bolton-le-Sands, Carnforth.   **01524 823316**
A restaurant seating 70. 'Difficult to fault this restaurant. Decor and
welcome second to none. Service efficient and courteous.' FS. 'Sampled
my usual bench mark meal of Shami Kebab, which was excellent,
followed by Chicken Madras, which was standard curry house.' MB.

CLITHEROE

DIL RAJ
7-9, Parsons Lane, Clitheroe.   **01200 27224**
A medium sized establishment, seating fifty-two diners. 'Has been a
favourite of ours for 3 years. Staff friendly and decor nice and clean. On-
view kitchen makes interesting feature. Sag Gosht and Gobhi Gosht are
particularly good as are Tandoori dishes. Home delivery service.' AP.

SHAH ANAZ
35-37, Whalley Road, Clitheroe.   **01200 24999**
A large restaurant seating 80 diners. 'Very polite staff. Very good food,
no complaints, except for the English Spring Chicken.' SP. **Serves you
right for ordering an English dish in an Indian restaurant**. Branches:
Agra, Horsehill Farm, Hapton, Nr Burnley. Akash, 198-200, Duckworth
Street, Darwen. Akash Takeaway, 87, Whalley Road, Accrington.

DARWEN

ANAZ
110-112, Duckworth Street, Darwen.   **01254 703357**
'We chose from the very extensive menu, Chicken Sambar, which is
tender juicy chicken cooked in a very spicy lentil sauce and absolutely
delicious. Lightest of Nans. First class.' MB.

TO FIND OUT HOW TO JOIN OUR DISCOUNT SCHEME SEE PAGE 288

SHANTEE
161-163, Duckworth Street, Darwen.   **01254 774335**
'Very good family run restaurant. Very friendly caring team. High
quality food at reasonable prices.' JN. Open seven days a week.

FLEETWOOD
MANZIL
3, Poulton Street, Fleetwood.   **01253 772580**
'Very small, thirty seats. Very clean, as you'd expect, and tastefully
decorated. Fresh and crisp Popadoms. Lamb Tikka Badami excellent,
mild, rich, lovely tender lamb in sauce with ground almonds and whole
peanuts. Chicken Jalfrezi - hot! Waiter brought in a karahi, crackling,
spluttering, smoking and steaming - the Jalfrezi that is not the waiter!
First rate Sag Paneer.' BR.

GREENHALGH
ASHIANA
Fleetwood Road, Greenhalgh.   **01253 836187**
'In a large imposing building, conveniently next to the pub. A smart
establishment to which no expense has been spared. Very comfortable
seating for eighty to ninety diners. Sampled my old favourites, Shammi
Kebabs, excellent. Chicken Madras, a little overspiced perhaps but
delicious and a first class Naan.' MB.

LANCASTER
NAWAAB
32, Parliament Street, Lancaster.   **01524 847488**
'Of exceptional quality, serving wonderful food.' DB.

SHABAB
23, Castle Hill, Lancaster.   **01524 388454**
'Situated in a fine and imposing building, in the area of Lancaster Castle.
The food was superb and very reasonable priced. Excellent Vegetable
Patra. Portions perfectly adequate.' DM.

LEYLAND
INDIAN COTTAGE   **CC DISCOUNT**
115, Towngate, Leyland.   **01772 457236**
Opened in 1987 by Rojob Ali. Seating forty six diners. Hours: 12 noon
to 2.30pm and 6pm till midnight. Friday and Saturday till 1am and
Sunday 4.30pm to midnight. Manager, Hir Miah has promised to give a
special deal to Curry Club members on Sundays. If you would like to dine
between 4.30pm and 8pm and you order two main courses, he will
charge for one. What a great deal that is, so go along and take up his offer.

MUGHAL
Thornlees, Wigan Road, Leyland.   **01772 622616**
'Very tastefully decorated with no-smoking area. Will go again and
again. Menu superb. Free popadoms with dishes of onion and spices.
Food of a very high standard.' KP.

VICEROY TANDOORI AND BALTI   **CC DISCOUNT**
3, Golden Hill Lane, Leyland.   **01772 621031**
A good Balti house serving all your old favourites in a restaurant seating
eighty diners. Proprietor, Makhlisur Rahman, who opened the Viceroy
in 1987, will give a discount to Curry Club members, see page 288 for
details. Hours: 12 noon to 2pm and 6pm till midnight.

FIND OUT HOW TO JOIN OUR DISCOUNT SCHEME ON PAGE 288

LONGRIDGE
POLASH
23-33, Berry Lane, Longridge.   **01772 785280**
'Tropical fish tank. Food excellent, Shammi Kebabs, Chicken Madras
and Pillao rice all first class. The Nan was a little on the crispy side.
Extensive menu with Balti dishes, 146 dishes and accompaniments.
There is something for everyone.' MB. Hours: 5.30pm till midnight,
Sunday 3pm till midnight. Fully licensed and air-conditioned. Sister
restaurant: Polash, 67-71a, Curzon Street, Burnley, tel: 01282 31112

THE

POLASH

AIR CONDITIONED
Tandoori Restaurant
(FULLY LICENSED)

Monday - Saturday:
5.30pm - 12 midnight
Sunday: 3.00pm - 12
midnight

**29/33, BERRY LANE, LONGRIDGE,
PRESTON, LANCASHIRE.**
Telephone: 01772 785280

Takeaways 10%
Discount

We will be happy to do outside catering for a large number of people
Orders over £25 delivered free of charge within 5 miles

MORECAMBE
MORECAMBE TANDOORI
47, Marine Road West, Morecambe.   **01524 832633**
A good standard restaurant seating forty-five diners. You will be happy
to find all your favourite tandooris and curries on the menu. Hours: 12
noon to 2pm and 6pm till midnight.

NELSON
MADHUBON
62, Manchester Road, Nelson.   **01282 691282**
Previously the Shabana. 'Service excellent, decor very pleasant. Food an
absolute delight. Lamb Sambar (very good lemon flavoured sauce),
Chicken Darjeeling (came with onion rings). Very hot towels and orange
slices finished off a great meal.' AS.

ORMSKIRK
PASSAGE TO INDIA
Moor Street, Ormskirk.   **01695 578979**
'Small, tastefully decorated impeccably clean restaurant serves a decent
range of dishes cooked and presented with above average care.' AGJ.

PRESTON
DILSHAD
121-122, Friargate, Preston.   **01772 250828**
'Has built itself a good reputation. Very modern and tastefully decorated
for around sixty people. Sampled Nargis Egg for starters, which was
excellent. Tandoori Mixed Grill again excellent, seved with a curry
sauce, which was a little over the top with garlic. I didn't mind, but it kept
my work colleagues well away.' MB.

NAAZ
Club Street, Bamber Bridge, Preston.   **01772 626695**
A large restaurant seating a hundred with two bars and alcove seating.
'Baltis first class.' MB. 'Large parties now assemble to enjoy the ambience,
especially the performance of the cheerful waiters doing 'wheelies' with
the serving trollies!' AE. 'Food second to none - specialities Hasina
Kebab and Chicken Tikka Shahee, but my favourite Chicken Tikka
followed by a Madras.' JW. Hours: Monday to Friday 12 noon to 2.30pm
and 6.30pm till 11.30pm. Saturday and Sunday 12 noon to midnight.
Other branch a takeaway: Naaz, School Lane, Bamber Bridge.

NEW KISMET   CC DISCOUNT
20, Derby Street, Preston.   **01772 251880**
A deceptively large restaurant seating seventy-six diners. Decorated in
pale blues. Seating arranged in partially screened off booths for four.
Colonial fans, suspended ceiling with spot lights, blue chintz Austrian
blinds and Indian paintings. 'Six of us from work decided to give it a try.
Although the food was on the whole excellent, the service was abysmal
and there were no plate warmers.' MB. Hours: 5pm to 3am, obviously
for insomniacs. Owner SN Ahmed, will be giving a discount to Curry
Club members, see page 288. Branch: Shiraz, 23, Berry Lane, Longridge.

PRACHEE
Preston New Road, Newton, Preston.   **01772 685896**
'Had a takeaway, service good. Chicken Madras, very hot and spicy,
very large juicy pieces of chicken.' JH.

SAGAR PREMIER
Clayton Brook Road, Bamber Bridge. Preston.   **01772 620200**
'Seats 120 people and is "THE BUSINESS". Very smart and very comfortable and gets very busy. Tried Kahri Chicken on waiter's recommendation, first class.' MB. Branches: Sagar, Blackrod and Sagar, Accrington.

ST ANNES ON SEA
MOGHUL   CC DISCOUNT
12, Orchard Road, St Annes-on-Sea.   **01253 712114**
A very sunny restaurant decorated in pastels, servi g fifty diners all the
usual Dansak, Madras, Vindaloo and Baltis and Karahis. Manager MD
Liaquat Ali has promised to give a discount to Curry Club members, see
page 288 for details. Branches: Sunam, 93-99, Redbank Road, Bispham,
Blackpool. Aliraj, 65, Topping Street, Blackpool.

WHALLEY
TRISHNA
25, King Street, Whalley.   **01254 822394**
'Very nice restaurant, bigger inside than it first appears (seats seventy-
two diners). Food absolutely gorgeous - could not fault it. Biggest Naan
bread ever seen! Polite service. On leaving, ladies get a flower, men a
lollipop.' S + P. Opening hours: 12 noon to 2.30pm and 6pm till midnight.

DAO SIAM AT THE JUDGE WALMSLEY
Billington, Whalley.   **01254 822172**
'Owners Paul and Buaphat Cryer have transformed the first floor of their
pub into a first class restaurant. In the comfortable lounge, you peruse
the extensive menu. Paul flits from table to table offering advice. When
you have made your choice, you are then taken upstairs, where your
starters await you. Famous Thai Green Curry Chicken was absolutely
fabulous, perfectly spiced, full of flavour. Gang Massaman, mild curry
fillet of beef cooked in coconut milk. We were recommended one fried
rice - but I think two would have been better - there's no accounting for
greed!! Open from Tuesday to Saturday evenings only.' MB.

LEICESTERSHIRE

HINCKLEY

LEEJA
93-95, Castle Street, Hinckley. **01455 616055**
'I have always been perfectly satisfied with the food and good friendly
service. Following the Brummie craze, they have opened a Balti room.
MAKE SURE THIS ONE IS IN THE NEXT GUIDE!!' MJG. Now it is!

LEICESTER

AKASH
159, London Road, Leicester. **0116 255 9030**
'No sooner than we were seated, the menus and free popadoms arrived
complete with obligatory mango chutney, onion salad and delicious red
sauce. Onion Bhaji very delicately spiced, excellent Pakuras (sic), crunchy
and more flavoursome. Service, was hotter than a Phall. Waiters were
quick, enthusiastic and very attentive.' LO1. 'We love the Akash.' J & PR.

BOBBY'S GUJARATI VEGETARIAN
154, Belgrave Road, Leicester. **0116 266 2448**
'Busy restaurant and takeaway. Cafeteria type atmosphere, you pay at
till. Unlicensed. Good breads, excellent service.' KF. 'Very good.' DG.

CURRY FEVER **TOP 100 - CC DISCOUNT**
139, Belgrave Road, Leicester. **0116 266 2941**
Opened in 1978, by Sunil and Anil Anand. (Relations of Madhu's
Brilliant and The Brilliant in Southall - see separate entries). Has recently
been extensively refurbished and now offers an exclusive atmosphere to
between sixty-five to seventy diners. 'Fantastic - Pili Chicken Masala - the
best.' GKG. You will find all your favourite curries and accompaniments
on their varied menu plus a few chef specialities. Karai (sic) and Balti
dishes are also featured. Hours: 12 noon to 2.30pm and 6pm till 11.30pm,
Friday and Saturday till midnight. Closed all day Mondays except on
Bank Holidays. We are glad you agreed that this is TOP 100 and have
pleasure keeping it there. Sunil Anand, will give a discount to Curry
Club members, see pages 288 for details. See page 173.

CURRY HOUSE **CC DISCOUNT**
63, London Road, Leicester. **0116 255 0688**
'Food absolutely superb served by very friendly waiters eager that you
enjoy. Sheek Kebabs served on a bed of fresh salad with fresh tangy
yoghurt sauce. Really excellent Chicken Vindaloo and Pilla Rice full of
flavour. Mandatory Nan was simply perfect.' MB. Chief Cashier, Mrs
Lipinski will give a discount to Curry Club members, see page 288.
Hours: 11am to 2pm and 6pm till 11.45pm. Branch: The Jewel in the
Crown, 98-100, Leicester Road, Wigston Magna, Leicester.

FRIENDS TANDOORI **TOP 100 - CC DISCOUNT**
41-45, Belgrave Road, Leicester. **0116 266 8809**
Opened in 1982 by TS Pabla. A massive restaurant seating one hundred
diners plus and with a separate lounge to have drinks and peruse the
menu, or to have coffee in after your meal. The interior is attractive with
its spiral staircase, enormous 'hookah' and works of art. The food from
the carefully selected menu is superb, we hear. And Oz Clark had a hand
in the excellent wine list. There are even 18 whiskeys. A caring restaurant
which deserves to be in our TOP 100. Manjit Pabla will give a discount
to Curry Club members, see page 288. Hours: Monday to Saturday 12
noon to 2.30pm and 6pm till 11.30pm, Sunday 6pm till 11.30pm.

GRAND DURBAR   CC DISCOUNT
294, Melton Road, Leicester.   **0116 266 6099**
Opened in 1988 and seating eighty diners. Free home delivery service
available within a five mile radius. Manager Kibria Wahid will offer a
discount to Curry Club members, see page 288. Hours: 12 noon to 2.30pm
and 6pm till midnight.

KHYBER   CC DISCOUNT
116, Melton Road, Leicester.   **0116 266 4842**
A small restaurant, seating forty, opened in 1984 which has built up a
good and reliable reputation for local customers. Owner, A Raval, will
give a discount to Curry Club members, see page 288 for details. Hours:
12 noon to 2pm and 6.30pm till 11.30pm.

NASEEB BALTI HOUSE   CC DISCOUNT
201, Melton Road, Leicester.   **0116 266 9047**
Opened in 1985 by Surinder Singh. A small and cosy restaurant seating
thirty four diners, so on weekends, be sure to book your table, so as not
to be disappointed. All the usual curries and Baltis on the standard curry
house menu. And the infamous, 'Tropical Balti' - chicken, meat and
prawns. Also a vegetarian version - chana, saag, mushroom and corn -
sounds delicious. Mr Singh will give a discount to Curry Club members,
see page 288. Hours: 6pm to 1am, seven days a week.

SHARMILEE VEGETARIAN   CC DISCOUNT
71-73, Belgrave Road, Leicester.   **0116 2 61 0503**
Opened way back in 1973 by Gosh brothers. Hours: Tuesday to Thursday, 12 noon to 2.30pm and 6pm till 9pm, Friday, Saturday and Sunday
12 noon to 9pm. Manager, LK Goswami will give a discount to Curry
Club members, see page 288.

SUNAR GOW
44b, Main Street, Broughton Astley, Leicester.   **01455 285900**
Managing owner, Harun Miah runs a sixty-two seater restaurant, serving all the usual curries. Hours: 5.30pm till midnight.

LOUGHBOROUGH
AMBER TANDOORI
5a, High Street, Loughborough.   **01509 215754**
'Decor is pleasant and clean. Food and service always good and prompt.'
MG. Hours: 12 noon to 2.30pm and 5.30pm till 12.30am. Till 1.30am on
Friday and Saturday evenings.

MELTON MOWBRAY
PARI TANDOORI   CC DISCOUNT
38, Leicester Street, Melton Mowbray.   **01664 410554**
Home delivery service available. Menu offers all the usual curries,
Tandooris and Baltis. Babul Ali will give a discount to Curry Club
members, see page 288. Hours: 6pm till midnight.

OUR TOP 100 RESTAURANTS ARE LISTED ON PAGES 35 AND 36.

DO YOU AGREE WITH OUR LIST OR DO HAVE YOU YOUR OWN

FAVOURITE(S) WHICH YOU THINK SHOULD BE NOMINATED.

LET US KNOW YOU VIEWS PLEASE. WRITE TO THE EDITOR.

LINCOLNSHIRE

BOSTON

STAR OF INDIA   TOP 100 - CC DISCOUNT
110-112, West Street, Boston.   01205 360558

Owned by Tanvir Hussain and seats fifty-two diners. He tells us that the
toilets have been refurbished and retiled, they used to have roller towels
but now they have installed hand-dryers. And his prices have not
changed, and Mr Hussain has promised to give a discount to Curry Club
members at his quieter times, see pages 288 for details, what a great deal.
'Very pleasant decor, typical Indian restaurant style enhanced by large
numbers of cotton flowers. Service attentive but not intrusive. Balti
Chicken was quite delicious. Keema Nan was piping hot and filled with
ample quantity of minced meat. Highly recommended.' MS-R. 'Best
ever Tandoori Chicken starter followed by superb Dhansak.' AG.
Opening hours: 12 noon to 2.30pm and 6pm till midnight. Repeated
praise keeps the Star in our TOP 100. Other branches which are both
takeaways and fast food outlets: Chilli Master, 2, Red Lion Street,
Stamford, Lincs and Chilli Masters, 11, Winsover Road, Spalding, Lincs.

BOURNE

PRINCE OF KASHMIR   CC DISCOUNT
8, Abbey Road, Bourne.   01778 393959

Seats 44 and serves reliable favourites such as Dansak (sic), Biriany (sic),
Malayan, Koorma (sic) and Rogon (sic). Dial-a-curry takeaway service
with free delivery within 10 miles. On the menu I noticed a chilli Nan!
Manager, A Arshad will give a discount to Curry Club members, see
page 288 . Hours: 5.30to midnight, Friday and Saturday to 12.30am.
Branch: Kashmir Balti House, Lincoln Road, Peterborough, Cambs.

LINCOLN

RAJ DOUTH
7, Eastgate, Lincoln.   **01522 548377**
'Quality of the food could not be faulted but the portions were a touch on the small side. Interesting starter was Pandur - stuffed aubergine.' SA.

LOUTH

HELAL
1, Mercer Row, Louth.   **01507 607960**
Well established (1975) huge (100 seats) restaurant. 'An attractive restaurant if rather dimly lit. Friendly service. Meal was very good indeed. Each dish had its own characteristics with delicious gravies. Chicken Tikka Dopiaza was outstanding.' DCC. 'Good value.' CP.

THE AGRA

99, East Road,
Sleaford, Lincolnshire.
NG34 7EH

To book your table telephone:
01529 414162

SLEAFORD

AGRA   **CC DISCOUNT**
99, East Road, Sleaford.   **01529 414162**
'This is a very fine curry house, offering a vast choice and they will even cook what you want. Chef specialities are both good value and nice to see, Chicken Tikka Massala and Madras are very good.' RT. Managing Director, Leeneth Karim, has promised to give a discount to Curry Club members , see page 288. 12 noon to 2.30pm and 5.30pm to 11.30pm.

SPALDING

CHILLI MASTERS
11, Winsover Road, Spalding.   **01775 762221**
A Hot and Spicy Restaurant, offering Pizza, (make your own, toppings 45p and 55p each - garlic and chilli free!!) Curry, Balti, Tandoori, Doner Kebabs, Southern Fried Chicken and Burgers. Fast and free delivery service available ilocally Hours: 5pm to 1am, Friday & Saturday till 3am. Branch at 2 Red Lion St, Stamford.

SHAHEEN
2, Pinchbeck Road, Spalding.   **01775 767852**
'Quantities vary from adequate to very generous and the quality very good. Coffee pot is never ending and we recommend a visit.' MS.

STAMFORD

RAJ OF INDIA   **CC DISCOUNT**
2, All Saints Street, Stamford.   **01780 53556**
'Excellent evening out, good and attentive service. Nicely decorated and furnished. Food well presented, hot and good portions. Lamb Tikka Massala particularly good.' JAG. Owner Rohom Ali offers a discount to CC members, see page 288. Hours: 12 noon to 3pm and 6pm to midnight.

GREATER MANCHESTER

Although Greater Manchester was introduced as a county in 1965, it is still disregarded by many of its residents who prefer to refer to the counties which Greater Manchester gobbled up eg: parts of Lancashire and Cheshire. We have adhered strictly to the official current Greater Manchester territory for town locations in this guide.

ALTRINCHAM

MUGHAL
86, Park Road, Timperley, Altrincham.

CC DISCOUNT
0161 973 4513

The popular Tondori Royale became the Mughal in 1994 and remains just as popular. Co-owner M Hoque will give a discount to Curry Club member, see page 288 Hours: 5pm till 12am. Branch: Tondori Royale, 682-84, Burnage Lane, Manchester. M19.

SHERE KHAN
Old Market Place, Altrincham.
0161 926 8777

'Situated next to the Orange Tree Pub (CAMRA award winner). An upmarket restaurant matched by upmarket prices. Restaurant on two floors. Dhansak sauce rich and creamy, Chappatis nice and large.' SN.

ASHTON-UNDER-LYNE

INDIAN OCEAN
83, Stamford Street East.
0161 343 3343

'A home made taste to the food. What really made the place was the sizeable and beautiful room they called the wine bar with extensive bar counters, good beer and satellite TV.' RH. Hours: 12 noon to 2.30pm and 5pm till 11pm. Sundays 4pm till 10.30pm only. Free delivery service.

JALAL-ABAD
24-26, Cotton Street East.
0161 343 4844

'Sizeable portions. Quality of food was outstanding. A small restaurant comfortable and tastefully decorated.' CB. Hours: Monday to Saturday 12 noon to 2.30pm. Sunday Family lunch 12 noon to 5pm. Monday to Thursday 5pm to 11.30pm. Friday, Saturday, Sunday 12 to midnight.

BOLTON

AMIR
2, Broadgate, Ladybridge, Bolton.
01204 660525

'A large restaurant seating 100 people. Shammi Kebabs were a real treat, good quality ground lamb, expertly spiced. Chicken Samba was well spiced and absolutely full of flavour to the last bite. Naan bread fresh and moist. Parking no problem.' MB.

ANAZ TAKEAWAY
138, St Helens Road, Bolton.
01204 660114

'The shop is absolutely spotless, service first class and I was offered a fresh cup of coffee whilst I waited. Very extensive menu, Shami Kebab, Chicken Madras rice and chips with Nan. All done perfectly. Only fault no yoghurt sauce.' MB.

LEENA
131-133, Bradshawgate, Bolton
01204 383255

'Gets rave reviews locally. Called in for Sunday lunch. Shami Kebab and Onion Bhajee for starters, Kebabs made the text book way with lentils, really tasty. Lamb Rogan Josh, first class, full of flavour, peppers, pimentos and tomatoes in a rich creamy sauce - excellent!!' MB.

SUNAR GAW   CC DISCOUNT
310, Manchester Road, Bolton.   01204 364915
Formerly Taj Mahal. Sunar Gaw means Golden Village. Opened in 1992
by Abdul Shahid and Abdul Hannan, the former is the manager front of
house, the latter chef behind the scenes. Seats forty-four diners, so do
book for weekends. Hours: 5.30pm till midnight. Abdul Shahid has
promised to give a discount to Curry Club members, see page 288.

BURY

TANDOORI NIGHTS
135, Rochdale Road, Bury.   0161 761 6224
'This little takeaway is brilliant. You can see them cooking the food - open
counter - very friendly and free chutney.' PJ. Hours: 5.30pm to 11.20pm,
Friday and Saturday till 12.30am and Sunday 4pm till 11pm.

CHEADLE

ALIGARH
202, Wilmslow Road, Heald Green, Cheadle.   0161 436 8809
'Another little gem. Worth going just for the domed ceiling. The food
ain't bad either. Shami Kebab (what else) a little dry but none the less very
tasty. Chicken Madras (what else) was also good.' MB. 'Nice restaurant,
very well decorated, clean. Good service from well dressed waiters.
Kebab Puri and Chicken Tikka starters excellent. Dhal the worst one I've
had. I shall return.' PH.

DUKINFIELD

INDIA COTTAGE
Foundry Street, Dukinfield.   0161 343 5961
'A huge restaurant seating 120 and it could take more. Situated in a
modern brick building, previously a nightclub. Roomy waiting area near
the bar with large bowls of Bombay Mix. Service excellent. Food
excellent, satisfied with portions, Garlic Chicken particularly good.' BG.
'Best Lamb Tikka ever. Lal Qila is delicious. Lamb Tikka Dupiaza is
superb! For the fire-eaters try the Jalfrezi - full of green chillies and ginger
- mind blowing! Quantities huge, one meal could be enough for two.' DP.

MANCHESTER

Manchester and its large suburbs have recently been re-post coded. For
the purpose of this guide we have put all M postcodes into Manchester
and have divided the area into Central and East, South, West and North,
using major roads as arbitrary boundaries.

MANCHESTER CENTRAL M1 TO M4

ASHOKA   TOP 100
Basil House, 105, Portland Street, Manchester. M1.   0161 228 7550
A massive restaurant seating 100. 'After initially viewing the menu my
impression was that the starters were slightly expensive - however this
changed as the food arrived - twice the quantity expected! All dishes
sampled were very tasty. Pleasant relaxed atmosphere and surroundings. Definitely worth a visit.' MB. 'Chicken Jalfrezi not as hot as I prefer
it to be but never-the-less excellently prepared. Lamb Moghlai very rich
but mild decorated with edible silver.' SPH. 'I chose to eat here based on
the glowing report in the GCG and I was not disappointed. It's an
impressive place all round - from the decor and general ambience to the
food. Free Popadoms and chutney on the table and nibbles while I
studied the menu. Chicken Curry absolutely superb, mild, rich and
aromatic, like an extremely good Korma. Pullao Rice fabulous and
fragrant.' BR. 'Totally impressed by the Indian atmosphere that oozed
from every corner. Essential Indian background music and Indian

'Objects of Art' adorn alcoves and walls. Waiters are dressed in traditional Indian costume and very polite and attentive. All food absolutely full of the most delicious flavours. Really succulent, juicy Sheek Kebab. Chicken Masala and Vegetable Curry both wonderfully hot and spicy with perfect Pillau Rice. Deserves all the accolade that it receives.' MB. And one is that it remains in our TOP 100. Hours: 12.30pm to 2.30pm and 5.30pm till 11.30pm. Not open for lunch on Sundays.

AL KHAYYAM
47, Rochdale Road, Manchester. M4.   **0161 839 0601**
'Very comfortable and smacks of class. First class standard curry house food. Service very friendly and attentive.' MB. 'An excellent restaurant with quick friendly service. Tandoori Mixed starter is a very substantial meal. Shahi Passanda, Chicken Jalfrezi and Buttered Chicken were rich and satisfying. Prices are higher but worth every penny.' BHB.

BALTI
63, Bridge Street, Manchester. M3.   **0161 832 9393**
Formerly Peppers. We have received mixed reports on this restaurant, since the spread of the Balti. 'Baltis tasty but could have done with more lamb and prawns. Popadoms and Naan excellent. Staff friendly, initial service good but took ages to pay the bill.' PT.

GAYLORD   CC DISCOUNT
Amethyst House, Spring Gardens, Manchester. M2.   0161 832 6037
'I looked at my watch it was 12.45pm, sudden pain flashed through my stomach, I needed a fix and fast. I looked round to get my bearings I was on Brown Street. I looked up there was a street sign pointing to Gaylord. Sweat started to ooze from my forehead running down my face in long cool riverlets, I staggered up the short street and into Marriots Court; I could see the entrance, would I make? The pain was worse so I quickened my stride and into the restaurant area. I was aware of a person stood next to the bar at the top of the stairs; I looked up, God I thought, I must be mad, I'm hallucinating, Henry Kissinger has come to meet me.
"Are you OK Sir?" a voice enquired.
"Henry." I said, "quick I need a fix."
"Henry! I'm not Henry! I'm Raman Kapoor the manager. I'll show your seat, Sir. You have got it bad...."
He hurried off to return a few minutes later with a fresh Popadom and a tray full of the most wonderful chutney you've ever tasted. This was followed in no time at all by a sizzling Sheek Kebab, the taste of which was out of this world. Next I sampled from the regular menu a dish of Chilli Chicken again the taste was unbelievable, this was accompanied with Pillau Rice and a fresh Nan which I watched the Chef prepare through the glass wall into the kitchen.
Suitably fixed I found myself back on the street. How lucky we are having one of the best restaurants in the country right here in Manchester.' MB. Your remarkable hallucinatory report is one among many praising the Gaylord. Mr R Kapoor will give a discount to Curry Club members, see page 288. Recent health problem demoted this restaurant from our TOP 100, but we believe it should be retained in the Guide.

KAILASH
34, Charlotte Street, Manchester. M1.   **0161 236 6624**
Nepalese restaurant situated in the basement. 'As you descend the steps you are met with the most wonderful spicy smells imaginable. Tandoori Fish for starters, the only way to eat fish as far as I'm concerned. Specialities of the house include Rogan Josh and Jalfrezi which are first class. Perfect rice and bread. Parking a nightmare as this restaurant is in Chinatown.' MB.

TO FIND OUT HOW TO JOIN OUR DISCOUNT SCHEME SEE PAGE 288

KIEZMAT
25-29, Great Ducie Street, Manchester. M3.   **0161 834 1088**
'A very spacious restaurant, upmarket with comfortable seating. Food is good standard curry house stuff. All the staff from the old Kismet have moved to this establishment.' MB.

RAJDOOT   **TOP 100 - CC DISCOUNT**
Carlton House, 18, Albert Square, Manchester. M2.   **0161 834 2176**
'Still up there amongst the very best. Exceptionally well presented and comfortable. The stools in the waiting area may be uncomfortable for tall people, but this would soon be forgotten whilst you dip into bowls of fresh Bombay Mix. Extensive menu with emphasis being on Moghul cuisine. No standard curry but what the hell, who needs it with food like this. Shish Kebab excellent, Lamb Rogan Josh first class, really tasty, kept me going.' MB. The Rajdoot is the creation of architect Des Sharda who also owns the Rajdoot in Bristol, Birmingham and Dublin. The Rajdoot is noticeable for its authentic elegant and exotic atmosphere, indeed it was one of the first to present itself in an upmarket and attractive way, and the architect's training shows with the Indian arts and crafts, colour styles and general layout. This restaurant along with the other three Rajdoots in this group offer Curry Club members a discount. See page 288. We are happy to keep this restaurant in our TOP 100 .

MANCHESTER EAST
Including: M11 - M31, M18, M34, M35, M40, M43.

LA MIRAGE TANDOORI
67-69, Kenyon Lane, Moston. M40.   **0161 681 9373**
After being a regular customer here for many years and never been disappointed, I feel La Mirage should be given recognition for its excellent curries and tandoori dishes. The decor is not brilliant, but the meals, service and prices are. The best Madras in Manchester.' BT.

MANCHESTER SOUTH
Including: M14 - M16, M19 - M13, M32, M33.

GREAT KATHMANDU
140, Burton Road, West Didsbury. M20.   **0161 434 6413**
'Service excellent is bordering somewhat on the irritational side, I was asked by at least five waiters whether I wanted a drink or any popadoms to which I answered that I had ordered a pint of lager when I came in. I still had to ask for it again after all that. I chose from a fairly extensive menu, Shami Kebabs which were excellent this followed by, yes, you've guessed it, Chicken Madras (for a change) which was really tasty as was the Pillao rice. Nan was fresh, light and extremely big. 'MB.

KHANDOKER   **CC DISCOUNT**
812, Kingsway, East Didsbury. M20.   **0161 428 4687**
An evenings only establishment 5pm till 12.30am, seating sixty. Popular, it seems with students and locals. Proprietor, Mr Khandoker Sufi Miah has promised to give a discount to Curry Club members, see page 288.

SONAGRA
2691, Barlow Moor Road, Chorlton-cum-Hardy. M21.   0161 861 0334
'Our local is an absolute jewel! You are greeted with old world charm and made to feel special. Tastefully decorated. Food is divine .' VH.

TONDORI ROYALE
628/9, Burnage Lane, Burnage. M19.   **0161 432 0930**
'It was packed! It is not difficult to work out why when you taste the cuisine. Atmosphere is electric and food well worth the 40 mile trip.' MB.

WILMSLOW ROAD RUSHOLME - M14

Rusholme is Manchester's main Asian area and its Wilmslow Road is the
equivalent of Birmingham's Bristol Road. Wilmslow Road extends for
nearly 6 miles south from Manchester Centre. Whilst it does not have the
glamour of Southall, or the intensity of Bradford, there are a good many
cheap Indian snack, sweet and curry houses. Here are some of your
favourites:

EASTERN TOUCH
76, Wilmslow Road, Rusholme. M14.　　　　　　　　**0161 224 5665**

'My favourite. Lino floor and glass topped tables - more a cafe really.
Warm Popadoms, chutney and sauces are brought to the table immediately - free to all diners. Standard but comprehensive menu. Kebabs
cooked freshly over charcoal in the corner of the restaurant, piping hot,
highly spiced and juicy served with a large plate of tomatoes, onion and
lettuce. Chicken Madras, prime quality, tender and succulent, very hot,
sauce is rich and fiery, perfect for mopping up with a meaty Keema Nan
Not licensed, I bring my own.' PW.

NAWAB
100, Wilmslow Road, Rusholme. M14.　　　　　　　**0161 225 9616**

'The food is good and the service for drinks is fair. Certainly good value
for money.' MB.

SANAM SWEET HOUSE　　　　　　　　　　**CC DISCOUNT**
145-151, Wilmslow Road, Rusholme. M14.　　　　　**0161 224 8824**

A humungus restaurant seating 160 plus 200 for function room. So
popular locally that it's often full with queues as well. Manager AQ
Akhtar will give a discount to Curry Club members, at his quieter times,
see page 288. Hours: Noon to midnight. Branch: Abduls, 121, Wilmslow
Road, Rusholme; 298, Oxford Road and 318, Wilmslow Road, Fallowfield.

SANAM TAKEAWAY
167, Wilmslow Road, Rusholme. M14.　　　　　　　**0161 257 3557**

'More of a kebab style takeaway than a restaurant, serving only starters.
Easily missed as the frontage covers no more than about ten feet. Dingy
decor and formica tables belie the standard of the food. Samosas both
meat and vegetable are the best I've ever eaten. Shikh Kebabs (three to
a portion) are superb. All served on a metal dish with no cutlery but a
warm, large and deliciously moist Nan. Not the place to take a girlfriend
but a must for those late nights out with the boys.' DB.

SANAM
215, Wilmslow Road, Rusholme. M14.　　　　　　　**0161 224 8570**

On two levels. The waiter could have done with a clean shirt but apart
from that the place was spotless. You can see your meals being cooked
in the open kitchen. The food is brilliant, Popadoms were fresh and crisp
and came with a tray of various onions and chutneys. Colleague swore
blind he had the best Chicken Tikka Masala. Not licensed.' MB.

SANGAM
13-15, Wilmslow Road, Rusholme. M14.　　　　　　**0161 257 3922**

'Upmarket, bright and clean. Licensed. Lamb Chop Tikka, one of the best
and most filling starters I have had. Will visit again.' RC.

SHERE KHAN
52, Wilmslow Road, Rusholme. M14.　　　　　　　**0161 256 2624**

Opened in 1987 and has built up a regular clientele in this 'Curry Golden
Mile'. Fully licensed and air conditioned. Hours: 12 noon to 12 midnight.
Branches: Mister Khan, 36, Wilmslow Road, Rusholme and Shere Khan,
9-10, Old Market Place, Altrincham.

SHEZAN
119, Wilmslow Road, Rusholme. M14.   **0161 224 8168**
A massive restaurant seating 120 diners. 'Yet another brilliant and fairly
cheap restaurant. Service was a little on the slow side, but the food was
quite superb.' MB. Owner Mr Masued Ahmed has promised to give a
discount to Curry Club members, see page 288. Hours: 12 noon and 1am.

TABAK
199-201, Wilmslow Road, Rusholme. M14.   **0161 257 3890**
'Another of those little gems. A large restaurant seating over 200 people.
Karahi Nawabi Bataire, quails. Afghanibashyan, tender juicy lamb chop
marinated in cream, spices and barbequed - not to be missed.' MB.

TANDOORI KITCHEN
131-133, Wilmslow Road, Rusholme. M14.   **0161 224 2329**
'Not licensed, no objection to bringing your own Glass topped tables.
Shamee Kebab made with lentils, served with plenty of salad and
chutney. Chicken Madras very tasty and, plenty of it. Service good.' MB.

MANCHESTER WEST
Including: M5 - M7 Salford, M27 - M31, M38, M41, M44, M46.

CADISHEAD M44
SUNDORBON
40, Liverpool Road, Cadishead. M44.   **0161 775 2812**
Formerly Mohti Mahal. A large restaurant seating eighty diners. Hours:
6pm till 12.30am. Branch: Asha Takeaway, 151, Laird Street, Birkenhead.

ECCLES M30
PASSAGE TO INDIA   **CC DISCOUNT**
168, Monton Road, Monton, Eccles. M30.   **0161 787 7546**
Opening hours: 12 noon to 11.30pm. Opened in 1988 by M Hassan
Choudhury and H Uddin, a large establishment seating ninety diners.
Mr Choudhury has promised to give a discount to Curry Club members,
see page 288. Branch: Gate of India, Swinton.

URMSTON M41
STANDARD
Higher Road, Urmston. M41.   **0161 748 2806**
'A largish restaurant seating seventy six diners. 'Interior is well above
average - not standard. Comfortable seating. Service I received was
beyond reproach, nothing was too much trouble. Sheek Kebab must rate
as the biggest I've ever had and one of the tastiest. Portions were so large
that it would have been impossible to eat it all in one session, so I took half
home with me. Restaurant prepares its own mango chutney, which they
sell along with a variety of pickles, chutneys and curry pastes. Nothing
is standard about this restaurant. Well worth a visit.' MB. Hours: 12
noon to 2pm and 5.30pm till 11.30pm.

MANCHESTER NORTH
Including M8, M9, M24 Middleton, M25 Prestwich and M26 Radcliffe.

MIDDLETON M24
RHODES TANDOORI TAKEAWAY
606, Manchester Old Road, Rhodes, Middleton. M24.   0161 655 3904
'Very friendly. Chicken Malaya enjoyed as well as the Bhindi Bhaji which
was well sized with lots of okra.' SN & RA. Hours: 4pm till 12 midnight
every day. Branch: Lees Tandoori, 54, High Street, Lees, Oldham.

PRESTWICH M25
GARDEN OF INDIA
411, Bury Old Road, Prestwich. M25.

CC DISCOUNT
0161 773 7784

Opened in 1984 by Hafizur Rahman. An88seat restaurant. Chicken Sambar, very reminiscent of a Dhansak, but not as sweet, which was a very pleasant change and one which I shall look out for again. Chicken Paneer met with total approval.' SN & RA. 'Have visited several times and have always found it quite acceptable.' MB. Manager, Rony Rahman will give a discount to Curry Club members, see page 288. Hours: 12 noon to 2.30pm and 6pm till 11.30pm.

WHITEFIELD M25
DWATS TAKEAWAY
184, Bury New Road, Whitefield. M25.

0161 796 5976

Takeaway only establishment. 'Shami Kebabs best in the UK. Despite many hours of grilling (is that a joke Mike!) for the recipes to no avail, and many hours experimenting in my own kitchen I'm afraid that the unique flavour is just out of reach. Same applies to their curries, a unique flavour and consistent. Baltis first class.' MB.

FORTS OF INDIA
7-11, Radcliffe New Road, Whitefield. M25.

CC DISCOUNT
0161 766 5873

Opened by Abdul Haris and seating seventy diners and twenty in the lounge. 'Decor is very much up market. Staff dressed in traditional costume. Cheap it is not, but never-the-less the food is absolutely wonderful and well worth the cost. Parking is not a problem.' MB. Mr Haris will give a discount to Curry Club members, see page 288. Hours: 12 noon to 2.30pm and 6pm till 11pm, Sunday 1pm till 11pm.

KIPLINGS INDIA
24, Elm Square, Bury New Road, Whitefield. M25.

0161 796 0557

A very impressive upmarket restaurant from the outside, plate glass windows with Austrian blinds. Inside, white linen, Chippendale style chairs, large bar and plants hanging from suspended ceilings. 'Menu is quite extensive with all the favourites and a selection of Balti dishes - I think they are all buying Pat's BALTI CURRY COOKBOOK. Extremely tasty and delicately spiced Shish Kebab followed by a Chicken Madras - what else! - which for me personally was perfect as I like the bite. Service could have been a little smoother and quicker. If you are looking for somewhere to celebrate something special, then look no further.' MB.

RADCLIFFE M26
ALISHAN
21-23, Church Street, Radcliffe. M26.

0161 725 9910

'Madras, one of the best. This little 40 seater restaurant continues to get good reports locally, and not without good reason. We've been here several times and have yet to fault it. Chicken Sambar, first class.' MB.

RADCLIFFE CHARCOAL TANDOORI
Blackburn Street, Radcliffe. M26.

0161 723 4870

'Very smart, upmarket restaurant with alcoves . Bar has large ornamental fish tank built in. Restaurant area is . Chicken Madras and Pullao Rice were perfect, so were the Chappatis. Cheerful and efficient service.' MB.

TASTE OF INDIA TAKEAWAY
74, Water Street, Radcliffe. M26.

CC DISCOUNT
0161 725 9129

'Yet another cheap and handy takeaway restaurant in my home town. Not that I'm complaining, it's just that I can't resist popping in to try them all out. A standard curry house, .' MB. Proprietor, Budur Miah will give a discount , see page 288. Hours: 5to midnight, Friday / Saturday till 1am.

OLDHAM

LIGHT OF BENGAL   **CC DISCOUNT**
114, Union Street, Oldham.   **0161 624 4600**
Large restaurant seating 80. Opened in 1980, by Abdul Hannan who is also front of house manager, to see that things go smoothly. Mr Hannan has promised to give a discount to Curry Club members, see page 288. Hours: Sunday to Thursday 5.30pm to1am. Friday and Saturday , till 1.30am. Branch: Bengal Brasserie, 31/33, Milnrow Road, Shaw, Oldham.

PANAHAR TANDOORI
175, Park Road, Oldham.   **0161 773 7784**
'Service excellent in small, intimate restaurant. Specialities, particularly the Lamb Pasanda, are wonderful - dip your Naan!. JH.

RAMSBOTTOM Known to residents as 'Rammy.'

EASTERN EYE
38, Bolton Street, Ramsbottom.   **01706 823268**
'Have dined here on many occasions and have never had a bad meal yet, indeed the only complaint is the restaurant is quite small with low ceilings which allow it to get a little warm when it gets busy. Though license, you may be asked to visit the pub over the road whilst your table is cleared and prepared. Chicken Tikka absolutely perfect. ' MB.

MOGHUL DYNASTY   **TOP 100**
51, Bolton Street, Ramsbottom.   **01706 821510**
'Superb, high ceilings, pillars and hanging baskets. Friendly attentive service. First class food, generous amounts.' JN. 'Chilli Massala Tandoori Chicken was out of this world, absolutely full of the most wonderful flavour. Washed down with wonderful Cobra lager.' MB. Just for MB, as he constantly tells us its **the best**, we give it our Top 100 award.

TANDOORI GHAR

INDIAN CUISINE

64, Drake Street, Rochdale,
Greater Manchester. OL16 1PA

For Reservations: 01706 46296

ROCHDALE

TANDOORI GHAR
64, Drake Street, Rochdale.   **01706 46296**
Serving all the usual curries plus Balti dishes. 'Cosy comfortable nothing out of the ordinary but pleasant. Chicken Madras superbly spiced.' MB. Hours: 12 noon to 2pm and 6pm till midnight, Friday and Saturday 6pm till 2.30am. Takeaway meals 15% discount before 8pm, 10% after 8pm.

STOCKPORT

ATITHI TAKEAWAY
43, London Road South, Poynton, Stockport.   **01625 858090**
'Open kitchens, very clean. Free coffee and Mix while waiting. Quality consistent and generous. Chicken Tikka Sambar v. good. For garlic / chilli lovers - North IndianGarlic Chicken.' EF. Hours: 4. till 11pm.

KUSHOOM COLY
6, Shaw Road, Heaton Moor, Stockport.   **0161 432 9841**
'I have never heard any Indian music in this place, usually Glen Miller or similar. However, the food is plentiful and if you like garlic then this is the place to go.' GC. 'Simple decor. Menu features the usual range of favourites. Jalfrezi coked the way I prefer it, very spicy and liberal use of green chillies.' PH. Hours: 6pm till 2am. Home delivery service.

MARPLE MASSALLA   CC DISCOUNT
105, Stockport Road, Marple, Stockport.   **0161 427 2558**
Formerly Mysore, a long standing haunt under this name since 1994. Manager, A Choudhury will give a discount to Curry Club members, see page 288. Hours: 5pm till 11.30pm, Friday and Saturday till midnight.

MEGHNA INDIAN   CC DISCOUNT
55, Dairyground Road, Bramhall, Stockport.   **0161 440 9464**
Opened in 1989 by Mohammed Abdul Ashik, who can be found managing front of house in this sixty seater restaurant, making sure things run smoothly for all you curryholics. Mr Ashik will give a discount to Curry Club members, see page 288. Hours: 5pm till 11.30pm, Sundays 3pm till 11.30pm. 10% discount on takeaway meals.

PHOOLBAGH   CC DISCOUNT
345, Edgeley Road, Cheadle Heath, Stockport.   **0161 427 3496**
Gous Miah opened this restaurant in 1977, quite some time ago now, so he has proven himself in running a good competent restaurant offering all your favourite curries and a few specialities thrown in for the more adventurous. But be sure to book for weekends as it is a small restaurant seating only forty. Mr Miah has promised to give a discount to Curry Club members, see page 288. Hours: 6pm till 1am.

ROMILEY TANDOORI
6-7, The Precinct, Romiley, Stockport.   **0161 430 3774**
'A very plush establishment, clean and serves excellent food. Shami Kebab very tasty served with red mango chutney and yoghurt sauce. Mild but tasty Chicken Madras. Service polite and attentive.' MB.

TANDOORI PARLOUR
115, Buxton Road, Heaviley, Stockport.   **0161 483 9112**
'A cosy restaurant seating about forty-eight diners. Choose from a very extensive menu all the usual standard curry house cuisine with one or two surprises thrown in, such as Malayan and Ceylonese dishes. Service polite and attentive. Parking not a problem. Fair prices.' MB.

WIGAN
AJMEER MANZIL   CC DISCOUNT
76, Market Street, Wigan.   **01942 35910**
Opened in 1970 by G Uddin and seats seventy-two diners. A realiable restaurant serving good reliable curries, Baltis and Korais with all your favourite accompaniments. An unusual bread on the menu - Pyaaz Puri - fried, thin bread with spicy onion. Mr Uddin, will give a discount to Curry Club members, see page 288. Hours: 5pm till 1am. Branch: Bombay Duck Takeaway, 50, Frog Lane, Wigan. and Taste of Bengal, 11, High Street, Standish, Wigan.

SAMUNDAR   CC DISCOUNT
81, High Street, Golborne, Wigan.   **01942 717730**
Evening hours only (5.30pm to Midnight). Standard competent formula curries from chef Bashir Uddin at Feroze Ali's restaurant, we hear, and they give discounts to Curry Club members, see page 288.

MERSEYSIDE

FORMBY

JEWEL IN THE CROWN
126-128, Church Road, Formby.   **01704 873198**
'We feel privileged to have such a fine curry house so close. We have never been disappointed.' DG. Hours: 12 noon to 2pm and 5.30pm till midnight. Friday and Saturday till 12.30am, Sunday 6pm till midnight.

LIVERPOOL

ALLERTON TANDOORI   **CC DISCOUNT**
79, Allerton Road, Liverpool.   **0151 722 1940**
Opened in 1985 by Mr A Rahman and seating sixty-two diners. In those ten years, he has built up a good trade, serving the locals reliably good curries with all their favourite accompaniments. He has also promised to give a discount to Curry Club members, see page 288. Minimum charge £7.50. Hours: 5.30pm till 1am.

JEWEL OF INDIA   **CC DISCOUNT**
9-11, Allerton Road, Woolton, Liverpool.   **0151 421 1264**
Very popular establishment, which though newish, knows the business of curry. Owner, Mr D Miah has promised to give a discount to Curry Club members, see page 288. Hours: 12 noon to 2pm and 5.30pm till midnight.

KOHINOOR   **CC DISCOUNT**
62, South Road, Waterloo, Liverpool.   **0151 928 6788**
A new restaurant on the curry scene. Opened last year by Mashood
Uddin and Andrew Davis. Mr Uddin will be found front of house,
making sure his new venture runs smoothly and has promised to give a
discount to Curry Club members, see page 288. Hours: 5pm till midnight, Friday and Saturday till 2am.

TAJ MAHAL
57, South Road, Waterloo, Liverpool.   **0151 928 7050**
'Superb restaurant - noted as being one of the best in north Liverpool.
Pleasant decor and surroundings though the background music can be
rather intrusive at times. Service rather slow but the food makes up for
it.' PS. 'Popadoms were very light and crispy. Vegetarian Thali very
good.' GF. Hours: 12 noon to 2.30pm and 5.30pm till midnight. Friday
and Saturday 2am. Sunday 2pm till 1am.

WIRRAL

HESWALL TANDOORI
52, Pensby Road, Heswall, Wirral.   **0151 342 8614**
A cosy establishment seating only thirty-two diners. Essential to book on
Friday and Saturday nights. 'Standards of this small restaurant remain
consistently high. Dishes have a distinctive taste and one can always be
sure of enjoyable food and attentive service.' Dr PAWW. Hours: Sunday
to Thursday 6pm till 11.30pm. Friday and Saturday 5.30pm till midnight.

KAYUM
225, Seabank Road, New Brighton, Wirral.   **0151 691 1919**
'Asked the waiter to chose the starters, we couldn't make up our mind
and were going to share anyway. Eight of us consumed a mountain of
fresh Popadoms and chutneys while we waited. Impressive Onion Bhaji,
good and spicy, Prawn Puri - excellent, Shish Kebab and Samosa - good,
but the star was Stuffed Pepper - magnificent. Chicken Tikka Rogan Josh
- superb, Chicken Tikka Bhuna a little too hot. Portions were a bit on the
small side. I recommend a visit.' DB.

RAJ BALTI
513, Pensby Road, Thingwall, Wirral.   **0151 648 5949**
A small restaurant seating forty-eight diners, so be sure to book a table
at weekends or you will miss out on all your favourite curries with
accompaniments. Mr Miah has promised to give a discount to Curry
Club members, see page 288. Hours: 5pm till 11.30pm. Branch: Dilshad
Balti, 132, Hagley Road, Oldswinford, Stourbridge. Dilshad Balti, Unit
6, Penkridge Retail Park, Wolverhampton Road, Penkridge.

TANDOORI MAHAL
24/26, King Street, Egremont, Wirral.   **0151 639 5948**
'Popadoms warm and crisp, chutney tasty and fresh. Chicken Tikka was
superb although the Madras sauce wasn't as hot as it could have been.
Loads of rice and salad. My girlfriend ordered mixed Kebab and Chicken
Tikka but she had had one too many and by the time the food came she
couldn't face it. I could!' DB.

The editor of this Guide welcomes your views
on the restaurants and take-aways we list in its
pages, and on any you visit anywhere. Please
send your reports to : The Editor, P.O. Box 7,
Haslemere, Surrey, GU27 1EP. Please enclose
an addressed envelope if you want a reply.

MIDDLESEX

GREATER LONDON

Now the western part of (outer) Greater London, Middlesex once contained most of London. It was 'abolished' when Greater London was formed in 1965. Confusion exists because the Post Office still use Middlesex as a postal county. Post codes add to the confusion. Enfield, for example is EN1, 2, 3 in postal Middlesex but is in (Herts) GL geographical. Potters Bar EN6 is the same. Barnet, is in postal Herts with EN4 and 5 code. It used to be in geographical Middlesex but is now GL borough! There is talk of reviving the county of Middlesex. It would help beleaguered guide editors!

EDGWARE

SHREE GANESHA VEGETARIAN
4, The Promenade, Edgwarebury Lane, Edgware.   **0181 958 2778**

Proprietor, Ramchandra Tiwari opened his restaurant in 1990, with his wife Hemantika running the kitchens making sure you are served only the very best vegetarian cuisine. Unusual dishes on the menu such as, Kaddu Curry (spicy pumpkin curry) and Lotus Stem Curry. They also serve two of my absolute favourites, Bhel Poori - Bombay street food and Masala Dosa - South Indian pancake with spiced potatoes and coconut chutney. Hours: evenings only 6pm till 10.30pm, plus Sunday lunch.

FELTHAM

INDIAN PALACE II   CC DISCOUNT
414, Staines Road, Bedfont.   **0181 751 5822**

Proprietor, Dilshad Miah has promised to give a discount to Curry Club members, see page 288. Hours: 12 noon to 3pm and 6pm till 11pm.

HAMPTON

MINAR
195, High Street, Hampton Hill.   **0181 979 0642**

'Visited for Sunday Buffet. At least 16 selections. Unlimited Popadoms and coffee. Staff very smart and polite. Highly recommended.' RP.

HARROW

EASTERN EYE   CC DISCOUNT
20, Station Parade, Northolt Road, Harrow.   **0181 422 5323**

Opened in 1988 by H Rahman and seats fifty-two diners. 'Good welcome. Chicken Tikka and Chat very tasty ample starters.' DD. Manager, HR Kamazy has promised to give a discount to Curry Club members, see page 288. Hours: 12 noon to 2.30pm and 6pm till midnight. Branches: Red Rose Tandoori, Hayes and Red Rose Tandoori, Stanmore.

HAYES

THAMOULINEE   CC DISCOUNT
128a, Uxbridge Road, Hayes.   **0181 561 3723**

Opened in 1990 and owned by Mr and Mrs Hyacinth. You will find Anthonypillai front of house and Mary Jasmine in the kitchen preparing excellent Sri Lankan dishes. South Indian food also featured on the menu, such as Dosas, plain or Masala. Sri Lankan specials include Kothu Rotti - chopped rotti with vegetables, onions and spices, String Hoppers, Sambals and Maldive Fish. 'Excellent value for money. Portions are a good size. Everything is freshly cooked and service is prompt.' AG. Mr Hyacinth has promised to give a 10% discount to Curry Club members, see page 288. Hours: 12 noon to 2.30pm and 6pm till midnight.

HILLINGDON

HILLINGDON TANDOORI
CC DISCOUNT
6, Byron Parade, Uxbridge Road, Hillingdon.
0181 561 7055
Opened in 1985 by Islam Uddin. Serving competent and reliable good curries to a loyal local trade. Manager, R Miah has promised to give a discount , see page 288. Hours: 12 to 2.30pm and 6pm till midnight. Branch: Iver Curry and Tandoori Centre, 26, High Street, Iver, Bucks.

HOUNSLOW

ASHNA
368, Staines Road, Hounslow.
0181 577 5988
Serving pure vegetarian cusines. 'A most friendly family establishment with a growing number of regulars. Masala Dosa is brilliant and Special Mushroom Curry is a weekend delight. .' RGM. Also runs a Video shop, selling and hiring all the latest Indian and Western films - just down the road at 362. All this and Bhel Poori too!

ISLEWORTH

OSTERLEY PAVILION
CC DISCOUNT
160, Thornbury Road, Osterley Park, Isleworth.
0181 560 6517
A smart establishment with careful service and a wide ranging menu. Proprietor, A Siddiqui (who opened his restaurant way back in 1986) has promised to give Curry Club members a discount at his quieter times, see page 288. If dining at the weekend, prebook your table, seats only fifty. Hours: Monday to Sunday 12 noon to 2.45pm and 6pm till midnight.

OSTERLEY PAVILION

INDIAN RESTAURANT

*160, Thornbury Road,
Osterley Park,
Isleworth, Middlesex.
TW7 4QE*

To Book Your Table Telephone:
0181 560 6517 & 0181 847 2690

REGALE INDIA CUISINE
CC DISCOUNT
545, Twickenham Road, Isleworth.
0181 744 3118
Formerly Curry palace. A small but bright establishment seating only forty-four diners. Trailing plants hang from the ceiling and wicker fans decorate the neutral walls. Owner, Aziz Ahmed, has promised to give a discount to Curry Club members, see page 288. Hours: 12 noon to 2.30pm and 6pm till 11.00pm.

NORTHOLT

EMPRESS OF INDIA
CC DISCOUNT
40-42, Church Road, Northolt.
0181 845 4361
Opened in 1977, by trio, R Ali, S Zaman, HR Khan. Serving all your usual favourites, Tandoori, Jhelfraisi (sic), Korma, Rogan (sic) and Dansak (sic) with all the traditional accompaniments. Manager, AT Choudhury, has promised to give a discount to Curry Club members at his quieter times, see page 288. Opening hours: 12 noon to 2.30pm and 6pm till 11.30pm. Friday and Saturday till midnight.

NORTHWOOD

RUCHITA
19, Joel Street, Northwood.

CC DISCOUNT
01923 825546

A popular local curry house. Proprietor, MA Matlib, has promised to give a discoun to Curry Club members, see page 288. Hours: 12 noon to 2.30pm and 6pm till 11.30pm, Friday and Saturday till midnight.

VICEROY
48, High Street, Northwood.

CC DISCOUNT
01923 827856

Popular establishment. Proprietor and manager, Mofiz Miah, has promised to give a discount to Curry Club members, see page 288. Opening hours: 12 noon to 2.30pm and 6pm till midnight, seven days a week.

PINNER

VILLAGE TANDOORI
426b, Rayners Lane, Pinner.

CC DISCOUNT
0181 866 7363

Formerly Taj Mahal. A snug little restaurant seating just thirty-two diners. Booking essential at weekends to avoid waiting. Manager, Lipu Miah, has promised to give a discount to Curry Club members, see page 288. Opening hours: 6pm till midnight, till 12.30am on weekends.

RUISLIP

PERSAD TANDOORI
36, High Street, Ruislip.

CC DISCOUNT
01895 630102

A standard curry house serving competent curries with accompaniments. Seats forty-two, so book on Fridays and Saturdays. Managing partner, Mr Choudhury will give a discount to Curry Club members at his quieter times, see page 288. Fully licensed. Opening hours: 12 noon to 3pm and 6pm till midnight. Branch: Golden Curry, 81, High Street, Yiewsley, West Drayton, Middx.

RUISLIP TANDOORI
115, High Street, Ruislip.

CC DISCOUNT
01895 632859

A regular entrant in our guide. Owned by Mr KB Raichhetri who hails from Nepal. He's usually there and welcomes a chat about Nepalese food. Sunday Buffet lunch - eat as much as you like. Special set lunch menu available. Menu includes specials such as Bangalore Phall Chicken and Prawn Pepper Massala. Opening hours: 12 noon to 2.30pm and 6pm till 11.45pm, Friday and Saturday till midnight. Mr Raichhetri will give a discount to Curry Club members at his quieter times, see page 288.

SOUTHALL

There are a number of sweet / snack centres, cafés and restaurants to be found. Most are on the Uxbridge Road, called The Broadway as it passes through Southall. Also there are others on South Road and the Green. These places and others around cater largely for their indigenous Asian population. This may inhibit others from entering. It should not. In our experience everyone is treated equally and all are welcome. However, if you are looking for lush decor, candlelight, carnations for the lady, etc., you will not find it. Neither will you find 'haute cuisine'.

But you will find good authentic cuisine at straightforward, functional eating houses usually with formica tables. The food is served fast, whether in self-service café or in a sit-down restaurant. Below we examine our (and our correspondents'), favourite eating holes. The indigenous population is largely Sikh and Punjabi, resulting in a fascinating and generally peaceful mix of Indian and Pakistani carnivores, enhanced by East African Asians.

P.S. I wonder if Sue Lawley would let me take Southall to her Desert Island as my luxury?

BABU TANDOORI
156, The Broadway, Southall.   **0181 574 1049**

'Try Lamb or Chicken curry or Mixed Vegetable or Bhindi curry. Best Tikka I have ever tasted. You don't have to spend a fortune to have a brilliant meal.' JW.

BRILLIANT   TOP 100 - CC DISCOUNT
72-74, Western Road, Southall.   **0181 574 1928**

Established in 1975 when one Mr Anand settled in the UK, having left Kenya. He brought with him a large energetic family, of which more later, and a tradition of Indian cooking at restaurant level which went

(continued overleaf)

back generations. Southall was the place Mr Anand chose to set up The Briliant. I said last time that the food is like Indian home cooking. I should qualify that a little. It is indeed unlike any standard curry house. As to home Indian cooking - it is unlike, that too - because it is 'Kenyan Asian' Indian cooking and that makes a subtle difference. And it is cooking at the hands of a master. I have had the privilege of meeting Mr Anand. Better still I have had the pleasure of having a meal cooked by him for me. It was an outstanding combination of taste. Now virtually retired Mr Anand has passed his cheffing skills on to his sons and they (KK and DK Anand) run The Brilliant. That is not the end of it. You will find Anands popping up 'everywhere'. Another two sons run Madhus Brilliant also in Southall, and relatives run The Curry Craze in Wembley and The Curry Fever in Leicester (see entries). And yes, in my view the food lives up the restaurant's name. It is Brilliant. Why? It starts with your arrival. Before you order, two delicious fresh chutneys arrive on the tables. One is carrot sticks in vinegar the other mint with chilli. Order Popadoms and chomp away. Star starters are Butter Chicken and Jeera Chicken, both huge - the former cooked in butter ghee with red spices, the latter with cummin. Other starters include Onion or Potato Bhajias - cooked in a light spicy batter. Main courses include a choice of chicken, lamb, mince and very fresh vegetables. I won't single out any in particular. They are all equally good, and the breads are a delight. Despite seating a humungous 120, it is advisable to book. 'Service friendly and informal. Food was excellent, I had Palak Chicken and Pilau Rice - lovely flavour and texture. Definitely go again.' SP. 'Restaurant bursting full with Indian and English gourmets and the service was very solicitious indeed.' GG. 'Food of excellent quality and large portions. Service very friendly and helpful.' MF. Opening hours: 12 noon to 3pm and 6pm till 11.30pm. Closed Mondays. . Decidedly The Brilliant remains in our TOP 100 and the Anands give a discount to Curry Club members at their quieter times, see page 288.

KARAHI TANDOORI KABAB CENTRE   CC DISCOUNT
161, The Broadway, Southall.   **0181 574 3571**

This restaurant is the new branch of the erstwhile neighbouring Tandoori Kebab Centre. Located at the Western end of Southall's main drag, one is attracted by the display of food in the window counter and an inviting spacious (sixty-six) layout, spotlessly clean formica café style but with waiter service. The display contains the normal items (for Southall) Samosas, Pakoras, Indian Sweetmeats, Salads and Breads. But among all this are two very unusual items (for Southall) - Bhel Puri and Gol Goppas with Jeera Pani. The former consists of cold crunchy sev, savoury rice crispies and potato laced with tamarind chutney, chillies and herbs. The latter are tiny crisp puris served with spiced potato, imli, and cummin spiced water. Both are specialised tastes but are very welcom in Southall. Behind a further long counter are the chefs cooking the Tandooris, Kebabs and Curries in front of you. And there are the Karahis - two handled woks in which the Curries are cooked. Of course Karahi is another word for Balti. Indeed Karahi is the universal word all over the subcontinent. Here it is all done superbly well. And at a very reasonable price. Open 9am, till midnight. Gets very busy at peak times, particularly with the younger local Asians. Unlicensed so BYO. Owner, AF Chaudhury has promised to give a discount to Curry Club members at his quieter times, see page 288. Hours: 9 am to midnight. Branches: Tandoori Kabab Centre, and Tandoori Express on Jalebi Junction, Southall, Middx. See entries overleaf.

MADHUS BRILLIANT   SPECIAL AWARD -- CC DISCOUNT
39, South Road, Southall.   **AND TOP 100   0181 574 1897**

Madhus Brilliant opened in 1980 as a breakway from literally the parent company, The Brilliant (see entry above). Two Anand sons Sanjeev (chef) and Sanjay (front of house) decided to do things their way. All the delicious items on the Brilliant's menu were offered, but the brothers added a tandoor, which gave a new dimension to their cooking. Madhu's seats over 100 on two floors. It is licensed but very relaxed and informal and often very busy, being highly patronised by the local Asian community. Guide fame has increased its white custom and everyone is made very welcome indeed. The menu is very similar to the Brilliant's in taste and concept, from the chutneys to the starters and the main courses. We get many reports from afficionados. One regular (DM) goes here at least twice a week. 'Smallish choice on the menu but all cooked wonderfully well. Alu Tikki was superb! Highly rated.' DM. 'Alu Tikki, a potato, chick pea and yoghurt dish, excellent flavour and texture, highly recommended. Chicken Tikka Masala and Palak Paneer, rich flavours and textures. Must rate as one of the best meals.' SP. 'My first try of Cobra in Cobra glass - verdict - excellent. Karahi Gosht, lamb simply outstanding, I can honestly say was the best tasting dish I have ever experienced. A truly memorable meal. Although I live eighty miles away, I will be bring my wife here soon.' SP. 'Methi Chicken full of flavour, vegetable dishes made with fresh vegetables and delicately spiced. Nans high quality. Portion size quite large. House wine very reasonable and drinkable.' MF. Sanjay is the entrepreneur of the Anand family. His outside catering for Asian weddings has now become a huge business with two or three engagements a week with up to 1000 guests a time. Watching an operation of this size is fascinating. It is no mean feat either and Sanjay has developed techniques both behind the scenes and front of house which make the process look easy. He operates just as slickly on a smaller scale too. What an idea for your next party! See page 6. Meanwhile, visit the restaurant, which we have no hesitation in keeping firmly at the top of our TOP 100.Hours: Wednesday to Monday excluding lunch Saturday and Sunday 12.30pm to 3pm and 6pm till 11.30pm (midnight Friday and Saturday).Mr Anand gives a discount to Curry Club members, at his quieter times (can't imagine when they are! always full), see page 288. Madhu's is the recipient of our SPECIAL AWARD for overall excellence.

MAHARAJA
171-173, The Broadway, Southall.   **CC DISCOUNT**
0181 574 4564
One of Southall's oldest, the Maharaja just carries on currying. 'The menu does not offer starters in the normal way, just could not eat it as there is no portion control of this very excellent food. This was our local, a mere 100 miles round trip!' GC. Managing partner, Harbans Singh Sandhu will give a discount to Curry Club members, at his quieter times, see page 288. Opening hours: 12 noon to 3pm and 6pm till 11.30pm.

MOTI MAHAL
94, The Broadway, Southall.   **0181 574 7682**
Unlicensed. Looks like a café. Food pretty spicy, meaning spicy rather than hot.' GG.

OMIS
1, Beaconsfield Road, Southall.   **TOP 100**
0181 571 4831
A small café style establishment serving chats and snacks as well as curries and breads. With just forty-two seats and despite its out of the way location it is always full of local Asian cognoscenti. Since I was taken there by Indian journalist KN Malik, 'I want to show you Indian food at its best,' and our subsequent Guide entry, Omi's has attracted more adventurous white diners. The menu is deceptively short but is enhanced with ever changing daily specials. The food is fresh in taste and is all delicious. Mykesh Kharbanda is the owner/chef. We like his food and his idiosyncrasies. The place doubles for a van hire. So you can get one phone call for a Saag Chicken with Peshwari Nan to go and the next for a driver and Transit Van! We still give it an idiosyncratic editorial TOP 100. Opening hours: Monday to Thursday 10.30am to 9pm. Friday and Saturday 10.30am to 9.30pm. Sunday closed. See overleaf.

SAGOO & THAKHAR (ASIAN TANDOORI CENTRE)   TOP 100
114, The Green, The Roxy, Southall.   0181 574 2579
and 157, The Broadway, Southall.   0181 574 3476
The partnership of Messrs Sagoo and Thakhar resulted years ago in two
unlicensed cafés open all hours (well nearly anyway - 9am until 10.30pm
daily) whose purpose was to serve Indian food to the local community
for breakfast, lunch, tea and dinner. Strategically located at either end of
Southall with Mr Sagoo at one and Mr Thakhar at the other. Your editor
has been going to both S and Ts alias The Asian Tandoori Centre (both)
or the Roxy Café (the Green) for decades and I still do not know who is
Mr Sagoo and who is Mr Thakhar. The clientelle is very predominantly
local Asians with a smattering of whites (though I've yet to see whites
eating curry at 9am!). The Roxy is the larger of the two but both serve
identical food (well almost identical - there are minor difference with a
few items), canteen style from long service counters. You take your tray,
then queue (almost inevitably in peak times), then ask the staff, who have
remained unchanged for as long as I have known it, to give you your
choice. Although the place has a business-like atmosphere, it is a very
welcoming place. As with all things Southall, get in there and enjoy it.
You'll never feel intimidated. 'A return to my favourite! It is a canteen
style service, is cheap and food is outstanding. My kind of place. How
you do not make the Roxy the best in Britain is beyond my comprehen-
sion. Indian food that one seldom finds in other restaurant in Britain,
such as Chan Bhatura and Aloo Tikki with all the trimmings! Fried
Karela, absolutely excellent!! I usually go for one of everything - it is that
good. Simply the best.' BG. I introduced Dominique to the delights of
Sagoo and Thakhar a decade ago. Such is her enjoyment of them both
(especially the carrot, onion and imli chutney) that during the writing of
this very Southall part of this Guide (after a 10 hour day at it) she
announced to me. 'Take me to The Roxy.' We went (a sixty mile round
trip). This is what Dominique had to say: When we arrived there was a
big queue at the counter, the restaurant area was full, we squeezed in the
door - not just because I was so full but the shop floor was packed with
bodies. Finally it was my turn - I gave my order to the assistent and yes
please can I have a LARGE portion of your carrot, onion and imli
chutney. He spooned large quantities of it into a plastic bag, sealed it and
popped it into my box. 'Can I have another one just like that please?'
I leaned over the counter. He laughed, 'Another one!' 'Yes please - just
like the first one' I smiled. Sagoo and Thakhar must turn round hundreds
of covers every day, yet the food is consistent, excellent authentic and
very delicious. Helpings are enormous (but if you over order they'll give
you takaway containers later). You can BYO as far as we know, but why
bother with the food as absorbing as this? And there's Lhassi too. A
recent innovation is , in any case, a license. You can buy cold beer,etc. If
Sue Lawley won't let me take Southall to her Desert Island maybe she'll
let me take Sagoo and Thakhar! Both branches decidedly in our TOP 100.

SAHAANA
80, South Road, Southall.   **0181 574 9209**
What's the most unlikely thing to find in carnivorous Punjabi oriented
Southall? Answer... a Sri Lankan restaurant! New since the last guide
(and despite that, it has already changed name (from Bharath to Sahaana).
It's not vegetarian but the contrast between its South Indian and Sri
Lankan food to Punjabi / Southall food could not be greater. Maybe this
is why (despite a bog-standard (for Southall) display of take-out samosas,
pakoras, sweetmeats in the front half of the venue) it was almost empty
when we tried it. Says editor DBAC: 'Sri Lankan restaurants are rare
enough. To find one in Southall...! We started with two masala popadoms
with home-made coconut chutney, while we looked at the menu. Rasam,
Masala Dosa with Sambar and more of that wonderful coconut chutney.
3 x 1/2 lager. All for a huge £11.00! I felt so full, I couldn't finish my Dosa
(which was so big, both ends fell off the dinner plate.) I wanted to finish
it but I couldn't I'd have been sick - total greed! Hours: 11am to 11pm.

SHAHANSHAH VEGETARIAN   **CC DISCOUNT**
60, North Road, Southall.   **0181 574 1493**
A cosy little establishment, seating just thirty diners. As its name
indicates, it is an all vegetarian restaurant and sweet centre. Proprietor,
Baljinder S Gill (his wife Harbans runs the kitchen) will give a discount
to CC members, see page 288. Hours2: 10am to 8pm (Tuesday closed).

TANDOORI EXPRESS
ON JALEBI JUNCTION   **CC DISCOUNT**
93, The Broadway, Southall.   **0181 571 6782**
A branch of the well established Tandoori Kebab Centre (see below)
located on the opposite side of the road. Owner Abdul Chaudhry
wanted a venue aimed at Southall's trendy youth. Opened in 1986, it
does indeed pull in the younger Asians, as do his equally popular other
branches. It not only has a 'zippy' name, it has a bright frontage
'enhanced' by a pink neon sign, and on the pavement outside resides a
horse cart and an Indian barrow which add considerable atmosphere. It
is, at times, full of Asian youngsters. On a typical occasion they were
mostly female who were enjoying chatting up the waiters in strong
cockney accents. The food is Pakistani tandoori and karahi cooking at its
best with all the usual home-made curries, fresh melt in the mouth breads
and snack foods such as Samosas, Aloo Tikki and Gol-Gappay. Great
value for money. Great food to eat at any time of day or night. And the
array of Indian sweets at the counter is most alluring. Assistant manager,
S Majeed, has promised to give a discount to Curry Club members, see
page 288. Hours: 9am to 11pm.

TANDOORI KABAB CENTRE   **CC DISCOUNT**
163, The Broadway, Southall.   **0181 571 5738**
Opened in 1965 and must be one of the oldest establishments in Southall.
Seats an unbelievable 400 (I'm glad I don't have anything to do with the
washing up!). Menu contains all the usual tandoori dishes, plus Dehi
Bhalla and Katlama for starters. For main course Maghaz Masala, lamb
brains cooked in the traditional way. Paneer Ka Naan - bread stuffed
with cheese. Eatable food, day and night. 'Very friendly service along
with good very reasonably priced food. Decor is very basic but who cares
at the price. Came out stuffed full!' SB. Manager Dalawar Chaudhry has
promised to give a discount to Curry Club members see page 288. Hours:
9am to 11pm. Free local delivery service for orders over £10.00. Branches:
Tandoori Express and Karahi Kebab Centre, Southall - see above.

TO FIND OUT HOW TO JOIN OUR DISCOUNT SCHEME SEE PAGE 288

SUDBURY

GANGES   CC DISCOUNT
769, Harrow Road, Sudbury.   **0181 904 0011**
Seating just forty diners, so best to book for weekends. Sunday lunch
buffet - children half price. House special include Kurchi Lamb - for four
diners (complete meal - 12 hours notice) £35.95, Kurchi Murg - for two
£26.96.Manager, Jomilul Haque will give a discount to Curry Club
members, see page 288. Hours: 12 noon to 2.30pm and 6pm till 11.30pm.

TEDDINGTON

BENGAL BRASSERIE   CC DISCOUNT
162, Stanley Road, Teddington.   **0181 977 7332**
A smart and well established restaurant, since 1986. Seats forty-four
diners. Serves all your favourite curries, tandooris, breads and rices with
a few chef specialities too, such as Bengal Special and Shahi Vegetable.
Fully licensed and 10% discount on takeaways. Managing partner, Ali
Kausar has promised to give a discount to Curry Club members, see page
288. Hours: 12 noon to 2.30pm and 6pm till midnight.

BILAS TANDOORI   CC DISCOUNT
4, Broad Street, Teddington.   **0181 977 1529**
A popular local haunt. Area manager, ZT Fruki has promised to give a
discount to Curry Club members, see page 288. Hours: 12 noon to 2.30pm
and 6pm till 11.30pm, till midnight on weekends. Branches: Sopna
Tandoori, 175, High Street, Hampton Hill, Middx and Tandoori Grill,
188, Castelnau, Barnes, London. SW13.

TWICKENHAM

STANDARD TANDOORI   CC DISCOUNT
68, Heath Road, Twickenham.   **0181 892 7072**
Opened in 1975, by A Moin. A reliable restaurant seating forty-eight
diners and serving competent curries. Menu includes Chilli Masalla for
the hotheads! Manager, A Lais, has promised to give a discount to CC
members, see page 288. Hours: 12 noon to 2.30pm and 6pm till midnight.
Branch: Woking Tandoori, 45, Goldworth Road, Woking, Surrey.

WEMBLEY

Rapidly gaining ground as the second Southall. But I don't agree with
Robin Weir that it has overtaken it - not quite yet anyway. Unlike
Southall its large Gujarati East African population gives Wembley food
a different (predominatly vegetarian) taste from Southall. As with
Southall there are many good sweet / snack shop / cafés and restaurants
crammed with Indian goodies. Here are your popular favourites....

CHETNA'S BHEL PURI   TOP 100
420, High Road, Wembley.   **0181 903 5989**
'Very popular family restaurant serving vegetarian food. Bhel Poor and
Aloo Papdi Chat. Deluxe Dosas and vegetarian Thali main course.' DB.
'Service friendly and efficient, very busy, queuing! Starters were well
received, different and delicious. Particularly Aloo Papdi Chat Bhel
Poori.' CRR. 'So busy people queued on pavement until their number
was called. Bhel Puri to start, soaked in curd and tamarind, all gorgeous,
washed down with lassi ,followed by Dosas and Rasmalai. Great
bustling atmosphere and superb food.' JM. This queuing lark has
annoyed some of our reporters (mainly weekend peak times) and it is a
recent phenomenon. 'Pity you made it a TOP 100. Never had to queue
before... still worth it though. And I still haven't converted my boyfriend
off the comical Chetna Pizza to curries. I'll keep trying... maybe by the
next Guide.' BD. We'll keep it in our TOP 100 despite the queues!

CURRY CRAZE   **TOP 100 - CC DISCOUNT**
8-9, The Triangle, Wembley Hill Road, Wembley.   **0181 902 9720**
Seats 100 diners and owned by a husband and wife team, Mr and Mrs
Malhotra, who are also in charge of front of house and the kitchen, and
are part of the Anand family. (See Brilliant, Southall). Its name reflects
the curry's popularity and judging by reports received it is a popular
venue. Menu lists all the favourite curries, Khorma (sic), Biriani, Keema
and Kofta. Specials include their famous Butter and Jeera ChickenHouse
specialities include Masaladar Chicken on the bone and Palak Lamb.
Fully licensed. This is Kenyan Asian food at its best and like its Southall
sisters, it deserves a TOP 100 accolade - so we've given it one. Mr
Malhotra will give a discount to Curry Club members, see page 288.
Hours: 12 noon to 2.30pm and 6pm till 11pm, closed on Tuesday.

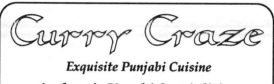

Curry Craze

Exquisite Punjabi Cuisine
Authentic Karahi Specialities

VEG SPECIALITIES INCLUDE: **NON-VEG SPECIALITIES INCLUDE:**

* ALOO TIKKI * BHEL *   * BUTTER CHICKEN * JEERA CHICKEN *
* CHILLI CORN *   * METHI CHICKEN * CHILLI CHICKEN *
* PANEER TIKKA* PANEER PAKORA *   * KARAHI CHICKEN * KARAHI LAMB *
* PANI PURI *   * KARAHI PRAWNS * ETC

SUNDAY BUFFET 12-2.30pm
Eat as much as you like

* COMFORTABLE SEATING FOR 100 *

PRIVATE PARKING WITH VALET SERVICE ON REQUEST AFTER 7PM

Highly Recommended by Major Food Critics

Specialist Caterers for all Occasions

8-9, NEELD PARADE, THE TRIANGLE,
WEMBLEY HILL ROAD, WEMBLEY.
0181 902 9720 & 0181 902 3440

KARAHI KING
213, East Lane, Wembley.   **0181 904 2760**
As its name suggests it's all manner of carnivorous curries cooked and
served in the karahi (in view) eaten with fresh melt-in-the-mouth bread
and no cutlery in true Asian manner. Unlicensed so BYO and enjoy.

MARU'S BHAJIA HOUSE
230, Ealing Road, Alperton, Wembley.   **0181 903 6771**
Unlike the Bhajis at the formula curry house, Ashok Maru's Bhajias are
not only correctly spelt, they are correctly cooked and a phenomenon,
strong enough to give his place its name. Elsewhere also called Pakoras
they are besan batter coated potato slices, deep-fried and served with
Imli Chutney. Try the Gol Goppas with Jeera Pani and Potato Curry (ask
how to eat them). 12 noon to around 9pm daily, closed on Tuesday.

MARUTI BHEL PURI
238a, Ealing Road, Wembley.   **0181 903 6743**
Vegetarian. Bombay street food features well on the menu. Masala and
Plain Dosas with Sambhar (sic) and the all important coconut chutney.
Unusual dishes include Karahi Sev Tomato and Karahi Corn-On-The-
Cob. Hours: 12 noon to 10pm. Closed Tuesdays. Fully licensed.

SAKONI
119-121, Ealing Road, Wembley.   **0181 903 9601**
Vegetarian snacks from Gujarat and Bombay here, and one of the few
places we know where you can get Pao Bhaji Bombay's popular equivalent of our beans on toast - only there and at the Sakoni it is vegetable
curry in a toasted bun. Juices ,and for those who can take its bitter-sweet
contrasts - pan. A mighty one-pop mouthful!

WOODLANDS   **CC DISCOUNT**
119-121, Ealing Road, Wembley.   **0181 903 9601**
The third London branch of a famous chain of restaurants from India
which specialise in South Indian vegetarian food. The food is described
in the entry for Woodlands, 77, Marylebone Road, London. W1 and they
have another branch at 37, Panton Street, London. SW1.

WEST DRAYTON
GOLDEN CURRY
81, High Street, West Drayton.   **01895 443435**
'A lovely place to go for a midweek curry. Managed to talk Paul into
going out when we were meant to be saving for a holiday. Special
Chicken Jalfri Masala - super scrummy . A side dish of Tofu and Peas,
Bombay Aloo and mixed vegetables.Brought a doggy bag home as there
was so much in a portion!. Friendly waiters with funny wiggles!!' SW.

NORFOLK

DISS

DISS TANDOORI
1-3, Shelfanger Road, Diss.

CC DISCOUNT
01379 651685

Opened in 1986 by Mobashir Ali and Jalal Khara and seats fifty-two diners. Mobashir will be found front of house greeting customers and Jalal is the power house in the kitchen, cooking all your favourite curries and accompaniments plus a few specials as well such as Balti, Zal Frezi (sic) and Trays (must be a Thali). They have agreed to give a discount to Curry Club members, see page 288. Hours: 12 noon to 2.30pm and 6pm till 11.30pm.

KINGS LYNN

INDIA GATE
41, St James Street, Kings Lynn.

01553 776489

Formerly the Kismet. 'Decor pastel blues and pinks with ornate plaster coving round the ceiling with ornate plaster frames round the Indian picture scenes. Food absolutely first class throughout. Value for money.' MB.

NORTH WALSHAM

PRINCE OF BENGAL
13a, Mundesley Road, North Walsham.

CC DISCOUNT
01692 500119

Proprieror Folik Miah Choudhury can be found in the restaurant welcoming guests in for their meal. He will give a discount to Curry Club members, see page 288. Hours: 12 noon to 2.30pm and 6pm till 11.30pm. Branches: Prince of Bengal, 40, Cromer Road, Sheringham, Norfolk. Prince of India, 32, High Street, Princes Risborough, Bucks. Prince of India, 7, Upper High Street, Thame, Oxon.

NORWICH

NORWICH TANDOORI
98, Magdalen Street, Anglia Square, Norwich.

CC DISCOUNT
01603 621436

'Straightforward comfortable interior. Lamb Pasanda best tried so far in the city. Chicken Tikka Pasanda, mildly creamy cooked with butter, almonds and sultanas, exceeded expectations.' TW. Kuit Meah, managing owner of this fifty seater restaurant has promised to give a discount to Curry Club members, see page 288. Hours: 12 noon to 3pm and 6pm till midnight.

PRINCE OF INDIA
19, Prince of Wales Road, Norwich.

01603 616937

'Beamed ceilings and divided alcoves to give a cosy atmosphere. Food is quite good. When ordering Popadoms, be sure to ask for the chutneys and onions, or you'll end up with nothing. Shami Kebabs quite delicious as is the Madras. Service slow when empty.' MB. Chef Specialities Peshwari Dishes and Korai Gosht from the Khyber Pass (so they tell us!). 'We found the food to be tasty and competently spiced and presented. Service was good considering the restaurant was packed to capacity. Noticed at least fifteen people in the "Bombay Mix Zone" waiting to be seated.' LO1. 'Started with Masalla Popadoms, pickles and chutneys which included an onion, lettuce and mint salad. There was an average amount of food but it was of good quality.' MSS. Opening hours: 12 noon to 3pm and 6pm till midnight.

THETFORD

NEMI INDIAN CUISINE   **CC DISCOUNT**
17, White Hart Street, Thetford.   **01842 761260**

A snug restaurant, seating forty-eight diners. 'For starters I sampled Nargis Kebab, a hard boiled egg covered with spicy mince meat , unbelievably tasty. Methi Murgh, Bombay Potato and Pillau Rice, absolutely terrific. Well worth a visit.' MB. 'Had been booked into Center Parc for a weekend break - sort of middle class Butlins where instead of donkey rides and funfairs there are all manner of 'healthy' activities. A peep through Nemi's window worried us as only four people eating in on a Saturday night. Usual discussions about whether or not to eat here, a major argument was swiftly averted much to relief of our rumbling stomachs. We had come for a takeaway, service was polite and efficient. The food was brown gravy variety, competently prepared and spiced and certainly good value.' LOI. Owner, Abdul Rouf will give a discount to Curry Club members, at his quieter times, see page 288. Hours: 12 noon to 2.30pm and 6pm till midnight.

NORTHAMPTONSHIRE

IRTHLINGBOROUGH

EASTERN SPICE   **CC DISCOUNT**
56-60, High Street, Irthlingborough.   **01933 650044**

Menu lists all the curry house favourites with a few additions. Kalmi (chicken) Kebab, Murgh Bemisall (tikka) and Murgh La Jawab (tandoori). Hom delivery service available,. Manager, Golam Sarwar will give a discount to Curry Club members, see page 288. Hours: 12 noon to 2.30pm and 6pm till 11.30pm.

TANDOORI NIGHTS   **CC DISCOUNT**
48, Station Road, Irthlingborough.   **01933 652675**

A small but cosy restaurant housed in an old Tudor building seating just thirty-five diners. Usual curry house menu, serving all your favourite dishes with accompaniments. Chef and owner Moyna Miah has promised to give a discount to Curry Club members, see page 288. Hours: 12 noon to 2.30pm and 6pm till 11pm. Weekends till midnight.

KETTERING

RAJ   **CC DISCOUNT**
50, Rockingham Road, Kettering.   **01536 513606**

'Bhindi Bhaji, fresh bindi, nicely cooked. Excellent Pasanda and Madras, beautiful Chupattis. Attentive and informative service. Minor drawback is the cost, more expensive than others in area.' TP. Separate Balti menu with every different combination including Balti Shahjahan - chicken, mince meat, almonds, coconuts and sultanas. Manager, Goyas Miah will give a discount to Curry Club members, see page 288. Hours: 12 noon to 2.30pm and 6pm till midnight. Home delivery service .

RED ROSE   **CC DISCOUNT**
1, George Street, Kettering.   **01536 510120**

Opened in 1991 and seats eighty diners. Tandooris, Tikkas, Korai (sic), Kormas and Jal-Frezi (sic) is on the menu including a satisfactory section on Balti. Manager Matin Rashid will give a discount to Curry Club members, see page 288. Hours: 12 noon to 2pm and 6pm till midnight. Friday and Saturday till 12.30am. Free delivery service.

NORTHAMPTON

ANCIENT RAJ   **CC DISCOUNT**
12, High Street, Long Buckby,Northampton.   **01327 842193**
Nothing ancient about this restaurant. It opened in 1993 and is already
very popular. Manager, Raj Miah will give a discount to Curry Club
members, at his quieter times, see page 288. Opening hours: 12 noon to
2.30pm and 5pm till 11pm. Branch: The Raj, 50, Rockingham Road,
Kettering, Northants. (see entry under Kettering)

STAR OF INDIA   **CC DISCOUNT**
5, Abington Avenue, Northampton.   **01604 30664**
Opened in 1982 by Abdul Noor and seats forty diners. You'll find
everything from Tandoori and Tikka to Madras and Vindaloo and
everything in between at this reliably good curry house. Manager,
Bodrul Islam will give a discount to Curry Club members at his quieter
times, see page 288. Opening hours: 12 noon to 2.15pm and 6pm till
midnight, Friday and Saturday till 1.30am.

TAJ MAHAL
7,Marefair, Northampton.   **01604 31132**
This restaurant has maintained its position in the Guide, firstly, because
it is Northampton's oldest, having opened in 1952, indeed, that rates it
with the country's first ten Indian restaurants. Secondly, its hours of
opening, Friday and Saturday night are remarkable, closing at 3am. This
is typical Curry House, nothing more and nothing less. With over forty
years in the business, you would expect them to be good at the job. I can't
imagine why they find it necessary to stay open till 3am, but for those
who hound up and down the M1 (yes there are some of use that do it in
the wee hours) they are just a hop and a jump away from junctions 15 and
16. Anything is better than motorway food, anytime of day or night. As
for the quality of the food, who cares at that hour of the morning?

WELLINGBOROUGH

AKASH TANDOORI
36, Cambridge Street, Wellingborough.   **01933 227193**
'Popadoms crispy and Tikka tender. Chicken Shashlik, fresh and spicy
with a Nan bread. Restaurant clean and service good.' DDC. Menu says,
"Dining without wine is like a day without sunshine".

It is the purpose of this Guide to report trends, to note
the bad things, and praise the good. Entry into any
guide, big or small, famous or little known, can affect
a restaurant, sometimes adversely. But a guide c an do
no more than report facts. Clients ultimately are the
lifeblood of a restaurant. And clients should make their
views known - praise and complaints alike - to the
restaurant, there and then, not next day. They should
also inform us of their views.

TO FIND OUT ABOUT HOW YOU CAN JOIN
THE CURRY CLUB MEMBERS' DISCOUNT
SCHEME, PLEASE TURN TO PAGE 288.

NORTHUMBERLAND

ALNWICK

ALNWICK TANDOORI
17, Clayport Street, Alnwick.

CC DISCOUNT
01665 510772

Owned by Abdul Khalique and Abdul Tahid. Mr Khalique will be found in the restaurant welcoming guests into their restaurant and Mr Tahid will be found in the kitchen cooking up all our favourite curries and accompaniments. The Alnwick Tandoori has promised to give Curry Club members at its quieter times, see page 288. Opening hours: 5.30pm to 11.30pm, seven days a week.

BERWICK-UPON-TWEED

MAGNA
39, Bridge Street, Berwick-upon-Tweed.

CC DISCOUNT
01289 302736

The Magna has been in our guide since we started it in 1984. 'And no wonder,' says Curry Club member Michael Fabricant MP. It's a family (Khan) business and the food which is well described on the menu is equally well cooked. Managing partner, Jahangir Khan will give a discount to Curry Club members at his quieter times, see page 288. Opening hours: 12 noon to 2.30pm and 6pm till midnight, closed for Sunday lunch.

MAGNA TANDOORI RESTAURANT
Fully Licensed
39 BRIDGE STREET
BERWICK-UPON-TWEED
INDIAN CUISINE
Northumberland
01289 302736/306229

CRAMLINGTON

LAL QILA
Dudley Lane, Cramlington.

CC DISCOUNT
01670 734268

Opened in 1987 but new to the Guide. Here because of satisfied reports received. Seats fifty-four diners and serves everything from Karahi to Balti and in between. Manager, Abdul Karim will give a discount to Curry Club members, at his quieter times, see page 288. Opening hours: 12 noon to 2.30pm and 6pm till 11.30pm. Sunday 7pm to 11.30pm only. Branch: Tandoor Mahal, 17, Bridge Street, Morpeth. Morpeth Takeaway, 10, Chantry Place, Morpeth.

CORBRIDGE

THE VALLEY   **TOP 100 - CC DISCOUNT**
SPECIAL AWARD: THE BEST IN THE NORTH
The Old Station House, Corbridge.   **01434 633434**

It is a pleasure to report on something quite unique, and probably un-copiable on the Indian restaurant scene. It's Syed Nadir Aziz's Valley restaurant. Known universally as Daraz, he has been involved in curry restaurants in the north-east since 1973 (including Newcastle's Moti Mahal and Daraz). In 1991 he came across Corbridge station building in the beautiful Tyne valley. Built in 1835 for Stephenson's railway, it is now disused as a station, although it is on the important Newcastle to Carlisle railway. Indeed trains stop at Corbridge station throughout every day, but passengers do not use the old building any more. That is not until Daraz breathed new life into it. He turned it into a stylish up-market Indian restaurant. Its USP which has attracted wide media attention is its location and the fact that they offer a unique train service whch is ideal for a celebration or special treat. Uniformed staff welcome you at Newcastle Central Station, and escort you by train to The Valley Restaurant to enjoy a meal which you have chosen while sitting on the train and has been telephoned through to the restaurant via a mobile. This service is for parties of 10 or more. Of course individuals can make their own way there and back by scheduled train - but beware a fairly early last train. One wag tells me that he books his takeaway by phone and collects it en-route without leaving the train on his way home from work! As to the restaurant, there is a reception room and seventy seats in four connecting rooms (one of which opens onto the westbound platform). Decor is lush and Indian in feel (turquoise and gold predomi-nate). And the food? The menu is extensive and all the currinary correct favourites are there. Chef Abdul Khalick's specials are much in demand. We hear of 'the creamiest Shah Jahani Pasanda and Luari Mangsho - lamb with fresh herbs and spices - a dish 'unique to the Valley' according to Daraz. We have placed this restaurant into our TOP 100 for originality and flair as well as for food. Come on members, try it and tell us all about it, we would all like to know. Owner, Syed Nadir Aziz (or Daraz for his friends) has promised to give a discount to Curry Club members, at his quieter times, see page 288. Opening hours: 6pm till 11pm, closed on Sundays. Branch: Moti Mahal, 14, Maple Avenue, Dunston, Gateshead. We are pleased to give this restaurant our BEST IN THE NORTH (of England) AWARD.

HEXHAM

ABBEY TANDOORI   **CC DISCOUNT**
28, Priestpopple, Hexham.   **01434 603509**

A plainly decorated restaurant but neat and tidy. Seats forty. A good selection of Tandoori dishes on the menu with, as they call them "sup-porting dishes" four different Nans. Manager, Miah Sahid has promised to give a discount to Curry Club members, at his quieter times, see page 288. Hours: 12 to 2pm and 6pm till 11.30pm, Sunday 6pm till 11pm only.

MORPETH

TANDOORI MAHAL   **CC DISCOUNT**
17, Bridge Street, Morpeth.   **01670 512420**

Branch of Lal Qila in Cramlington. 'An absolutely first class establish-ment. Prices fair, service good, decor of a very high standard, parking no problem.' MB. Assistant manager, Awlad Miah has promised to give a discount to Curry Club members, see page 288. Hours: 12 noon to 2.30pm and 6pm till midnight. Sunday 7pm till 11.30pm only.

TO FIND OUT HOW TO JOIN OUR DISCOUNT SCHEME
SEE PAGE 288

NOTTINGHAMSHIRE

MANSFIELD
MODHU MITHA
11-15, Ratcliffe Gate, Mansfield. 01623 651203
'Interior has been decorated in cool greens and seats around seventy. Extensive menu but standard curry house stuff. Food quite delicious and always plenty of it. Fresh Bhindi in the Bhajee.' MB.

NEWARK
ASHA
2, Stodman Street, Newark. 01636 702870
'Decor, very wine bar. Chicken Tikka Masala pleasant but lacked the creaminess that I am used to. Well recommended.' DH.

NOTTINGHAM
BEESTON TANDOORI CC DISCOUNT
150-152, High Road, Beeston, Nottingham. 0115 922 3330
A small but cosy restaurant seating forty diners. Chef Recommendations include Uri and Muki Special, which are described as fairly dry but well spiced. You are advised to book your table for Friday and Saturday evenings. Owner, S Choudhury gives a discount to Curry Club members, see page 288. Hours: 12 noon to 2.30pm and 6pm till midnight.

CHAND   CC DISCOUNT
26, Mansfield Road, Nottingham.   **0115 947 4103**
A fairly plainly decorated restaurant in dark red velvet and white walls.
Hanging plants and colonial fan. Menu contains a very good selection
both in quality and quantity of vegetarian dishes. Dhava Thaum - garlic
mushrooms, Begum Bahar - mild and sweet with fruit and nuts. Balti
dishes are also on the menu. Proprietor, MP Aslam has promised to give
a discount to Curry Club members, at his quieter times, see page 288.
Opening hours: 12 noon to 2pm and 6pm till midnight. Branch: Bombay
Bicycle Takeaway, 511, Alfreton Road, Nottingham,

GOLDEN TANDOORI BALTI
276, Alfreton Road, Nottingham.   **0115 942 0046**
'Standard curry house decor but the food, advertised as Pakistani, was
excellent. Chicken Karahi - delicious, Meat Balti - melt in the mouth
pieces of lamb and well flavoured, spiced sauce.' CF & AW. 10%
discount with takeaway orders. They also run a delivery service.

THE INDIAN
7, Bentinck Road, Nottingham.   **0115 942 4922**
A very upmarket restaurant, tastefully decorated to a very high stand-
ard. Cream walls, ornate white plaster work, tiled floor, large palms in
white pots and carpets hanging from walls. 'Aubergine Paneer and
Garlic and Mushroom Baji for starters, served with crisp salad. Murgh
Makhani, Chicken Tikka cooked with garlic, coriander and brandy and
I can honestly say it was among the best curries I have ever eaten. Rice
portions were large. Staff extremely friendly and food is outstanding.'
CY. Hours: Tuesday to Sunday 6pm till midnight (

KASHMIR   CC DISCOUNT
60, Maid Marian Way, Nottingham.   **0115 947 6542**
A large restaurant seating between ninety and one hundred diners.
Opened in 1988 by AD Satti, who has promised to give a discount to
Curry Club members, at his quieter times, see page 288. Hours: 6pm till
1am, Friday and Saturday (for all of you night owls!) till 2.30am.

LAGUNA
43, Mount Street, Nottingham.   **0115 941 1632**
'Serves the rice that I judge all other by - always fluffy and al dente and
never sticky. Decor well above average, chairs are comfortable. Starter
prices a bit steep. Lamb Badam Pasanda was rich and tasty. As Arnie
says, "I'll be back!"' PR. 'Cobra lager available. Overall excellent quality
food and big portions. Authentically praised by my Asian friends.' AT.

MAHARANI   CC DISCOUNT
7, Hockley Street, Notingham.   **0115 950 6785**
Well established tandoori house. Owner, manager Mr Bashir will give
a discount to Curry Club members, at his quieter times, see page 288.

MEHRAN II   CC DISCOUNT
948-950, Woodborough Rd, Mapperley, Nottingham.   **0115 955 1005**
A pretty and informative menu with some interesting dishes.
Sommerkhand - cooked with strawberry, cherries, fresh cream and
pistachio (sounds good - doesn't it). Sassi - cooked with banana,
pineapple and fresh cream. Awami - cooked with Keema, fresh tomatoes
and omelette. Siaherr - cooked with tomatoes, garlic and green peppers
in mustard oil. Balti and Karahi dishes are also featured on the menu.
Managing owner, Akram Dhareeja has promised to give a discount to
Curry Club members, at his quieter times, see page 288. Hours: Lunch:
Monday to Saturday 12 noon to 2pm. Dinner: Monday to Sunday 6pm
till 1am. Branches: Mehran, 2, Cromford Road, Langley Mill, Derbys and
Mehran Takeaway, 245, Nottingham Road, Somercotes, Derbys.

MOGAL E AZAM
7-9, Goldsmith Street, Nottingham.

CC DISCOUNT
0115 947 3826

'Visited several times over the past two years, consistently good food and attentive service. My friend amused the waiters by ordering the hottest curry on the menu and then spent the evening with sweat streaming down his face. In fairness they warned him against it!' AT. 'The restaurant has a wall gallery of star's autographed photo's thanking him for his superb meals and service.' GW. Opened in 1977 by Mr SN Miah, who has promised to give a discount to Curry Club members, see page 288. Hours: 12 noon to 2.30pm and 5.30pm till 1.30am.

MOUSHUMI
124, Derby Road, Stapleford. Nottingham.

CC DISCOUNT
0115 939 4929

A tastefully decorated restaurant decked out in sea greens and stained wood. Large and expensive engraved glass panels divide the restaurant. Proprietor Sanawor Ali has promised to give a discount to Curry Club members, see page 288. Hours: 12 noon to 2.30pm and 6pm till 11.30pm.

NEW KOH-I-NOOR
25-27, Bridgford Road, West Bridgford, Nottingham.

CC DISCOUNT
0115 981 1645

A small restaurant seating forty diners. 'I am always impressed with the freshness of the vegetables here. My mother fell in love with the Peshwari Nan .' PR. Managing owner, Mr Ibrahim will give a discount to Curry Club members, see page 288. Hours: 5.30pm to 12.30am, seven days a week. Branch: Plaza Tandoori, 15, Main Road, Gedling, Notts.

NOOR JAHAN
41, Mansfield Road, Nottingham.

CC DISCOUNT
0115 947 6449

Opened in 1971 and changed ownership twice since. Under new management of Motahir Khan who will give a discount , see page 288.

PAPPADUM BALTI
207, Radford Road,Nottingham.

CC DISCOUNT
0115 978 0972

A cute little restaurant seating just 24. Owner, Manager and creator of curries in the kitchen, Tariq Mahmood promises to give discounts to Curry Club members,see page 288. Opening hours: Sunday to Thursday 6pm till 1am. Friday and Saturday 6pm till (for curry insomniacs) 3am.

SAAGAR
473, Mansfield Road, Sherwood, Nottingham.

TOP 100 - CC DISCOUNT
0115 962 2014

Seats on two floors up to 80 diners. Balti dishes on the menu, along with Jalfarazi (sic), Kurma (sic) and Danshak (sic). 'Enjoyed a superb meal - tasty, well presented food. Huge portions, every table was asking for doggybags. King Prawn Pakora were like cricket balls - a meal in themselves.' AT. 'Clean, fresh atmosphere. Chicken Tikka Kashmir, an enormous portion.' CS. 'We are great supporters of the Saagar.' JT. Managing owner, Mohammed Khizer gives a discount to Curry Club members, see page 288. Hours: 12 to 2.30pm and 5.30pm till 12.30am. Remains in our Top 100.

SHABAZ
142, Alfreton Road, Nottingham.

0115 979 0061

'Food is always of the highest quality. My favourite.' LW. Hours: 6pm till 3am, Friday and Saturday 6pm till 4am. Insomniacs take note.

SUTTON-IN-ASHFIELD
BEKASH
83, Outram Street, Sutton-in-Ashfield

CC DISCOUNT
01623 559955

Friendly, competent food and service at Masuk Miah's Bekash. We reported last time they adore children here. Judging by reports received adults adore the Bekash to. And they give a discount to Curry Club members, see page 288.

OXFORDSHIRE

ABINGDON
PRINCE OF INDIA   **CC DISCOUNT**
10, Ock Street, Abingdon.   **01235 523033**
We hear good things about the Prince, especially the Sunday lunch
buffet. Manager, A Sulman will give a discount to Curry Club members,
see page 288. Hours: 12 noon to 2.30pm and 6pm till midnight. Branch:
Prince of India, 31, High Street, Wallingford.

BANBURY
MOGHUL
58, Parsons Street, Banbury.   **01295 264177**
'I have used this place for years when in town (keeps the same chef)
lovely inside, good food, first class service.' PJ.

SHEESH MAHAL
45, Bridge Street, Banbury.   **01295 266489**
'Decided to visit on a friend's recommendation. Tandoori Fish for
starters, very good. Chicken Moghalai, excellent, Nan breads were
massive. Coffee pot and cream were left on our table so we could help
ourselves.' JSK. Hours: 12 noon to 2.30pm and 6pm till midnight.

BICESTER
SAHANA   **CC DISCOUNT**
15, Market Square, Bicester.   **01869 245170**
'Having visited every Indian restaurant in Oxford and surrounding area
in the past ten years, this must rate highly. The menu is wide and varied.
The friendly and efficient service is second to none. Decor is basic but
clean and tidy.' CFB. 'Upon entering the restaurant one already had the
feeling of comfort with the light dimmed to the right level. Sheek Kebab
very good and Samosa was thoroughly cooked. Dansak was of good
consistency, an excellent sweet and sour taste. Good food at an afford-
able price.' RC.Proprietor, A Uddin will give a discount to Curry Club
members, see page 288. Hours: 12 noon to 2.30pm and 6pm to 11.30pm.

CHIPPING NORTON
ANARKALI   **CC DISCOUNT**
6, West Street, Chipping Norton.   **01608 642785**
'Good selection on menu, good sized portions. Best ever Naans, light and
fluffy. Onion Bhajees out of this world. Bank holiday weekend and was
busy but manager still had time to talk to us.' PA. Proprietor, A Uddin
will give a discount to Curry Club members, see page 288. Hours: 12
noon to 2.30pm and 6pm till 11.30pm. Branch: Moreton Tandoori, High
Street, Moreton-In-Marsh, Glos.

HENLEY-ON-THAMES
GAZAL   **CC DISCOUNT**
53-55, Reading Road, Henley-on-Thames.   **01491 574659**
A gazal is a gentle Indian love song. It has nothing to do with guzzling.
I hope that puts one reporter right. He loves the place though. Director,
Anwer Naseem will give a discount to Curry Club members, see page
288. Hours: 12 noon to 2pm and 6pm till 11pm.

VICEROY
40, Hart Street, Henley-on-Thames.   **01491 577097**
A large restaurant seating 100. A good and reliable establishment
serving all the usual curries and accompaniments with a few specials
thrown in such as Chingri Jhol - king prawns served in a skillet and
Karahi Kebab Khyberi - from the Khyber Pass.

OXFORD

ALCAZAR
1, The Parade, Windmill Road, Headington, Oxford.   **01865 60309**
'A smallish restaurant serving Balti food. My wife and I both had Balti
Mughlai, an elegant subtly flavoured dish as good as anything we have
ever had in an Indian restaurant. Pulao Arasta Deluxi, very finely
flavoured rice. Service was efficient, courteous and good humoured.
Impressed.' Dr GG. 'Mediterranean-feel decor, white walls and tiled
floor. Boasts a cushioned area, one can languish upon thick cushions and
enjoy a relaxed a unique feast.' DH.

AZIZ   **TOP 100**
230, Cowley Road, Oxford.   **01865 794945**
'Tastefully simple decor, airy and bright. Ada Gosht superbly flavoured
and most delicious. Korai Murgh was tender and tasty, and both served
in ample quantity. Outstanding Pullao rice in texture and fragrance.
Service was slow, excusable because the restaurant was well attended.'
Dr JCC. 'Excellent quality, charming service. Very comfortable and
relaxing atmosphere.' RT. Decoration immediately impressed. Tables
simply but elegantly set with crisp white linen. Good vegetarian selection on menu. Generous quantities and delicately flavoured. Emphasis
on subtlety. A splendid meal.' WC. A new entry to our TOP 100.

JAMAL'S
108, Walton Street, Oxford.   **01865 310102**
'My Vindaloo was not a good tingle but a bit of a volcano! Very good
portions, Chapatis lovely and moist. Highly recommended.' GH. 'Very
comfortable restaurant, pleasing decor. Food absolutely delicious! We'll
go again.' JW. 'Good value with delicious food.' CME.

KASHMIR HALAL   **CC DISCOUNT**
64, Cowley Road, Oxford.   **01865 250165**
Opened in 1970 by Said Meah and seats fifty diners. A comprehensive
menu listing all your favourite curries and accompaniments. Mr Meah
has promised to give a discount to Curry Club members, see page 288.
Hours: 12 noon to 3pm and 6pm till midnight.

OXFORD TANDOORI   **CC DISCOUNT**
209, Cowley Road, Oxford.   **01865 241493**
A small establishment seating forty-four diners. A good reliable curry
house serving competent curries. Proprietor, Tosir Ali has agreed to give
a discount to Curry Club members, see page 288. Hours: 12 noon to
2.30pm and 6pm till midnight.

POLASH TANDOORI   **TOP 100.**
25, Park End Street, Oxford.   **01865 250244**
'Cannot fault the food, but consider it expensive for the small portions.'
CME. 'Capacious restaurant is bright, simply attractive and welcoming.
A truly extensive menu and bar facilities offer all one could wish. Food
is excellently prepared, Parathas clean and tasty. Passanda Gosht
creamy and spicy with tender lamb. Highly recommended.' Dr JCC. 'I
had a Murgh Jalfrezi which was ridiculously hot with green chillies in
abundance - to be fair the manager did warn me. Staff were very
courteous and apologetic when we were stranded with Popadoms but no

pickle tray.' ND. The cooking by Mohana Pilliai is well above average and some of the specials are unusual featuring duck, venison, pheasant and chitol and buaal - Bangladeshi fish. We are happy to retain the Polash in our TOP 100 and welcome more reports. Manager Gous Uddin will give a discount to Curry Club members, see page 288. Hours: 12 noon to 2.30pm and 6pm till 11.30pm.

STANDARD
117, Walton Street, Oxford.   **01865 53557**
A small restaurant seating forty, so be sure to book on Fridays and Saturdays. You will find all the usual curries and accompaniments on the menu. Hours: 12 noon to 2.30pm and 6pm till 11.30pm.

TAJ MAHAL
16, Turl Street, Oxford.   **01865 243783**
The Taj Mahal is on the first floor above Whites in the middle of a beautiful part of Oxford. There since 1937. It was the third curry restaurant in England at the time and the first outside London. 'Varied menu, we chose from the specials. Massive quantities of quality food. Waiter was happy to explain dishes to an American lady sitting on the next table.' JF. 'A smart, comfortable restaurant with splendid views. Karahi Chicken - exceptional, Methi Gosht and Vegetable Curry - very good. We rate them pretty highly.' Dr GG. 'Birianis remain outstanding. Huge portions.' Dr AGJ.

WALLINGFORD
PRINCE OF INDIA   **CC DISCOUNT**
31, High Street, Wallingford.   **01491 835324**
This standard curry house seats forty diners and serves all the usual tandooris and curries that you are expecting. They also do a free home delivery service, minimum order £10.00. Manager, A Sulman will give a discount to Curry Club members, see page 288. Hours: 12 noon to 2.30pm and 6pm till midnight.

WITNEY
CURRY PARADISE
39, High Street, Witney.   **01993 702187**
House specials include Makhnee (sic), (Chicken Tikka Masala) Shak Shu-Ka (sic) (a mild mince dish) and Achaar Lamb (pickled). Korai dishes are also to be found but as of yet no Baltis. Head chef M Uddin is so eager that you try his wonderful curries that he has promised to give Curry Club members a discount at his quieter moments in the kitchen, see page 288. Hours: 12 noon to 2.30pm and 6pm till 11.30pm.

The editor of this Guide welcomes your views on the restaurants and take-aways we list in its pages, and on any you visit anywhere. Please send your reports to : The Editor, P.O. Box 7, Haslemere, Surrey, GU27 1EP. Please enclose an addressed envelope if you want a reply.

TO FIND OUT ABOUT HOW YOU CAN JOIN THE CURRY CLUB MEMBERS' DISCOUNT SCHEME, PLEASE TURN TO PAGE 288.

SHROPSHIRE

BRIDGNORTH
EURAISA
21, West Castle Street, Bridgnorth. 01746 764895
Menu contains all your favourite curries and accompaniments. A long established restaurant (1975) means that you can be sure of competent service and food, and we generally receive good reports about it.

LUDLOW
SHAPLA BALTI
58, Broad Street, Ludlow. 01584 875153
'Pleasant decor, fairly clean and tidy with prompt service. Good value and worth a visit.' DG. Hours: 12 noon to midnight.

OSWESTRY
SIMLA CC DISCOUNT
42, Beatrice Street, Oswestry. 01691 659880
Opened in 1976 and seats a hundred. 'Onion Bhajee, decor and service were good.' SP. Owner, Sufu Miah will give a discount to Curry Club members, see page 288. Hours: 12 noon to midnight. Branch: Simla, 4-5, Victoria Square, Grapes Hill, Llangollen, Clwyd. Reports please.

SHREWSBURY
CASTLE INDIAN TAKEAWAY CC DISCOUNT
74, Castle Foregate, Shrewsbury. 01743 231808
You will find all the usual curries on the menu, from Rogon Juice (sic) and Birwani (sic) to Pal (sic). Home delivery service available, minimum order £10.00. Opened in 1985 by Abul Lais and J Hussain, who will give a discount to Curry Club members, see page 288. Hours: evenings only, 5.30pm till midnight. Branch: Curry House, 29, Mardol, Shrewsbury.

SHALIMAR CC DISCOUNT
23, Abbey Foregate, Shrewsbury. 01743 366658
Opened in 1989 and seats seventy-five diners. Serves all the usual curries and accompaniments, but Tandoori dishes are their specialitiy. Proprietor, Mr Uddin will give a discount , see page 288. Hours: 12 to 2.30pm 5.30pm till midnight. Branch: Bilash, 7, Horse Fair, Rugley, Stafs.

TELFORD
DHAKA CC DISCOUNT
35-37, Tan Bank, Wellington, Telford. 01952 243487
Karahi Kabab Kyberi and Butter Chicken are chef specialities, and there are also three Balti dishes on the menu. Proprietor, MU Ahmed will give a discount , see page 288. Hours: 12 noon to 2pm and 6pm till midnight.

MISTER DAVES BALTI HOUSE CC DISCOUNT
15, Burton Street, Dawley, Telford. 01952 503955
Balti everything on the menu, there isn't one they don't do. Proprietor, M Kirton will give a discount to Curry Club members, see page 288. Hours: evenings only, 6pm till midnight.

WHITCHURCH
JAYS TANDOORI AND BALTI
9, High Street, Whitchurch. 01948 662478
'When I'm in town I'm in Jays. I love their food.' PJ. Hours: evenings only, 6pm till 1am, Friday and Saturday till 2am.

SOMERSET

BRIDGWATER

ENGLISH RAJ INDIAN
CC DISCOUNT
54, Clare Street, Bridgwater.
01278 424416

Owned by A Kalam since 1978 who is also head of the kitchen. 'Popadoms light and crisp. Nargis Kebab, quite spicy. Prawn and Mushroom Curry, Madras hot, lots of prawns and the portion was a good size.' FEG. Balti is on the menu. Mr Kalam will give a discount to Curry Club members, see page 288. Hours: 12 noon to 2pm and 6pm till 11.30pm.

TASTE OF INDIA
CC DISCOUNT
31-33, Penel Orlieu, Bridgwater.
01278 446666

Opened 1989 and seats forty-five diners. Balti can be found on the menu along with all your old favourites. Farid Hassan, sole proprietor, has promised to give a discount to Curry Club members, see page 288. Hours: 12 noon to 2pm and 5.30pm to midnight. Reports welcomed.

TAUNTON

GANGES BALTI HOUSE
93-95, Station Road, Taunton.
01823 284967

My twelve year old daughter (fast becoming a curryholic) votes her Chicken Tikka Masala her favourite.' BG. 'Onion Bhajia, flavour out of this world. Tikka Masala superb, Chilli Masala best I have ever tasted. Rice well cooked. I liked Mushroom Pilau which although not on the menu the waiter assured me he could do without any problem. Pity we live 250 miles away.' JW. Hours: 12 to 2.15pm and 6pm to midnight.

WELLINGTON

TASTE OF INDIA   CC DISCOUNT
2, North Street, Wellington.   **0123 667051**
A cosy little restaurant seating thirty diners. Serving all the usual curies and accompaniments to locals as well as visiting holiday makers. Mr Choudhury, owner and head chef, will give a discount to Curry Club members, see page 288. Hours: 12 noon to 2pm and 6pm till midnight. Closed all day on Tuesday.

WINCANTON

MIAH'S   CC DISCOUNT
4, Church Street, Wincanton.   **01963 33417**
'Very good restaurant with excellent food.' AHS. Manager, Akthar Hussain has promised to give a discount to Curry Club members, see page 288. Hours: 12 noon to 2.30pm and 6pm till 11pm. Branches: Humaira, 112, Judd Street, London WC1 and Raj of India, 28, Salisbury Street, Shaftesbury, Dorset.

STAFFORDSHIRE

BURTON-ON-TRENT

GEORGE'S TANDOORI   CC DISCOUNT
48-49, Station Street, Burton-on-Trent.   **01283 533424**
Specials include: George's Special Cocktail - 1/4 Tandoori Chicken, Sheesh Kebab, Chicken and Lamb Tikka prepared in a wok with a mild sauce, all for £6.75. Under breads is a 'G & T Nan' - not a gin and tonic but garlic and tomato! Balti dishes are also available. Free home delivery service - minimum order £10.00 within a five mile radius. Proprietor, Davinder Gidda will give a discount to Curry Club members, see page 288. Hours: 6pm till 1am, seven days a week. Reports welcomed.

CANNOCK

BENGAL BRASSERIE   CC DISCOUNT
4, Market Street, Hednesford, Nr Cannock.   **01543 424769**
Serving all the usual curry house fare including Balti dishes. Home delivery service available, within a three mile radius for a minimum order of £10.00. Proprietor, Mr Miah will give a discount to Curry Club members, see page 288. Hours: 6pm till midnight. Reports welcomed.

SALEEM NAGH
Queen Square, Cannock.   **01543 505089**
'Decor is tastefully luxurious in pastel pinks and greys. Service is prompt and courteous. Starters are plentiful and are served, cooked and enjoy the same quality as the main courses. Each visit has been a real evening out in a relaxed are friendly atmosphere, which judging by its increasingly growing popularity is a view shared by many.' AK.

CODSALL
RAJPUT
The Square, Codsall.   **01902 844642**
'After eventually deciding it wasn't a pub (it's a Tudor building) we entered and were immediately impressed by the layout of the reception area. Upstairs restaurant seems a little cramped. Service polite and friendly. Food very good, ordered my usual Chicken Tikka Masala.' DG.

LICHFIELD
BENGAL   **CC DISCOUNT**
42, Bore Street, Lichfield.   **01543 263772**
A huge restaurant seating 100. Under the same ownersip since 1976 and has built up a good local trade for serving competent curries and accompaniments. Managing owner, Shofique Rahman will give a discount to Curry Club members, see page 288. Evenings only, 5pm till 1am.

THE EASTERN ~EYE~

19b, Bird Street, Lichfield, Staffordshire.
Telephone: 01543 254399

EASTERN EYE   **TOP 100 - CC DISCOUNT**
19b, Bird Street, Lichfield.   **01543 254399**
Owner by Mr Salam and was in our last guide. 'Very pleased to add my endorsement to this restaurant. Cosy atmosphere, friendly helpful staff and my Lamb Madras far and away the best I have ever had.' BF. MP and Curry Club member, Michael Fabricant, eats here when in his constituency. 'Service very attentive, infact I think I was asked about three times if I was enjoying the meal, once is enough. Food excellent, Chicken Tikka Masala was probably the best I've ever had. A cut above the rest, I will use it for special occasions rather than on a regular basis, it's a bit pricey.' DG. 'Tandoori Bombay Fish is exquisite.' BF. 'Still in the top league. I've even started to use this place for my takeaways. Puts other restaurants in the shade.' DG. 'Comfort and decor still as good as before. Kohla Puri fresh and spicy. Nans and popadoms were beautiful. Quantities more than sufficient. Highly recommended.' DB. Mr Salam gives a discount to Curry Club members, see page 288. Hours: 5pm till midnight.

RAJ DUTH
21, St Johns Street, Lichfield.   **01543 264552**
Karahi and Balti dishes on the menu. Hours: 5pm till 12.30am. Fridays and Saturday till 1am. Reports welcomed.

NEWCASTLE-UNDER-LYME

BILASH   CC DISCOUNT
22, Keele Road, Newcastle-under-Lyme.   **01782 614549**
'It is by far the plushest restaurant in town with wood panel decor, nice
cutlery and comfortable seating, but food is a little lacking.' DE. Manager, Abdul Matin will give a discount to Curry Club members, see page
288. Hours: 5pm till 12.30am. Branches: Bilash, Baildon, West Yorks.
Monzil, 44, Broad Street, Hanley, Stoke On Trent. Asha Takeaway, 22a,
Higherland, Newcastle, Staffs. Reports welcomed.

RUGELEY

GANGES   CC DISCOUNT
5, Horsefair, Rugeley.   **01889 582594**
'The longest established restaurant in Rugeley. In the twelve years I have
been visiting this restaurant I have always found the food to be excellent,
coupled with good friendly service. I can recommend this restaurant to
novices and veterans alike.' DE. Mahbub Ahmed Choudhury will give
a discount to Curry Club members at his quieter times, see page 288.
Opening hours: 5.30pm to 1am.

STOKE-ON-TRENT

AL SHEIKH'S BALTI CENTRE   TOP 100
15, Howard Place, Shelton, Stoke-on-Trent.   **01782 285583**
'Ah paradise found!! Al Sheikh's should go straight into the Top 100 and
as the DJs say 'climbing fast'. Armed with cans of lager, it is unlicensed
and a BYO, we booked for 9pm but of course the table was not ready, we
were ushered to the pub across the road. A waiter came over to get us
once our table was ready - now that's customer service! Food matched
up to the setting, Liver Tikka superb. Baltis are very good, rich and tasty.
Large Nan, one recommended between a couple. The best curry experience.' SN & RA. 'A great atmosphere with friendly staff. Wonderful
Baltis.' PC. 'Magnificent and plentiful food plus fast and attentive
service. I'm desperately trying to organise some more business trips to
the Midlands.' EJR. So for SN & RA it goes into our TOP 100.

BALTI PALACE   CC DISCOUNT
39-41, Hope Street, Hanley, Stoke-on-Trent.   **01782 274744**
A large menu contains just about everything from Tandoori to Baltis.
Free home delivery service within five miles for an order over £10.00.
Students with their ID cards get a 10% discount. Proprietor, Nuruz
Zamal will give a discount to Curry Club members, see page 288. Hours:
6pm till 1.30am, weekends till 2am.

MONZIL   CC DISCOUNT
44, Broad Street, Hanley, Stoke-on-Trent.   **01782 280150**
Seats a massive 120 diners. Manager, A Matin will give a discount to
Curry Club members, see page 288. Hours: 7pm till 3am. (See Bilash,
Newcastle Under Lyme, for branches).

UTTOXETER

KOHI NOOR   CC DISCOUNT
Queen Street, Uttoxeter.   **01889 562153**
Serving competent and reliably good curries and accompaniments since
1986. Managing owner, S Miah will give a discount to Curry Club
members, see page 288. Hours: 5.30pm to midnight. Branch: Kohi Noor,
Rink Shopping Centre, Rinkway, Swadlincote, Derbys.

SUFFOLK

FELIXSTOWE
BOMBAY NITE   **CC DISCOUNT**
285, High Street, Felixstowe.   **01394 272131**
Owner, Mahbub Alam, who will be found front of house greeting his customers, gives a discount , see page 288. Hours: 12 noon to 2.30pm 6pm to 11.30pm. Branch: Bombay, Orwell Place, Ipswich.

HADLEIGH
ROYAL BENGAL
51, High Street, Hadleigh.   **01473 823744**
'Small restaurant but very comfortable. Menu is quite extensive and full of old favourites. Speciality Tandoori dishes are recommended.' MB.

IPSWICH
TAJ MAHAL   **CC DISCOUNT**
40-42, Norwich Road, Ipswich.   **01473 257712**
Opened in 1985 and seats sixty diners. Serving competent curries and accompaniments. Manager, Muktar Ali gives a discount to Curry Club members, see page 288. Hours: 12 noon to 2pm and 6pm till midnight.

LOWESTOFT
AHMED   **CC DISCOUNT**
150, Bridge Road, Oulton Broad, Lowestoft.   **01502 501725**
A cute little restaurant with just 28 seats. 'Brilliant.' PJ. Proprietor, Boshor Ali will give a discount to Curry Club members, see page 288. Hours: 12 noon to 2.30pm and 6pm till 11.30pm. Branch: Jorna Indian Takeaway, 29-33, Wherstead Road, Ipswich, Suffolk.

SEETA   **CC DISCOUNT**
176, High Street, Lowestoft.   **01502 574132**
Tiny (28 seats), pretty establishment. All the usual curries and accompaniments on the menu, including Scampi Kurma, Biriani etc. Owner, M Uddin will give a discount to Curry Club members, see page 288. Hours: 12 noon to 2pm and 6pm till 11.30pm. Closed on Tuesdays.

NEWMARKET
NEWMARKET INDIAN CUISINE
150, High Street, Newmarket.   **01638 660973**
'Small, friendly restaurant. Very busy. Wide selection on menu. Mela full of flavour. Madras spicy, hot but not too hot.' MG.

STOWMARKET
ROYAL TANDOORI
16/18, Tavern Street, Stowmarket.   **01449 674392**
'Food was gorgeous.' PJ. Hours: 12 noon to 3pm and 6pm till 11.30pm.

WOODBRIDGE
ROYAL BENGAL   **TOP 100 - CC DISCOUNT**
6, Quay Street, Woodbridge.   **01394 387983**
'Service friendly and efficient.' PD. 'Shami Kebab was a little on the small side, but what it lacked in size it more than made up for in flavour. Chicken Madras was absolutly first class. .' MB. Manager, Mr Khan gives a generous discount to Curry Club members, see page 288. Hours: 12 noon to 2.30pm and 6pm till 11.30pm. Remains in our TOP 100.

SURREY

Parts of Surrey were absorbed by Greater London in 1965. We note affected boroughs with the letters GL.

ASHTEAD

MOGHUL DYNASTY   **CC DISCOUNT**
1, Craddock Parade, Ashtead.   **01372 274810**
Manager, Abdul Mannan will give a discount to Curry Club members, see page 288. Hours: 12 noon to 2.30pm and 5.30pm till 11pm. Branch: Cannon Tandoori, 7, Station Parade, Cannon Park, Edgware, Middx.

BANSTEAD

BANSTEAD TANDOORI   **CC DISCOUNT**
6, High Street, Banstead.   **01737 362757**
Manager, Abdul Noor will give a discount to Curry Club members, see page 288. Hours: 12 noon to 3pm and 6pm till 11.30pm.

BYFLEET

RED ROSE OF BYFLEET   **CC DISCOUNT**
148-150, High Road, Byfleet.   **01932 355559**
An attractively decorated restaurant with plaster cornices and dado rails. Ivys and palms divide tables and chandeliers hang from the ceilings. King Prawn dishes are house specialities. Managing partner, Shuel Miah will give a discount to Curry Club members, see page 288. Hours: 12 noon to 2.30pm and 6pm till 11.30pm. Branch: Red Rose In Surbiton, Red Rose of Chessington and Gaylord in Weybridge.

CAMBERLEY

DIWAN EE KHASS
365, London Road, Camberley.   **01276 66606**
'Chicken Jalfrezi tends to be on the hot side and is usually made even hotter for me. Staff appreciate my desire for hot food - if I don't have the Jalfrezi I choose the Meat Phall. Situated in a poor location so not that busy, my dread is that they will close and leave a gaping hole in my life and stomach. Introduced a special - Islamabad Balti.' BG.

RAJ
Yorktown Road, College Town, Camberley.   **01276 33224**
'A standard curry house with quick and efficient service. Try Bhoona Chicken or Chicken Dhansak.' EM.

ANCIENT RAJ
9, The Parade, Frimley High Street, Frimley, Camberley. 01276 21503
'We had intended to have a Pizza, however, my addiction to spices led us to the Ancient Raj. Good and busy atmosphere for a Monday night. All in all we thoroughly enjoyed our experience. Our only other visit was several weeks ago when we took the children to the Sunday buffet, £7.95 for per adult and £5 for the brats. Excellent value.' BG.

CARSHALTON GL

ASIA STANDARD   **CC DISCOUNT**
140-142, High Street, Carshalton.   **0181 647 0286**
A reliable good curry house. Managing owner, Abdul Hannan will give a discount to Curry Club members at lunch times, see page 288. Hours: 12 noon to 2.30pm and 6pm till 11.30pm.

CLAY OVEN TAKEAWAY   **CC DISCOUNT**
15a, Gordon Road, Carshalton Beeches.   **0181 647 94190**
A takeaway only establishment, opened in 1992. Hermon Miah will give
a discount to Curry Club members, see page 288. Hours: 5.30pm to
11.30pm. Branch: Gaylord, 141, Manchester Road, Isle of Dogs. E14.

ROSE HILL TANDOORI   **CC DISCOUNT**
320, Wrythe Lane, Rose Hill, Carshalton.   **0181 644 9793**
First of all apologies to Mr Rahman for getting tha name of his restaurant
wrong, it is in fact Rose Hill Tandoori and not Rose of India. We are very
sorry and hope this didn't cause too much confusion. Opened in 1985
and seats an intimate thirty-two diners. The menu offers all your
favourite curries and accompaniments and on a quick look at the drinks
menu I see Confederates Coffee - made with Southern Comfort - that's a
new one on me, sounds good too. Owner, Mr SalequrRahman will give
a discount to Curry Club members, see page 288. Hours: 12 noon to
2.30pm and 5.30pm till midnight. There is also a delivery service.

CHIPSTEAD
CHIPSTEAD TANDOORI   **CC DISCOUNT**
32, Station Approach, Chipstead.   **01737 556401**
Manager, Abdul Munaim will give a discount to Curry Club members,
see page 288. Hours: 12 noon to 2.30pm and 6pm till 11.30pm. Branches:
Delhi Brasserie, 134, Cromwell Road, Kensington, London. SW7 and
Delhi Brasserie, 44, Frith Street, Soho. London. WC2.

COBHAM
COBHAM TANDOORI   **CC DISCOUNT**
12c, Anyards Road, Cobham.   **01932 863842**
A small but comprehensive menu, serving all the usual curries and
accompaniments, but not a Samosas in sight! Managing partner, Mr
Yakub will give a discount to Curry Club members, see page 288. Hours:
12 noon to 2.30pm and 6pm till 11.30pm.

CROYDON GL
BANANA LEAF   **CC DISCOUNT**
27, Lower Addiscombe Road, Croydon.   **0181 688 0297**
One of the few South Indian restaurant serving authentic food. Owner,
Mr D Sitharaman is also the head chef, creating all your favourites and
some of his in the kitchen. Manager, Mr V Thambi will give a discount
to Curry Club members, see page 288. Hours: 12 noon to 2.30pm and 6pm
till 11.30pm. Fully licensed.

DEANS   **CC DISCOUNT**
241, London Road, Croydon.   **0181 665 9192**
Deans is a massive restaurant seating 150 diners and serving Pakistani
food. A small but typically Pakistani menu, serving Karahis and Handis.
Manager, Zaka Ud Din will give a discount to Curry Club members, see
page 288. Hours: 12 noon to 3pm and 6pm till midnight. Fully licensed.

INDIA PALACE   **CC DISCOUNT**
79, High Street, Croydon.   **0181 686 6730**
A massive restaurant seating 140 diners. It is a new restaurant which
opened last year. Tastefully and peacefully decorated in pastels, with
clean lines and high backed chairs. The head chef is Indian, so hopefully
you will be treated to some really authentic cuisine, Goan dishes are
house specialities. Sylvia MacPherson-Grant (the accountant) has
authorised the manager, Francis Letoit to give a discount to Curry Club
members, see page 288. Hours: 12 noon to 3pm and 6pm till 11pm, closed
on Sunday. Branch: India Palace, 112-114, Edgware Road, .London. W1.

ROYAL TANDOORI 2
226, Addington Road, Selsdon, Croydon.   **0181 651 3500**
An attractive restaurant decorated in green, with engraved glass panels
separating diners. Restaurant is partitioned by plants, which splits up a
rather large and long room. A few interesting dishes on the menu
include, Veal Karahi, Quail Karahi and Tandoori Trout. Home delivery
is available. Hours: 12 noon to 2.30pm and 6pm till 11.30pm, weekends
till midnight. Branch: Royal Tandoori (1), 209, Godstone Road,
Whyteleafe, Surrey.

SOUTH INDIA
16, London Road, Croydon.   **0181 688 6216**
Owned by Mr Dinamani and Mr Vaman, the former is heading the
kitchen and the latter is front of house manager. A South Indian
restaurant serving lovely dishes such as Masala Dosai with Sambar and
Coconut Chutney! Hours: 12 noon to 2.30pm and 6pm till 11pm.

DORKING
MOGHUL
187, High Street, Dorking.   **01306 876296**
'Wide choice of meals consumed, all up to usual high standards.' PW.

EAST MOLESEY
GOLDEN CURRY
19, Hampton Court Parade, East Molesey.   **0181 979 4358**
Opened the year I was born, way back in '66. Waiter, Abdul Karim serves
all our usual favourite curries and accompaniments at a good curry
house standard. Hours: 12 noon to 2.30pm and 6pm till midnight.

PALACE
20, Bridge Road, East Molesey.   **0181 941 3540**
A pretty Victorian conservatory has expanded this restaurant to seat
sixty diners. Hours: 12 noon to 2.30pm and 6pm till 11.30pm.

EPSOM
LE RAJ   **TOP 100**
211, Firtree Road, Epsom Downs.   **01737 371371**
'A well established restaurant with a regular following of customers.
Very smart, clean and tidy decor. Service is prompt and attentive. An
ideal setting for that special occassion, but I feel they put extra tables in
as it was cramped.' RP. 'The food is better that I have ever had, service
was slow. Bindi was nice and firm. Pickles were home-made not out of
a jar.' JP. Owner, chef Enam Ali pionered his curry in the sky venture,
Le Raj Avion. Originally he served curries aboard a passenger aircraft
chartered for the purpose from London City airport. In addition, for that
special night out, he organises a romantic night trip in a four seater
aircraft from Biggin Hill followed by a candle-lit Le Raj dinner for two.
Enam's cooking is light and innovative, and includes some Bangladeshi
specials. For those who like things spicy, ask and you shall receive.
Positively in our TOP 100. See advertisment on page 42.

EWELL
BOMBAY   **CC DISCOUNT**
332, Kingston Road, Ewell.   **0181 393 0445**
A very long standing and capable curry house. Manager, F Miah will
give a discount to Curry Club members, see page 288. Hours: 12 noon to
2.30pm and 6pm till midnight. See advertisement on page 215.

TO FIND OUT HOW TO JOIN OUR DISCOUNT SCHEME SEE PAGE 288

CURRY HOUSE
1, Cheam Road, Ewell.   **0181 393 0734**
'Ghost Methi was particulary delicious and had a crunchy texture from
fresh onion. Tarka Dhal also deserves a mention, perfect for dipping
Nans into. Food was piping hot and the portions adequate.' Dr JP.

FARNHAM
DARJEELING
25, South Street, Farnham.   **01252 714322**
'Everything about this restaurant is good. The decor is subtle, low light,
tropical fish. Good carpeting and sumptuous table linen and crockery.
The menu is extensive. Service is very good. Waiters are friendly but
unobtrusive. Food is excellent, subtly spiced, generous portions, excellent quality. Our favourite restaurant'. JW. Seats forty-six diners so
booking at weekends is necessary. Hours: 12 noon to 2pm and 6pm till
11.30pm. Branches: Viceroy, 1a, High Street, Hartley Witney, Hants.
Banaras, 40, Downing Street, Farnham, Surrey.

SHOMRAAT
133, Upper Hale Road, Upper Hale, Farnham.   **01252 735175**
'Extensive menu, large portions and excellent quality food. Discreet
service but friendly. Pleasing decor, marble pillars, chintz curtains and
comfortable beech chairs. Spring Lobster Masala, mouth watering
flavour.' JW. 'On collecting our takeaway we found the staff and
restaurant to be very pleasant. Food was above average.' PD.

FETCHAM
FETCHAM TANDOORI
248, Cobham Road, Fetcham.   **01372 374927**
Service was pleasant, though distant. Onion Bhajia was large and crisp.
Phall was tasty (I was expecting a super fire eater experience - instead I
received a Phall barely hotter than a Madras), together with the Pillau
Rice, and Mushroom Bhaji plentiful.   Restaurant scrupulously clean,
decor predominantly green, brown, pleasantly relaxing.' BP-D. Hours:
12 noon to 2.30pm and 6pm till 11pm, Friday and Saturday till midnight.

GODALMING
FARNCOMBE TANDOORI
18, Farncombe Street, Farncombe, Godalming.   **01483 423131**
'Wide menu of standard dishes. Just the right amounts of food. Very
tasty Sag Aloo and Butter Chicken. Pleasant service at the right time.'
BH. Hours: 12 noon to 2.30pm and 6pm till 11.30m, till midnight on
Friday and Saturday nights. Branch: Chalfont Tandoori Takeaway, 4,
Station Approach, Little Chalfont, Amersham, Bucks. See their adver-
tisement on page 215.

GUILDFORD

CHAMPAN TANDOORI
High Street, Bramley, Guildford.   **01483 893684**

DBAC has been here and can says it is a delightful little restaurant. Seating is split between two rooms, the smaller one is almost like a private dining room and would be great for a party, seats about ten. I always order Chicken Tikka Masala as my bench mark and can tell you that it is superb, the chef has added mango chutney which gives it a slightly sweet but tangy flavour. 'Small but cosy room. Best Chicken Murgh I've ever had - so garlicky - a new recipe they informed me!' SV.

KOHINOOR   CC DISCOUNT
24, Woodbridge Road, Guildford.   **01483 306051**

'Gets busy at the weekends. Service and food is excellent and this is rapidly becoming my favourite in Guildford.' CD. 'My wife's Pasanda was the most delicious she has ever eaten. Very reasonable prices considering the location. Tables very close to each other.' EJR. Owner and chef, Azizur Rahman will give a discount to Curry Club members, , see page 288. Hours: 12 noon to 2.30pm and 6pm till 11.30pm.

HASLEMERE

SHAHANAZ   EDITOR'S CHOICE
Kings Road, Haslemere.   **01428 651380**

An insight from the deputy editor: 'I have included this restaurant, not because of its authentic Indian cuisine, you won't find it, but because it is my local and it does do really good standard curry house food, cooked the Bangladeshi way, which I happen to adore. It's a small restaurant seating around 25, and I've never actually eaten in here. I have picked up many a takeaway, and had even more delivered, which is a God send in Haslemere, the town that humanity forgot. I have known standards to drop a fraction when they are busy on a Friday or Saturday night, so I try to do things like restaurant roundup for the Curry Club magazine or typing this guide during the week, then desperate urges don't overcome me. Because it is our local, I'm not very adventurous and order the same thing every time, almost without fail. Bombay Potato is wonderful, with onions and capsicums. Nans are large and fresh. Popadoms always crisp and light, and they do a great onion chutney. A new addition to the menu is Balti, there is a large day-glow-yellow piece of card stuck in the window, saying *'we now serve BALTI'*. Pat's "Balti Curry Cookbook" launched Balti around the country. Someone even said it 'Baltified Britain' and now we can get it in our home town. Great! It's astonishing how quickly it has come full circle.' Dominique.

HINDHEAD

RAJAH
Headley Road, Grayshott, Hindhead.   **01428 605855**

'First impressions of this restaurant were good. A friendly welcome greeted us and the restaurant itself was nicely laid out. Material from the ceiling formis a canopy. Tandoori Chicken lovely with mint sauce.' PD.

KINGSTON GL

GOLDEN CURRY   CC DISCOUNT
36-38, High Street, Hampton Wick, Kingston-upon-Thames.   **0181 977 1422**

The menu lists all our favourite curries and accompaniments, with a few specials as well, such as Chicken Rejala - fairly hot with yoghurt and black pepper. Free home delivery service available.Owner, Mabashar Ali will give a discount to Curry Club members, see page 288. Hours: 12 noon to 2.30pm and 6pm till midnight.

MONTY'S TANDOORI
53, Fife Road, Kingston-upon-Thames.

CC DISCOUNT
0181 546 1724

A modern restaurant, with a light and airy feel. South Indian face masks decorate the white walls and hang from cream drapes. Hand painted silk pictures of Indian scenes cover the walls, the floor is tiled. ' Service is excellent, unobtrusive, polite and no mistakes. Food is plentiful and piping hot.' ST. Owner, Kishor Shrestha gives a discount to Curry Club members, see page 288. Hours: 12 noon to 3pm and 6pm till midnight.

LEATHERHEAD

CURRY QUEEN
41, Church Street, Bookham, Leatherhead.   01372 457241

'Have always been impressed with the constant high standard of cooking. Delicious Chicken Tikka and Butterfly Prawns. Wonderful Naan bread. A true feast at a reasonable price.' EJR.

OXTED

MAHATMA COTE
111, Station Road, Oxted.   01883 722821

'I suppose it had to happen. It's the old gag about, "What do you call an Indian cloakroom attendent?" "Mahat - Macoat" Vintage Milligan !! Interior is first class with alot of attention being paid to the presentation. Good crips white linen, decent cutlery and glassware. A reluctance to leave the pickle tray behind after we had eaten our popadoms. Onion Bhajias a bit on the big side, only two per portion. Dhansaks well upto standard, hot and spicy with plenty of lentils to thicken the gravy. Bhindi and Brinjal both more than acceptable.' CD. Daily specials also available.

PURLEY GL

INDIA PALACE
11, Russell Parade, Russell Hill Road, Purley.

CC DISCOUNT
0181 660 6411

Well liked curry house. Owner, Z Haq will give a discount to Curry Club members, see page 288. Hours: 12 noon to 2.30pm and 6pm till 11.30pm.

REIGATE

REIGATE TANDOORI
10, West Street, Reigate.   01737 245695

'The best in Reigate by a wide margin. Food arrived very well presented and tasted fresh and authentic. I recommend this well appointed restaurant, especially the Sunday Buffet.' AD.

RICHMOND GL

INDIAN TANDOORI
113, Kew Road, Richmond.   0181 940 4308

Very basic decor but always clean. Everyone gets Popadoms and chutneys while they peruse the menu. Food was excellent, just the right heat, flavours wonderful.' JMW.

STAINES

ANCIENT RAJ
157, High Street, Staines.

CC DISCOUNT
01784 457099

'This restaurant is appropriate for all occasions, from takeaways to family celebrations. A stylish setting, pinks and creams, but not overpowering. Moghal swordsmen figures decorate the walls. We are impressed with the consistent high standard of well presented and hot food. Reasonably priced.' SR. Owner chef, Syed Joynul gives a discount to CC members, see page 288. Hours: 12 to 2.30pm & 6pm to 11.30pm.

SURBITON GL

AGRA TANDOORI   CC DISCOUNT
142, Ewell Road, Surbiton.   **0181 399 8854**
This is a good and reliable curry house, serving competent curries and
their accompaniments. Owner and manager, HK Paul will give a
discount to Curry Club members, see page 288. Hours: 12 noon to 2.30pm
and 6pm till midnight.

AJANTA   CC DISCOUNT
114, Ewell Road, Surbiton.   **0181 399 1262**
Looking at the menu you will find all your usual favourite spicy starters
and main courses. A new addition to the menu is Balti . Head waiter,
Rubel Ahmad will give a discount to Curry Club members, see page 288.
Hours: 12 noon to 2.30pm and 6pm till midnight. Branches: Shapla,
Bristol Road, Selly Oak, Shapla, Shirley, Birmingham.

RAJ   CC DISCOUNT
163, Ewell Road, Surbiton.   **0181 390 0251**
'More than enough to eat for very modest prices. Convivial surroundings, proprietor always very attentive and polite. Food of consistently
good quality, always a pleasure to eat there. Owner, Aziz Miah will give
a discount to Curry Club members, see page 288. Hours: 12 noon to
2.30pm and 6pm till midnight.

SARADA   CC DISCOUNT
286-288, Ewell Road, Surbiton.   **0181 399 0745**
A medium sized restaurant seating forty-eight diners. All the usual spicy
dishes on the menu, including Rougan Josh (sic), Jalfrazzi (sic) and
Bangalore Phal. There are not, as yet, any Balti dishes but there are,
however, Korai dishes instead. Owner and manager, Nani Gopal Seal
will give a discount to Curry Club members, see page 288. Hours: 12
noon to 2.45pm and 6pm till midnight.

SUTTON GL

BENGAL TANDOORI   CC DISCOUNT
260, High Street, Sutton.   **0181 643 8214**
Perusing the menu you will find Balti and Karai (sic) dishes, along with
all your favourite curries and accompaniments. Owner and manager,
Sufi Miah will give a discount to Curry Club members, see page 288.
Hours: 12 noon to 2.,30pm and 6pm till midnight.

SAVAR
7, Cheam Road, Sutton.   **0181 661 9395**
'Food was all freshly cooked. Specialities include fish dishes and also
venison. Chicken Jalfrezi was tasty and spicy, Pilau rice had no artifical
colouring but had a good spicy and minty flavour.' JS. Hours: 12 noon
to 3pm and 6pm till 11.30pm, till midnight on Friday and Saturday.

TOLWORTH GL

JAIPUR   CC DISCOUNT
90, The Broadway, Tolworth.   **0181 399 3619**
'A thoroughly enjoyable restaurant.' DRC. 'One of my regular haunts.'
PD. Owner S.U.Ali will give a discount to Curry Club members, see page
288. Branch: Jaipur, 49, Chertsey Road, Woking.

VIRGINIA WATER

VICEROY OF INDIA   CC DISCOUNT
4, Station Approach, Virginia Water.   **01344 843157**
A well respected local curry house, serving all your favourites. Owner
M.S.Ali will give a discount to Curry Club members, see page 288.

WEYBRIDGE

GOLDEN CURRY   CC DISCOUNT
132, Oatlands Drive, Weybridge.   01932 846931
A number of good reports received all give the thumbs up, though we
hear that the green flock wallpaper is no more! Owner Enayeth Khan will
give a discount to Curry Club members, see page 288.

THE HUSSAIN   CC DISCOUNT
47, Church Street, Weybridge.   01932 844720
Garlic chicken was memorable, even next day, according to one wag. All
reports speak well of the Hussain, and owner M. Suleman will give a
discount to Curry Club members, see page 288.

WHYTELEAFE

CURRY GARDEN   CC DISCOUNT
242, Godstone Road, Whyteleafe.   01883 627237
Good reports received. Branches: Canterbury, Ashford, Blackheath,
Whitstable and Southgate, N14. Owners Akhlaqur and Rahman will
give a discount to Curry Club members, see page 288.

WOKING

KHYBER PASS   CC DISCOUNT
18, The Broadway, Woking.   01483 764710
It's a standard curry house, green decor and Hindi arches. 'Food is
always good. Of particular interest to us is the lime pickle on the chutney
tray.' DRC. Manager Jafar Abdul Wahab, will give a generous discount
to Curry Club members, see page 288. Branches: Khyber Pass, 12, Lower
Guildford Road, Knaphill and 54, Terrace Road, Walton on Thames.

SUSSEX

For the purposes of this Guide, we combine East and West Sussex.

BEXHILL-ON-SEA

ANWAR   CC DISCOUNT
2, Sackville Road, Bexhill-on-Sea.   **01424 210205**
A brightly decorated standard curry house complete with Hindi arches.
Managing owner, Jamir Uddin will give a discount to Curry Club
members, see page 288. Hours: 12 noon to 2.30pm and 6pm till midnight.

SHIPLU   CC DISCOUNT
109, London Road, Bexhill-on-Sea.   **01424 219159**
Sparkling blue and silver marble- effect decor make this standard curry
house stand out from the rest. 'Service couldn't be bettered, all dishes
were well cooked and presented in adequate quantities.' DJB. Managing
owner, Abdul Kalam Azad will give a discount to Curry Club members,
see page 288. Hours: 12 noon to 2.30pm and 6pm till midnight.

BOGNOR REGIS

MAGNA   CC DISCOUNT
33, Argyle Road, Bognor Regis.   **01243 828322**
'Has become a favourite, it also appears to be very popular with other
locals, which suggests consistent good quality and service.' JO. Owner,
Rup Miah will give a discount to Curry Club members, see page 288.
Hours: 12 noon to 2.30pm and 5.30pm till 11.30pm.

PASSAGE TO INDIA
11, The Square, Barnham, Bognor Regis.   **01243 555064**
'Prices reasonable, as is the service, quality and quantity. Waiters go out
of their way to be helpful and kind to the children.' JO. 'Kitchen staff
flexible to accomodate ones tastes.' RI. Hours: 12 noon to 2.30pm and
6pm till 11.30pm, Friday and Saturday till midnight.

ELMER TANDOORI
76-78, Elmer Road, Middleton-on-Sea, Bognor Regis.   **01243 582641**
'Clean and comfortable decor, if uninspiring. Service friendly and
efficient even when busy. For flavour and texture its hard to beat.' JD.
'On the whole, quality is very good, but the standard of the Nan bread has
been known to vary.'JO. 12 to 2.30pm; 6 to 11pm, Friday/Saturday 12.

BRIGHTON

ANCIENT CURRY DOME   CC DISCOUNT
6, George Street, Brighton.   **01273 670521**
Takeaway only establishment, serving all the favourites including Balti
dishes. Chef, owner Ali Hassan will give a discount to Curry Club
members, see page 288. Hours: 12 noon to 2pm and 5pm till midnight.

BLACK CHUPPATI
New England Road, Brighton.   **01273 699011**
'Decor very plain, food marvellous, authentic recipes. Prices higher than
other restaurants.' RD. 'Relaxed atmosphere, beautiful home-style food.'
HH.

VICEROY OF INDIA   CC DISCOUNT
13, Preston Street, Brighton.   **01273 324733**
Established in 1985 and a good reliable curry house. Managing owner,
Mhoammed Ali will give a discount to Curry Club members, see page
288. Hours: 12 noon to 3pm and 6pm till midnight.

CHICHESTER

PEACOCK   **CC DISCOUNT**
Eastgate Square, Chichester.   **01243 775978**
'Wide choice on menu with perfectly adequate quantities.' JO. Manager, MA Miah will give a discount to Curry Club members, at lunchtimes, see page 288. Hours: 12 noon to 2.30pm and 6pm till 11.30pm.

CRAWLEY

BENGAL SPICES   **CC DISCOUNT**
71, Gales Drive, Three Bridges, Crawley.   **01293 571007**
A pretty green and gold restaurant with engraved glass screens, dividing diners. Balti features on the menu. Owner, AH Anwar will give a discount to Curry Club members, see page 288. 12 to 2.30; 6pm till 11pm.

RAJ   **CC DISCOUNT**
8, Broadfield Barton, Broadfield, Crawley.   **01293 515425**
A well established restaurant (1982), serving competent curries to a loyal following. Partner, MSU Ahmed will give a discount to Curry Club members, see page 288. Hours: 12 noon to 2.30pm and 6pm till 11.30pm.

CROWBOROUGH

AKASH BALTI   **CC DISCOUNT**
24, Crowborough Hill, Jarvis Brook, Crowborough.   **01892 661881**
Free Onion Salad with every takeaway order, free house wine with orders over £20. Balti featured on the menu and the manager, MD Adbul Kahir will give a discount to Curry Club members, see page 288. Hours: 12 noon to 2.30pm and 6pm till midnight.

EAST GRINSTEAD

SHAPLA
94, Railway Approach, East Grinstead.   **01342 327655**
Takeaway only, doing competent curries, 12 noon to 2.30pm and 5.30pm till midnight. Branch: Badsha, 10, West Cross, Tenterden, Kent.

EASTBOURNE

INDIAN PARADISE   **CC DISCOUNT**
166, Seaside, Eastbourne.   **01323 735408**
A bright restaurant serving competent curries and accompaniments to a local following for the last fourteen years. Owner, A Khalique will give a discount to Curry Club members, see page 288. Hours: 12 noon to 2.30pm and 6pm till midnight. Delivery service available.

HAILSHAM

RAJ DHUTT   **CC DISCOUNT**
48, High Street, Hailsham.   **01323 842847**
'Glass boothed seating allows for privacy. Popadoms light and served with sweet yoghurt. Onion Bhajis the biggest I've seen and full of onions. Jalfrezi, fresh chillies, hottish with plenty of meat.' GH. Managing owner, A Salik will give a discount to Curry Club members, see page 288. Hours: 12 noon to 2.30pm and 6pm till 11.30pm.

HASTINGS

SHIPLU   **CC DISCOUNT**
177a, Queens Road, Hastings.   **01424 439493**
'Tastefully decorated and clean. Service a little on the slow side but friendly. Popadoms warm and crisp, Onion Bhajia large, couldn't be beaten. Bangalore Phall not on the menu but asked for it and got it, very hot as it should be.' BP-D. Managing owner, Mr Hoque will give a discount to CC members, see p 288. 12 noon to 2.30; 6pm till midnight.

HAYWARDS HEATH
CURRY INN
58, Commercial Square, Haywards Heath.
CC DISCOUNT
01444 415414
'We were warmlywelcomed into this well decorated restaurant. Really good Prawn Butterfly. Lamb Chilli Masala extra hot was superb.' JLG. Manager, Ahad Miah will give a discount to Curry Club members, see page 288. Hours: 12 noon to 2.30pm and 6pm till 11.30pm.

HORSHAM
CURRY CENTRE
43, London Road, Horsham.
01403 254811
'Our regular haunt for over twenty years. Thoroughly recommended for consistent food. Excellent Niramish.' DRM.

HOVE
AL RIAZ
244, Portland Road, Hove.
CC DISCOUNT
01273 722332
Not decorated in an typically Indian style, pastel blue linen, grey walls. Comfortable velvet chairs to sit in while you peruse the menu or order a takeaway. Book for a table in the conservatory. Proprietor and chef Khorshier Riaz Khan will give a discount to Curry Club members, see page 288. Hours: 12 noon to 2.30pm and 5.30pm till 11.30pm. Delivery service available.

ASHOKA
95-97, Church Road, Hove.
CC DISCOUNT
01273 734193
A large establishment seating over one hundred diners. All the usual curried favourites on the menu. Owner, Rafique Miah will give a discount to Curry Club members, see page 288. Hours: 12 noon to 3pm and 6pm till midnight.

BALI BRASSERIE
Kingsway Court, First Avenue, Hove.
CC DISCOUNT
01273 323810
A very modern and stylish restaurant serving Indonesian and Malaysian cuisine. Delights include: Indonesian Sausage - tasty sausage filled with prawns, fish and vegetables. Part of the restaurant is a glamourous bar - with slightly different hours. Partner, Mrs B Calais will give a discount to Curry Club members, see page 288. 12 to 2pm;7.30pm till 10.30pm.

HOVE TANDOORI
175, Church Road, Hove.
CC DISCOUNT
01273 737188
A bright, if slightly gawdy curry house, serving good curry house food (Balti also included) at reasonable prices. Owner, Sofir Ahmad will give a discount to Curry Club members, see page 288. Hours: 12 noon to 2.30pm and 5.30pm till midnight. Delivery service available.

KARIM'S TANDOORI
15, Blatchington Road, Hove.
01273 739780
Starters are brilliant especially Nagis Kebab. Garlic Nan very tasty.Curries delicately spiced, but small portions.' ADS. 'Restaurant underground, so rather cold, but food and service made up for this.' PA. 6 till 11.30pm. Branch: Tandoori Nights, 2, Coombe Terrace, Lewis Road, Brighton.

KASHMIR
71, Old Shoreham Road, Hove.
01273 739677
Always consistently good quaity food. Absolutely delicious, large quantities and service friendly.' ADS. Balti also featured on the menu. Hours: 12 noon to 3pm and 6pm till midnight. Home delivery service

NEWHAVEN

VICEROY   **CC DISCOUNT**
4, Bridge Street, Newhaven.   **01273 513308**
An attractive restaurant seating forty diners. You will find all your usual
favourites with some unusual specials. Duck curries and Balti also
feature on the menu. Manager, Roshon Ali will give a discount to Curry
Club members, see page 288. Hours: 12 noon to 2.30pm and 6pm till
midnight. Delivery service available. Branch: Mayfield Tandoori, High
Street, Mayfield, Sussex.

NUTLEY

GANGES   **CC DISCOUNT**
High Street, Nutley.   **01825 713287**
Proprietor, M Haque will give a discount to Curry Club members, see
page 288. Hours: 6pm till midnight.

PETWORTH

VICE REGAL LODGE   **CC DISCOUNT**
East Street, Petworth.   **01798 43217**
A family restaurant. Cooking is done by the owners wife, Yasmin.
'Excellent quality, Prawn Rezala especially.' CK. All the usual curries
and accompaniments are present on the menu. Proprietor, MY Choudhury
will give a discount to Curry Club member, see page 288. Hours:
12.30pm to 2pm (by reservation only) and 6pm till 11pm.

RINGMER

RINGMER TANDOORI   **CC DISCOUNT**
72, Springett Avenue, Ringmer.   **01273 812855**
Balti dishes feature on the menu along with all our regular favourites.
Owner, MA Uddin will give a discount to Curry Club members, see page
288. Hours: 12 noon to 2.30pm and 6pm till midnight.

STEYNING

MAHARAJA
The Street, Bramber, Steyning.   **01903 812123**
"Good helping of Chicken Biriani well presented. Right balance of
ingredients. Nan bread light and fluffy. One of our favourites.' SR.
'Immediately impressed with the ambience. Quality of food was excel-
lent. 'GC. Hours: 12 noon to 2.30pm and 6pm till 11.30pm.

WORTHING

SHAFIQUES   **CC DISCOUNT**
42, Goring Road, Worthing.   **01903 504035**
'Baltis were excellent. Mattar Paneer, peas and cottage cheese cooked
with herbs - lovely.' NJD. Proprietor, Shafique Uddin will give a
discount to CC members, see page 288. 12 noon to 2.30 ; 5.30 to 11.30pm.

TASTE OF BENGAL   **CC DISCOUNT**
203, Heene Road, Worthing.   **01903 238400**
Takeaway only establishment. 'Quick and friendly service. Portions
generous. Excellent Vindaloo.' SB. Proprietor chef, Adbul Kalam will
give a discount to Curry Club members, see page 288. 12 to 2.30; 5.30pm
till midnight. Branch: Golden Bengal, 40, Lyndhurst Road, Worthing.

**TO FIND OUT ABOUT HOW YOU CAN JOIN THE
CURRY CLUB MEMBERS' DISCOUNT SCHEME,
PLEASE TURN TO PAGE 288.**

TYNE AND WEAR

GATESHEAD

THE LAST DAYS OF THE RAJ   **CC DISCOUNT**
218, Durham Road, Shipcote, Gateshead.   **0191 477 2888**
A takeaway establishment on ly, serving good curries: 12 to 2.30pm and
6 to midnight, closed for lunch on Sundays and Bank Holidays. Branch:
Last Days of the Raj, 168, Kells Lane, Lowfell, Gateshead. See page 288.

LAST DAYS OF THE RAJ CUISINE   **CC DISCOUNT**
565, Durham Road, Low Fell, Gateshead.   **0191 487 6282**
Serving competent takeaways only. Hours: 12 noon to 2.30pm and 6pm
till midnight, closed for lunch on Sundays and Bank Holidays.

NEWCASTLE UPON TYNE

DARAZ   **CC DISCOUNT**
4, Holly Avenue West, Jesmond, Newcastle.   **0191 281 8431**
All your favourite curries on the menu including Karahi but no Balti as
of yet. Hours: 12 noon to 2.30pm and 5.30pm till 11.30pm. Proprietor,
Imran Haider Choudhury will give a discount see page 288.

BALTI HOUSE   **CC DISCOUNT**
4, Waterloo Street, Newcastle.   **0191 232 7952**
A sixty four seater restaurant with a cocktail bar for you to make a night
of it! Hours: 6pm to midnight. Branch: Balti House, 18a, The Garth, Front
Street, Winlaton, Blaydon. Proprietor, Firuzul Islam Khan. See page 288.

RUPALI   **TOP 100 - CC DISCOUNT 20%**
6, Bigg Market, Newcastle.   **0191 232 8629**
'Superb menu - the best. Personal attentive service from Mr (Lord)Latif.'
DW. See page 36. Lord Harpole is full of tricks and fun. Get him talking.
He's hon chairman Curry Club North East. And try his world's hottest
curry! Recently redecorated following a fire, it remains in our Top 100

SACHINS   **TOP 100**
Old Hawthorn Inn, Fourth Banks, Newcastle.   **0191 261 9035**
Busy, charismatic place, where you can be sure of getting good Punjabi
curries, i.e. the ones we all love. Scottish owner Liam Cunningham, adds
flair, but be advised to book. It remains in our Top 100. See page 243.

SHIKARA   **CC DISCOUNT**
52, St Andrew's Street, Newcastle.   **0191 233 0005**
Seats a massive 150 diners on two floors. 'Buffet night very busy, so book
a table. Great value for money.' MS. ' Impressive menu.' DC'. Hours:
12 noon to 2.30pm and 6pm to 11.30. Owner, Saif Ahmed. See page 288.

VUJON   **TOP 100 - CC DISCOUNT**
29, Queen Street, Newcastle.   **0191 221 0601**
'Very stylish decor. Comfortable well lit and very clean. No standard
curries, but starter and main courses proved interesting and a good
choice.' KDF. Remains in our Top 100, and gives discounts. See page 288.

SOUTH SHIELDS

TANDOORI INTERNATIONALE
97, Ocean Road, South Shields.   **0191 456 2000**
'Main courses enjoyagble, good portions, prices are a little higher.' ED.
'I particularly recommend the Nargis Kofta.' DM.

NASEEB
90, Ocean Road, South Shields.   0191 456 4294
'My Sylhet Mixed Special was good.' DM.

STAR OF INDIA   CC DISCOUNT
194, Ocean Road, South Shields.   0191 456 2210
'Visited for the special offer three course meal, beautifully prepared and presented.' TH. Balti dishes on the menu. 12 to 2.30pm; 5.30 to1am, Friday / Saturday 2am. Branches: Royal Bengal, Prince Regent St, Stockton ; Shapla, 192, Northgate, Darlington. Discount, see page 288.

SUNDERLAND
CITY TANDOORI
27, Fawcett Street, Sunderland.   0191 567 0535
'Extensive menu with all the old favourites (Baltis). Food well presented. Good view into the kitchen - nothing to hide - reassuring.' CF & AW.

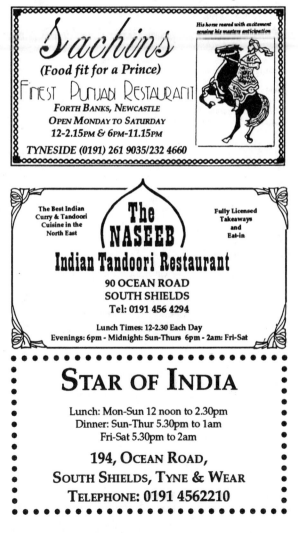

GRANGE TOWN TANDOORI KITCHEN CC DISCOUNT
1, Stockton Terrace, Grangetown, Sunderland. 0191 565 5984
Another takeaway only establishment. Balti and other favourites on the menu. Hours: 12 noon to 2pm and 5.30pm till midnight, Friday and Saturday till 12.30am. Owner, Shofozul Islamwill give a discount to Curry Club members, see page 288. Home delivery service.

WALLSEND
LIGHT OF INDIA
120, High Street East, Wallsend. 0191 234 5556
'Manager, Mr Salik is always very helpful. Food more than enough does an excellent Chicken Tikka Chilli Mosala (sic).' MS. Hours: 12 noon to 2.30pm and 6pm till 12.30am, closed Sunday lunch.

WHICKHAM
JAMDANI CC DISCOUNT
3, The Square, Front Sreet, Whickham. 0191 496 0820
Well established curry house, since 1978. Seats 38 diners, so booking at weekends is advised. Hours: 12 noon to 2.30pm and 6pm till 11.30pm. Will give a discount to Curry Club members, see page 288.

MOTIJHEEL CC DISCOUNT
9, Front Street, Whickham. 0191 488 0851
A takeaway establishment serving the full menu. Hours: 12 noon to 2pm and 6pm till 11.30pm. Manager, EH Choudhury. See page 288.

WINLATON
BALTI HOUSE CC DISCOUNT
18a, The Garth, Front Street, Winlaton. 0191 414 2223
A small restaurant seating just thirty-four diners all the usual favourites plus Balti. Owner, FI Khan has promised to up his takeaway discount from 15% to 20% for Curry Club members, see page 288. Hours: 6pm till midnight. Branch: Balti House, 4, Waterloo Street, Newcastle.

WHITLEY BAY
HIMALAYA CC DISCOUNT
33, Esplanade, Whitley Bay. 0191 251 3629
Reliable curry house. Hours: 12 noon to 2.30pm and 5.30pm till midnight. Owner, Abdul Goffar will give a discount, see page 288.

SHAHENSHAH CC DISCOUNT
187-189, Whitley Road, Whitley Bay. 0191 297 0503
'Food first class. Chicken Tikka terrific, full of flavour.' MB. 'My local for a year.' SN. 'We found the restaurant busy in a quiet and efficient way. To drink, Cobra lager, the perfect accompaniment.' PAP. See page 288

TAKDIR CC DISCOUNT
11, East Parade, Whitley Bay. 0191 253 0236
Serving all the usual curries and accompaniment with a few interesting house specials. Hours: 12 noon to 2pm and 5.30pm till midnight. Owner, M Rahman will give a discount to Curry Club members, see page 288.

TO FIND OUT HOW TO JOIN OUR DISCOUNT
SCHEME SEE PAGE 288

WARWICKSHIRE

ALCESTER

BALTI CELLAR　　　　　　　　　　　　　　**CC DISCOUNT**
7, Market Place, 316 High Street Alcester.　　　　**01789 764635**
Director, MM Hussain will give a discount to Curry Club members, see
page 288. Hours: 5.30pm till midnight, till 1am on Friday and Saturday.

ROMNA TANDOORI　　　　　　　　　　　　**CC DISCOUNT**
25, High Street, Alcester.　　　　　　　　　　　**01789 762252**
Proprietor, Rofik Ullah will give a discount to Curry Club members, see
page 288. Hours: 5pm till midnight.

HENLEY IN ARDEN

ARDEN TANDOORI　　　　　　　　　　　　**CC DISCOUNT**
137, High Street, Henley In Arden.　　　　　　**01564 792503**
Manager, Angur Miah will give a discount to Curry Club members, see
page 288. Hours: 12 noon to 2.30pm and 5.30pm till 11.30, midnight on
Friday and Saturday.

KENILWORTH

BALTI TOWERS
149, Warwick Road, Kenilworth.　　　　　　　**01926 851156**
'Attached to Kenilworth Lodge Hotel. Food dominated by Balti dishes,
large, fluffy Naans to accompany. Well sized portions.' SN & RA. Balti
Towers also at 50, Clarendon Street, Leamington Spa.

LEAMINGTON SPA

ASHOKA   **TOP 100**
22, Regent Street, Leamington Spa.   **01926 428272**
'Consistently the best. Variety and quality of food speaks for itself. Free
popadoms when collecting a takeaway' SN & RA. Hours: 6pm (Sunday
6.30pm) till 2am, Friday and Saturday till 3am. Remains in our Top 100.

HUSSAINS RAJ BHUJ
58, Bath Street, Leamington Spa.   **01926 888869**
'Food well worth the queue for a table. Chicken Chilli Balti was very hot
with high quality chicken. Nans very fluffy and light.' SN & RA.
'Excellent value. Balti Mince with green chilli is particularly tasty.' S &
AR. 'Service good considering how busy the place became. Kathlama
(cross betweenYorkshire pudding and a pancake filled with vegetable
curry) quite delectable.' AS.

NUNEATON

SUNDARBON
39, Attleborough Road, Nuneaton.   **01203 344243**
'Very very good.' PJ. Hours: 5pm till midnight, Friday till 1am.

RUGBY

DILRUBA   **CC DISCOUNT**
155-157, Railway Terrace, Rugby.   **01788 542262**
Serving good curries and accompaniments since 1983. Owner, Liaquat
Ali will give a discount to Curry Club members, see page 288. Hours:
6pm till 1am, Friday and Saturday till 2am, Sunday till 1.20am.

Titash International Balti Restaurant

OPEN DAILY
5PM TO
MIDNIGHT

65, Church Street, Rugby, Warwickshire. CV21 3PT

01788 574433/4

TITASH INTERNATIONAL BALTI   **CC DISCOUNT**
65, Church Street, Rugby.   **01788 574433**
A well respected Balti house. Owner Mashuk Ali will give a discount to
Curry Club members, see page 288. Hours: 5pm till 12.30am. Branch:
Titash International Balti, 290, Ormond Road, Frankley. See page 246.

STRATFORD-UPON-AVON

LALBAGH BALTI   **CC DISCOUNT**
3, Greenhill Street, Stratford-Upon-Avon.   **01789 293563**
'Good menu choice including Balti dishes. Average to generous portions. Excellent Sag Prawns.' GM. Manager, Suruz Ali will give a
discount to Curry Club members, see page 288. Hours: 12 noon to 2pm
and 5.30pm till 12.30am.

HUSSAIN'S
6A, Chapel Street, Sratford-Upon-Avon   **01789 205804**
Noon to 1130pm, reflecting its approach to its tourist trade

WEST MIDLANDS

BIRMINGHAM CENTRAL

BALTI SOCIETY
68, New Street, Birmingham, B2   **0121 643 9493**
'Balti Society is licensed and tends to attract a younger clientele later on
but still stays true to its Balti roots with a good range of traditional dishes.
My Balti Chicken Tikka Masala was mild but tasty although this Balti
House tends to make their Baltis saucier than most and certainly it was
on the rich side. However, tear drop Nans were on hand to soak up the
sauce.' Andy Munro. Sun to Thurs 6pm to 1am. Friday/Sat to 1.30am.

DAYS OF THE RAJ   **TOP 100 - CC DISCOUNT**
51, Dale End, B4.   **0121 236 0445**
Owners Kulair and Singh spared no expense when it opened in 1986, and
it continues to get good reports: 'Superbly cooked meal with individual
flavours coming through.' TMC. 'Food absolutely superb, though the
service less than warm.' DRC. 'Excellent rice.' CM. 'As good as ever.
There is only one problem two doors marked *Officers* and *Ladies*. I am
neither, and always feel that I should use the door downstairs marked
Private.' DMc. Remains in our TOP 100.

DIGBETH BALTI TOWERS
1-2, Barn Street, Digbeth.   **0121 643 8667**
'Has an excellent range of Baltis and starters all at reasonable prices.
Pakora which was championship class served up superbly fresh with a
spicy taste. The usual tasty dips were on hand for dunking purposes.
Balti Chicken Korma served up sizzling, although it was not in the
carnation cream category it has a lot more character than some of the
blander Balti Kormas I have tasted. Chicken content was excellent and
the dish was well spiced whilst retaining the traditional mildness of a
Korma. Fresh, doughy teardrop Nans'. Andy Munro.

MAHARAJAH   **TOP 100**
23, Hurst Street, B5.   **0121 622 2641**
'They tell me 90% of patrons are regulars and I can believe it - they all
seem to know each other and greet each other like friends. (being from
Sussex I always make an effort to visit it when on business). The service
is friendly and the food fragrant and freshly prepared, the Keema Nan
the is as good as I've tasted anywhere.' DL says it's the best Indian he has
ever visited by miles. Also not a local he has been 12 times in 24 months.
He warns they close on Sundays and for two weeks in the Summer. So
book to be sure. Says in our TOP 100.

MILAN INDIAN CUISINE   **CC DISCOUNT**
93, Newhall Street, B3.   **0121 236 0671**
Harish Patel's pleasant restaurant serves a wide range of tandoories and
a few Baltis. For a total change try Chef Balbir's Indo Chinese Manchu-
rian dishes. Will give a discount to Curry Club members, see page 288.
Branches: Milan Sweet Centre, 191, Stoney Lane, Sparkbrook and Milan
Sweet Centre, 238, Soho Road, Handsworth, Birmingham.

MOKHAM'S OF DIGBETH   **CC DISCOUNT**
140, Digbeth High Street, Birmingham, B%   **0121 643 7375**
Says Andy Munro: 'Mokham's pride themselves on their cooking so you
may have to wait as all the food is freshly prepared. Tandoori Sheeksh
Kebab is certainly one of the best I have ever tasted. 'Balti Exotica' of
meat, chicken, prawns, mushroom and pasta without doubt unique in
my experience. A very substantial dish, served up in the traditional black
bowl, it was beautifully spiced and the pasta blended superbly but when

combined with my nan bread it left me feeling like Pavarotti.' Unlicensed. Hours: Seven days a week - 12pm to 2.30pm and 6pm till late. Owner Naz Khan will give a discount to Curry Club members, see p 288

RAJDOOT   TOP100 - CC DISCOUNT
12, Albert Street, B4.   **0121 643 8749**
Des Sarda's Rajdoot has branches in Bristol and Manchester (see entries on pages 102 and 187 and ad on page 12). The chefs here are Nepalese and their cooking is as delicate as you'll find. For those who enjoy spicier fare, you only have to ask. Pat Chapman filmed here with Noel Edmonds for his BBC-TV Addicts series recently. Surprisingly Noel professed not to like curry. After some persuasion by Pat, Noel finally took a bite of Tandoori Chicken then another bite and another! A potential convert and nowhere better to do it! Des has promised to give a discount to Curry Club members, see page 288. See also page 12.

BIRMINGHAM SOUTH AND SOUTH EAST

B8, 9, 10, 11, 12, 13 POSTCODES
BALTI AREA

*Moseley, Small Heath, Sparkhill and Sparkbrook are the Birmingham suburbs where Balti began in Britain, and now proliferates. Their Asian population is largely North Pakistani, and it is from here Balti originated. We asked **Andy Munro** to contribute his views on his 20 favourite Balti Houses, and they appear on these and the preceeding pages, courtesy of **What's On Birmingham and Midlands**, and their **Essential Street Balti Guide**. To find out what Balti is, see our glossary on page 38.*

ADIL 1   CC DISCOUNT
148-150, Stoney Lane, Sparkbrook, B11.   **0121 449 0335**
ADIL 2
130, Stoney Lane, Balsall Heath, B12.   **0121 449 9296**
Adils 1 and 2 may not be where to take your girlfriend if you are planning to propose. If it's romance she wants, she'll turn you down!! But a great place to go for fun and good food. 'Service and comfort poor. Quality good and quantities very good. Value for money excellent.' RHA. 'It was wonderful, a superb tasty meal in a busy and fascinating restaurant. We purchased our wine next door and weren't charged corkage. Green Chilli Bhajia eye watering. Huge Nans and mopped our hot black balti pans clean! Pity we don't live nearer.' GM. Manager, M Ashraf will give a discount to Curry Club members, see page 288. Hours: 12 noon to 12 midnight. Branch: Waterfront Balti, 127-129, Dudley Road, Brierely Hill.

ALAMGEER   CC DISCOUNT
811, Stratford Road, Sparkhill, B11.   **0121 778 2388**
A small restaurant seating just thirty diners. Baltis and curries on the menu. Owner, G Arif will give a discount to Curry Club members, see page 288. Hours: 6pm till 2.30am. Reports please.

ALI BABA
250, Ladypool Road, Sparkbrook,B11   **0121 449 4929**
Despite the smart decor prices have been kept at traditional levels and as we studied the menu we were served up tasty mint dips and Poppadoms. Tandoori chicken breast is superb if slightly hot. Main course Baltis are served up in traditional black bowls and I opted for a well spiced Balti Chicken and Mushroom mopped up with a small nan although family sizes are available. Unlicensed. Hours: 12 to 2.30pm and 5pm till late.

GRAND TANDOORI
345, Stratford Road, Sparkhill, B11.   **0121 772 5610**
'Very popular. If you order anything other than a Balti they get confused. Not licensed.' J & A McL.

I AM THE KING OF BALTI
230-2, Ladypool Road, Sparkbrook.,B12　　　**0121 449 1170**
Says Andy Munro: 'The menu bears the legend, "We at King Balti stand for food easily digestible, lingering in taste, pleasing in flavour and fascinating to look at". Chicken Pakora came in a number of tasty strips with side salad and free dips. Sheekh Kebabs are charcoal barbecued whilst the restaurant also does a King Kebab which would probably have stretched Henry VIII himself. Baltis are served up in small shiny bowls but are certainly not short on quantity and quality. My Balti Kashmiri Chicken was full of tasty chunks of meat and enough fruit to satisfy even the man for Del Monte. Mega nans are available plus a range of varieties such as Peshwari.' Hours: Monday to Thursday 3pm to 12.30am, Friday and Saturday 1pm to 1.30am and Sunday 1 pm to 12.30am.

IB NE GHANI
264-266, Green Lane, Small Heath, B9.
CC DISCOUNT
0121 772 8138
Competent curries at this establishment. Owner, Dawood Hussain will give a discount to Curry Club members, see page 288. Hours: 5pm till 1am, Friday and Saturday 4pm till 2am.

IMRAN
264, Ladypool Road, Sparkbrook, B12.　　　**0121 449 1370**
'Baltis, superb. Family Nan, unbelievable - 3 feet by 2 feet. BYO from "offy" next door. Excellent value for money.' RS. Says Andy Munro: 'Imran is one of Birmingham's oldest established Balti Houses and indeed is one of several that claim to have been around at the time of the first ever splitting of the Nan bread in Birmingham. The restaurant is spacious and includes a see through Kebab cooking area for those who like to see a Sheekh Kebab being cooked live. Predictably Sheekh Kebabs and Tikkas have a tasty charcoaled flavour. My main course Balti Chicken and Mushroom was served up in a shiny bowl and had an impressively spicy kick. Nans are available in the usual range of sizes and unusually you can also get a family Chapatti. Other unusual items include the Quail Balti (a dish which has now achieved almost protected status).' Hours: 12 noon till midnight.

KASHMIR LAKE BALTI
127-129, Ladypool Road, Sparkbrook, B12.
CC DISCOUNT
0121 440 1238
Managing owner, Jabber Karim will give a discount to Curry Club members, see page 288. Hours: 12 noon to 2.30pm and 6pm till late.

KASHMIR LODGE
132, Stratford Road, Sparkbrook, B12　　　**0121 773 1632**
Says Andy Munro: 'It is housed in a former bank - the sort of grandiose building used before such establishments became virtually an excuse for a hole in the wall. Prices remain at a credible street level. There is a good range of Baltis including Balti Tinda (sweet potato) or Balti Karele (bitter gourd). Chicken and Mushroom was fairly spicy with tender meat. The accompanying Nan was fresh and yeasty.' Licensed. Hours:12 noon to 2.30pm and 6pm to midnight.

KILIMANJARO
9a, Walford Road, Sparkbrook, B11.　　　**0121 771 3994**
'Bills itself as a Kenyan restaurant. Menu out of the ordinary. Kuku Parka - half a chicken marinated in coconut milk and spices, slowly grilled and served with saffron rice and a bread made of coconut flour. Quite simply marvellous.' GGP.

KHYBER
365, Ladypool Road, Sparkbrook, B12.　　　**0121 449 5139**
'One of the spit and sawdust Balti houses that proliferate in Sparkbrook. Tandoori Chicken very tasty. Chicken Tikka absolutely superb.' GGP.

KING'S PARADISE
321, Stratford Road, Sparkhill, B12.

CC DISCOUNT
0121 753 2212

Says Andy Munro: 'King's Paradise is a restaurant which has changed its name and management more times than local club Birmingham City but now seems to have found the right combination. Efficiently run it is smartly decorated but even smarter are the prices. Particularly recommended is a substantial Kings Paradise Kebab. There is an excellent selection of Baltis and my Balti Lamb and Okra was very pleasingly spiced although perhaps the okra were more 'swartzennegars' than 'ladies' fingers. Has its own car park adjacent to a car repair business and if you are lucky enough to park it in the wrong place you may get a car respray and a free service whilst you are dining!' Owner, Mahboob Hussain will give a discount to Curry Club members, see page 288.
Hours: 12.30pm to 2.30pm and 5.30pm till 1am, weekends till 2am.

MINAR BALTI HOUSE
7, Walford Road, Sparkbrook, B11.

0121 773 5734

'Hadji Chop for starter, spicy kebab dipped in egg and deep-fried, very tasty.' GGP. Says Andy Munro: 'Minar is tucked away off the main road but luckily a little bird told me about it (I hasten to add not a Minar bird). Mushroom Bhajias are beautifully fresh and the Hadji Chops are homemade masterpieces. Liver Tikkas are amongst the options for the more adventurous. There is a good range of Baltis served up in a customary black bowl and include such gems as Balti Chutney Kofta. There is a superb range of Nans including a fairly unique prawn variety.'
Hours: 6pm to midnight, Sundays till 11pm.

PEARL OF KASHMIR
310, Highgate Road, Sparkbrook, B11

0121 772 6085

Says Andy Munro: 'Deceptively small from the outside, it is surprisingly spacious and airy inside aided by several extremely efficient fans. Free dips are an ideal accompaniment to a distinctly orangy (in taste as well as colour) Pakora. Main Baltis are robustly spiced and portions are good. The Balti was a trifle oily but never-the-less very tasty. Yeasty Nan breads were an ideal accompaniment. Menu has one or two suprises.'
Unlicensed. Hours: 12 noon to 2.30pm and 6pm to 1am.

PLAZA TANDOORI BALTI
278, Ladypool Road, Balsall Heath, B12

CC DISCOUNT
0121 449 4249

Says Andy Munro: 'Most of Brum's Balti Houses are Muslim run but 'Sikh and you shall find' and the Plaza is one of the very few run by Sikhs. I opted for a reasonable priced Lamb Tikka (£1.40) and this was an excellent start. My Balti Chicken and Mushroom was served up in a small cast iron Balti as opposed to the traditional bigger steel type.

However, it was brimful of quality meat and spicy sauce. I decided on a standard Nan but next time I think I will try the Plaza's Special Rogani Nan (baked with mixed nuts, sultanas and egg sauce).' Unlicensed.'Very attractive, upmarket decor. Nargis Kebab, the largest I have ever seen. Very crispy Vegetable Samosa, nicely spiced.' GGP. Hours: 5pm till midnight. Partner, RS Ghatoor will give a discount to Curry Club members, see page 288.

PUNJABI PARADISE
377, Ladypool Road, Sparkbrook, B12.   **0121 449 4110**
'Chicken Tikka, Onion Bhajia and Kulfi simply second to none. Adequate comfort but crowned at weekends.' CM. Says Andy Munro: Let your taste buds decide" is the challenge from the management and mine definitely voted unanimously in favour. Starters to be recommended include a top quality chicken Pakora which proves the chef obviously knows his goujons. Yeasty nan breads are on hand to dip into the depths of sizzling volcanic black bowls. This is one of the lighter Baltis but is exceptionally tasty with a strong coriander flavour sauce surrounding tender breast of chicken. Smart but unpretentious decor with traditional glass top tables.' Unlicensed. Hours: 5pm to 2am.

ROYAL AL-FAISEL

TANDOORI RESTAURANT

136-140, STONEY LANE, SPARKBROOK,
BIRMINGHAM. B12 8AQ
0121 449 5695 / 8902

Open: 11.30am to Midnight - 7 Days a Week
Own Drinks Welcome * Private Car Park
ONE OF BIRMINGHAM'S OLDEST BALTI HOUSES

ROYAL AL FAISAL
136-140, Stoney Lane, Balsall Heath, B12.   **0121 449 5695**
'Also spelt, by themselves, Faisel. Very busy. BYO. Nan breads huge, about 3 foot long! Superb flavour, excellent value.' SP. Says Andy Munro: 'Al fFaisal's is probably most famous for its 'Karak' Nans which were probably the first mutant Nans to appear in Birmingham's Balti Houses. Starters include some extras such as Egg Bhaji, Nargis Kebab, and if you have just won the pools - Tandoori King Prawn at £4.95. My main course Balti Chicken and Mushroom was pungently spicy but probably not as much as the unusual Balti Chicken and Mince with Special Green Chilli which must be worth a shot for those who are willing to ask committing'Balticide'.' Unlicensed. Hours: 11.30am till midnight.

ROYAL NAIM   AWARD WINNER -CC DISCOUNT
417-419, Stratford Road, Sparkhill, B11.   **0121 766 7849**
A massive restaurant seating 175 diners on two floors.Says Andy Munro: 'Royal by Naim and Royal by nature. King size portions served in king sized premises. Free creamy yoghurt dips are wonderfully smooth and spicy and keep the taste buds occupied as you study the menu which lists over a hundred Balti dishes. Chicken Tikka is the piece de resistance - gargantuan in portion but its quantity does not compromise its quality. Main courses include Balti Chicken Tikka Masala with extra spice which may cause taste buds to overload and 'affishionados' are recommended to try an excellent Balti Fish Masala. The Royal Naim makes all its own

sweets and for chocoholics, its chocolate Barfi is undoubtedly worth the CBM. Owner, M Nazir will give a discount to Curry Club members, see page 288. Hours: 12 noon to 1am, Friday and Saturday till 3am. Branch: Royal Stirchley Tandoori and Balti House, 1526-1528, Pershore Road, Stirchley. B30. Gets our BEST BALTI HOUSE AWARD.

SANAMS TANDOORI
80-82, Stoney Lane, Balsall Heath, B12.   **0121 771 4715**
'Unpretentious and simple. Complimentary popadoms. Fish pakora delicious. Onion Bhajia, slices of onion deep-fried. Quantities generous. Garlic Nan was garlicky indeed! Tropical Balti, sauce enhanced rather than drowned flavour of prawns. Competitive prices.' GD-G.

SHAHI NAN KABAB
353, Stratford Road, Sparkhill, B11   **0121 772 2787**
'Sheekh Kebabs roasting on an open fire', in the words of that famous Asian Xmas Ballad. Starters include the endangered Liver Tikka, which was surprisingly quite mildly spiced, and charcoaled Kebabs. Black bowled Baltis are served up by men in short sleeves (no posy designer gear here) and were complimented by bubbly Nans. There is an excellent range of Shahi snacks including a large Rolly Polly (three Kebabs in a Paratha with salad and chutney) - whether you get a certificate and a photograph if you finish it is another matter! . Noon to midnight.

SHEREEN KADAH
543, Moseley Road, Balsall Heath, B12   **0121 440 4641**
Says Andy Munro; 'The Kebabs and Tikkas are barbecued on an Olympic-style flame. In the display cabinet is a selection of Kebabs on an array of sharp skewers which look like a Zulu armoury after an attack on Rorke's Drift. Free dips are brought to the glass topped table as the main courses are awaited. If you want to push the boat out a King Prawn Balti at £4.50 is a real catch. ' Unlicensed. Hours: 11am to Midnight.

MOSELEY - B13
K2   CC DISCOUNT
107, Alcester Road, Moseley, B13.   **0121 449 3883**
Managing owner, M Naim tells us that he caters for people with a discerning taste in food, music and ambience. A banality free atmosphere. Pleased to hear it! He will also give a discount to Curry Club members, see page 288. Hours: 12 noon to 2pm and 6pm till 11.30pm.

KABABISH   CC DISCOUNT
29, Woodbridge Road, Moseley, B13.   **0121 449 5556**
Serves your favourite Baltis and curries. 'Best Naan bread in town!' RA. Manager, Mohammed Farooq will give a discount to CC members, see 288. Hours: 12 noon to 2.30pm and 6pm till midnight. Branch: Kababish, 2, Robin Hood Lane, Hall Green and , 266, Jockey Road, Sutton Coldfield.

NIRALA
580, Moseley Road, Moseley, B13   **0121 440 7600**
Says Andy Munro: 'A sight for pubbers and clubbers leaving Birmingham City centre after a night on the town. The window is lit up by its famous charcoal barbecue which is used to cook its equally famous Tikkas. Mr Mirala, can be seen silhouetted against the light of the flame like the driver of the Flying Scotsman whilst the rest of the Balti house is definitely Pullman class. Sheeskh Kebabs and Tikkas are predictably excellent, and to follow there is a choice of over 80 Balti dishes and almost before I could finish my free dip, my chosen Balti Chicken and Mushroom put in a sizzling appearance.' 'Service is speedy. Quantities are much larger. Balti Chicken with vegetables, superb value . Balti Chicken andMushroom, quintessential experience.' GGP.Unlicensed.

ROYAL NAWEED
44, Woodbridge Road, Moseley, B13.　　　　**0121 449 2156**
'Free popadoms with dips. Baltis very good. Huge Naan, eventually
defeated us. No frills, clean, excellent value.' MJG.

BIRMINGHAM - EAST AND SOUTH EAST
B 25 to 28　(POSTCODE ORDER)

YEW TREE COTTAGE TANDOORI

Balti & Tandoori Restaurant (Licensed)

43, Stoney Lane,
Yardley, Birmingham.
B25 8RE

Open 7 Days a Week:	**Table Reservations:**
Mon to Thur - 5pm to 1am	**Evenings - 0121 784 0707**
Fri & Sat - 5pm to 2am	**& 0121 786 1814**
Sunday - 6pm to 1am	**Day - 0831 430542**

YEW TREE COTTAGE　　　　　　　　**CC DISCOUNT**
43, Stoney Lane, Yardley, B25.　　　　**0121 784 0707**
A very large comprehensive menuwith favourite curries and Baltis.
Manager, J Chaudhuri will give a discount to Curry Club members, see
page 288. Hours: 5pm (Sunday 6pm) till 1am, Friday/Saturday till 2am.

ASHA
2250, Coventry Road, Sheldon, B26.　　　　**0121 743 6572**
'Good food, especially the Chicken Tikka Masala.' CM.

SHABAR TANDOORI
4, Arden Oak Road, Sheldon. B26.　　　　**0121 742 0636**
'One of our favourites for authenticity.' J & A McL.

TITASH INTERNATIONAL
2278, Coventry Road, Sheldon, B26.　　　　**0121 722 2080**
Chicken Tikka Omelette and Baranasi Nan (pineapple) on the menu
along with all your favourite Baltis and curries.

J JAY'S
1347, Stratford Road, Hall Green, B28.　　　　**0121 777 3185**
'Service exceptionally friendly. Boti Kebab, tender and tasty. Tandoori
Chicken Masala and Karahi Chicken superbly cooked.' J McL.

KABABISH
2, Robin Hood Lane, Hall Green, B28.　　　　**0121 745 5445**
'Standard of food is very high and consistent in each of the three
establishments.' RHA. Hours: 12 noon to 2.30pm and 6pm till 11.30pm.
Branches: Kababish, 29, Woodbridge Road, Moseley and Kababish, 266,
Jockey Road, Sutton Coldfield.

PURPLE ROOMS
1076, Stratford Road, Hall Green, B28.　　　　**0121 702 2193**
'Popadoms fresh tasting. Baltis of excellent quality. Hot towels and
mints to finish.' J McL.

BIRMINGHAM - NORTH
B23, 24,43 (POSTCODE ORDER)

SAMRAT TANDOORI   **CC DISCOUNT**
710, Chester Road, Erdington, B23.   **0121 384 5900**
A large menu with all our favourite curries, Baltis and accompaniments. Owner, Niresh R Dey will give a discount to Curry Club members, see page 288. 12 noon to 2.30pm and 6pm till midnight. Delivery service.

STOCKLAND BALTI   **CC DISCOUNT**
221 Marsh Lane, Erdington, B23.   **0121 377 8789**
A takeaway establishment, serving competent curries to a regular crowd. Manager, Noor Ali will give a discount to Curry Club members, se page 288. Hours: 5pm till 12.30am, Friday and Saturday till 1am.

INDIA GARDEN
992, Tyburn Road, Erdington, B24   **0121 373 9363**
A competent curry house serving competent curries. Hours: 12 noon to 12.30am, Thursday and Sunday till 1am, Friday and Saturday till 2am. Branch: Bashundora, Guildhall, Lichfield Road, Sutton Coldfield. Reports please.

DILKUSH TANDOORI
514, Queslett Road, Great Barr, B43.   **0121 325 1774**
Specials on the menu include Balti and Chicken Shillong - chicken and orange curry. Hours: 5pm till 12.30pm. Branch: Dilshad, 24b, Anchor Road, Aldridge.

RAJ INDIAN
30, Birmingham Road, Great Barr, B43.   **0121 357 8368**
A takeaway establishment. Extensive menu with all regular curries and Baltis with accompaniments. Delivery service available. Hours: 5.30pm till 12.30am. Branch: Raj, 21, Queen Street, Droitwich, Worcs. Arden Tandoori, 137, High Street, Henley in Arden, Solihull.

BIRMINGHAM - NORTH WEST
B16, B19

J JAYS
2, Edgbaston Shopping Centre, Five Ways, B16.   **0121 455 6871**
'Extensive menu including wide range of vegetable dishes.' RA.

OMARS KASHMIRI
167, Hagley Road, Edgbaston, B16.   **0121 454 7104**
'Plenty of choice, food excellent, especially Naan bread. Value for money.' E & O L. Hours: 6.30pm till 11.30pm, Sunday Buffet from 1pm.

AZIM
106, Lozells Road, Birmingham, B19.   **0121 523 5349**
Extensive Balti menu plus all the usual curries and accompaniments. 'Clean and nicely decorated. Menu under glass topped tables. Good range of Baltis as well as traditional curry dishes. Balti Meat Spinach succulent with flavour.' GH. Hours: 12 noon to 1.30am.

RED PALACE
1-11, Constitution Hill, Hockley. B19.   **0121 236 8097**
'Extensive buffet lunches served daily are superb. .' RHA.

BIRMINGHAM - SOUTH WEST

B15, B29, B30, B32, B45, B66

SHIMLA PINKS
214, Broad Street, Birmingham, B15.   **0121 633 0366**
'Nans the best I've had. Bhuna Chicken particularly good. Service
courteous. Plenty of space. Strange decor.' MJG.

DILSHAD INTERNATIONAL   CC DISCOUNT
618-620, Bristol Road, Selly Oak, B29.   **0121 472 5016**
A huge restaurant seating 100 diners. Head waiter, Zakaria Altafi gives
a discount to Curry Club members, see 288. Hour: 5.30 to3am, Friday/
Saturday to4am. Branch: Balti Night, 1480, Pershore Road, Strichley.

KHAN BALTI   CC DISCOUNT
632, Bristol Road, Selly Oak, B29.   **0121 471 3844**
Get all your favourite Balti combinations here. Manager, M Taj will give
a discount to Curry Club members, see page 288. Hours: 5pm till 2am.
Branch: Khanum, 510, Bristol Road, Selly Oak, Birmingham.

KHANUM   CC DISCOUNT
510, Bristol Road, Selly Oak, B29.   **0121 471 4877**
Extensive menu serving all our favourite curries . Owner, M Suleman
will give a discount to Curry Club members, see page 288. Hours: 5pm
till 2am, weekends till 3am. Branch: Khan's, 632, Bristol Road, Selly Oak.

BALTI BAZAAR
1267-69, Pershore Road, Stirchley, B30.   **0121 459 4517**
'Wide ranging menu, all very reasonably priced. Tandoori Chicken, well
marinated, Meat Samosa, very spicy and tasty. Substancial helping of
Balti Chicken Aloo Gobi, chicken came in very big lumps.' GGP. Andy
Munro says: 'Bazaar in name and bizare in menu. Moreish aptly
describes the food as well as the style of decor. Chicken Tikka Puri - the
bread was crispy but moist and the Tikka was quality. I know a number
of people who insist the Balti Chicken Keski is an absolute must for what
must have been an equally tasty Balti Chicken Shim (chicken cooked
with spiced green beans). The chefs special Bazaar Nan actually contains
fresh fruit.' Unlicensed. Hours: 5pm to midnight.

RAJPOOT   CC DISCOUNT
1831-1833, Pershore Road, Cotteridge, B30.   **0121 458 5604**
A large restaurant seating ninty-four diners all their favourite curries
and Balthis (sic). Proprietor, Watir Ali will give a discount to Curry Club
members, see page 288. Hours: 6pm till 2am.

ROYAL STIRCHLEY BALTI & TANDOORI
Pershore Road, Stirchley, B30   **0121 433 4320**
Usual starters are available at Balti house budget prices and my Chicken
Pakora was served up in a large portion accompanied by a discreet little
side salad. Free dips were tasty if napalm strength. There are almost a
100 Balti dishes available, I decided on a Balti bowl standard Meat and
Mushroom. Family Nans are a must for all large partied mopping up.
Unlicensed. Hours: 5.30pm till late.

YASSER TANDOORI   CC DISCOUNT
1268, Pershore Road, Stirchley, B30.   **0121 433 3023**
A sixty-eight seater restaurant serving competent curries. Manager, A
Hussain wil give a discount to Curry Club members, see page 288.
Hours: 4pm till 1am, Friday and Saturday till 2am.

INDIA GARDEN   **CC DISCOUNT**
417, Hagley Road West, Quinton, B32.   **0121 421 3242**
A licensed restaurant with special Happy Hour Menu - good value.
Hours: 5pm till 1am, Thursday, Friday and Saturday till 2am. Branch:
Balti Palace, 349, Birchfield Road, Perry Barr, Birmingham.

HIMALAYA
1716, Bristol Road South, Longbridge, B45.   **0121 453 4336**
Extensive menu with all your favourite curries and accompaniments.
Not licensed , so BYO. 'Have tried a good selection of everything and
nothing has been a disappointment.' MR. Hours: 5.30pm till 12.30am.

COVENTRY

BOMBAY PALACE
64, Earlsdon Street, Earlsdon, Coventry.   **01203 677851**
'Plentiful and very tasty Chicken Chat. Fairly hot Chicken Ceylon,
immense helpings. Service quick and pleasant.' GGP.

THE DAYS OF THE RAJ
87-89, Radford Road, Coventry.   **01203 597001**
'Very smart upmarket decor. Shashlick chicken was unbelivably tasty.
Balti Lamb exceptionally spicy and really tasty.' PJ

ISTIFA BALTI
6, Hales Street, Coventry.   **01203 224311**
'The food here is good and so are the prices. There is only one thing that
is really bad about this place, and that's the music, all one tape of it. An
awful waiter is more entertainment value than frustrating and he has
special magic powers! The Balti that on-one ordered magically changes
as he circles the table! Within three circuits a Chicken Rogan has become
a Chicken Dupiaza, WOW! Unlicensed.' LO1.

KOH I NOOR
63, Well Street, Coventry.   **01203 223637**
'A large Balti house with bouncers on the door. Popadoms warm and
crisp.' LO1.

MOONLIGHT BALTI
196, Foleshill Road, Coventry.   **01203 633414**
'Average menu, good food served hot and fresh. Is licensed but you can
BYO. Good value for money.' HM. 'Onion Bhajia warm and crisp,
copious salad. Balti Chicken Dupiaza, very tasty chicken, lots of sauce,
big helping. Peshwari Nan , very buttery and hot.' GGP.

RAJDOOT
29, City Arcade, Coventry.   **01203 223195**
'Wide and varied menu, quantities generous. Very tasty Chicken Hakime
(Chef's invention), with green chillies and a hot and sour sauce.' GGP.

KING WILLIAM IV PUB   **TOP 100**
1059, Foleshill Road, Coventry.   **01203 686394**
'As it is also a pub we thought a game of darts and a pint before moving
on to the food. Aromas wonderful, impossible to concentrate, so we
elbowed a few old locals out of the way and grabbed a table. Food
delicious. Balti dish, tender meat in a rich sauce with really, really hot
chilli peices. Portions large. Nan breads among the best, coriander
leaves in them, yummy.' KC. 'Menu provides an enormous range of
different meals at very reasonable prices. Helpings very generous.' GGP.

TO FIND OUT HOW TO JOIN OUR DISCOUNT
SCHEME SEE PAGE 288

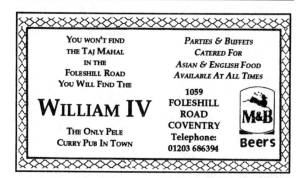
DUDLEY
MR DAVE'S BALTI HOUSE
947, High Street, Dudley.   01384 400288
'This was great. Like a café. Basic menu. Absolutely delicious Balti
Special, huge portion, fantastic!' MS.

HALESOWEN
BALTI TOWERS   CC DISCOUNT
85, Long Lane, Halesowen.   0121 559 5118
Good selection of Balti dishes with regular curries too. Managing owner,
Mohammed Sadique will give a discount to Curry Club members, see
page 288. Hours: 6pm till 11.30pm, Sunday 12 noon to 2.30pm and 6pm
till 11.30pm. Fully licensed.

DILSHAD INTERNATIONAL   CC DISCOUNT
14-15, Halesowen Road, Halesowen.   0121 421 6549
Opened in 1990 and has built up a regular loyal following. Manager, Anawarul Abaden will give a discount to Curry Club members, see page 288. Hours: 6pm till midnight. Branch: Dilshad International, 49-51, Market Street, Kingswinford.

RED PEPPERS   CC DISCOUNT
8, Hagley Street, Halesowen.   0121 550 8588
A small restaurant seating forty-four diners, gets busy at weekends, so best to book. Owner, Mostaqul Islam will give a discount to Curry Club members, se epage 288. Hours: Sunday to Wednesday: 6pm till midnight. Thursday: 12 noon to 2.30pm and 6pm till midnight. Friday and Saturday: till 1am. Home delivery service.

KINGSWINFORD
DILSHAD INTERNATIONAL   CC DISCOUNT
49-51, Market Street, Kingswinford.   01384 294861
A popular eating place, serving the locals all their favourite Baltis, curries and accompaniments. Owner, Mohammed Miah will give a discount to Curry Club members, see page 288. Hours: 6pm till midnight. Branch: Dilshad International, 14-15, Halesowen Road, Halesowen.

MR DAVE'S BALTI HOUSE
847, High Street, Kingswinford.   01384 400288
'Is licensed, but it ain't cheap - so bring your own. Service extremely efficient and friendly, food was of a high standard. Very reasonable prices.' DG.

KNOWLE
BILASH   CC DISCOUNT
1608, High Street, Knowle.   01564 773030
'Need to reserve a table. Varied selection of starters and main meals. Very good quality.' J & A McL. Partner, N Ali will give a discount to Curry Club members, see page 288. Hours: 5.30pm till midnight.

NETHERTON
CLASSICAL BALTI HOUSE   CC DISCOUNT
63, Halesowen Road, Netherton.   01384 240230
A small restaurant so book for a table at the weekends. Happy Hour special menu, between 6pm and 9pm. Manager, R Khan will give a discount to Curry Club members, see page 288. Hours: 6pm till 2am, weekends till 3am.

SEDGLEY
BALTI BAZAAR   CC DISCOUNT
2, Bull Ring, Dudley Street, Sedgley.   01902 671759
An upmarket restaurant with an extensive menu offering a full range of Baltis and curries. Seats forty-four diners, so book at weekends. Owner, AB Miah will give a discount to Curry Club members, see page 288. Hours: 5.30pm till 11.30pm. Friday and Saturday till 12.30am.

SOLIHULL
KUNJON
79, Hobs Moat Road, Solihull, B72.   0121 722 2982
'A restaurant offering very high class standards and service. Well prepared and cooked but rather mild.' PJ.

RAJNAGAR INTERNATIONAL
256, Lyndon Road, Olton, Solihull, B72.   **0121 742 8140**
Comprehensive menu with Balti and Kadai (sic) dishes with all the other favourites. 'Kitchen boasts a large window, guests can watch the preparations of their meal. Varied menu.' J & A McL. Evening hours.

STOURBRIDGE
DILSHAD   **CC DISCOUNT**
132, Hagley Road, Oldswinford, Stourbridge.   **01384 372762**
A fifty seater establishment serving competent curries and accompaniment to the local curry eating population. Proprietor, R Miah will give a discount to Curry Club members, see page 288. Hours: 5pm till midnight. Branch: Dilshad, 6, Penkridge Retail Park, Wolverhampton Road, Penkridge, Staffs.

MR DAVE'S BALTI HOUSE
15, High Street, Lye, Stourbridge.   **01384 891353**
'Decor superior, trendy and distinguished. Adequate menu. Very generous quantities, especially the main courses.' GGP.

INDIA HOUSE
22, Lower High Street, Stourbridge.   **01384 393361**
An evenings only establishment serving good curry house food. Hours: 6pm till midnight. Friday and Saturday till 1am.

KINVER TANDOORI INTERNATIONAL
50, High Street, Kinver, Stourbridge.   **01384 877448**
'Meal excellent, all tender meat portions are very generous and dishes very individual. Onion Kulcha Nan truly superlative, deliciously puffed up and served hot.' SF.

KAMRAN

34, High Street, Lye, Stourbridge.   **01384 893030**
Unlicensed, so BYO, waiters will chill and serve. What service! Hours:
5.30pm till midnight. Home delivery service available.

SHANAJ   CC DISCOUNT
122, High Street, Kinver, Stourbridge.   **01384 877747**
A busy curry house serving good curries from their standard menu.
Owner, Makmad Ali will give a discount to Curry Club members, see
page 288. Hours: 5.30pm till 11pm, Sunday 1pm till 11pm.

SUTTON COLDFIELD

BASHUNDORA
Guildhall, Lichfield Road, Sutton Coldfield, B74.   **0121 354 8397**
A popular cury house with a loyal following of customers. Hours: 12
noon to 2pm and 6pm till midnight. Reports please.

THE CROWN
Walsall Road, Four Oaks, Sutton Coldfield, B74.   **0121 308 1258**
'An Indian restaurant in a pub, surroundings excellent and clean, service
same. Korai Chicken, Tikka Jalrezi, all superb. Popadoms and Kulcha
Nan were the best.' DB.

INDUS TANDOORI
11, Kings Road, New Oscott, Sutton Coldfield, B73.   **0121 355 5089**
'Quality of starters very good, Sheek Kebab and Chicken Tikka as good
as anywhere I have been.' RHA. 'Comfortable, relaxed restaurant.' BE.

JAHED CUISINE OF INDIA
425, Birmingham Rd, Wylde Grn, S'n Coldfield, B72.   **0121 382 2105**
'Wide menu selection, excellentfood, beautifully presented.' PW.

KABABISH   CC DISCOUNT
266, Jockey Road, Sutton Coldfield, B73.   **0121 355 5062**
Follows the same format as the others in the group. Hours: 5pm till
11.30pm. Manager, Mr M Sadiq will give a discount to Curry Club
members, see page 288. Branches: see separate entries.

WALSALL

KHAN
89, Ablewell Street, Walsall.   **01922 20376**
'Popadoms crisp. Generous quantities. Murghi Shah Passanda (sic)
ranked as one of the best. Faultless service. Comfort , decor modest.' JB.

KISMET
20, Aldridge Shopping Precinct, Walsall.   **01922 59861**
All our favourite curries and accompaniment served from a comprehensive menu.Hours: 5.30pm till 12.30am. Branch: Romna Takeaway, 25,
High Street, Alchester, Warwickshire. Reports please.

PAPRIKA
78, Bradford Street, Walsall.   **01922 29944**
'A good value restaurant which always delivers first rate meals. Decor
very simple. Advisable to book at weekends. Staff helpful.' DG.

TO FIND OUT HOW TO JOIN OUR DISCOUNT
SCHEME SEE PAGE 288

POLASH BALTI
10, Anchor Parade, Aldridge, Walsall.   **01922 51442**
Standard curries served from a standard menu at reasonable prices.
Hours: 5pm till 12.30am.

SHAHI GRILL   CC DISCOUNT
89, Bridge Street, Walsall.   **01922 24079**
A good standard curry house serving good standard curries to the local
curry eating population. Owner Chef, Mozmil Ali will give a discount
to Curry Club members, see page 288. Hours: 6pm till 1am, Friday and
Saturday till 2am.

WARLEY
AL MOUGHAL   CC DISCOUNT
622, Bearwood Road, Smethwick, Warley. B66.   **0121 420 3987**
Book at wekends, tends to get busy. Serving competent curries to a loyal
local following. Owner, Saeed Moughal will give a discount to Curry
Club members, see page 288. Hours: 6pm till midnight. Reports please.

NAWAB   CC DISCOUNT
544, Hagley Road West, Oldbury, Warley.   **0121 422 1767**
Monday night: Nawabi Night special menu! Thursday night, Balti night!
Managing owner, Ashraf Uddin will give a discount to Curry Club
members, see page 288. Hours: 6pm till 2am, Friday and Saturday till
3am. Home delivery service available.

ROWLEY VILLAGE   **TOP 100**
10, Portway Road, Rowley Regis, Warley.   **0121 561 4463**
Mr Moin Udin's restauraunt has come to our notice from a number of
good reports. His large and attractive menu, featuring a panther as its
logo, contains many goodies. DC loves the Chicken Nan, and we hear
good things about the Karahi dishes. These combination dishes, such as
Chicken, Prawn and Meat Bhuna, or Sagwalla and Dhansak Kurma(sic)
are a type of Balti, and are 'more than delicious' JR. We have placed this
restaurant in our Top 100. Its hours are evenings only: 5.15 to midnight.
See advertisement on page 20.

BROMWICH
SHALIMAR
145, High Street, West Bromwich.   **0121 553 1319**
'I have eaten here regularly over ten years and have been impressed by
their excellent quality food. Friendly unobtrusive service. Reasonable
prices.' SCH.

WOLVERHAMPTON
AL AMIN   **CC DISCOUNT**
4, Lane Green Road, Codsall, Bilbrook, Wol'ton.   **01902 846344**
Gets busy at weekends, so best to bok a table or be disappointed. Owner,
Hannan Ali will give a discount to Curry Club members, see page 288.
Hours: 5pm till midnight, closed Sunday.

BILASH
2, Cheapside, Wolverhampton.   **01902 27762**
'Sampled the midweek lunch buffet, which was excellent. MB. 'Kitchens
were visable behind a fully glazed wall and the food was superb.' IB.

HABIB INDIAN CUISINE   **CC DISCOUNT**
46, Queen Street, Wolverhampton.   **01902 772155**
Serves competent curries and accompaniment from an extensive menu.
Chef, Habibur Rahman will give a discount to Curry Club members, see
page 288. Hours: 6pm till midnight, Friday and Saturday till 2.30am.
Branch: Maharaja Takeaway, Highbridge Road, Sutton Coldfield.

NEEL AKASH
31, School Street, Wolverhampton.   **01902 34511**
'Only a small concern but this helps of atmosphere. Staff helpful and
polite, they smile as well. Popadoms warm, plates are pre-warmed and
foo well presented and savoury.' DG. Free delivery service.

PURBANI   **CC DISCOUNT**
41-43, Birch Street, Wolverhampton.   **01902 24030**
Seats a massive 130 diners. Menu contains all our favourite curries and
side dishes. A popular curry house serving competent curries to a local
following. Owner, L Hussain (since 1978) will give a discount to Curry
Club members, see page 288. Hours: 5pm till 12.30pm. Branch: Raj Balti,
66, Bradford Street, Walsall.

Owners of restaurants selected to appear in
this Guide are invited to advertise only after
their restaurant has been selected for entry.
  We thank those who have done so. It helps to
keep the price of the Guide as low as possible.

WILTSHIRE

CHIPPENHAM
AKASH TANDOORI AND BALTI
19, The Bridge, Chippenham.   **01249 653358**
A smallish restaurant seating forty-six diners, serving competent curries

MELKSHAM
MELKSHAM TANDOORI   **CC DISCOUNT**
26, Church Street, Melksham.   **01225 705242**
A well established restaurant, since 1985, serving all our favourites.
Owner Chef, Abdul Wahid will give a discount to Curry Club members,
see page 288. Hours: 12 noon to 2pm and 6pm till midnight. Branches:
Nawab, Old Cowmbran, Gwent and Saadi Takeaway, Bradford on
Avon, Wilts.

SALISBURY
ASIA   **CC DISCOUNT**
90, Fisherton Street, Salisbury.   **01722 327628**
'Tastefully decoarted and clean. Rhogan Josh hotter than expected but
very enjoyable. Bombay Potato excellent.' AJA. 'All round it is a terrific
place to eat.' SB. Owner, Siraj Uddin Ahmed will give a discount to Curry
Club members, see page 288. Hours: 12 noon to 3pm and 5.30pm till
midnight. Branches: Light of Asia, Andover, Hants and Polash, Oxford.

SWINDON
CURRY GARDEN   **CC DISCOUNT**
90, Victoria Road, Swindon.   **01793 521114**
An extensive menu serving all our favourite curries, Baltis and accompaniments. Owner, L Miah will give a discount to Curry Club members, see
page 288. Hours: 12 noon to 2.30pm and 5.30pm till midnight.

GOLDEN DELIGHT
47, High Street, Cricklade, Nr. Swindon.   **01793 750303**
A small reliable restaurant seating forty-four diners, so book for weekends. Manager, Makram Ali will give a discount to Curry Club members,
see page 288. Hours: 12 noon to 2.30pm and 6pm till midnight.

JEWEL IN THE CROWN
15-16, Victoria Road, Swindon.   **01793 522687**
A large establishment seating 120 diners. 'I requested a Phall to the
amusement of the waiters. The Chef came out of the kitchen just to
confirm my order. Best Korma my wife has ever had.' WJR. 'Enjoyed a
Balti.' JPH. Hours: 12 noon to 2.30pm and 5.30pm till midnight.

KHYBER
5/6, Victoria Road, Swindon.   **01793 523992**
Another huge restaurant seating 128. Hours: 12 noon to midnight, Thursday, Friday and Saturday till 1am.

RAFU'S TANDOORI   **CC DISCOUNT**
29-30, High Street, Highworth, Swindon.   **01793 765320**
Yet another huge restaurant seating 110. 'A marvellous experience.' RG. 'Our favourite.' CM & SD. 'I have always enjoyed the quality and variety of their dishes.' DES. Manager, Safu Miah will give a discount to Curry Club members, see page 288. Hours: 12 noon to 3pm and 6pm till midnight. Branch: Rafu's, 188-189, Victoria Road, Swindon.

ROBIS BALTI KITCHEN   **CC DISCOUNT**
1, Victoria Road, Swindon.   **01793 511919**
A reliable good restaurant seating 62 diners. Owner, Tohur Uddin gives a discount to Curry Club members, see page 288. 5pm to midnight. Branch: Nisha Indian Takeaway, 24, Greenhill Street, Stratford-on-Avon.

TROWBRIDGE
ROSE OF INDIA TAKEAWAY
Unit 5, Court Mill Centre, Castle Street, Trowbridge.   **01225 776457**
A takeaway establishment serving all the usual curries.

WARMINSTER
BOMBAY HOUSE,
60-62, East Street, Warminster.   **01985 846951**
An extensive menu full of our favourite curries. House Specials include Lobster Chilli Mussala. Home delivery service.

YORKSHIRE NORTH

BRIDLINGTON
BRIDLINGTON TANDOORI
124, St John Street, Bridlington.   **01262 400014**
'BEST Chicken Madras that I've EVER tasted, expertly spiced with a most delightful lemony flavour.' MB. Hours: 12 noon to 2.30pm and 6pm till midnight. Branch: Wold Tandoori, 81, Middle Street South, Driffield, West Yorks.

HARROGATE
RAJPUT
11, Cheltenham Parade, Harrogate.   **01423 562113**
'Asked for Lamb Curry between Madras and Vindaloo, just right. Garlic Nan bread melted in the mouth.' GH.

SANGAM
3, Bower Street, Harrogate.   **01423 507206**
'Popadoms big, warm and crisp. Chapattis were excellent and moist.' GH. Hours: 6pm till 12.30am, Friday and Saturday till 1.30am.

RICHMOND
RICHMOND TANDOORI
32a, Market Place, Richmond.   **01748 850338**
Hours: 6pm till midnight, Saturday and Sunday 3pm till midnight. Branch: Sultan Takeaway, 62, Front Street, Winlaton, Blandon, T & W.

RIPON
MOTI RAJ   CC DISCOUNT
18, High Skellgate, Ripon.   **01765 690348**
Owner, Abdul Malik will give a discount to Curry Club members, see page 288. Hours: 5.30pm till midnight. Delivery service available.

SCARBOROUGH
SCARBOROUGH TANDOORI
50-52, St Thomas Street, Scarborough.   **01723 352393**
'Service a little on the miserable side. Chicken Madras, Lamb Rongan Gusht (sic) absolutely first class, full of flavour. .' MB. 'Mixed Kebabs as good as ever. Keema Nan the best I've ever had.' CP. Hours: 12 noon to 2.30pm and 6pm till midnight. Friday and Saturday till 12.30am.

SKIPTON
AAGRAH   TOP100 - CC DISCOUNT
4, Unicorn Hs, Devonshire Pl, Keighley Rd, Skipton.   **01756 790807**
'Always been very pleased. Nothing is too much trouble and children are well catered for. Menu has expanded, especially vegetarian and Balti dishes. Quality food. Highly recommended.' AP. 'Exceptionally pleased with both the food and the service. Vegetarian menu is most innovative and varied.' JH. 'Ample portions and reasonable prices.' ED. 'Complimentary Popadoms. Food was absolutely superb with many dishes that I hadn't encountered.' IS. Managing Partner, Mostafizur Rahman will give a discount to Curry Club members, see page 288. Hours: 6pm till midnight, Sunday till 11pm. Branches: Aagrah, 27, West Gate, Shipley; Aagrah, 483, Bradford Road, Rudey and Aagrah, Aberford Road, Garforth. See advertisement on page 260.

RAJ   CC DISCOUNT
11, Keighley Road, Skipton.   **01756 795697**
Serving all the usual curries and accompaniments with a few specials.

Manager, MA Miah will give a discount to Curry Club members, see page 288. Hours: 12 noon to 2.30pm and 6pm till midnight, Sunday 5.30pm till 11pm.

ROYAL BENGAL   **CC DISCOUNT**
21, Keighley Road, Skipton.   **01756 792473**
Owner, Raza Miah, will give a discount to Curry Club members, see page 288. Hours: 12 noon to 2pm and 6pm till 11.30pm. Branch: Prince of Bengal, 1b, Court Lane, Skipton.

YORK
GARDEN OF INDIA
5, Fawcett Street, York.   **01904 645679**
'Four of us embarked on the place ordering different meals, so I got a chance to taste them all. Standard was exceptionally high.' MB.

MOGUL
39, Tanner Row, York.   **01904 659622**
'Food, decor and value for money all excellent.' AA

RISE OF THE RAJ
112, Micklegate, York.   **01904 622975**
'Decor is excellent. Food and value for money average.' AA.

TAJ MAHAL
4, Kings Staith, York.   **01904 653944**
'Food and prices excellent.' AA.

YORKSHIRE SOUTH

BARNSLEY
JALSA
7, Pitt Street, Bransley.   **01226 779114**
A popular curry house with a loyal local following. Proprietor, E Rahman will give a discount to Curry Club members, see page 288. Hours: 6pm till midnight.

INDIAN GARDENS
16, Peel Square, Barnsley.   **01226 282612**
'Good and wide choice menu. Prawn Bhajee excellent. Baltis arrived in steel karahis accompanied by Peshwari Nan and Keema with garlic (included all this year's garlic bulb harvest).' TH. Hours: 6pm till 12.30am.

K2
5 Royal Street, Barnsley.   **01226 299230**
'Unlicensed. Excellent Chicken Pakoras and Mushroom Bhajias. Chicken Karahi with a very tasty Peshwari Nan.' TH.

DONCASTER
INDUS   **CC DISCOUNT**
24-26, Silver Street, Doncaster.   **01302 323366**
A massive restaurant seating 175 diners. 'Short menu. Very smart and upmarket. Meal was excellent with good portions, waiters fast and efficient.' GJP. Partner, Nayeem Din will give a discount to Curry Club members, see page 288. Hours: 12 noon to 2pm and 7pm till 12.15am. Branches: Grand St Leger Hotel and Restaurant, Doncaster. Sahib, 138, West Street, Sheffield.

TAJ MAHAL   **CC DISCOUNT**
32, Hallgate, Doncaster.   **01302 341218**
'Plush restaurant with luxurious bar area. Friendly relaxed service.
Generous Prawn Puri.' PW. Owner, Javed Akhtar will give a discount
to Curry Club members, see page 288. Hours: 12 noon to 2.30pm and 6pm
till midnight. Branches: India Gate, 9, Fitzwilliam Street, Peterborough.
Taj Mahal, 37-39, Lincoln Road, Peterborough. Home Delivery service.

PENSISTONE
TASTE OF INDIA
56, Bridge Street, Penistone.   **01226 766951**
A standard curry house serving standard curries and accompaniments
at reasonable prices. Hours: 12 noon to 2.30pm and 6pm till midnight.

SHEFFIELD

BEKASH   **CC DISCOUNT**
349-351, Ecclesall Road, Sheffield.   **01742 664168**
A pretty and modern restaurant seating fifty-two diners. Owner, Ala
Uddin will give a discount to Curry Club members, see page 288. Hours:
12 noon to 2pm (closed Monday) and 6pm till midnight. Friday and
Saturday till 1.30am. Sunday Buffet: 12.30pm till 5pm.

CURRY HOUSE   **CC DISCOUNT**
91, Leppings Lane, Hillsborough, Sheffield. **01742 334462**
A takeaway only establishment serving popular curries and accompaniment. Waiter, Shipon Ali will give a discount to Curry Club members,
see page 288. Hours: 5pm till midnight.

EVEREST   **CC DISCOUNT**
59-61, Chesterfield Road, Sheffield.   **01742 582975**
A large restaurant seating eight-six diners. Menu contains favourite
curries and accompaniments. Manager, Mohammed Nasim will give a
discount to Curry Club members, see page 288. Hours: 6pm till 3am.

HIMALAYA   **CC DISCOUNT**
13-15, Convent Walk, Sheffield.   **01742 724134**
'Serves the best starters. Mixed Kebab a meal in themselves - big with
plenty of raw onions - gorgeous. Tried a Tindaloo once - I had to have
three pints of lager with it to put the fire out.' WDM. Director, Azir
Uddin Ahmed will give a discount to Curry Club members, see page 288.
Hours: 12 to 2.30pm and 6pm till midnight. Friday/Saturday till 1am.

KASHMIR PALACE   **CC DISCOUNT**
34, Sandygate Road, Crosspool. Sheffield.   **01742 666008**
A huge restaurant seating 100 diners and serving good curries to the local
curry eaters. Proprietor, MJ Malik will give a discount to Curry Club
members, see page 288. Hours: 6pm to midnight, Friday /Saturday 1am.

RAJ   **CC DISCOUNT**
234, Abbeydale Road, Sheffield.   **01742 586776**
A very upmarket and tastefully decorated restaurant seating thirty-four
diners. Partner, Mohammed Tafique will give a discount to Curry Club
members, see page 288. Hours: 6pm till 1am.

TANDOORI HOUSE   **CC DISCOUNT**
64, Abbeydale Road, Sheffield.   **01742 508043**
Takeaway establishment with a delivery service available. Manager,
Anjum Sohail will give a discount to Curry Club members, see page 288.
Hours: 5.30pm till midnight, Friday and Saturday till 1am.

TO FIND OUT HOW TO JOIN OUR DISCOUNT SCHEME SEE PAGE 288

YORKSHIRE WEST

BATLEY

PARADISE
1, Field Lane, Batley.   **01924 472017**
A family business, with Sarfraz managing front of house and Mohammed as head chef. Hours: 5.30pm till 1am.

SPICE GARDEN
2, Market Place, Birstall, Batley.   **01924 471690**
'Bhuna Prawn Puri and Mixed Special Rhogan Josh were tres bon! A
comfortable place, nicely decorated.' DMI.

BRIDGHOUSE

THIPTI   **CC DISCOUNT**
6, Huddersfield Road, Bridghouse.   **01484 719818**
'Decor good. Not expensive.' BG. Proprietor, Mokaddas Ali will give a
discount to Curry Club members, see page 288. Hours: 6pm till midnight, Friday and Saturday till 1am.

BRADFORD

*With its Asian population largely Pakistani, and very well establiashed, Brad-
ford has a more than interesting curry background, lthough, the restaurants
sweet shops and cafes are much more widely spread around, than say Southall.
They are unmissable for the curry-holic, of course, giving excellent,
uncompromising ethnic food, at real value for money prices. With more such
establishments per head of the population, than any other city in Britain,
Bradford remains 'Curry City U.K'. Here are your favourites:*

AMEER   **CC DISCOUNT**
415, Thornton Road, Thornton, Bradford.   **01274 833673**
A sixty seater establishment serving good standard curries. Owner, P
Qureshi will give a discount to Curry Club members, see page 288.
Hours: 5.30pm till 1am. Licensed.

ASHA   **CC DISCOUNT**
31, Cheapside, Bradford.   **01274 729358**
"Special Feast Night" on Sunday and Thursday. Owner, Abdul Anwar
will give a discount to Curry Club members see page 288. 6 to midnight.

BOMBAY BRASSERIE   **CC DISCOUNT**
Simes Street, off Westgate, Bradford.   **01274 737564**
A massive restaurant seating 120 diners. 'Surroundings are unbelievable, a renovated Old Church. Service is good. Chef makes Nan breads
inside a small glass fronted kitchen.' NDM. Director, Shaukat Ahmed
gives a discount, see page 288. Hours: 12.30 to 2.30pm; 6pm to 11.30pm.

BOMBAY TANDOORI
3B, Wilton Street, Bradford.   **01274 721879**
'Decor simply but very clean. Shown to a spacious table. Service
excellent, friendly and unobtrusive. Bombay Murgh E Special - absolutely superb, flavours delighted my tastebuds.' JP. Hours: 5pm till late

EASTERN DELIGHT
30, Little Horton Lane, Bradford.   **01274 393014**
'Ordered my usual Sheek Kebab which arrived at lightning speed with
fresh salad and yoghurt, excellent if a little tough. Keema Madras with
rice and Chapattis to use instead of cutlery, full of flavour, up to the last
bite.' MB.

HANSA'S GUJARATI VEGETARIAN
44, Great Horton Road, Bradford.   **01274 730433**
A vegetarian restaurant. 'Spinach and Potato Curry was lovely leaving
a taste that developed for many hours after the meal - first class. Well
worth another visit for a taste of something different.' GH.

INTERNATIONAL TANDOORI   CC DISCOUNT
40-42, Manville Terrace, off Morley Street, Bradford.   01274 721449
'Pleasant surroundings and waiters. Meat Vindaloo has plenty of meat
in a thick gravy, hot enough without blowing my head off.' GH.
'Upmarket but prices are good.' RS. Manager, Raja Yasin Khan will give
a discount to Curry Club members, see page 288. 12 noon till 3.30am.

K2   CC DISCOUNT
116, Lumb Lane, Bradford.   **01274 723704**
A popular local curry house serving good curries at reasonable prices.
Manager, Abdul Ghatoor will give a discount to Curry Club members,
se page 288. Hours: 11.30am till midnight. Branches: Kasher Kashmiri,
119-121, Oak Lane, Bradford. Aftab Takeaway, Gleedless, Sheffield.

KARACHI
15-17, Neal Street, Bradford.   **01274 732015**
'Spinach Mince Curry was terrific particularly with raw puréed green
chilli on top. Chicken Tikka also brilliant.' GH. 'Extremely cheap.' RS.

KASHMIR   CC DISCOUNT
27, Morley Street, Bradford.   **01274 726513**
Seats a massive 200 diners. 'Meat and Mushroom Vindaloo acceptable,
Chappatis only warm.' RS. We have received a letter from one of our
members, telling us that the proprietor, Mr Latif refused to acknowledge
the Curry Club Discount Scheme, well, he has again, for this edition of the
guide, ticked the box and signed underneath to authorise participation,
so lets see what happens this time. 'Meal was excellent and the value is
fantastic.' RB. 'Meat Spinach Curry was tasty and thick textured.' GH.
Mohammed Latif will give a discount to Curry Club members, see page
288. Hours: 11am to 3am. Branch: Taj Mahal, 25, Morley Street, Bradford.

KHADIM'S   CC DISCOUNT
103, Carlisle Road, Bradford.   **01274 541699**
A small and friendly restaurant seating just twenty-six diners. Popular
curries on the menu. Proprietor, Khadim Hussain will give a discount to
Curry Club members, see page 288. Hours: 12 noon to midnight.

KHYBER
6, The Green, Idle.   **01274 613518**
Menu lists allthe favourite curries and accompaniments at reasonable
prices. Hours: 4pm till 11.30pm.

MOGHAL   CC DISCOUNT
790, Leeds Road, Bradford.   **01274 733324**
Another small and friendly establishment, seating twenty-eight diners
all their favourites including Balti. Owner, Mohammed Akbar will give
a discount to Curry Club members, see page 288. Hours: 10am till 2am.

MUMTAZ PAAN HOUSE
386-396, Great Horton Road, Bradford.   **01274 571861**
A large restaurant seating 150 diners. 'Masla Fish, the best starter I've
ever had. Portions are plentiful. Alcohol free zone. Service is slow, be
patient, it's worth it.' RB. 'Decor is fantastic, with fans to keep you cool.
Excellent quality and consistent flavour.' KI. Hours: 11am till 1am.

TO FIND OUT HOW TO JOIN OUR DISCOUNT SCHEME SEE PAGE 288

NAWAAB   **TOP 100**
32, Manor Row, Bradford.   **01274 720371**
'Impeccable service. Large pickle tray waiting on each table, Popadoms crisp. So many excellent main dishes to choose from, we have been through most of them, everyone being of a very high standard. It isn't the cheapest but for the quality who can complain.' NDM. Hours: 12 noon to 2pm and 6pm till 12.30am. Branch: Nawaab, 35, Westgate, Huddersfield. (see separate entry). Both branches get a TOP 100 award.

RAWAL   **CC DISCOUNT**
3, Wilton Street, off Morley Street, Bradford.   **01274 720030**
'Metalic blue decor. Open kitchen. Chicken Tikka starter would have made a good main course. Wonderful Lassi.' DS. Head waiter, Mobin Iqbal will give a discount to Curry Club members, see page 288. Hours: 5.30pm till 2am, Friday and Saturday till 3am.

SABRAAJ
20, Little Horton Lane, Bradford.   **01274 724316**
'Relaxed, friendly, speedy service. Excellent quality, food prepared with fresh herbs and spices.' N & M I.

SHABINA
258, Great Horton Road, Bradford.   **01274 737212**
'Very basic, no table cloths, cheap and cheerful. No drinks license. Food mild.' BG.

SHISH MAHAL   **CC DISCOUNT**
6, St Thomas Road, Bradford.   **01274 723999**
A fifty-four seater establishment, serving popular curries and accompaniments. Owner, M ohammed Taj will give a discount to Curry Club members, see page 288. Hours: 4pm till 3am.

SHIRAZ
133, Oak Lane, Bradford.   **01274 490176**
'Wide range of excellent value appetizers. Extensive vegetarian dishes.' PH. Balti on the menu.

TAJ MAHAL   **CC DISCOUNT**
25, Morley Street, Bradford.   **01274 724947**
A large restaurant seating eighty diners. 'Very cheap.' RS. Owner, Mohammed Latif will give a discount to Curry Club members, see page 288. Hours: 5pm till 3am. Branch: Kashmir, 27, Morley Street.

DEWSBURY

GULSHAN
Northgate House, Northgate, Dewsbury.   **01924 456289**
'An incredible eating experience. Basic, service is via a counter, where the kitchen can be seen. Cooking is undertaken by Asian women who are veiled. Food is great. Chicken Dhansak, highly recommended. The sanitary facilities - upstairs through a rom of sleeping people (Asians), we won't tell the Health Dept because we want the Gulshan to stay as it is.' ID. Home delivery service. Hours: 10am to 2pm and 5pm till 2am.

SANAM   **CC DISCOUNT**
28, Wellington Road, Dewsbury.   **01924 454248**
A family run business. Restaurant seats sixty diners. Manager, Mohammed Shiraz will give a discount to Curry Club members, see page 288. Hours: 6pm till midnight. Branch: Paradise, 1, Fields Street, Batley.

TO FIND OUT HOW TO JOIN OUR DISCOUNT SCHEME SEE PAGE 288

HALIFAX

SULTAN MAHAL   **CC DISCOUNT**
20b, Westgate, Halifax.   **01422 350209**
Menu contains all your favourite curries and accompaniments at reasonable prices. Owner, Mohammed Fazil will give a discount to Curry Club members, see page 288. Hours: 5.30pm till 1am.

HUDDERSFIELD

BANYAN TREE   **CC DISCOUNT**
274, Bradford Road, Fartown, Huddersfield.   **01484 535037**
A massive restaurant seating 200 diners. 'A lot of money has been spent on its appearance. Dining area is really impressive. Kitchen is glass fronted.' NDM. Proprietor, Joe Saleem will give a discount to Curry Club members, see page 288. Hours: 6pm till midnight, Friday and Saturday till 1am. Delivery service available.

NAWAAB   **TOP 100**
35, Westgate, Huddersfield.   **01484 422775**
A beautiful restaurant with arches and pillars, the ceiling are a plasterers' paradise. Balti features on the menu along with other popular curries and side dishes. 'Very busy and popular but worth the wait. Plush decor, service prompt. Food wonderful.' SP. 'Smaller than the Bradford branch but just as classy. An old building that they have refurbished to a very high standard.' NDM. Hours: 12 noon to 2pm and 6pm till late. Branch: Nawaab, 32, Manor Row, Bradford. Both restaurants in our TOP 100.

SHABAB
37-39, New Street, Huddersfield.   **01484 549514**
'Good quality food, lovely surroundings, chairs uncomfortable, expensive.' NDM. 'Interesting and different curry house fayre. Friendly and efficient service.' N & M I. 'Exceptional value for money lunch buffet.' BG. 'Service worked like a well oiled machine. Quantities good.' RC.

KNOTTINGLEY

JEWEL IN THE CROWN
110, Weeland Road, Knottingley.   **01997 607233**
'Provides excellent food at reasonable prices. Service friendly and efficient. Recommend the Mixed Grill.' IB. Hours: 6pm till midnight.

LEEDS

AAGRAH   **TOP 100 - CC DISCOUNT**
Aberford Road, Garforth, Leeds.   **0113 287 6606**
'Extensive menu with lots of unusual dishes. Delicious quantities, freshly prepared using herbs and spices. Attentive and efficient service but not rushed. Beautiful and comfortable decor, palacially fitted. Busy so book a table.' N & M I. 'Potato and Cauliflower dish was very good indeed.' PJ. Managing owner, M Aslam will give a discount to Curry Club members, see page 288. Hours: 6pm till 11.30pm, Friday/ Saturday till midnight. Branches: Aagrah, 483, Bradford Road, Pudsey; Aagrah, 27, Westgate, Shipley and Aagrah, Devonshire Place, Skipton. All branches remain in our TOP 100, for providing consistently good curries. See page 260.

AYESHA
Victoria Road, Leeds.   **0113 275 8826**
'Asked for a hot and spicy version of Vegetable Korma, which was not on the menu - no problem - absolutely beautiful. Chicken Masala tasted fantastic - very Balti influenced. Large portions. Great value. No alcohol on premises due to religious beliefs.' CS. Hours: 6pm till late. Delivery service available.

DARBAR   **TOP 100**
16-17, Kirkgate, Leeds.   **0113 246 0381**
'An undiscovered gem! Impressive presentation of dishes, Tandoori
Prawns were almost luminous. We will be back.' AH. 'Very impressive,
smart decor, excellent service, very good food. Wonderful!!' PJ. 'Outstanding restaurant. Enormous Mixed Grill. Tandoori Murgh Massala
comes with exquisite sauce. All helpings are generous. Sumptuous
decor.' D O'R. A new and deserved entrant to our Top 100.

DAWAT
4-6, Leeds Road, Kippax, Leeds.   **0113 287 2279**
A sweet little restaurant seating just twenty-six diners. Owned by Mr
Arora with cooking done by Mrs Arora. 'Food cooked to order. Fish
Tikka is delicious.' BPW. Hours: 6.30pm till 11pm.

EAST INDIA   **CC DISCOUNT**
Unit 8, Arndale Centre, Crossgates, Leeds.   **0113 260 2530**
Managing owner, Abdul Ahad will give a discount to Curry Club
members, see page 288. Hours: 5.30pm till midnight.

HANSA'S GUJARATI VEGETARIAN   **CC DISCOUNT**
72-74, North Street, Leeds.   **TOP 100**   **0113 244 4408**
'I particularly enjoyed the crunchy spicy flavour of the Shrikhand.' DM.
'As a non-vegetarian I went with an open mind. Food was fine but
portions small.' DB. 'Exquisite Lassi, portions small.' DO'R. Proprietors,
Mr and Mrs Dabhi will give a discount to Curry Club members, see page
288. Hours: 12 noon to 2pm(Thursday/Friday only), 6pm till 11pm
(Monday to Thursday), till 11.30pm Friday / Saturday. Remains in our
Top 100, but bigger portions please.

KHYBER PASS
65, Haddon Road, Burley, Leeds.   **0113 278 9656**
'Quantities were large. Vegetable Korma, tangy, creamy and divine.
Disappointed to find tinned potatoes with my spinach but the rich
delectable sauce more than compensated. Comfort/decor are basic.' CS.
'Excellent value for money. Consistently good food. .' LJM.

MOGHUL
8 The Green, Town Street, Horsforth, Leeds.   **0113 259 0530**
Pretty double-fronted establishment, housed in a stone building, with
comfortable high-backed chairs. A wide variety of favourites, including
Balti. Set menu good value, including lunches.

OLD DELHI
104,Burley Road, Leeds.   **0113 242 2026**
'A curry house with a difference, no standard curries on the menu but
Haleem, Shola and Shimla. Vast vegetarian menu. Quality good, prices
reasonable. No license, but pub next door lets you take your drinks with
you. If busy, waiters collect you from the pub when a table is ready.' RB.

PAHLGAM TANDOORI   **CC DISCOUNT**
159, Dewsbury Road, Beeston, Leeds.   **0113 270 4028**
'Decorated to a high standard. Lage portions, all very tasty.' KI.
Manager, Pervaiz Hussain will give a discount to Curry Club members,
see page 288. Hours: 5pm till 1am, Thursday and Sunday till 2am, Friday
and Saturday till 3am. Delivery service available.

RAIES TANDOORI   **CC DISCOUNT**
162, Roundhay Road, Leeds.   **0113 249 2493**
A thirty-two seater establishment, tends to get busy at weekends, so
book. 'Best dishes are Mixed Starter, Chicken Tikka Masala and Karahi
Gosht.' KI. Not licensed. Owner, MA Kiani will give a discount to Curry
Club members, see page 288. Hours: 5.30pm till 2.30am.

SHEESH MAHAL ASIAN CUISINE   **CC DISCOUNT**
348, Kirkstall Road, Leeds.   **0113 230 4161**
Menu lists all our favourite curries and side dishes at reasonable prices.
Proprietor, Azram Choudhry will give a discount to Curry Club members, see page 288. Hours: 5pm till midnight.

TANDOORI MAHAL   **CC DISCOUNT**
6-8, Merrion Street, Leeds.   **0113 245 2907**
'Good selection on pickle tray. Good quantities. Side dish of Bhindi
properly cooked.' SR. Proprietor, Zaman Miah will give a discount to
Curry Club members, see page 288. 12 to 2.30pm and 6pm till midnight.

PUDSEY

AAGRAH   **TOP 100 - CC DISCOUNT**
483, Bradford Road, Pudsey.   **01274 668818**
The restaurants with the beautiful chairs from Pakistan. The Aagrah
group is owned by three brothers. All four restaurants are listed as TOP
100 establishments. 'Murgh Saag tasted great. Chicken Zafrani we had
never come across but did enjoy. Service very rushed.' NDM. 'Good
menu. Felt rushed.' M O'H. Mohammed Aslam will give a discount to
Curry Club members, se page 288. Hours: 6pm till 11.30pm, till midnight
on Friday and saturday. Sunday 12 noon to 11.30pm. In our TOP 100, but
get that service problem sorted out. See below and overleaf.

SHIPLEY

AAGRAH   **TOP 100 - CC DISCOUNT**
27, Westgate, Shipley.   **01274 594660**
Seats forty-five diners. Partner, M Sabir will give a discount to Curry
Club members, see page 288. Hours: 6pm till midnight, till 12.15am on
Friday and Saturday. In our TOP 100. See above and overleaf.

BAILDON TANDOORI   **CC DISCOUNT**
6, North Gate, Baildon, Shipley.   **01274 582500**
Seats fifty-two diners, serving popular curries and accompaniments.
Owner, Mohammed Snober will give a discount to Curry Club members,
see page 288. Hours: 6pm till midnight.

WAKEFIELD

RAJ POOT
134, Kirkgate, Wakefield.   **01924 371215**
',Quality is excellent, Chicken Tikka Masala delicious.' N & M I.

WETHERBY

JAFLONG TANDOORI
31, High Street, Wetherby.   **01937 587011**
'A small restaurant. Food very good indeed, service 1st class.' DC O'D.

**Devonshire Place,
Keighley Road,
Skipton, North Yorkshire.
01756 790807**

**483 Bradford Road,
Pudsey, Leeds,
West Yorkshire.
01274 668818**

**27, Westgate.
Shipley, Bradford,
West Yorkshire.
01274 549660**

**Aberforth Road,
Garforth, Leeds,
West Yorkshire.
0113 287 6606**

CHANNEL ISLANDS
GUERNSEY
L,EREE
TASTE OF INDIA   CC DISCOUNT
Sunset Cottage, L'Eree.   **01481 64516**
'Two Popadoms waited at the table which was neatly laid out. Fish
Tikka, marinated in a sauce, very succulent. First rate Methi Gosht with
highly flavoured sauce.' JT. Owner, Tony Fernandes will give a discount
to Curry Club members, see page 288. Hours: 12 noon to 2pm and 6pm
till 11pm. Branch: Taste of India, 2, Mill Street, St Peter Port.

ST PETER PORT
TASTE OF INDIA
2, Mill Street, St Peter Port.   **01481 723730**
'Popadoms, onion salad and mint sauce waiting on the table. Sampled
Sardines on Puree, rich. A clean and well decorated restaurant, service
good.' JT. Branch: Taste of India, Sunset Cottage, L'Eree.

JERSEY
ST HELIER
SHEZAN
53, Kensington Place, St Helier.   **01534 22960**
'A small restaurant seating 40. Sheek Kebab to my mind almost perfect.
Balti Gosht, absolutely wonderful. Expensive but worth it.' MB.

TAJ MAHAL CENTRAL
La Motte Street, St Helier.   **01534 20147**
'Classy and luxurious restaurant. You are surrounded by running water
and tropical fish. Had best ever Tarka Dal.' TM.

ST AUBIN
SHAPLA
Victoria Road, St Aubin.   **01534 46495**
'Interior decor, to a very high standard with rich reds, golds and blues.
Hasna Kebabs, pieces of lamb marinated in yoghurt and spices and
tandooried with onions, peppers and tomatoes, really very tasty indeed.
Chicken Jalfrezi, aroma teriffic. Simply perfect Lamb Rogan Gosht. ' MB.

ISLES

ISLE OF LEWIS
STORNOWAY
ALI'S
24, South Beach Street, Stornoway.   **01851 706116**
Menu includes all the favourites. 'Had a good sound meal.' DMcK.

ISLE OF MAN
DOUGLAS
TAJ MAHAL
3, Esplanade Lane, Douglas.   **01624 74741**
'"Welcome" the sign said, what is didn't say was, "Britains most expensive restaurant" - Chutney Mary was cheaper. But it was worth it. All
very tasty and well presented. Friendly staff.' MB.

RAMSEY
SPICE OF LIFE
8, Peel Street, Ramsey.   **01624 816534**
'Sensationally good. Sauces excellent - we got the impression someone
has been on a curry cooking course - and passed! Prices ridiculously
high. Bizare note on the door, *"we do not serve drunks"* .' D McC.

ORKNEY
BIRSAY
HEIMDALL
Earls Palace, Birsay.
'Operates from a farm house kitchen, with an adjoining three table café
area. Humble menu. Portions are handsomely ample and reveal a
scintillant flavouring only arrived at by using fresh spices and herbs.' ES.
Hours: Friday, Saturday and Sunday 5pm till 10pm.

KIRKWALL
MUMTAZ
7, Bridge Street, Kirkwall.   **01856 873537**
'Comfortable and modern restaurant. All food very tasty. Service good
and efficient.' PAW W. Hours: 12 noon to midnight.

SHETLAND
LERWICK
RABE INDIAN
26, Commercial Road, Lerwick.   **01595 3349**
'Warm decor. Well cooked Indian cuisine at reasonable prices. Samosas,
Bhajia and Chicken Tikka Masala were all delicious.' AIE.

ISLE OF SKYE
PORTREE
GANDHI
Bayfield Road, Portree.   **01478 612681**
'Don't be put off by the horrendous tartan carpet that awaits your
entrance. Food took a long time to come. When it did come, however,
it was excellent.' SN. 'Pleasant surprise. Bank holiday and was packed,
we were seated promptly, a bit of a delay but service friendly. Delicious
food. Gobi Panir - spicy cauli- cheese unusual.' E O'D.

ISLE OF WIGHT
COWES
COWES TANDOORI   **CC DISCOUNT**
40, High Street, Cowes.   **01983 296710**
Seats sixty-four diners. A good selection of curries and side dishes on the
menu along with some specials such as Podina Gusht and Garlic Chicken.
Owner, Ashid Ali will give a discount to Curry Club members, see page
288. Hours: 12 noon to 2.30pm and 6pm till midnight.

NEWPORT
NABAB PALACE   **CC DISCOUNT**
84, Upper Street, James Street, Newport.   **01983 523276**
Seats fifty-four diners. Serves good, competent curries and accompaniments at reasonable island prices. Owner, Jila Miah will give a 10%
discount to Curry Club members, see page 288. Hours: 12 noon to
2.30pm and 6pm till midnight.

NORTHERN IRELAND

BANGOR
ALI KEBABAS and SIMA'S
9 and11, Crosby Street, Bangor.   **01247 271722**
All the usual curries and side dishes on the menu.

BELFAST
ASHOKA
365, Lisburn Road, Belfast.   **01232 660362**
A smart and upmarket restaurant. Specialities include Karahi dishes.

BENGAL BRASSERIE
339, Ormeau Road, Belfast.   **01232 647516**
'Decor very palatial and comfortable, but very poor lighting. Very good
selection on menu. Sparse portions. Quality excellent.' AS.

CAFE INDIA
60, Great Victoria Street, Belfast.   **01232 243727**
A restaurant with atmosphere. Menu contains Karai and Balthi (sic).

JHARNA
133, Lisburn Road, Belfast.   **01232 381299**
Seats 80. Decorated in burgundy and jade green with gold. Popular
curries on the menu.

MAHARAJA
62, Botanic Avenue. Belfast.   **01232 234200**
Set meals on the menu are value for money.

RAJPUT
461, Lisburn Road, Belfast.   **01232 662168**
A good restaurant for popular curries and side dishes.

HOLYWOOD
BOKHARA
149-1533, High Street, Holywood.   **01232 426767**
'Spicing is not subtle but portions are enormous. Sag dishes are particu-
larly delicious and the Brinjal Bhaji is one of the best I have ever had.
Service is good if you get a Bangladeshi waiter and hilarious if you get an
Irish waitress.' RBS.

NEWTOWNARDS
EASTERN TANDOORI
16, Castle Street, Newtownards.   **01247 819541**
'Food is of an exceptionally high standard.' AM. . Branches: Eastern
Tandoori, Old Parish Hall, Deansgrange, Dublin and Eastern Tandoori,
1, New Street, Malahide, Dublin.

GANGES   **CC DISCOUNT**
69, Court Street, Newtownards.   **01247 811426**
'Very good portions with doggie bags provided. Best Nan bread I've
tasted. Service is excellent. Prices have increased dramatically.' AS.
Hours: 12 noon to 2pm and 5.30pm till 11.30pm. Friday and Saturday till
midnight. Sunday 5pm till 11pm only. Discount for members, see p288.

REPUBLIC OF IRELAND

CORK

DELHI PALACE
Washington Street, Cork.   00 353 21 276227
'Menu not extensive, but most favourites are there. Bhajia and Tandoori Chicken were both excellent. Sag Gosht, tender and tasty. Murgh Makhani rich and buttery.' JS.

RANI'S
Princes Street, Cork.   00 353 21 273690
'Small, neat restaurant, seats about twenty six. Samosa was crisp with a tasty filling. Lamb Pasanda well cooked and quite delicious.' B & AB.
'Lamb Bhuna full of flavour. Chicken Pasanda, rich. Fragrant Pullao Rice. Adequate quantities.' JS. Open: every evening in tourist season.

DALKEY

AL MINAR   CC DISCOUNT
21, Castle Street, Dalkey.   00 353 1 284 0900
Opened in 1985 and has established itself as a reliable curry house serving good food. Waiter, Michael Rahman will give a discount to Curry Club members, see page 288. Hours: 12 noon to 2.30pm and 6pm till 11pm. Sunday Buffet 1pm till 5pm.

DUBLIN

CHANDI
174, Pembroke Road, Ballsbridge, Dublin.   00 353 1 668 1458
'Large restaurant on three floors. Vegetable Kebabs, tasty. Prawn Bhuna, quite spicy. Generous portions.' FEG. Hours: 12.30pm and 2.30pm and 6pm till 11.30pm. Sunday 6pm till 11.30pm. Branch: Chandni, 123-125, Masons Hill, Bromley, Kent. UK.

EASTERN
34-35, South William Street, Dublin.   00 353 1 671 0428
'Decor extremely pleasing, Indian carving etc. Food very good, my German colleague very impressed.' SP. Branches: Eastern, Old Parish Hall, Deansgrange, Dublin and Eastern, 1, New Street, Malahide, Dublin. Newly opened: Eastern, Emmet Place, Cork.

RAJDOOT   BEST IN IRELAND AWARD   CC DISCOUNT
26, Clarendon St, Westbury Centre, Dublin.   00 353 1 679 4274
'Comfortable and smart surroundings. Excellent supply of nibbles while we waited for a table. Complimentary Popadoms and chutneys. Started with Kidney Massalla followed by Lamb Jalfrezi, the best every tasted. Washed down with Guinness - we were in Ireland! Service impeccable, deserves TOP 100.' JM. Manager, Raghbir Singh will give a discount to Curry Club members, see page 288. Hours: Monday to Saturday 12 noon to 2.30pm and 6.30pm till 11.30pm. Branches: Rajdoot, 12-22, Albert Street, Birmingham; Rajdoot, Carlton House, 16-18, Albert Square, Manchester; Rajdoot, 83, Park Street, Bristol; Rajdoot, Lamo de Espinosa, Fuengirola, Malaga, Spain. See page 12. A Top 100 restaurant, deseving our BEST IN IRELAND AWARD.

SHALIMAR
17, South Great George Street, Dublin.   00 353 1 671 0738
'Standard curry house fayre.' SP. Set meals on the menu are good value.

SCOTLAND

BORDERS

KELSO
SWAGAT
Inch Road, Kelso.   **01573 225159**
'This tiny restaurant is difficult to find. Mr Kumar, the proprietor has converted his garage into a restaurant. Sounds awful, doesn't it - well it isn't. The food, service, prices are all excellent, I cannot commend this little place enough.' JR.

CENTRAL

BRIDGE OF ALLAN
BENAZIR TANDOORI   **CC DISCOUNT**
23, Henderson Street, Bridse of Allan.   **01786 833710**
'Very small restaurant, (thirty diners) but the food, menu, quality, price and service were excellent. So you forgot about how squashed you were.' CR. Owner, I Mohammed will give a dscount to Curry Club members, see page 288. Hours: 4pm till 11.30pm.

DUNBLANE
INDIA GATE
Fourways,Perth Road, Dunblane.   **01786 825394**
'Exceedingly large portions, everyone was feeling full after the starters! Very large Nans. To sum up this restaurant, 'lots' to eat, 'lots' of taste, but not 'lots' of price.' SH.

FALKIRK
MEHRAN   **CC DISCOUNT**
4, Weir Street, Falkirk.   **01324 622010**
All our favourites on the menu including some extras, Nehari, Nantara and Achari. Chicken and Mushroom Samosa sounds good too. Partner, Arif Shakir will give a discount to Curry Club members, see page 288. Hours: 12 noon to 2pm and 5pm till midnight. Thursday to Sunday 5pm till 1.30am. Delivery service available.

GRANGEMOUTH
SHAHI TANDOORI
6a, Union Road, Grangemouth.   **01000 665055**
Standard curry house menu with a few specials. Hours: Sunday to Thursday 5pm till midnight. Friday 12 noon to 2pm and 4pm till 1am. Saturday 4pm till 1am. Delivery service available.

STIRLING
BAGHDAD   **CC DISCOUNT**
16-18, Barnton Street, Stirling.   **01786 472137**
A huge restaurant seating 140 diners. Balti Nights are every Monday, Buffet Night on Wednesday. Manager, Rauinder Singh Purba will give a discount to Curry Club members, see page 288. Hours: 12 noon to midnight. Sunday 3.30pm till midnight. Delivery service available.

EAST INDIAN COMPANY and VARSITY BLUES
7, Viewfield Place, Stirling.   **01786 471330**
'Down a flight of stairs to a dark oak panelled room, a fire burning
brightly, walls huge with pseudo paintings. We sat at a highly polished
mahogany reproduction table. We found no argument with their claim
that, "The Key to our success is a delicacy of flavour." PW. Home
delivery service.Branch: Shimla Pinks (Glasgow and Birmingham),
Killermont Polo Club - see separate enties.

TAJ MAHAL   **CC DISCOUNT**
39, King Street, Stirling.   **01786 470728**
A large restaurant seating 100 diners. 'The humble Sheek Kebab deserves a special mention. Chef makes Nan bread to demand in front of
the customer.' DL. Head waiter, Neil Ambasana, will give a discount to
Curry Club members, see page 288. Hours: 12 noon to midnight.

DUMFRIES & GALLOWAY

DUMFRIES
JEWEL IN THE CROWN   **CC DISCOUNT**
48-50, St Michael Street, Dumfries.   **01387 64183**
Try the Bengali Chicken, a mild curry with bamboo shoots and sultanas.
Nan breads come under the title of 'Supporting Sundries of Tandoori
Dishes'. Manager, Mr A Muhit will give a discount to Curry Club
members, see page 288. Hours: 12 to 2.30pm and 5.30pm till 11.30pm.

STRANRAER
SHISH MAHAL
41, Hanover Street, Stranraer.   **01776 703987**
'My favourite meal is their Jaipuri Masala, chicken, King prawns and
mushrooms cooked in the tandoor with a rich sauce.' FB. Hours: 12 noon
to 2pm and 5pm till 1.30am. Saturday: 12 noon to 1.30am. Sunday 4pm
till 12.30am. Free delivery service.

FIFE

CUPAR
MALIA
27, Crossgate, Cupar.   **01334 557844**
'Chana Puri as meal in itself, spicy with thin crispy puri - lovely. Others
in my party cleared their plates - obviously a good sign.' GS.

DUMFERMLINE
KHANS   **CC DISCOUNT**
33, Carnegie Drive, Dumfermline.   **01383 739478**
Seats a massive 160 diners. 'Good value for money. Portions are large
and they also make a mean Phal!' Balti is included on the menu along
with delights such as Bombay Tiffin, served with Tamarind chutney. LR.
Manager, Ismail Khan will give a discount to Curry Club members, se
page 288. Hours: 12 noon to 2.30pm and 5.30pm till 11.30pm.

GLENROTHES

NURJAHAN   CC DISCOUNT
Coslane, Woodside Road, Glenrothes.   **01592 630649**
A large establishment seating 110 . Decorated in pinks to a very high
standard. Roomy carver chairs at all tables. A restaurant for a special
occasion. Striking menu with photographs, of spices and dishes of curry
and breads. Proprietor, Manirul Islam will give a discount to Curry Club
members, see page 288. Hours: 12 noon to 2pm and 5pm till 11pm.

KIRKCALDY

AMRITSAR
274, High Street, Kirkcaldy.   **01592 267639**
'Regular customers are recognised and welcomed. Gourmet nights - eat
as much as you like - are excellent value when you are feeling very
hungry.' SH. 'Portions more than generous.' IR.

ROSYTH

TASTE OF INDIA
130, Admiralty Road, Rosyth.   **01384 413844**
'Restaurant decor good and spacious. Starters set a high standard of
promises to come - the main courses let down. Raita that accompanies
the Pakoras was made with yoghurt, mint and mango, very tasty.' NS.

ST ANDREWS

BABUR   CC DISCOUNT
89, South Street, St Andrews.   **01334 477778**
A large restaurant seating 105 diners. 'The decor is splendid and I speak
as an architect, ideally arranged for an intimate meal. We ordered the
Emperor's mid-day feast, ate well and demolished several bottles of
Cobra lager.' PLS. Marketing Executive Tony Hussain will give a
discount to Curry Club members, see page 288. Hours: 12 noon to 3pm
and 5pm till midnight. Fax (on same line) for a copy of their menu.

NEW BALAKA BANGLADESHI   AWARD WINNER   TOP 100
3, Alexandra Place, St Andrews.   **01334 474825**
An upmarket and sophisticated restaurant, decorated in pinks. Palms
divide tables and Indian art hangs from the walls.   Unusual dishes on
the menu include: Mas Bangla - salmon marinated in lime, turmeric and
chilli, fried with mustard oil, garlic, onion, tomato and aubergine. Hours:
12 noon to 1am (Friday and Saturday only), 5.30pm till 1am.We have
many reports about Mr Rouf's excellent food and restaurant, which
ensure not only his Top 100 placing, but our BEST IN SCOTLAND
AWARD.

GRAMPIAN

ABERDEEN

CROWN TANDOORI
145, Crown Street, Aberdeen.   **01224 210288**
'Well furnished. Immediately served with popadoms as soon as I sat
down. Boti Kabab was delicious - very tender and full of flavour.
Portions are small, thought I'd been served a starter by mistake!' RC.

GATE OF INDIA
33, Summer Street, Aberdeen. **01224 624752**
'Waiters amused as I managed to eat my way through a Phal. A well run
restaurant with above average service and excellent food.' GS.

ELGIN
NASEEB **CC DISCOUNT**
54, High Street, Elgin. **01343 550250**
Good curries at reasonable prices in pleasant surroundings. Owner,
Nemat Ali gives a discount to Curry Club members, see page 288. Hours:
5pm till midnight. Branch: Nemat, 52, West Church Street, Buckie.

QISMAT
202-204, High Street, Elgin. **01343 541461**
'Service polite and prompt. Large portions from extensive menu. Tried
Chicken Balti for the first time, with extra chilli. Offers good food in good
surroundings.' AM. Hours: 12 noon to 2pm and 5pm till midnight,
Sunday 5pm till midnight.

ELLON
NOSHEEN
Bridge Street, Ellon. **01358 724309**
'Good food with ample portions. A bit expensive but worth it.' AMcW.

FORRES
PRINCE OF INDIA **CC DISCOUNT**
64, High Street, Forres. **01309 673475**
Opened in 1985 and has built up a good loyal following for serving good
curries at sensible prices. Manager, Harunur Rashid will give a discount
to Curry Club members, see page 288. Hours: 12 noon to 2pm and 5pm
till midnight. Branch: Prince of India, Station Road, Pitlochry.

INVERURIE
ALO CHAYA **CC DISCOUNT**
56, Market Place, Inverurie. **01467 624860**
A well established restaurant, since 1987. 'Waiters efficient and friendly.
Buffet night is worth a visit.' AMcW. Owner, Syed Mujibul Hoque will
give a discount to Curry Club members, see page 288. Hours: 12 noon to
2.30pm and 5.30pm till 11.30pm.

TURRIFF
SHOMI
24, Balmellie Street, Turriff. **01888 562636**
'Buffet nights are basic but good value.' AMcW.

TANDOORI RESTAURANT

202-204, High Street,
Elgin, Morayshire, Grampian.
IV30 1BA

01343 541461 & 01343 540785

HIGHLAND

AVIEMORE
ASHA
43, Grampian Road, Aviemore.　　　　　　　　**01479 811118**
'Our first impression of the menu was that it seemed expensive, but most main courses included rice. Katta Murgh Masala was very tasty with a tang of lime.' EO'D. Hours: 12 noon to 2pm and 5.30pm till 11.30pm.

FORT WILLIAM
INDIAN GARDEN
88, High Street, Fort William.　　　　　　　　**01397 705011**
'Service slow but the food's good.' GM. This restaurant has been under the present ownership for ten years and seats sixty diners.

INVERNESS
RAJAH INTERNATIONAL
2, Post Office Avenue, Inverness.　　　　　　　**01463 237190**
A spacious restaurant seating sixty diners. HB says, 'The best curry experience in over ten years.' Hours: 12 noon to midnight.

NAIRN
AL RAJ　　　　　　　　　　　　　　CC DISCOUNT
25, Harbour Street, Nairn, Inverness.　　　　　**01667 455370**
Opened in 1984 and has built up a good reputation for good curries and accompaniments at reasonable prices. Restaurant seats seventy diners and has a private party room. Mobarok Ali, the Honorable Owner, will give a discount to Curry Club members, see page 288. Hours: 12 noon to 2pm and 5pm till 11pm.

LOTHIAN

EDINBURGH
BALLI'S TANDOORI　　　　　　　　　　CC DISCOUNT
89, Hanover Street, Edinburgh.　　　　　　　　**0131 226 3451**
Balti and Nentara on the menu. Owner, A Rarwaiz will give a discount to Curry Club members, see page 288. 11am to 2pm;5pm till midnight.

BANGALORE TANDOORI　　　　　　　　CC DISCOUNT
52, Home Street, Edinburgh.　　　　　　　　　**0131 229 1348**
'Had a good Chicken Biriani .'PB. Owner, Mahmood Khan will give a discount to Curry Club , see p288. Hours: 5pm to 1.30am, Fri/ Sat 2am.

CAFÉ INDIA
29, West Maitland Street, Edinburgh.　　　　　**0131 220 0603**
'An airy restaurant with high ceilings. . Popadoms - nice, but price of pickle tray O.T.T. Dopiaza was superb. Chapati's good too.' AG.

GULNAR'S PASSAGE TO INDIA　　　　　CC DISCOUNT
46, Queen Charlotte Street, Leith, Edinburgh.　**0131 554 7520**
'Complimentary Popadoms while you were ordering. Chicken Dupiaza delicious , not too many onions.' AG. Manager, Mohammad Saleh gives a discount to Curry Club members, see page 288.

INDIA GATE
23, Brougham Place, Edinburgh.   0131 229 1537
Boal fish and Nentara on the menu of this popular Indian restaurant.

INDIAN CAVALRY CLUB
3, Atholl Place, Edinburgh.   0131 228 3282
'Smart upmarket restaurant. Service quick, though waiter forgot side
plates. Food excellent. The hottest Jalfrezi I have tasted. Prices high but
on the whole worth it.' EM. For vegetarians and other diners try the
Pineapple Samber, pineapple in a lentil and tamarind sauce.

JAIPUR MANSION
10, Newington Road, Edinburgh.   0131 662 9023
A newly opened establishment. Very upmarket. Wonderful menu with
wonderful food. Tessrio, mussels seasoned with coriander, turmeric,
garlic, cumin and lightly fried. Bhari Hui Simla Mirch, lean minced lamb
or boneless chicken pieces with an amalgam of traditional herbs and
spices. Once cooked, stuffed into fresh bell pepper and shallow fried.
Balti Karahi and Nentara is also on the menu. Wine list is very impressive
too. Hours: 12 noon to midnight.

KALPNA
2-3, St Patrick's Square, Edinburgh.   0131 667 9890
Established in 1983. Serves well respected curries.

LANCERS BRASSERIE   **TOP 100 - CC DISCOUNT**
5, Hamilton Place, Edinburgh.   0131 332 3444
A beautifully decorated and stylish restaurant, pink suede on the walls,
tiled floor, highly polished tables, a really smart eating atmosphere.
Downstairs is a private dining room for approximately a dozen diners.
Chippendale- style furniture, banquet style. Prints of times gone by of
the Raj decorate the walls. Great for a special treat, eg: a birthday party.
A small but selective menu. Don't expect a standard curry house, it isn't.
'Decor nice but expensive.' AG McW. Owner Wali Udin gives. a
discount to Curry Club members, see page 288. Hours: 12 noon to 2.30pm
and 5.30pm till 11.30pm. Branches: Verandah, Suruchi, and Maharaja's

MAHARAJAH'S   **CC DISCOUNT**
17-19, Forrest Road, Edinburgh.   0131 220 2273
A modern and luxuriously decorated restaurant in salmons pinks and
subtle greys. Great swags of material hang from the ceiling giving a
tented effect. Partner, Razu Khan will give a discount to Curry Club
members, see page 288. Hours: 12 noon to 2pm and 5.30pm till 11.30pm.
In connection with Verandah, Lancers and Suruchi in Edinburgh.

MONSOON VILLAGE
13, Dalry Road, Haymarket, Edinburgh.   0131 346 0204
A small restaurant seating 42. Well established and well liked.

OMAR KHAYYAM
1,Grosvenor Street, Edinburgh.   0131 225 2481
'Food and service first class.' ES. 'Nan breads the biggest I've ever
encountered, perfect light texture. Chicken Bhuna was perfect in a sauce
like nectar. Chicken Dopiaza - mouthwatering stuff.' FB.

PATAKA
190, Causewayside, Edinburgh.   0131 668 1167
'Menu is superb. All sorts of lovely variations on the normal theme.
Complimentary popadoms and pickles are on the table when you sit
down.Had Tamatar Wali Josh, which was not unlike an ordinary Rogan
Josh except it was more delectable with a very rich sauce. Delightful melt
in the mouth Green Herb Chicken. Large quantities, sheer glutony!' AG.

RAJ
91, Henderson Street, Leith, Edinburgh. 0131 553 3980
Tommy Miah's potentially luxurious restaurant, complete with a lot of original Victorian style. Tommy is currently running 1983 prices promotion. Good value for money, especially since portions are huge. Homemade Mango chutney is served with Popadoms on every table.

SHAMIANA
14, Brougham Street, Edinburgh. 0131 226 2265
A family owned and run business. Seats forty-three diners. Tends to get busy at weekends so please book your table. Hours: 6pm till 11.30pm.

SINGAPORE SLING CC DISCOUNT
503, Lawn Market, The Royal Mile, Edinburgh. 0131 226 2826
Not a curry restaurant, but there is a curry or two on the menu. A smallish restaurant, seating 45, gets busy at weekends, so book a table. Proprietor, C Pang will give a discount to Curry Club members, see page 288. Hours: 12.30pm to 2.30pm and 6pm till 11pm, Friday and Saturday till midnight. Branch: Singapura, 69, North Castle Street, Edinburgh.

SURUCHI
14a, Nicholson Street, Edinburgh. 0131 556 6583
Suruchi means, in most Indian languages means good taste. Restaurant decor has been imported from India. Jaipur blue/turquoise tiles adorn the walls. Proprietor, Herman Rodrigues, is also a photographer and his many works cover the walls. Table linen is vegetable dyed pink and table wear is beaten coppered brass. A real Indian Meal in this vegetarian restaurant. See ad on previous page.

TANDOORI LAND CC DISCOUNT
63, Clerk Street, Edinburgh. 0131 667 1035
What a title!! A small restaurant seating 32. Owner, S Chowdhury will give a discount to Curry Club members, see page 288. Hours: 5pm till midnight. Branch: Morningside, 128, Morningside Road, Edinburgh.

VERANDAH TOP 100
17, Dalry Road, Edinburgh. 0131 337 5828
A pretty restaurant creating an illusion of sitting on a Verandah somewhere in Asia. Cane chairs to sit on, bamboo slatted blinds cover the walls. Hours: 12 noon to 2.15pm and 5pm till midnight. Branch: Maharajah, 17-19, Forrest Road, Edinburgh. See ad on previous page.

MUSSELBURGH
SHISH MAHAL CC DISCOUNT
63a, High Street, Musselburgh. 0131 665 3121
Seats fifty diners. All the popular curries and side dishes on the menu. Owner, Idris Khan will give a discount to Curry Club members, see page 288. Hours: 12 noon to 2pm and 5pm till midnight. Home deliveries .

STRATHCLYDE

ARDROSSAN

SANGEET CC DISCOUNT
51, Glasgow Street, Ardrossan. 01294 601191
An intimate restaurant seating thirty-six diners. Owner, Fawad Khan
will give a discount to Curry Club members, see page 288. Hours: 12
noon to 2pm (Thursday to Friday only) and 5pm till 12.30am.

GLASGOW

ALI BABAS BALTI BAR
51, West Regent Street, Glasgow. 0141 332 6289
'Glasgow's first Balti house. Five different Pakoras and Balti, nice. .' CW.

ALISHAN TANDOORI
250, Battlefield Road, Battlefield. 0141 632 5294
Menu includes a good range of popular curries along with specials such
as Nantara, Masaladar, Chasni, Achaari and Nashidar.

AMBALA SWEET CENTRE
178, Maxwell Road, Glasgow. 0141 429 5620
Takeaway establishment, serving a small range of compentently cooked
curries and snacks.'Lamb Bhoona is amazing!. DF. Hours: 10am to 10pm.

ASHOKA WEST END
1284, Argyle Street, Glasgow. 0141 339 0936
'Very hospitable. Tandoori Chicken Chat Drumsticks, pleasant. Roghan
Josh was excellent.' CW. Hours: 5pm till midnight.

ASHOKA ASHTON LANE
19, Ashton Lane, Glasgow. 0141 357 5904
'Chicken Massala Dosa was excellent, filled with strips of tandoori
chicken and a massive portion of rice. A recommended oasis.' CW.

ASHOKA
268, Clarkston Road, Glasgow. 0141 637 5904
Try House Specialities such as Goanese Delicacy, Mewa Massala and
Kerela Chilli Chicken. Hours: 5pm till midnight.

BALBIR'S VEGETARIAN ASHOKA CC DISCOUNT
BALBIR'S ASHOKA TANDOORI
108, Elderslie Street, Glasgow. 0141 221 1761
Balbirs Vegetarian Ashoka is upstairs. and serves purely vegetarian
delights such as Kachoris, stuffed lentil pastry, Patra, curried lotus leaf
rolls, andBhel Poori. Balbir's Ashoka Tandoori is downstairs and serves
meat curries. Try a Garam Masala curry sprinkled with green chillies. 'I
can vouch for this restaurant, it is excellent.'BS. Owner, Gian Singh will
give a discount to Curry Club members, see page 288. Hours: 5pm to
midnight, Friday /Saturday till 1am. Branches 141 & 149 Elderslie Street.

CAFÉ INDIA
171, North Street, Charing Cross, Glasgow. 0141 248 4074
Seats a massive 250 diners. Set menus are a speciality, and Gourmet
Night Extravaganza is every Monday from 7pm till 10.30pm.

CREME DE LA CREME
1071, Argyle Street, Finnieston, Glasgow. 0141 221 3222
Situated in a former cinema and aiming at an upmarket image. No
expense has been spared on creating style reminiscent of London's

Bombay Brasserie. Former stalls and dress circle are in use, thus a very large restaurant. 'Food good, Service poor.' BG. 'Service superb. Prices dear, but portions large.' D McK.'Tried the buffet, my first experience of this type of spice inhalation.As much as you like. All reasonable.' CW.

INDIA DINER
1191-1193, Argyle Street, Glasgow.
CC DISCOUNT
0141 221 0354
Head Waiter, Anmal Lak will give a discount to Curry Club members, see page 288. Hours: 12 noon to 2pm and 5pm till midnight.

KILLERMONT POLO CLUB
2022, Maryhill Rd, Maryhill Pk, Bearsden, Glasgow.   0141 946 5412
Two dining areas, one is oak panelled with Georgian-style chairs, polished tables and polo items decorated the walls. The other is more traditional with high-backed chairs, and flowing table linen.

KOH I NOOR
235, North Street, Charing Cross, Glasgow.   0141 204 1444
'An excellent meal. Meat Samosas came with a plateful of salad and chickpea in sweet curry sauce .It was so filling I had to leave most of my main course!' SF. 'Starters very impressive, quantities large. Garlic Nan not for the faint hearted: beautiful. Chicken Tikka Chasini and Chicken Nentara memorable.' HB. 'Absolutely superb.In a class of its own.' BS.

MOTHER INDIA CAFÉ BISTRO
28, Westminster Terrace, Glasgow.   0141 221 1663
A small, unlicensed restaurant, so BYO. Between 5.30pm and 7.30pm they serve Indian high tea. Reports please.

MURPHY'S PAKORA BAR
1287, Argyle Street, Glasgow.   0141 334 1550
'The best selction of Pakoras that you are ever likely to see'.CW. How about Haggis Pakora. Beam me up Scotty.'CW. Hours: 12 to midnight.

RAMANA
427, Sauchiehall Street, Glasgow.
CC DISCOUNT
0141 332 2528
Seats 120 diners. Hours: 12 noon to midnight. Owner, BS Purewal will give a discount to Curry Club members, see page 288.

SEPOY CLUB
62, St Andrews Drive, Pollokshields, Glasgow.   0141 427 1106
Former Victorian house now a hotel with Indian restaurant. Exquisite decor. Amazing range of meals. Beautifully presented Pakoras, but expensive. Sorbet to cleanse the palate followed by well presented Jaipuri, Green Herb Chicken, Tikka and Tandoori. A delight.' DF.

SHISH MAHAL
66-68, Park Road, Glasgow.
CC DISCOUNT
0141 334 7899
Opened way back in 1964 Managing partner, Nasim Ahmed will give a discount to Curry Club members, see page 288. Hours: 12 noon to 2pm and 5pm till 11.30pm. Friday/Saturday 12 noon to 11.30pm and Sunday 3pm till 11.30pm. Branch: Shish Mahal, 1348, Maryhill Road, Glasgow.

SPICE OF LIFE
1293, Argyle Street, Glasgow.   0141 334 0678
How about Banana Pakoras, or Garlic Mussel Poori. Goanese Lamb.

TURBAN TANDOORI
2, Station Road, Giffnock, Glasgow.
CC DISCOUNT
0141 638 0069
Specials include Nentara and Masaledar dishes. Proprietor, Kulbir Purewal will give a discount to Curry Club members, see page 288. Hours: 5pm till midnight. Delivery Service available.

EAST KILBRIDE
ATRIUM COURT   **CC DISCOUNT**
3, The Boardwalk, East Kilbride.   **013552 60681**
All the usual curries and a good selection of Pakoras and specials such as Nentara, Chasini and Karahi. Manager, JS Boparai will give a discount to Curry Club members, see page 288. Hours: 12 noon to midnight. Branch: Taj Palace, 2, Scholar's Gate, Whitehills, East Kilbride.

HAMILTON
SHANGRI LA
28-32, Castle Street, Hamilton.   **01698 285500**
Menu delights include: Reshmi Mushlee Masala - haddock with peppers, tomatoes, onions and chillies and Butter Chicken Masala - tikka sautéed with tomatoes and butter. Balti and Karahi also on the menu.

JOHNSTONE
ASHOKA
3, Rankine Street, Johnstone.   **01505 322430**
Same menu as Glasgow branches. Set meals are good value for money.

SHIMLA PINKS
4, William Street, off Houston Square, Johnstone.   **0105 22697**
Modern restaurant. Polished floors, tubular stainless steel chairs arranged round black tables. Branch: Shimla Pinks - Birmingham, Killermont Polo Club and East India Company and Varsity Blues.

KILWINNING
17TH -21ST LANCERS
3, Oswenad Road, Kilwinning.   **01294 557244**
'Our favourites are Lancers assorted Pakora, Lamb Jaipuri, Karahi Lamb Tikka Bhuna and Shahi Korma. Decor is styled as a regimental mess.' CA. 'Chicken Tikka was delightful. Korma came in a silver dish, sprinkled with almonds; creamy and rich consistency.' JD.

LARGS
KOH I NOOR
84, Gallowgate Street, Largs.   **01475 686051**
This restaurant is situated on the shore front and has a good view. 'Varied menu, good sized quantities, quality of meal very good.' WW.

PAISLEY
KOH I NOOR   **CC DISCOUNT**
40, New Sneddon Street, Paisley.   **0141 889 7909**
Specialities include: Nentara, Lyallpuri and Masala Karahi. Owner, A Ghafur will give a discount to Curry Club members, see page 288. Hours: 5pm till midnight.

TANDOORI KNIGHT   **CC DISCOUNT**
14, Moss Street, Paisley.   **0141 887 7693**
Seats ninety diners. Owner, Gurmakh Sing Purewall will give a discount to Curry Club members, see page 288. Hours: 12 noon to midnight.

PRESTWICK
TAJ   **CC DISCOUNT**
141, Main Street, Prestwick.   **01292 77318**
Seats a massive 150 diners. Owner, Rabinder Singh will give a discount to Curry Club members, see page 288. Hours: 12 to 2pm 5pm to12.15am.

RENFREW
CAFÉ INDIA
43, Hairst Street, Renfrew.   **0141 885 1066**
Kichori, Samosas and Puri for starters. Masaledar, Nentara, Garam
Masala curries for main course along with other popular favourites.

SALTCOATS
AKOSKA PALACE
66, Hamilton Street, Saltcoats.   **01294 466713**
'Special Assorted Ralwa - chicken and lamb tikka withBhuna sauce and
a sea of prawns, peppers and mince as well. Gave it the thumbs up.' CW.

TAYSIDE

BROUGHTY FERRY
GULISTAN HOUSE   **CC DISCOUNT**
Queen Street Halls, Broughty Ferry.   **01382 738844**
'Impressive decor. Some meals excellent. Tandoori dishes are normally
very good.' FC. Owner, MA Mohammed will give a discount to Curry
Club members, see page 288. Hours: 5pm till midnight.

VICEROY
44, Gray Street, Broughty Ferry.   **01382 477550**
'Food always superb, staff friendly. Generous helpings.' FC.

DUNDEE
CHAAND   **CC DISCOUNT**
104, Dura Street, Dundee.   **01384 456786**
Good curry house food on the menu. Owner, MA Kessar gives discounts
to Curry Club members, see page 288. Hours: 5pm till midnight.

SHABAB
34,Main Street, Dundee.   **01382 810916**
'Keema Nan, superb full of minced meat and ginormous. I am drooling
thinking of it.' If you can find a bigger Nan you'll be lucky.' FC.

SHEHZAD
24,Castle Street, Dundee.   **01382 200265**
'Always good value and tasty curries. Chicken Dhansak mouthwatering. Good sized portions and service prompt.' SH.

FORFAR
RUPALI
3-5, Queen Street, Forfar.   **01307 464480**
'Khachi Biryani is outstanding, huge portion. Big, fresh tasty Nan .' GS.

PERTH
AL FAROOQ
13, County Place, Perth.   **01738 442000**
'Garlic Nan was out of this world. Rapturous praise for the Vegetable
Thali and Lamb Achari Gosht described as brilliant.' AP.

SHALIMAR
Atholl Street, Perth.   **01738 634204**
'Small, cosy wonderfully decorated. Prawn Puri and Patia dishes are
excellent. Nans large and fluffy. Mouthwatering.' SH. .

WALES

CLWYD

COLWYN BAY
BENGAL PALACE   **CC DISCOUNT**
The Clock House, 55, Abergele Road, Colwyn Bay.   **01492 531683**
'A roomy restaurant with excellent service and very good food. Air conditioning is very effective and the whole experience was very pleasant,' A & CV. Manager, AM Khan will give a discount to Curry Club members, see page 288. Hours: 12 noon to 2.30pm and 6pm till 11.30pm.

**The Clock House
55/57 Abergele Road
Colwyn Bay
(01492) 531683/531884**

**Lunch: 12pm to 2.30pm
Dinner: 6pm to 11.30pm
Last Orders at 11.15pm**

**"Our menu is extensive,
but not expensive"**

SITAR
1 Bay View Road,Colwyn Bay.   **01492 533816**
'Provided us with good average food for several years.' A & CV.

DEESIDE
AMANTOLA INTERNATIONAL
Welsh Road, Sealand, Deeside.   **01244 811383**
'Like a trip to India, spoilt for choice. Free Popadoms with chutney and my favourite meal - Chicken Madras.' PJ. 'Impressive, seating for over 200 people and all in small cosy alcoves which are divided off into small roooms which are named after places in Bangladesh. Colourful restaurant decorated in rich golds, blues, reds and greens. Absolutely spot on, truly delicious Chicken Madras with Pilau Rice and Nan. Chinese food also on the menu.' MB. 'Onion Bhajis - good. Prawn Puri - excellent. Korai - superb.' DB. Delivery service available.

BENGAL DYNASTY   **AWARD WINNER**   **CC DISCOUNT**
106, Chester Rd East, Shotton, Deeside.   **TOP 100**   **01244 830455**
'Varied menu. Service of the highest rate. Quality food in good, average sized portions. Light, bright and pretty decor.' PM. 'Pickles seemed home-made and excellent.' DR. 'Jalfrezi with boiled rice, good portion.' DB. Executive partner, Monchab Ali will give a discount to Curry Club members, see page 288. Hours: 12 noon to 2.30pm and 5.30pm till 11pm. Branch: Bengal Dynasty, 1, North Parade, Llandudno, Gwynedd.They jointly win our BEST IN WALES AWARD. See advertisement on page 31.

LLANGOLLEN

SIMLA
4-5, Victoria Square, Llangollen.   **01978 860610**
'AboveAverage.' A & CV. Seats fifty diners and can fill up quickly on a
Friday and Saturday night, so book your table. Popular curries on the
menu. Hours: 12 noon to 2.30pm and 6pm till midnight. Sunday lunch
1pm till 2.30pm. Branch: Simla, 42, Beatrice Street, Oswestry, Shropshire.

SYLHET
36, Regent Street, Llangollen.   **01978 861877**
'Liked the look of this restaurant and we weren't wrong. Food was
excellent, waiter helpful and informative.' AS.

PRESTATYN
SUHAIL TANDOORI
12, Bastion Road, Prestatyn.   **01745 856829**
A former church. 'Service slow. Grand surroundings - layout being on
several levels surrounding a central altar-like bar. Dall Soup - excellent.
Korai arrived with a thick sauce full of large pieces of tender chicken.'
KB. Prices seemed a little expensive but quality and quantity made up
for it. Vegetable Korma looked and tasted good with lots of almonds.'
LC.

RHYL
INDIA GARDEN   **CC DISCOUNT**
41, Abbey Street, Rhyl.   **01745 350092**
'A very small but tastefully decorated and well served restaurant. Food
is good.' A & CV. Gourmet Nights every Tuesday and Special Banquets
on Friday. Owner, Abdul Shahid will give a discount to Curry Club
members, see page 288. Hours: 12 noon to 2pm and 5.30pm till 11.30pm.

Owners of restaurants selected to appear in
this Guide are invited to advertise only after
their restaurant has been selected for entry.
  We thank those who have done so. It helps to
keep the price of the Guide as low as possible.

Fully Licensed

Tandoori Restaurant

the Light Of Asia Restaurant

34, Eastgate
Aberystwyth
SY23 2AR

01970 615040

We Specialise in Tandoori and Balti Dishes

Curry to take out always available
Tandoori, Indian and English Dishes
Large Parties Catered For
(by prior arrangement)
Open Every Day
12 noon to 2.30pm & 5.30pm to Midnight

DYFED

ABERYSTWYTH

LIGHT OF ASIA   CC DISCOUNT
34, East gate, Aberystwyth.   01970 615040
Gets busy on Friday and Saturday nights, so best to book a table or be disappointed. Proprietor, Ansar Miah will give a discount to Curry Club members, see page 288.   12 noon to 2.30pm and 5.30pm till midnight.

ROYAL PIER TANDOORI
The Pier, Marine Terrace, Aberystwyth.   01970 624888
'Superb position on end of pier. Tandoori, Special Rice, Methi Gosht and Lamb Vindaloo all excellent.' DL.

CARMARTHAN

GARDEN TANDOORI
7, Barn Road, Carmarthen.   01267 235652
'The food and service is excellent - very friendly. Free Popadom while waiting.' PJ. Popular curries with some specials such as Tandoori Trout.

HAVERFORDWEST

TAJ MAHAL
2, Milford Road, Haverfordwest.   01437 73610
'Very good food from this tasty little place and good service.' PJ.

KILGETTY

SURMA   CC DISCOUNT
4, Commercial Hse, Carmarthen Rd, Kilgetty.   01834 811861
'Onion Bhajee, very good, Tikka Masala, very tasty, Chicken Patia, good but not as hot as menu suggested. Mushroom Pilau the best I've ever had. More than we could eat.' AD. Proprietor, Shahidul Islam will give a discount to Curry Club members, see page 288. Hours: 6pm till 11.30pm.

LAMPETER
SHAPLA   CC DISCOUNT
8, College Street, Lampeter.   **01570 422076**
A small restaurant seating forty diners. Serves good curries and accompaniments at reasonable prices. Manager, Shahid Noor will give a discount to Curry Club members, see page 288. Branch: Cross Hands Tandoori, 9, Carmarthen Road, Cross Hands.

LLANELLI
SHEESH MAHAL
53, Stepney Street, Llanelli.   **01000 773773**
A popular curry house serving popular curries.

PEMBROKE
PRINCESS OF INDIA   CC DISCOUNT
3-5, Bush Street, Pembroke Dock.   **01646 685394**
Competent curries and side dishes on the menu at the reliable good curry house. Will give a discount to Curry Club members, see page 288.

MILFORD HAVEN
OBSERVANT ADMIRAL   CC DISCOUNT
129-131, Charles Street, Milford Haven.   **01646 697490**
A small restaurant, seating thirty-six diners with a large function room for sixty-four. 'Balti Bindi Gosht - excellent quantity, quality good. Balti Murgh Masala - very generous portion, very wel marinated. Decor very pleasant, expensive carpet, service slow.' GGP. Owner, Victor C Heise will give a discount to Curry Club members, see page 288. Hours: 12 noon to 2pm and 5pm till late.

GLAMORGAN

For the purposes of this guide, we have combined Mid, South and West Glamorgan.

ABERDARE
GULSHAN
42, Canon Street, Aberdare.   **01685 871763**
Hours: 12 noon to 2pm and 6pm till midnight.

BARRY
MODERN TANDOORI TAKEAWAY
290, Holton Road, Barry.   **01446 746787**
A takeaway establishment only, popular curries and side dishes on the menu here. Hours: 5.30pm till 12.30am.

SHAHI NOOR
87, High Street, Barry.   **01446 735706**
A small restaurant, seating forty-four diners, that gets busy at weekends, so reserve your table. Hours: 12 noon to 2.30pm and 6pm till midnight.

BRIDGEND
DELHI DELI
59-61, Nolton Street, Bridgend.   **01656 647229**
'A quality restaurant. Decor unusual, blues and yellows. Murgh Kebab was good, tasty minced chicken. Lamb Gustaba an interesting Indian meatball.' PH. Sunday Buffet 12 noon to 3pm.

NATRAJ
16, Wyndham, Street, Bridgend.   **01656 667853**
Opened in 1989 and have built up a good local following, providing
competent curries at reasonable prices. Balti features on the menu,
Hours: 12 noon to 2.30pm and 5.30pm till midnight.

CARDIFF

BALTI WALLAH   **CC DISCOUNT**
72, Cowbridge Road East, Canton, Cardiff.   **01222 395959**
Seats sixty-five diners and serves popular curries and accompaniments.
Admin Manager, Andrew Hicks will give a discount to Curry Club
members, see page 288. Hours: 12 noon to 2pm (Monday to Saturday
only) and 5.30pm till midnight, till 1am on Friday and Saturday. Branch:
King Balti, 131, Albany Road, Roath, Cardiff.

BENGAL BRASSERIE
147, Cowbridge Road East, Canton, Cardiff.   **01222 226687**
'My favourite is the Lamb Tikka, moutwatering and I recommend the
Lamb Madras or Vindaloo. Side dishes are of a high standard and
reasonable priced.' M L-J.

INDIAN OCEAN
290, North Road, Cardiff.   **01222 621349**
'Very friendly place, not large but decor is smart. Chicken Tikka Masala
was delicious. Keema and Peshwari Nan were absolutely wonderful as
is the Quail and Tandoori Lamb Chops.' JL.

JUBORAJ   **CC DISCOUNT**
11, Heol-y-Deri, Rhiwbina, Cardiff.   **01222 628894**
A large restaurant seating ninety diners. 'Very inviting witha pleasant
atmosphere. Chicken Tikka Masala very pleasant.' JL. Managing
partner, Ana Miah will give a discount to Curry Club members, see page
288. Hours: 12 noon to 2.30pm and 6pm till 11pm. Branch: Juboraj II, 10,
Mill Lane, The Hayes, Cardiff.

KING BALTI   **CC DISCOUNT**
131, Albany Road, Roath, Cardiff.   **01222 482890**
A massive establishement seating 160 diners. 'Staff are very helpful and
the meals are the very best. Ample quantities - I'm a hearty eater.' M L-
J. 'The food is good, prices a little high.' JL. Admin manager, Andrew
Hicks, will give a discount to Curry Club members, see page 288. Hours:
12 to 2pm and 5.30pm till midnight, till 1am on Friday and Saturday.
Branch: Balti Wallah, 72, Cowbridge Road East, Canton, Cardiff.

STAR OF WALES
438, Cowbridge Road East, Canton, Cardiff.   **01222 383222**
'The quality and quantity is the reason to visit. I always ask for containers
to take the remains of my meal home.' M L-J. Hours: 12 noon to 2.30pm
and 6pm till 1.30am, till 2.30am on Friday / Saturday. Sunday 6 to 1am.

TASTE OF ASIA   **CC DISCOUNT**
236, City Road, Roath, Cardiff.   **01222 493994**
Opened in 1989 and has built up a good trade for serving competent
curries and side dishes. Proprietor, Kabir Miah will give a discount to
Curry Club members, see page 288. Hours: 6pm till midnight.

TASTE OF INDIA
103-5, Woodville Road, Cathays, Cardiff.   **01232 228863**
'My favourite.' BH. Good curries and accompaniments are on the menu
including a few specialities.

CATHAYS
AKASH
49, Crwys Road, Cathays.   **01222 383727**
'Menu offered all the usual favourites. Quantities supplied were very generous and well worth the money. We left absolutely bloated. Chicken Madras was mouthwatering.' JG.

BALTI HOUSE TANDOORI   CC DISCOUNT
14, Crwys Road, Cathays.   **01222 482923**
Balti features on the menu at this reliable curry house, there is even a Balti Grill and a Balti Koftha (sic) for a starter. Manager, Ali Akbar will give a discount to Curry Club members, see page 288. Hours: 5pm till 12.30am, Friday and Saturday till 1.30am. Branches: Modern Tandoori, 290, Holton Road, Barry. City Balti, 286, City Road, Roath, Cardiff. Taste of Paradise, Nolton Road, Bridgend.

MERTHYR TYDFIL
STAR OF INDIA   CC DISCOUNT
1, Morlais Building, High Street, Merthyr Tydfil.   01685 388344
A thirty-eight seat restaurant, tends to book up on a Friday and Saturday, so book. Balti on the menu along with other popular curries. Manager, Mohammed will give a discount to Curry Club members, see page 288. Hours: 12 noon to 2.30pm and 6pm till midnight. Branch: Brecon Tandoori, Glamorgan Street, Brecon, Powys.

PENARTH
PRINCE OF INDIA
13, Ludlow Lane, Penarth.   **01222 700137**
A tiny restaurant seating just twenty-eight diners. Hours: 6pm till midnight.

TROPICAL TANDOORI
14, Glebe Street, Penarth.   **01222 707555**
A takeaway establishment. Opened in 1986 and well known for serving up reliable curries and accompaniments at reasonable prices. Hours: 5pm till midnight.

PONTYPRIDD
RAJ BALTI
25, Toff Vale Shopping Centre, Pontypridd.   **01443 400652**
'Good decor, excellent service, seats over 100 diners. One of the best Sheek Kebabs every tasted. Excellent Balti Jalfrezi, very spicy, nicely hot. Balti Korma Maharaja, rich and creamy.' JO.

SWANSEA
BENGAL BRASSERIE
67, Walter Road, Uplands, Swansea.   **01792 643747**
'A beautiful incense aroma greets you and you are guided to tables cosily nestled behind slatted screens. Menu full of unusual dishes. Okra side dish, pungent and tasty.' DMcD. 'My favourite.' GJ. Hours: 12 noon to 2.30pm and 6pm till midnight.

EURO ASIAN
103/4, High Street, Gorseinon, Swansea.   **01792 891162**
Good and varied menu serving popular curries and side dishes. Hours: 5.30pm till 12.30am, till 1am Friday and Saturday. Sunday 6pm till midnight. Free home delivery service.

INDIAN COTTAGE **CC DISCOUNT**
69, Herbert Street, Pontardawe, Swansea. **01792 830208**
Seats fifty-sixe diners in comfortable surroundings. Competent curries on the menu. Chef, Abdul Razzak will give a discount to Curry Club members, see page 288. Hours: 12 noon to 2pm and 5.30pm till midnight, till 1am Friday and Saturday.

KILLAY TANDOORI
436, Gower Road, Killay, Swansea. **01792 205449**
'Small comfortable restaurant. Menu very full, portions adequate, quality good, service helpful.' A N-S.

RAJ BALTI HOUSE,
82, St Helens Road, Swansea. **01792 645383**
Hours: 6pm till 1am, every day.

RAJPUTANA
44, High Street, Gorseinon, Swansea. **01792 895883**
A takeaway, established in 1978. Serves standard curries and accompa niments at reasonable prices. Hours: 6pm till midnight, till 12.30am on Friday and Saturday.

SEAVIEW TANDOORI
728, Mumbles Road, Mumbles, Swansea. **01792 361991**
'Located right on the front overlooking the bay. Plain exterior reveals a smart, modern and spacious restaurant. Standard range of curry dishes of excellent quality.' PJ.

VICEROY OF INDIA **CC DISCOUNT**
50, St Helens Road, Swansea. **01792 466898**
'Serves absolutely first class cuisine. Delicious Shamee Kebab. Really wonderful Naan bread.' MB. Owner, Abdul Latif will give a discount to Curry Club members, see page 288. Hours: 6pm till 2.30am. Friday and Saturday till 3am. Sunday till 2am.

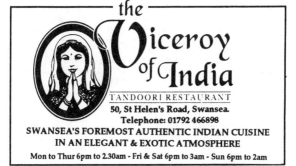

YSTRAD MYNACH
INDIAN PALACE **CC DISCOUNT**
12-14, Penallta Road, Ystrad Mynach. **01443 862894**
Specialities on the menu include: Balti, Karai and Tandoori dishes. Manager, Monir Miah will give a discount to Curry Club members, see page 288. Hours: 12 noon to 2.30pm (Thursday to Saturday only) and 5.30pm till 11.45pm.

GWENT

ABERGAVENNY

SUNDARBON
7, Monk Street, Abergavenny.

CC DISCOUNT
01873 852692

Menu lists all popular curries with a good selection of tandoories items. Manager, B Miah will give a discount to Curry Club members, see page 288. Hours: 12 noon to 2.30pm and 6pm till midnight.

BEDWAS

INDIAN COTTAGE
Bridge Cottage, The Square, Bedwas.

CC DISCOUNT
01222 860369

A small and cosy restaurant seating just thirty-two diners. Tends to gets busy at weekends, so booking is advisable. Manager, Mark Harris will give a discount to Curry Club members, see page 288. Hours: 6 to 12pm.

CAERLEON

BAGAN
2, Cross Street, Caerleon.

01633 430086

House specialities include: Lobster Dilruba and Tandoori Duck Mossallah (sic). Hours: 12 noon to 2.30pm and 6pm till 11.30pm.

CWMBRAN

KHAN
6, Commercial Street, Pontnewydd, Cwmbran.

CC DISCOUNT
01633 867141

This takeaway only establishment commenced trading way back in 1984. Reliable good, popular curries are on the menu here. Manager, Sirjat Khan will give a discount to Curry Club members, see page 288. Hours: 5.30pm till midnight, till 1am on Friday and Saturday.

NAWAB
25-27, Victoria Street, Cwmbran.

CC DISCOUNT
01633 874272

'Don't be put off by having to ring the door bell to gain entry. Food really is first class. Popadoms came with the most comprehensive tray of pickles and chutneys. Shami Kebab ordered got a Rashmi, wonderful. Absolutely delighful and full of flavour Chicken Madras.' MB. Proprietor, Abdul Faruq will give a discount to Curry Club members, see page 288. Hours: 12 noon to 2pm and 6pm till midnight.

MONMOUTH

MISBAH
9, Priory Street, Monmouth.

01600 714940

An intimate restaurant seating thirty diners. Weekends tend to get busy quickly, so reserving a table is necessary. Proprietor, D Miah will give a discount to Curry Club members, see page 288. Hours: 12 noon to 2pm and 6pm till 11.30pm.

NEWPORT

KING BALTI HOUSE
248, Corporation Road, Newport.

CC DISCOUNT
01633 266609

'Service was especially good, very friendly waiters. Balti Nan is about the size of A3 paper. A truly outstanding evening.' PH. Manager, SM Tarafdar will give a discount to Curry Club members, see page 288. Hours: 12 noon to 2pm and 6pm till 12.30am. Friday/ Saturday till 1am.

KOH I NOOR   **CC DISCOUNT**
104, Chepstow Road, Maindee, Newport.   01633 258615
Menu is fairly large with a good range of popular curries along with Balti and a Lobster Summerkand. Manager, Ullah Tahir will give a discount to Curry Club members, see page 288. Hours: 12 noon to 2.30pm and 6pm till 1.30am, Friday and Saturday till 2am. Sunday 6pm till 1am.

LAHORE
145, Dock Street, Newport.   01633 265665
A standard curry house serving reliable good curry house food at reasonable prices. Hours: 12 noon to 2.30pm and 6pm till 2pm. Branch: Eastern Tandoori, 11, Risca Road, Cross Keys. Gwent.

GWYNEDD

BANGOR

MAHABHARAT
5-7, High Street, Bangor.   **01248 351337**
'Spacious and comfortable restaurant. Standard curry house menu.
Service very efficient except for the late arrival of the mint sauce which
was supposed to accompany the starter. Portions very generous and
food of a high standard.' IM.

TANDOORI KNIGHTS
10, Holyhead Road, Bangor.   **01248 364634**
'Standard curry house menu. Service slow, portions average, but on the
whole a good meal. Naan bread the best I have ever had.' IM.

CAERNARFON

GANDHI
11, Palace Street, Caernarfon.   **01286 676797**
A standard menu containing all our regular favourites. 'Brilliant.' PJ.
Hours: 12 noon to 2pm and 5.30pm till 11pm. Sunday 5.30pm till 11pm.

HOLYHEAD

OMAR KHAYYAM   **CC DISCOUNT**
8, Newry Street, Holyhead, Anglesey.   **01407 760333**
A busy standard curry house serving reliable good curries. Mr Shiron
Miah, the owner, has offered a lunch time discount of 10% for Curry Club
members, see page 288. Hours: 12 noon to 2pm and 5.30pm till 11.30pm,
Sunday 5pm till 11.30pm.

LLANDUDNO

BENGAL DYNASTY   **TOP 100 - CC DISCOUNT**
1, North Parade, Llandudno.   **AWARD WINNER**   **01492 878445**
Llandudno is a really lovely seaside town jam packed with gorgeous
Georgian buildings. The Bengal Dynasty is situated in one of these fine
buildings. The menu contains all the usual curries and accompaniments
that most other Bangladeshi curry houses have but their food is really
nicely done, using good and tasty stocks and marinades. Manager, M
Ahmed will give a discount to Curry Club members, see page 288.
Hours: 12 noon to 2.30pm and 6pm till 11.300m. Branch: Bengal Dynasty,
104-106, Chester Road East, Shotton, Deeside, Clwyd. Both restaurants
remains in our TOP 100 and our BEST IN WALES AWARD.

LLANGEFNI

MOONLIGHT   **CC DISCOUNT**
40, High Street, Llangefni, Anglesey.   **01248 722595**
'A comfortable and well appointed restaurant. Chicken Tikka Masala
was mucht to my taste. Nan bread was freshly cooked and had an
excellent taste.' PAW W. Proprietor, Emdadur Rahman will give a
discount to Curry Club members, see page 288. Hours: 12 noon to 2pm
and 5.30pm till 11.30pm.

PORTHMADOG

PASSAGE TO INDIA   **CC DISCOUNT**
26a, Lombard Street, Porthmadog.   **01766 512144**
Established in 1985 and seats forty-four diners. Has built up a good trade
of locals and tends to get busy at weekends, so book to avoid queues.

Manager, Ruhel Rahman will give a discount to Curry Club members, see page 288. Hours: 12 noon to 2pm and 6pm till 11pm. Branch: Tandoori Temptations, 303, Stanstead Road, Forest Hill, London, SE23.

PWLLHELI
GLYNLLIFON
Abersoch Road, Llandebdrog, Pwllheli.　　　　**01758 740147**
'A very smart and pleasant country house restaurant. Menu changes every three days, with dishes I have never heard of. Not a curry house menu. All diners were given tandoori fish for a starter and main course was laid out on a large table for you to choose. Quality authentic real Indian food, which has not been altered to suit western tastes.' IM.

REDFORD TANDOORI
28, Penlan Street, Pwllheli.　　　　**01758 613884**
'Decor plain, service slow but attentive. All meals individually prepared - flavours really come through. Excellent value, thoroughly recommended.' DW. 'Very good.' PJ. Hours: 12 noon to 2pm and 6pm till 11.20pm. Friday and Sunday not open for lunch.

POWYS

BRECON
BRECON TANDOORI
Glamorgan Street, Brecon.　　　　**01874 624653**
A small and cosy restaurant seating thirty-eight diners and serving competent curries at reasonable prices.

NEWTOWN
SHILAM
49, Broad Street, Newtown.　　　　**01686 625333**
'I can highly recommend it. Menu has all the old favourites like Bhoona, Pasanda and Tikka Masala. Seats about forty-five and has a 'padded cell' at the rear for the most riotus of customers. Service excellent, polite and courteous. Portions generous.' ME.

LLANDRINDOD WELLS
DILLRAJ
Emporium Building, Temple St, Llandrindod Wells.　　**01597 823843**
A standard curry house serving good standard fayre. 'Enjoyed this one, right on the Welsh Border - Boy Oh.' PJ

WELSHPOOL
SHILAM
13, Berriew Street, Welshpool.　　　　**01938 553431**
'Exterior shabby, but interior very pleasant. Fantastic menu. Exception al Bhuna Prawn on Purée. Lamb Passanda the best we've vere had.' PM.

TO FIND OUT ABOUT HOW YOU CAN JOIN THE CURRY CLUB MEMBERS' DISCOUNT SCHEME, PLEASE SEE OVER.

CURRY CLUB MEMBERS'

DISCOUNT VOUCHER SCHEME

SAVE POUNDS ON DINING!

To make big savings on your curry meals or takeaways, you must become a
Curry Club member. It's easy: contact us at the address below.
Members get, amongst other things, a quarterly magazine, in which there
are four vouchers. So you get sixteen vouchers a year.

Each voucher is valid at any one of the restaurants who have agreed
to participate in this scheme. To identify them, look for
CC DISCOUNT at the top right hand of the restaurant's entry.

The actual discount each restaurant is willing to give varies from restaurant
to restaurant. Some will give a free bottle of wine, or free starters,
others 5% off the bill, and some are offering as much as 10%.

We have agreed with the restaurant owners that these discounts are available at
the discretion of the restaurant, at their quieter times, and that each Curry Club
member will book in advance when using a DISCOUNT VOUCHER.

To find out how much discount you can get, and when they will give it to you,
please PHONE THE MANAGER. (Where ever possible we have given the
name of the individual owner or manager, who has agreed to give the discount,
in the participating restaurant's entry.) Then please BOOK.

There is no limit to the number of people Curry Club members may take.
One voucher is valid for a discount on one meal, and
must be handed over when paying the bill.

REMEMBER, YOU MUST BE A MEMBER OF THE CURRY CLUB TO GET YOUR VOUCHERS. SO JOIN NOW TO SAVE POUNDS.

More information about the scheme and the Club from:

**THE CURRY CLUB
P.O.BOX 7, HASLEMERE
SURREY GU27 1EP**

Please send an S.A.E.